BATMAN
AND PSYCHOLOGY

A Dark and Stormy Knight

TRAVIS LANGLEY

WILEY

John Wiley & Sons, Inc.

Published by John Wiley & Sons, Inc., Hoboken, New Jersey
Published simultaneously in Canada

BATMAN is ™ and © DC Comics. Used with Permission. Illustration credits: pages 5, 8, 29, 35, 54, 67, 80, 90, 110, 130, 141, 151, 158, 178, 211, 237, 257, 266: Marko Head; pages 85, 124: Nick Langley; pages 94, 103, 227: Travis Langley.

For general information about our other products and services, please contact our Customer Care Department within the United States at (800) 762-2974, outside the United States at (317) 572-3993 or fax (317) 572-4002.

Wiley also publishes its books in a variety of electronic formats and by print-on-demand. Some content that appears in standard print versions of this book may not be available in other formats. For more information about Wiley products, visit us at www.wiley.com.

Library of Congress Cataloging-in-Publication Data:

Langley, Travis (date)
    Batman and psychology: a dark and stormy knight / by Travis Langley; foreword by Michael Uslan; introduction by Dennis O'Neil.
        p. cm.
    Includes bibliographical references and index.
    ISBN 978-1-118-16765-6 (pbk.: acid-free paper); ISBN 978-1-118-22636-0 (ebk); ISBN 978-1-118-23951-3 (ebk); ISBN 978-1-118-26425-6 (ebk)
    1. Batman (Fictitious character).   2. Psychology and literature.   I. Title.
    PN6728.B36L36 2012
    741.5'973--dc23

                                                            2011053474

Printed in the United States of America

10 9 8 7 6 5 4

For Rebecca, Alex, and Nicholas from everything I am today.

For my parents, Lynda and Travis Sr., from the kid who never goes away.

Contents

Acknowledgments

My Bat-Family

If I start naming everybody who ever helped me love Batman, I'll never stop. How far back do I go? To my mom who read me comic books when I was small? To Neal Adams whose art, by making Batman stories look so much more eerie than TV had led me to expect, motivated my preschool self to learn to read? To editor Bob Schreck and writer Kevin Smith, whose work reignited my habit of subscribing to monthly comics? Then how about more artists—Jim Aparo, Dick Giordano, Sheldon Moldoff, Irv Novick, Marshall Rogers, George Roussos—and writers, editors, actors, directors, still more artists . . . ? The long line of creative individuals who have kept our hero patrolling Gotham in print and on screen never stops, and I do thank them all.

This book begins one summer when *The Dark Knight* was packing audiences into movie theaters; when I read the book *Superman on the Couch,* in which Danny Fingeroth observed[1] that mental health professionals had written nearly nothing about comics in the fifty years since psychiatrist Fredric Wertham attacked the comic book industry; and when my son Nicholas went to San Diego Comic-Con to collect data for Matt Smith's ethological research[2] (no, not the Matt Smith who flies a TARDIS). Accompanying Nick there because I wanted to see their group's research presentation, I looked around

Comic-Con, I watched thousands of people bustling about in an environment that celebrated their passions, I met scholars writing on many comics-related topics, and it all came together for me: I needed to study comic book fans, and I needed to write about Batman.

Evan Gregory of the Ethan Ellenberg Literary Agency brought me to Wiley, Connie Santisteban, John Simko, Rebecca Yeager, and the whole Wiley team. When you're writing a book about Batman, you take it as a good sign when you learn your literary agent named his dog Bruce Wayne. My wife, Rebecca, a licensed therapist, helped me think through the therapeutic issues. My older son, Alex, thought I should organize my chapters around the villains—hence my compromise, my Case Files' featured foes. Artists Marko Head and Nick Langley created illustrations, including those at the beginning of every chapter, and I can't thank DC Comics V.P. Jay Kogan and Rights & Permissions Manager Thomas King strongly enough for the images from DC Comics/Warner Bros. publications. I must thank my first readers (Rebecca and Alex), second readers (Action Flick Chick Katrina Hill, Christopher Daley, Marissa Nolan-Layman, David Manning), supportive friends like Bruce and Kathy Smith and GeekNation.com's Clare Kramer and Brian Keathley, and a twitpal legion. Chris Spatz and Ralph McKenna at Hendrix College and then Terry Christenson, Arnold Gerall, Barbara Moely, my great mentor Ed O'Neal, and others taught me all kinds of psychology at Tulane University so I could misrepresent it here for you.

I've been fortunate to teach at a university that respects and supports comics scholarship. Communication professor Randy Duncan paved the way before me through his years of teaching *Comics as Communication*, guiding Henderson State University's comic book club, and building our library's Stephen R. Bissette Archives and graphic novel collection, which houses plenty of Batman titles thanks to librarians like Lea Ann Alexander. English instructor Eric Bailey helped me access key television episodes from decades-old master prints. Dean Maralyn Sommer, Undergraduate Research Chair Martin Campbell, John Hardee, Millie Bowden, Lecia Franklin, Carolyn Hatley, Linda Mooney, and Erma Johnson have helped our students and myself travel to conventions where we've collected interview and survey data for our ongoing ERIICA Project (Empirical Research on the Interpretation and Influence of the Comic Arts).[3] Those students impress me all the time: Erica Ash, Tommy Cash, Carly Cate, Summer Delezen, Robert O'Nale, Ashley Pitcock, Justin Poole, Nikki Robertson, Thomas Sepe, Jarod Shurtleff, Nicole Smith . . . they keep coming. Working in a department full of people I both respect and like— supportive and dedicated colleagues Aneeq Ahmad, Rafael Bejarano, and Paul Williamson—is truly a blessing, and words cannot convey the depths of my gratitude to our department chair, Todd Wiebers, for many reasons, not the least of which has been letting me teach courses like *Comics & Psychology*, *Psychology in Film*, and one titled *Batman*.

With Peter Coogan, once upon a time, Randy Duncan co-founded the Comics Arts Conference: San Diego Comic-Con's scholarly conference-within-the-con. Helping them and current CAC chair Kate McClancy organize the conference has been a privilege, and we all owe a huge debt to Eddie Ibrahim, Sue Lord, Gary Sassaman, and others who run SDCC and WonderCon. Mark Walters (Dallas Comic Con), Ben Stevens (Sci-Fi Expo), Lance Fensterman (New York Comic Con), and more con organizers created valuable opportunities for me.

One of the highlights of my year every summer lately has been conducting Comic-Con panels on the psychology of Batman together with fellow psychologist Robin Rosenberg and *The Dark Knight Rises* executive producer Michael Uslan. Great people have joined us along the way—like writer Len Wein (creator of Lucius Fox, Swamp Thing, and Wolverine), psychologist Andrea Letamendi, actress Lee Meriwether (*Batman: The Movie*'s Catwoman), journalist Nerdy Bird Jill Pantozzi, neuroscientist E. Paul Zehr (author of *Becoming Batman*), and comic book legend Denny O'Neil (the man who wrote the first comic books I ever read).[4] It's hard to imagine how we'll top that first time when *Batman* TV star Adam West, "The Laughing Fish" scribe Steve Englehart, and artist Jerry Robinson, whose achievements include creating the Joker with Kane and Finger, helped us discuss the Joker's psychopathy.[5] Nina West Tooley, James Tooley, Fred Westbrook, and Jens Robinson helped tremendously with that. Adam had never previously met Michael or Jerry in person. Since then, they've each commented on how enjoyable that historic day turned out to be;

Michael covers it in his autobiography, *The Boy Who Loved Batman*. While I have additional reasons for thanking every individual mentioned above, I must again thank two important and gracious human beings in particular: Michael Uslan for contributing this book's foreword and Denny O'Neil for the introduction. It is an honor, sirs.

Jerry Robinson's gone now, but I remain forever grateful to him. Hired in his teens to work on the art a few months after Kane and Finger created their masked avenger, Jerry contributed much to their mythos and brought those early days to life for me. He was always a warm and considerate man who spent as much time asking about me, my work, and my opinions as he spent answering my questions. I'll never get to meet the late Bob Kane or Bill Finger. We can't chat about their creations. I can't watch them greet fans, hear them recount anecdotes from their amazing lives, or thank them for everything they set in motion and all that their legacy has meant—not face-to-face anyway. This book is more than my answer to a question the man who played my childhood hero once asked me, as you'll soon see. It's my heartfelt "thank you" to Bob and Bill. Jerry too.

Batman creator Bob Kane's headstone. Photo by Lynda M. Langley.

Foreword

BY MICHAEL USLAN

Recently, *The New York Times* took DC Comics, the comic book industry generally, and Batman specifically over the coals for what they claimed might be an insensitivity toward all the supervillains like the Joker, Two-Face, the Scarecrow, and Catwoman, whom they apparently saw less as "villains" and more as mere victims of assorted types and degrees of mental illness.[6] Concerned psychiatrists and psychologists, it seems, feel that comic books denigrate these poor souls as "dangerous," "evil," and even "lunatics," mix-matching in the process such clinical appellations as "psychotics" and "schizophrenics" with "costumed crazies" and "homicidal maniacs." Some psychiatrists and psychologists argue that the comic book supervillain stereotypes promote shameful generalizations that continue to cause every new generation of comic book readers to fear or mock these afflicted and misunderstood antagonists.

Particularly targeted by these critics is the comic book institution known as Arkham Asylum (the word "asylum" no longer being a politically correct term of art) and the references to its patients as "inmates" (the latter word also no longer politically correct). The panels of the stories visually depict scenes of these afflicted victims sitting in barred cells (the word "cells" no longer politically correct in this context), wearing straitjackets or shackles (the word "straitjacket" no longer politically correct). Comic books are accused of ratcheting

Left to right: Comic-Con panelists Robin Rosenberg, Michael Uslan, Travis Langley, Adam West, Jerry Robinson. Photo by Alex Langley.

up bias, prejudice, and fear against the Joker and his compadres. Indeed, these psychiatrists and psychologists now see Batman as more of the bad guy than the so-called supervillains he opposes. They give no credit to the Dark Knight for his decades-long non-use of butterfly nets (while not specifically mentioned in the article, I'll venture to guess that the term "butterfly nets" is also no longer politically correct) to corral his opponents who break out of Arkham seemingly every Wednesday the new comic books go on sale.

The bipolar opposite of this rather sensationalistic approach to Batman and the comics with all the trumped-up charges against the Caped Crusader is the scholarly and insightful book you now hold in your hands. Superherologist Travis Langley is a university professor and an eminent scholar on the psychology of comic book superheroes and their real-life fans. *Batman and Psychology: A Dark and Stormy Knight* represents the culmination of his professional journal articles, chapters, blogs, many convention panels, and lifetime of contemplating the nature of heroes both factual and fictional, especially the one who guards Gotham. His professional credentials, mixed with his love for comic books and the character of Batman, create a fascinating, entertaining, and educational read. What makes Batman tick? Are superheroes with secret identities schizophrenic? Is Batman neurotic? Psychotic? And are Batman's rogues gallery of supervillains truly *not* rogues or supervillains, but rather victims of a heartless society who are in need of better understanding and far more compassion than shown to date by the Gotham City Police Department, Batman, Robin, Superman, and even the entire Justice League of America? Find your nearest couch, lie down, and let Dr. Langley explain it all.

Michael Uslan
Gotham City
2012

✿   ✿   ✿

Michael Uslan is a comics scholar, writer, and filmmaker experienced in taking on one Goliath after another. To get approval to teach the first course on comic book folklore at any accredited university, he asked a university dean to recount Superman's famous origin and then pointed out that the dean had just described the story of Moses. Michael has written some of our most enduring heroes' comic book adventures (*Batman*, *The Shadow*, *The Spirit*, *Archie*), but is best known for bringing our hero to the big screen as executive producer of every Batman movie since the 1980s—originally another giant battle because studio executives at the time had trouble believing audiences would want a serious Batman.

1

Beneath the Cowl

Who Is Batman?

Adam West once asked me if I thought Batman was crazy. *Batman and Psychology: A Dark and Stormy Knight* is my answer.

Since his debut in 1939's *Detective Comics* #27, Batman has thrilled billions across the globe over time, and through a multitude of media. Of the world's three best-known comic book heroes—the bat, the spider, and the man from another planet, a trio of orphaned boys—he's the one who works by night, needs a car to get him into town, and is the most mortal. He's the superhero with no superpowers, the one we can most easily believe might inhabit our world. While his secret identity is the most fantastic of the three, one charmingly handsome billionaire living in a grand mansion on top of a vast cave versus two nebbishy newspaper employees, that fantastic wealth helps us accept his masked identity as something that feels real. Someone has to pay for those wonderful toys. The real world has more people known to be superrich than superpowered. Batman is the hero even adults can envision existing in real life, with less suspension of disbelief. Even though he has opportunities few people enjoy, Bruce Wayne hails from a city, not a mythical island or distant world, and he builds himself into a hero through training and hard work—no radiation, secret formula, or magic ring required.

His origin is tragic and brutally believable. It taps the most primal of our childhood fears: A family outing twists into tragedy when a mugger guns his parents down before his eyes.

His films among the highest-grossing in history, this character has starred in more movies and television series, both animated and live-action, than any other comic book hero. Why does this brooding vigilante, this tormented soul who stalks the streets looking for trouble, dressed like a vampire, fascinate us so? Duality and obsession, his enemies' and his own, fill his stories. His enemies reflect and distort facets of himself. He's smug, he's sly, he's so intimidating that he can enter a room full of people who can fly, read minds, cast spells, or run faster than light, and yet they're the ones daunted by him—and that's what we love. Strong and smart, unfettered by fiscal limitations or anybody else's rules, he brings a deep wish of ours to life. Batman's the part of us that wants to scare all of life's bullies away.

In creating bright, shining Superman, Jerry Siegel and Joe Shuster caught lightning in a bottle. One sleepless night, Jerry conceived "of a character like Samson, Hercules, and all the strong men I ever heard of rolled into one—only more so."[1] Jerry and his artist friend Joe drew inspiration from divine heroes throughout the ages to create not just Superman himself, but the very concept of the costumed superhero. They made the meme. They launched modern mythology.[2] Superman became an immediate hit. On the heels of that first caped hero's success, publishers scrambled to concoct more. Superman's publisher hired young cartoonist Bob Kane to generate their next costumed do-gooder.[3] Ahead of all the upcoming Superman imitations, Kane and his collaborator Bill Finger pulled not from the superhuman figures who'd inspired Jerry and Joe, but instead from the dark mystery-men of silent movies and pulp fiction, most notably Zorro and the Shadow, extraordinary men but men nonetheless. Where Superman drew his might from Earth's sun, Batman found his in a city's darkness.* Jerry and Joe played with the bright and impossible; Bob and Bill expanded that meme by adding the coin's other side, the dark and improbably possible.

---

*"The first light had cast the first shadow."—Grant Morrison (2011), 26.

Nobody today gets to read that first Batman story without already knowing that the vigilante puzzling authorities will turn out to be the bored rich boy who spends his time, up until the final panel, as Commissioner Gordon's literary foil, a sounding board to whom Gordon can voice his thoughts—no more than we might scratch our heads over a classic Robert Louis Stevenson novel because we can't figure out mild-mannered Dr. Jekyll's connection to that lout Mr. Hyde. We know the name and face of the man behind the mask, but what lurks behind the face? The question *"Who is Batman?"* strikes deeper than Batman's cowl, Bruce Wayne's façade, or any name he chooses to use. It's a *who* question packed with *why*: Why does he fight crime? Why as a vigilante? Why the mask, the bat, and the underage partner? Why are his most intimate relationships with "bad girls" he ought to lock up? And why won't he kill that homicidal, green-haired clown?

Does Batman have bats in his belfry?

Right to left: Bat-Films executive producer Michael Uslan, *Batman* television actor Adam West, and psychologist/superherologist Travis Langley discuss Batman and the Joker at San Diego Comic-Con International. Photo by Alex Langley.

2

Which Batman?

"Will the real Batman please stand up?"
—message on a Joker playing card in *The Dark Knight* (2008 motion picture)

 efore we can analyze the character, we must define our parameters. Before we can explore the question of *who* along with all its *whys*, we first must consider *which* Batman we mean.

Even though Batman originated and endures as a comic book character, most of us first met him on TV. From the time I was a toddler, Adam West was the live Batman. I also watched the Caped Crusader in Saturday morning cartoons, pitted Batman and Robin toys against the Joker in his green plastic van, and, wearing a towel cape and black gloves, played like I was Batman. Voiced by Olan Soule, a more serious (though still upbeat) Batman teamed with Superman, Wonder Woman, and Aquaman to form an undersized Justice League, the original *Super Friends*, on Saturday mornings. Those television versions set me up for some big surprises when I finally got to read the comic books' darker stories for myself.

A generation later, my sons knew Batman best through *Batman: The Animated Series*. My older son, age eight when that show began, had known Batman from other media, but memory is a funny thing and the cartoon burned its way backward through time as if it had retroactively gotten there first. He remembers that as his earliest Batman even though he knows this cannot be right. My younger son discovered Batman more like I did, as a preschooler unbothered by details like the fact that Batman didn't really exist, which may be why, of the two boys, he became the bigger Bat-fan. His enthrallment started with *Batman Returns* toys that came out months before *Batman: The Animated Series* debuted; however, the most powerful impression seared into his young mind—for him, where Batman begins—was the edited-for-TV *Batman Returns* Batmobile breaking away parts of itself so it could speed through a narrow alley. His previous passion for toy cars locked onto that vehicle. Batman amazed him, and so did his toys.

Knowing that the man in the costume is a Six Flags performer doesn't reduce the child's awe over meeting Batman in person. Photo by Travis Langley.

Screen History

1940s Serials

Batman's screen history starts with the Columbia Pictures serial *Batman* (1943), starring Lewis Wilson and Douglas Croft as the first live-action Batman and Robin four years after the character's comic book debut. In the days when a typical Saturday for many meant sharing a community experience in the seats of their local theaters, watching a full-length feature plus newsreels, cartoons, comedic short films starring the Three Stooges or Our Gang, and at least one chapter of a film serial, *Batman* was new, not something they'd all known their whole lives. Through one cliffhanger after another for 15 weeks, they watched the Dynamic Duo fight American hoodlums, Japanese agent Dr. Tito Daka, and Daka's mind-controlled "zombie" slaves.

Fear is a recurring element in Batman's stories, but one fear in particular shaped this serial's creation—*xenophobia*, exaggerated fear of foreigners or strangers. Anti-Asian sentiment was not new to America during World War II, and the depictions and descriptions of the Japanese in this serial were overtly racist. The serial's narrator tells us that buildings in the city's Little Tokyo district have sat empty "since a wise government rounded up the shifty-eyed Japs,"[1] referring to the U.S. government's 1942 relocation and internment of over 100,000 American citizens and residents of Japanese ancestry into War Relocation Camps in the wake of Japan's attack on Pearl Harbor.[2] No such relocation occurred for any of German or Italian descent, only for those whose ancestors came from the Axis alliance's Asian member. "Daka, the sinister Jap spy," with his "twisted Oriental brain," embodied the Japanese alien that many feared still lurked in America, having somehow avoided getting rounded up—a point driven home when Batman tells Daka, "We've been searching for you ever since you killed those two agents assigned to your deportation!"[3]

The serial nonetheless contributed to Batman's mythos. Just as *The Adventures of Superman* radio program added Jimmy Olsen, Perry White, and the deadly Kryptonite to the Man of Steel's life, the *Batman* serial gave the Dark Knight his Batcave,[4] its entrance through a grandfather clock, and a leaner butler, Alfred, who sometimes helps the heroes in the field. A better written if more poorly acted sequel followed, 1949's *Batman and Robin*, free of the racist propaganda. Both serials did well at the box office, and yet the 1950s saw no new Batman on screen, perhaps because scathing critiques like Fredric Wertham's 1954 book *Seduction of the Innocent* incited a backlash against comic books. A 1965 theatrical reissue of the *Batman* serial, presenting all 15 half-hour chapters in one marathon showing, proved successful enough that it paved the way for new Batman cliffhangers, this time on TV.[5]

Batman (1966–1968 TV Series, 1966 Motion Picture)

> *"Some days, you just can't get rid of a bomb."*
> —Batman (Adam West), *Batman: The Movie*

The unintentional campiness viewers enjoyed in the re-released 22-year-old *Batman* serial inspired deliberate camp when executive producer William Dozier and writer Lorenzo Semple Jr. brought ABC a television series comedic enough to make adults howl and straight enough for kids to enjoy heroic derring-do. TV had depicted *Superman*, *The Lone Ranger*, and *Tarzan* with no less earnestness than their original source material. Among superhero shows, *Batman* was something new. Actors who could deliver the silliest lines straight-faced proved critical to the series' success. Dozier explained to actor Adam West "that it had to be played as though we were dropping a bomb on Hiroshima, with that kind of deadly seriousness."[6] West became their square, hard-nosed Batman. Adults got the jokes, kids got a kick out of seeing heroes fight bad guys, and it worked as intended.

The show rarely ventured into any overt psychological issues. "We were superficial," Adam West has remarked, "what did we know?"[7] Even when it did, the deliberate farce had no need for accurate depiction of mental illness or its treatment. Mind control popped up in several episodes, in no way resembling any real-world hypnosis or brainwashing techniques. In one episode, the Siren's voice compels Bruce Wayne to sign his fortune over to her and then jump off a building;[8] in another, the Sandman makes Robin activate the machine that will kill Batman if the Caped Crusader doesn't escape that week's cliffhanger.[9]

After Bruce Wayne makes the Joker a vice president of the Gotham National Bank as part of a plan to expose the clown's counterfeiting,[10] Commissioner Gordon decides the millionaire playboy has lost his marbles and has him committed. A straitjacketed Bruce escapes, rolling with the fall out the back of the Anti-Lunatic Squad's van. The story ends with a doctor giving Bruce a clean bill of health and pronouncing that the tumble from the van has knocked some sense back into him, thus restoring his sanity. The doctor's method for testing soundness of mind baffled me even as a child: He taps a reflex hammer to Bruce's knee.[11]

Despite all their antics, none of this Batman's enemies are ever labeled criminally insane. The flamboyant felons escape from Gotham State Prison, not Arkham Asylum. The most psychologically relevant story element, in terms of long-running characterization, is the curious condition of King Tut (see Case File 2–1: King Tut).

Batman (1989 Motion Picture)

"A lot of people think you're as dangerous as the Joker."
—Vicki Vale (Kim Basinger)

Fifty years after the character's comic book debut, director Tim Burton brought us a cinematic Batman who operates from the shadows. Executive producer Michael Uslan wanted Burton to base this one on the first year of Batman's *Detective Comics* stories (pre-Robin) plus adventures later separately written by Dennis O'Neil and Steve Englehart.[12] The popularity of Frank Miller's then-recent four-part graphic novel *The Dark Knight Returns* indicated that fans might be ready for darker Batman tales. Burton added his own flair: For the first time, we saw a neurotic Batman and an awkward Bruce Wayne. Although the movie did have a few odd bits of camp (remember the scruffy news anchors?), the strangest humor came from the Joker and suited his nature.

The script took a noirish approach and made Batman more believable by surrounding him with a noirish city. Burton's Gotham City looms, described in Sam Hamm's script as "if Hell had sprung up through the pavements and kept on going." Burton and production designer Anton Furst looked at New York and "decided to darken everything and build vertically and cram things together and then just go further with it in a more cartoon way," Burton explained.[13] "It has an operatic feel, and an almost timeless quality." The creators of *Batman: The Animated Series* adopted these principles as well. "This neo-Expressionistic, Germanic city"[14] with its Gothic architecture gave us an environment that *needed* Batman. He and his city go together. Each helps us believe the other.

Another important contribution Burton's film added was the Voice. As Batman, actor Michael Keaton dropped his voice, making it deeper and rougher, which helped us accept that people wouldn't recognize Batman as Bruce Wayne—on this one point, no suspension of disbelief was required. "Bruce Wayne is a man about town, a luminary, so people know his voice. So I came up with the idea of dropping his voice down," Keaton explained, "as Batman it comes from a lower thing that he drops down into, a place he has to reach to become a quasi-vigilante."[15] The comic book stories themselves now refer to Batman affecting a gruffer voice when costumed.[16]

In Burton's vision, Bruce Wayne spends his days sleep-deprived, his awkwardness no act. Instead of following the traditional depiction of Batman as formidably fit, physically as well as socially, Burton chose to humanize Bruce Wayne by making him weak. Auditioning one muscle man after another for the role, Burton had found himself unable to picture someone who already looked like an action-adventure hero deciding to dress up like a bat. Once he envisioned a weaker man wearing the costume in order to transform himself, the concept came together. "We just took off from the psychology of saying, 'Here's a guy who doesn't look like Arnold Schwarzenegger, so why's he doing this?' He's not trying to create an image for himself, he's trying to become something he's not."[17] Burton's Batman wears the costume as armor, a bulletproof exoskeleton that confers the power and strength he otherwise lacks. "He does it because he *needs* to, because he's not this gigantic, strapping macho man. It's all about transformation."[18]

While Burton's Bruce Wayne transforms back and forth between Batman and Bruce, psychopathic Jack Napier makes one irreversible transformation from a menacing, grim-faced gangster who kills for practical reasons into a cackling, clown-faced master criminal who kills for the dark humor of it all.*

Batman Returns (1992 Motion Picture)

> "Sickos never scare me. At least they're committed."
> —Selina Kyle (Michelle Pfeiffer)

For the sequel, Burton wanted to bring in Catwoman—to him, Batman's most interesting antagonist after the Joker—while studio execs insisted on using the Penguin, whom they saw as Batman's number-two foe, so this film wound up with both. "You could find the psychological profile of Batman, Catwoman, Joker, but the Penguin was just this guy with a cigarette and a top hat," Burton said of the challenge to characterize Oswald Cobblepot, the Penguin.[19] The profile did not gel until Burton gave the character another layer that would tie him into the motion picture's theme: duality.

In this sequel, Batman and Catwoman each have dual identities, their light and dark sides. Bruce and Selina, two uncomfortable, uncertain, unhappy people who can each walk unassumingly in daylight, transform into their confident, assertive counterparts by night. When all other party guests chat and dance at a masquerade, milling about in their costumes and masks, Bruce and Selina each arrive in formalwear, respectively tuxedo and gown, no masks other than their civilized fronts. "Selina, don't you see?" Bruce tells her toward the movie's end, right before he tears off his mask. "We're the same. We're the same, split right down the center."

In Batman Returns, the dark side is animal nature: the bat, the cat, and the chilly little bird. Unlike Bruce Wayne and Selina Kyle, who don animal outfits, Cobblepot was born a "freak" with flippers instead of hands. Whereas they decide to become nocturnal animals, he endeavors to become a man who can step into the light, except he tries to do so through trickery and without relinquishing his beastly nature.

---

*Only in this version is Jack Napier the man who will become the Joker. In other versions, the Joker's lack of any known alter ego is important.

In both of Burton's Bat-films, Bruce Wayne is distant, the villains steal the show, and the love interests hold our attention. Vicki Vale and Selina Kyle give us perspectives we follow through the course of each story. Though conscious of complaints that the Joker stole the first movie and that the second film showed Batman too little, Tim Burton felt these criticisms "were missing the point of the character. . . . This guy wants to remain as hidden as possible and as in the shadows as possible and unrevealing about himself as possible, so he's not going to eat up screen time by these big speeches and doing dancing around the Batcave." However sound Burton's reasoning may have been, those criticisms reflected one possible advantage that comics have over film—text, in the form of thought balloons and narration, that can let us get inside a character's head.

Batman Forever (1995 Motion Picture)

> *"I'll bring the wine. You bring your scarred psyche."*
> —Dr. Chase Meridian (Nicole Kidman)

When Tim Burton decided to help produce but not direct the next film, director Joel Schumacher arrived with a lighter, brighter vision of a grand Batman movie filled with spectacle and flash, although it did have its edge. The film explores Batman's origin in more detail than did the previous films. *Batman Forever* is partly "a retelling of the origin story in a way that attempts to take a little bit closer look at the psychology of Bruce Wayne and how he became older Bruce Wayne," according to screenwriter Akiva Goldsman.[20] Witnessing the murder of Dick Grayson's acrobat family makes Bruce reflect on his own beginning.

> Bruce (Val Kilmer): Just like my parents. It's happening again. A monster comes out of the night, a scream, two shots. I killed them.
> Alfred (Michael Gough): What did you say?
> Bruce: He killed them. Two-Face, he slaughtered that boy's parents.
> Alfred: No. No, you said, "I." "I killed them."

Bruce, having consulted with criminal psychologist Chase Meridian about the mysterious stalker leaving riddles at Wayne Manor, tells her he has never remembered much about the events surrounding his parents' deaths, that what he remembers comes to him mostly in dreams. However, since the Graysons' similar deaths, the memories have started haunting him while awake: Finding his father's journal after his parents' wake, young Bruce realized the crushing fact that his father would never write in it again. Chase says he's describing a *repressed memory*, "images of a forgotten pain that's trying to surface." With repression, which Freud considered the most important defense mechanism[21] even though modern empirical evidence now suggests it might occur rarely if at all,[22] the unconscious mind locks away feelings, desires, and experiences that the conscious ego cannot bear. Why would Bruce repress something so simple? And why would that memory's retrieval matter so much? Goldsman later explained:

> In the screenplay and in the movie that we shot, there is a very different center of the movie, where he opens up the book and the last entry is "Martha and I want to stay home tonight, but Bruce insists on going to see a movie." [Bruce] had repressed his fantasy that this was all his fault, that if he just hadn't made them go see a movie that night, they would never have been out and they would never have been killed. And so the whole movie was actually built around this kind of psychological reckoning. That's why the love interest is a psychologist.[23]

The film, despite editing out the repressed guilt that Bruce needs to resolve before he can accept Dick Grayson as a crime-fighting partner, retained issues important in many a Batman story: duality and obsession. Two-Face, the film's secondary villain, embodies both. Literally split down the center—his right side handsome, his left side acid-scarred—former District Attorney Harvey Dent compulsively tosses a coin to let fate make his decisions. Chase and Batman refer to him as having "multiple personalities" and yet, aside from his referring to himself in the plural, the film shows no signs that he has that condition. This Two-Face never acts torn between right and wrong. He always wants to do wrong. Leaving his decisions to a coin toss merely absolves him of responsibility for his actions. When the toss goes against his wishes, he shows disappointment, going so far as to toss it repeatedly until it lets him do the thing he desires. Although the trauma that scarred half his face brought out his dark side, we see no evidence that he switches between selves, no sign of any gaps in memory between good Harvey and bad.

Edward Nygma,* who is the film's central villain, the Riddler, appears to have *borderline personality disorder*, an unstable, incomplete identity characterized by chaos in one's thoughts, moods, actions, and self-concept, "one of the most frustrating psychiatric conditions to live with and to treat."[24] Edward's specific symptoms include *splitting*, categorizing people in positive and negative extremes, switching abruptly between idealizing and demonizing the same individual as indicated by his vacillating views toward Bruce Wayne. "You're my idol," he tells Bruce at their first meeting, when Edward initially impresses Bruce with his inventive ideas only to press too hard and botch his chance to get the multimillionaire to fund his research. Hero worship inverts into dangerous obsession. Eddie stalks Bruce, anonymously leaving him riddles with sinister overtones. "He's obsessed with you," Chase cautions Bruce. "His only escape may be to purge the fixation," referring to "potential homicidal tendencies."

Psychologist Chase and borderline Edward each spend the movie attracted, in different ways, to Bruce Wayne and each trying to get inside Batman's mind—in Edward's case, literally. Chase wants to be with Bruce and Edward wants to be like him. Chase attends a party with Bruce; host Edward wears a fake mole to match one on Bruce's (Val Kilmer's) face. Chase builds a file studying Batman; Edward builds his brainwave manipulator to steal information from people's heads, including Bruce Wayne's secrets. Edward's need for association with a more complete human being grows from idolizing and imitating Bruce to integrating into himself bits of information and intelligence from all who attach Nygmatech's 3-D boxes to their TVs. The machine overloads Edward's brain, leaving him disconnected

---

Batman Forever spelled his surname *Nygma* even though it's normally *Nigma*.

and confused in Arkham Asylum, under the delusion that he himself is Batman.

Out of all the Burton-Schumacher Batman films, none other shows Bruce Wayne as often nor depicts him so thoroughly as a meaningful character. This Bruce is braver, bolder, more comfortable in anything he wears. With no time to costume up and without hesitation, like James Bond in black tux, Bruce attacks Two-Face's thugs during a frantic attempt to stop a ticking bomb from killing hundreds at the circus. He does not become Batman. He *is* Batman.

> Bruce: You have a thing for bats?
> Chase: Oh, that's a Rorschach, Mister Wayne, an inkblot.
>   People see what they want. I think the question would be:
>   Do *you* have a thing for bats?

Some of the movie's campier moments distracted from its psychological breadth, as did its association with Schumacher's next Bat-film, which would become the campiest in more than thirty years.

Batman & Robin (1997 Motion Picture)

> *"This is why Superman works alone."*
> —Batman (George Clooney)

Because the film *Batman & Robin* provided little depth to Batman himself,* spotting Batman's character development at this point requires the viewer to step back and consider his personal arc over the course of the four films: In Burton's movies, Bruce Wayne starts off in *Batman* as a hollow figure, but he's at least trying to socialize and maintain some pretense of a life. By *Batman Returns*, he has stopped bothering to pretend. Gone is the party he threw at the start of the previous film. Now he sits home alone in the dark until the Bat-Signal flips his Batman switch and his ideal self springs to life. Selina must enter his life before he'll consider revisiting Gotham's social scene. This anti-heroine who challenges Batman as Catwoman and dates Bruce as Selina awakens his human nature in a way Vicki

---

*Batman & Robin's great lesson: Men have nipples; women don't. Decide for yourself what psychological issues figured into that costuming decision.

Vale never could—by attracting and matching both sides, bat and man. By the film's end, he has discovered he does want someone else in his life. The Schumacher films then show him progressively opening up more. In *Batman Forever*, he opens his psyche and heart to a psychologist and begrudgingly takes on a partner, followed by the movie *Batman & Robin*, where he welcomes Batgirl and the whole Bat-Family notion without hesitation.

Cartoons

Many cartoons have starred or guest-starred Batman and Robin. The Dynamic Duo teamed up with Scooby-Doo, joined the Super Friends, tolerated Bat-Mite, and—due to the restrictive nature of 1960s to 1980s standards and practices—improvised nonviolent ways to combat evil over the course of assorted Saturday morning programs that offered no depth, few psychological insights, and precious little to attract adults. Many[25] nevertheless consider Batman's definitive screen depiction to have been that of one particular cartoon, *Batman: The Animated Series*.

In 1992, Warner Bros. Animation followed the success of Tim Burton's *Batman* by developing a new animated program, which Bruce Timm masterminded. Filled with shadows, pathos, and wry wit, episodes retold comic book stories and mixed in new works from whole cloth. Its creators held to the principle that Batman was the character's true self and playboy Bruce Wayne simply his disguise. "He *is* Batman," said Kevin Conroy, the actor who voiced this Batman and Bruce Wayne. "He became Batman the instant his parents were murdered. Batman needs Bruce, however hollow that identity feels to him from time to time. Bruce keeps Batman human." Where some movies show Bruce's temptation to give up being Batman, this Batman's only temptation would have been to give up being Bruce. "The temptation is to retreat into the cave and never come out. To give up his disguise as Bruce Wayne and surrender himself completely to the darkness."[26]

Batman: The Animated Series left lasting marks on Batman's rogues gallery. Its version of Two-Face's origin integrated multiple personality in a way that made some sense, showing that its Harvey Dent always had a bad Harvey inside him waiting for trauma to bring it out. The series fleshed out Poison Ivy, introduced psychiatrist-turned-sidekick Harley Quinn into the Joker's life, and re-envisioned the previously two-dimensional Mr. Freeze into perhaps the most poignant opponent of them all (see Case File 2–2: Mr. Freeze).

Timm's Batman would continue his adventures in *The New Batman/Superman Adventures*, *Batman Beyond*, and *Justice League Unlimited*. Other, unrelated Batman cartoon series would follow, exploring new takes on the characters (the serious *The Batman*, the comedic *The Brave and the Bold*), along with unrelated animated films (e.g., *Batman: Under the Red Hood*) that each met popular demand for fresh exploits from our Dark Knight.

Batman Begins (2005 Motion Picture)

> "*A guy who dresses up like a bat clearly has issues.*"
> —Bruce Wayne (Christian Bale)

For the first time, a Batman movie's central figure was the man inside the mask, Bruce Wayne. Director and script co-author Christopher Nolan finally got to spin the kind of tale Joel Schumacher had yearned for the chance to tell, the cinematic counterpart to author Frank Miller and artist David Mazzuchelli's *Batman: Year One*. Whereas Tim Burton and his team had created a Gotham askew from our reality, built on massive soundstages with nightmare architecture and no hint that the rest of the planet might even exist, Nolan gave us a city as real as he could create with scenes shot in London and Chicago, no gigantic soundstage, and its hero roaming the planet. Quitting college, Bruce picks up skills outside Gotham until he is ready to bring his new knowledge home.

Batman Begins is about fear—what causes it, how it's overcome, and how it's instilled. Between scenes of Henri Ducard teaching Bruce advanced fighting techniques so that he might "turn fear against those who prey on the fearful," we see how 8-year-old Bruce gained the fears his adult self is learning to face. Before we first see the man, we see the child running, playing, and falling through an old well into a cave filled with bats. Nightmares haunt the boy. His father assures him that the bats flew out to frighten him only because they'd felt their own fear, because all creatures feel fear, "especially the scary ones." By daylight the family enters Gotham, the city his parents have worked hard to improve, a city that will never again look quite so bright, to attend a show that night. Performers' bat-like costumes frighten Bruce, so the Waynes leave the show early only to cross paths with the mugger and murderer Joe Chill. *Batman Begins* brings in an element strangely edited out of *Batman Forever*: If not for young Bruce's feelings, his fear in this case, they wouldn't have been in the wrong place at the wrong time. Twentysomething Bruce later tells Ducard, "My anger outweighs my guilt," without denying he feels guilty.

Once back in Gotham, Batman instills fear through intimidation and violence while Dr. Jonathan Crane, a.k.a. the Scarecrow, creates long-lasting fear via panic-inducing toxin. Crane and Ducard, a.k.a. Ra's al Ghul, mean to panic the whole city. Bruce, who has been so intent on making crooks feel fear, now fights to stop that toxin's spread. He fights fear itself. Robbed of revenge against Chill, Bruce has launched his assault on all criminals—every thug he slugs a pitiful substitute for his parents' killer—but he comes to recognize that justice is bigger than vengeance and that he can inspire much more. In the film's final scene, Jim Gordon shines the Bat-Signal while he voices concerns about escalation. He worries that Batman's example might inspire criminals to try to top him, criminals like a theatrical newcomer who killed guards and left a Joker playing card behind.

"This is your mask," Rachel Dawes says, touching Bruce's face in the film's last daylight scene. "Your real face is the one that criminals now fear." Not quite. While one face is truer to himself than the other, as this Bruce Wayne, Christian Bale actually plays three roles: the reckless billionaire playboy, the symbol who must be more than a man, and the flesh-and-blood mortal his surrogate father Alfred knows best.

The Dark Knight (2008 Motion Picture)

> *"They're wise to your act. You got rules. The Joker, he's got no rules. Nobody's gonna cross him for you."*
> —Sal Maroni (Eric Roberts)

The Dark Knight is about inspiration. Batman's example inspires fool-hardy copycat vigilantes, his threat inspires less fear once the criminals learn he won't kill, and Harvey Dent inspires the citizens of Gotham City. On the other side, there's the Joker out to inspire anarchy and coax everybody into revealing their darkest sides. Inspiration leads to escalation.

More than any other villains, the Joker and Two-Face reflect Batman himself as funhouse distortions, converses of who and what he is. The laughing, jesting, brightly colored Joker contrasts with the grim, dark Batman. The Joker is the Joker, no alter ego. The film's opening bank robbery shows him wearing clown mask over clown makeup. Under the surface there's only more Joker. He gives no history except inconsistent lies. When he finally considers the impact of his demand that Batman unmask, he retracts the threat and demands that Batman's identity remain undisclosed. He wants a Batman who has no other self, a Dark Knight whose only deeper layer is further darkness.

More obviously mirroring the hero overall, the Batman/Bruce Wayne duality, is Harvey "Two-Face" Dent—another man transformed by tragedy into a figure with two faces. From a dinner date of Bruce's to the Joker himself, people keep wondering if Harvey Dent, the face of honor and hope in corrupt Gotham City, might be the bat. At one point Harvey claims that he is, turning himself over to authorities and trusting Batman to do the right thing by "saving my ass." Worth noting from this film is one hint as to why their defining tragedies sent these two men down different forks in the road— Bruce into taking charge of his life, protecting the innocent, and fighting for what's right, and Harvey into trusting only 50–50 fate, seeking revenge, and threatening innocents while showing no sign of remorse. Long before fire scars Harvey down one side, police have already nicknamed him "Two-Face." Though we never hear why, it may mean they'd glimpsed some hypocrisy, a malevolent potential that the Joker would later lure out. When Gordon asks why Harvey won't let doctors treat his burns, Harvey's answer is to insist Gordon utter that nickname, after which Harvey says, "Why should I hide who I am?"

The Dark Knight includes depictions of mental illness. Harvey tries intimidating information out of one of the Joker's psychotic henchmen until Batman points out the uselessness of the attempt. "Schiff, Thomas. A *paranoid schizophrenic*, former patient at Arkham Asylum, the kind of mind the Joker attracts." For the most part, however bizarre he might appear, the Joker seems dangerously sane. He understands his actions; he uses order to sow chaos, developing well-orchestrated plans to foster anarchy; and although the people of Gotham will prove themselves better than he expects, he correctly anticipates many actions people will take and recognizes the reality around him. He has no hallucinations or obvious delusions. When he tells Two-Face he doesn't scheme, "I just do things," either he's lying or he has a view so warped that he fails to recognize his own scheming nature. We do not know.

However, there are moments that make the audience question the Joker's grip on reality. When he tells mobsters, "Why don't you give me a call when you want to start taking things a little more seriously? Here's my card," and drops a Joker card onto the table, is he toying with them or does he truly not realize that this card that has no contact information will not help them call? This character who attracts psychotic henchmen may have lingering symptoms from his own past psychosis. He keeps making involuntary, repetitive movements—flicking his tongue, smacking his mouth—which suggest *tardive dyskinesia*, a condition that arises as a consequence of long-term or high-dosage use of *antipsychotic* (*neuroleptic*) medication. Even after discontinuing the drugs' use, patients may show these tic-like actions for the rest of their lives.[27]

The film ends with Gordon smashing the Bat-Signal, the same bat symbol he'd shone in his first scene when he'd wanted to assure the folks of Gotham that their hero was out there. Together he and Batman will mislead them. After investing so much time trying both to make criminals cower and to help citizens have faith, they decide Batman cannot embody both chaos and order, both shadowed hero and light in the night. To preserve Harvey's value as the White Knight beyond his death, they'll keep the Face's sins secret and let the public think Batman may have committed murder. Batman will be only the Dark Knight. He may have underestimated his own power to shine.

The Dark Knight Rises (2012 Motion Picture)

> *"We were in this together, and then you were gone. And now this evil rises. The Batman has to come back."*
>
> —Commissioner Gordon (Gary Oldman)

Following the death of actor Heath Ledger, *The Dark Knight*'s Joker, filmmaker Christopher Nolan found himself without a story for the next film, initially saying he had "honestly no concept of what I would do next."[28] In time, he decided that instead of continuing to treat these films as Batman's early career, he would skip ahead and bring his Bat-films to an end with a story the comic books could not tell. "And in viewing it as the finishing of a story rather than infinitely blowing up the balloon and expanding the story," Nolan said, "viewing it as an ending, that sets you very much on the right track about the appropriate conclusion and the essence of what tale we're telling. And it hearkens back to that priority of trying to find the reality in these fantastic stories."[29] The old serials aside, what previous superhero movie series ever clearly concluded instead of fizzling out? Chris Nolan takes Batman into territory no movie superhero has dared visit before.

Ra's al Ghul and the Joker have each tried to teach Batman lessons about the darker side of human nature. He's not the only one they're trying to teach. Ra's wants the world to watch Gotham tear itself apart; the Joker wants Gotham's citizens to see for themselves the worst that they're ready to do. One thinks globally; the other thinks locally. Bane, too, means to bring out the worst in people before school finally lets out.

As if Gotham's police, the al Ghul legacy, a city's simmering tension, and outright riots weren't trouble enough, Batman has to juggle dealings with Selina Kyle and Bane: the woman who makes him and the villain who breaks him. Having sacrificed the Dark Knight's reputation in the previous film for the sake of White Knight Harvey Dent's memory, should Batman fade into urban legend hated and hunted or emerge like a supernatural figure risen from the grave? Without Batman, what is Bruce Wayne? Without heroes during times of peace, who's ready to oppose evil when new conflict appears? As things get bad and then get worse, Bruce will have to reconcile with his own creation, the Batman, as crime-fighter, symbol, and the truest part of himself so the hero can rise to the occasion. Bruce will have to push himself to the limits he has previously said Batman can't have. How deeply do the sacrifices cut? Who will occupy Gotham? With the haves feeding off the have-nots during troubled post-9/11, post-war times and evil men then pounding their messages into frustrated citizens, Bruce needs to determine once and for all what kind of hero, what kind of legend or man, people really need and what they need to know about him. What does it take to break the Bat—or to salvage a shattered symbol?

> *"There's a storm coming, Mister Wayne. You and your friends better batten down the hatches 'cause when it hits, you're all gonna wonder how you ever thought you could live so large and leave so little for the rest of us."*
> —Selina Kyle (Anne Hathaway)

The Source Material: Comic Books!

DC Comics stories have featured more than one Bruce Wayne in their ongoing series, plus many parallel universes, variant histories, possible futures, imaginary tales, and other "alternate" Batman yarns, the most influential of which is arguably Frank Miller's four-part graphic novel *The Dark Knight Returns* (1986). In terms of ongoing continuity through most DC Comics publications, despite history-altering crises along the way, there have been two: the Golden Age Batman and the repeatedly revised Silver Age/modern one.

The Golden Age Batman

In 1956, DC Comics began replacing existing characters like the Flash, Green Lantern, and Atom with new characters that had the same superhero names but different origins and costumes, often new secret identities and powers. DC left certain characters unchanged, including those they now dub the "Big Three": Superman, Wonder Woman, and Batman. When Barry Allen, a character whose debut as the new Flash launched the Silver Age,[30] crosses from his world (Earth-One) into a parallel universe (Earth-Two), he meets Jay

Garrick, who'd been the Flash during comics' Golden Age.[31] Earth-One's Justice League of America soon meets Earth-Two's Justice Society of America,[32] and things grow complicated. Once the continuity establishes that the new versions and similarly named old ones live in different worlds, DC indirectly created two Supermen, two Wonder Women, two Batmen. The Justice League's Batman, having interacted with Silver Age heroes like Allen, lives on Earth-One and, as such, has to be a different character from Earth-Two's Batman, who'd known Garrick in World War II.

The Golden Age Batman and Superman become best friends, both honorary members of the Justice Society. While that original Batman has allies, he has only one partner, his ward, Dick Grayson, a.k.a. Robin the Boy Wonder. This Bruce Wayne, having been raised by Uncle Philip and not by the butler Alfred Pennyworth, hires butler Alfred Beagle sometime after becoming Dick Grayson's surrogate father. Bruce marries Selina Kyle, the reformed Catwoman, and together they have a daughter, Helena. That world's Catwoman and then Batman each die when they come out of retirement for one last adventure apiece.[33] Adopting the *nom de plume* Huntress, Helena carries on the crime-fighting tradition.

The distinction between the original Batman and the modern is, to some degree, false. At no point did DC's creative teams decide, "This is our last issue starring the old Batman. Next month we pack and move to Earth-One." The earliest appearances retroactively became Earth-Two Batman's adventures, with no fine distinction as to when the new Batman's stories began.

The Silver Age/Modern Batman

DC and Marvel's superheroes live along a "sliding scale" of time. No matter when most modern heroes' first stories saw print, published adventures from the Silver Age onward took place no more than a decade or so ago within their fictional careers. Batman's 1960s adventures, those that remain canon, for him took place not long ago. Officially, though, most of those stories either never happened or took place in different ways. History changed and keeps changing. The Silver Age, which a new Flash heralded in 1956, ended around 1970

The Caped Crusader's kid-friendly adventures in early Silver Age comic books commonly saw him meeting space aliens (*Batman* #128, left) or mutating into one wacky form after another (e.g., #147's Bat-Baby, right) instead of delving into any deeper concerns. Photo by Lynda M. Langley.

when mainstream comic books lost much of their innocence: Batman's sidekick heads to college; Green Arrow's sidekick gets hooked on drugs, as does Spider-Man's best friend; the Green Goblin murders Spidey's girlfriend Gwen; and the Joker, now deemed insane, resumes his old habit of murdering people left and right.[34] A more serious Bronze Age ensued and lasted until *Crisis on Infinite Earths* (1985–1986) set off a rattling chain of Multiverse makeovers, and Reagan-era superhero deconstructions *Batman: The Dark Knight Returns* (1986) and *Watchmen* (1986–1987) inspired many creators to turn comics even darker deep into the long-lasting Modern Age, the Dark Age of tarnished heroes (see chapter 13).

Despite inconsistencies, revisions, and errors, the modern Batman has the longest semblance of a continuous fictional history. The Silver Age Batman both is and is not the same as the modern. Rather than create even more Batmen who might bump into each other while bouncing between even more universes, authors attribute changes between the Silver Age and today to reality-altering events (the Multiverse makeovers: the crossover epics *Crisis on Infinite Earths*, *Zero Hour*, *Infinite Crisis*, *Flashpoint*), much the way Marty McFly's family history keeps getting altered over the course of the three *Back to the Future* films. From Batman's silliest Silver Age stories to his return to grim avenger roots and everything beyond, each adventure in the mainstream Bat-comics' canon "really" took place even if later undone or altered by time travelers' interference and other butterfly effects, and he is the same entity whether he remembers it all or not.

More than one Robin has accompanied the modern Batman: Dick Grayson, Jason Todd, Tim Drake, Damian Wayne, and briefly a Girl Wonder, Stephanie Brown—two of whom die, although they both return (Jason getting convolutedly resurrected and Stephanie having faked her death). Robins keep growing up. Stephanie replaces Barbara Gordon as Batgirl, Tim replaces Jason as Red Robin, Jason adopts the Joker's old alias as the Red Hood, and Dick, after years of fighting crime under the name Nightwing, becomes a new Batman while Bruce is believed dead—some of those changes last, some don't. Having briefly (although perhaps not bindingly) married Talia al Ghul,[35] Bruce has allegedly fathered her son Damian.[36] This League of Assassins–trained lad becomes a grimmer Robin by brighter Batman Grayson's side[37] until Damian at last works with his father, while Bruce proceeds to recruit an international league of Batmen under the auspices of Batman, Inc.[38] Within the fiction, the Caped Crusader turns franchise.

Whose Belfry?

So which Batman do we mean—Golden Age, Silver Age, pre-Crisis, post-Crisis, post–Zero Hour, post–Infinite Crisis, Dark Knight, Bright Knight, Adam West, Michael Keaton, Kevin Conroy, Christian Bale, any other in between?

Yes. All of them.

When in doubt, assume the modern comic book character, but examples will come from them all. *Batman: The Animated Series* creator Bruce Timm has said that there are "so many different interpretations of Batman—everything from Adam West to Frank Miller to Tim Burton. . . . There's a certain validity to all those versions. They don't cancel each other out, they're all, to a degree, justifiable."[39] It's like reading contradictory legends of Robin Hood. If he doesn't wield bow and arrow and steal from the rich, he's not Robin Hood. No matter which Batman we consider, some things remain constant. In 1939, 1966, 1986, and today, wealthy Bruce Wayne—a bit smug in the knowledge that he can accomplish what sworn police officers either can't or won't—dresses up, plays detective, punches bad guys, and lives his double life, all so he can protect the innocent, infuse fear in evildoers, and fight his endless fight.

He will never finish avenging the parents who died before his eyes.

CASE FILE 2–1 King Tut

Real name: Professor William Omaha McElroy

First appearance: "The Curse of Tut," *Batman* season 1, episode 27 (April 13, 1966). Portrayed by Victor Buono.

Origin: After suffering a blow to the head during a student riot, Yale University Egyptologist William McElroy develops amnesia coupled with the belief that he is the reincarnated King Tutankhamen, the pharaoh who ruled circa 1333–1324 bce during Egypt's 18th Dynasty. As King Tut, he proceeds to steal Egyptian artifacts and tries transforming Gotham into a modern-day Thebes. Each time Batman and Robin finally knock the man out or trick him into ingesting his own scarab potion, he emerges from his delusion fully restored to his mild-mannered professorial self—until a future episode's random brick or flower pot falls on his head and turns him back into Tut. His henchmen often accept McElroy's delusion, such as when those falling flower pots also strike two students on their heads, upon which they kneel before Tut.[1]

"No! No violence! I can't stand violence! But I like torture. Hmm, it's good, clean fun."

—King Tut in the *Batman* television series
(episode 88, "Batman's Waterloo," March 9, 1967)

✿   ✿   ✿

Even though Chief O'Hara once leads the protesting professor away for incarceration,[2] McElroy when in his right mind never gets held criminally responsible for Tut's crimes and remains free to await his next concussion. McElroy takes personal responsibility for his actions by wearing a protective hat—attempting, albeit futilely, to prevent the next mishap. The insanity defense, much as it might seem to apply here, never gets mentioned. In fact, the heroes tell Tut he'll go to the penitentiary, and when Dr. Cassandra frees Batman's worst enemies so they can turn invisible and fight him in the dark for the program's penultimate episode,[3] King Tut escapes from jail along with the rest. So when he's McElroy, he goes free, but if Tut, he's locked up.

McElroy (Victor Buono): Did I do it again?
Batman (Adam West): You certainly did.
McElroy: Did I hurt anyone?
Batman: Only yourself, professor. Only yourself.

How might we diagnose Professor McElroy?

Amnesia (loss of memory) can be *biogenic* (biologically generated) or *psychogenic* (psychologically generated). However much King Tut's amnesia might appear to be biogenic—after all, head injury brings it on—repeated bonks to the noggin will not turn amnesia on and off, back and forth, like a brain damage light switch. Outside 1960s sitcoms, head injuries don't work that way. Psychogenic amnesia, however, conceivably could.

Simple *dissociation* is an everyday process in which different parts of the mind function at the same time without sharing information with each other—as in the case of *highway hypnosis*, when you're driving down the road and suddenly realize you don't remember the last five miles. Part of your mind was daydreaming while another part was driving the car. The *dissociative disorders* take dissociation to an unhealthy extreme, typically as a way to escape from facing trauma or other unpleasant reality, and usually include some degree of psychogenic amnesia. *Dissociative amnesia,* psychogenic memory loss far too broad for ordinary forgetfulness, would be an inadequate diagnosis, failing to account for McElroy's most prominent symptom: his assumption of a new identity.

Dissociative fugue involves confusion about one's identity or even assumption of a new identity together with amnesia for some or all of the person's previous life. "Fugue" means "flight"—the person flees his or her past life, abruptly disappearing without notice and traveling far away, usually in response to now-forgotten trauma, stress, or overwhelming life events. In most cases, the problem involves a single episode that lasts hours to months and abruptly ends in complete recovery, although longer-lasting cases do exist. Those few who experience reoccurring fugues periodically roam from home without knowing who they are, escaping their old identities entirely, as opposed to King Tut, who, rather than abandoning McElroy's past life, embodies the Egyptologist's area of expertise. Recurrent assumption of a particular alternate persona would better fit *dissociative identity disorder*, the modern name for *multiple personality.* Professionals uncomfortable with the idiosyncratic blow-to-the-head trigger for Egyptologist-to-Egyptian transformations might have to settle for *dissociative disorder not otherwise specified*, recognizing that his condition falls within the dissociative disorder category without pinning it down as any disorder specifically described in the American Psychiatric Association's *Diagnostic and Statistical Manual of Mental Disorders* (*DSM*).

Despite his *delusion* (a belief grossly out of touch with reality), specific *psychotic disorders* (disorders in which the person is grossly out of touch with reality) seem less likely than a dissociative disorder. Aside from believing himself to be Tut, he fully recognizes how the world works. He knows he is not in the fourteenth century BCE. Although he believes he is Tut's reincarnation, reincarnation is a popular belief worldwide—the norm in numerous cultures. If psychotic, his single delusion could qualify him for *delusional disorder*, specifically of the *grandiose type* because he believes himself to be such a famous personage. Depending on their reasons for buying into that belief, his henchmen might suffer either their own dissociative conditions or *shared psychosis* (see Case File 8–2: Harley Quinn).

> *"How many times must I tell you? Queens consume nectar and ambrosia, not hot dogs!"*
> —King Tut to Nefertiti in the *Batman* television series (episode 27, "The Curse of Tut," April 13, 1966)

CASE FILE 2–2 Mr. Freeze

Real name: Victor Fries

First appearance: *Batman* #121 (February, 1959) as Mr. Zero; renamed Mr. Freeze for 1966–1968 *Batman* television series[1] and subsequent comics.[2]

Origin: When cryogenics researcher Victor Fries learns that his wife, Nora, suffers from a rapidly progressing terminal illness, he suspends her in cryostasis and gets to work in pursuit of a cure. A ruthless executive tampers with the equipment and causes an accident that soaks Fries in cryopreservation fluids. Victor's body temperature plunges and his body chemistry changes in adaptation. Now he must wear a special refrigeration suit to maintain his subzero temperature while he seeks revenge on any he believes have wronged him and steals equipment and funds to continue his efforts to restore Nora.[3]

> *"It would move me to tears if I still had tears to shed."*
> —Mr. Freeze in "Heart of Ice," *Batman: The Animated Series*, ep. 17 (September 7, 1992)

❁   ❁   ❁

"Heart of Ice," the Emmy-winning episode of *Batman: The Animated Series*, established this origin, subsequently integrated into the comic books and one movie. Television turned Mr. Zero, one nearly forgotten gimmick villain among many, into the most tragically sympathetic member of Batman's best-known foes, Mr. Freeze, this cold-bodied man with the coldhearted personality who'll stop at nothing for the sake of the one person who ever warmed up his life. In the *stages of grief* Elisabeth Kübler-Ross[4] made famous (see next chapter for more detail), Victor Fries blasts his way through denial and anger into the bargaining stage, determined to fix what's wrong and save Nora's life. Any threat to that bargain fires up his anger.

In killing not only those who've wronged him but security guards and any other innocent person caught in his way, Victor Fries embarks on a quest on Nora's behalf regardless of what her wishes would have been, with some parallels to how Bruce Wayne as a young man at times disregards his late parents' wishes, ideals, and legacy. Bruce matures. In *Batman Begins*, he goes from cursing Wayne Manor as a mausoleum he'd gladly tear down brick by brick to mourning its loss when a villain burns it down and then planning to rebuild it exactly as before.

No actress voices Nora Fries. In cartoons and live-action film, she floats dreamily in frozen storage, a thing of beauty in a cryogenic snow globe. Victor's love is real, but by carrying out his murders and heists heedless of how she'd feel, he gives no thought to the fact that if he succeeds, she'll have feelings about everything he's done. He engages in her *objectification*—that is, he treats her more like a precious object and less like a human being. Objectification leads to *dehumanization*, forgetting that the other person has a mind and morality associated with personhood.[5] Victor's objectifying of Nora may result from her inanimate state; then again, distant, standoffish Victor, who never warmed up to anyone else, never having picked up a normal array of social skills or interpersonal perceptiveness, may always have objectified the beautiful woman to some degree.

For all his sociopathic shortcomings, Victor values Nora's well-being above his own, her happiness over his. In the comics and cartoons, her restoration is poignant, each format offering different reasons why, after doing everything for her sake, he can never touch his wife again. The animated film *Batman & Mr. Freeze: SubZero* ends with Nora cured and Victor presumed dead. Televised news of her restoration gives Victor a smile before he heads back into the Arctic snow, crying icy tears of joy as he lets Nora live without him, in peace.

3
The Trauma

"This is such a primal origin story. A kid watches his parents murdered in front of his eyes on a concrete altar of blood and at that moment sacrifices his childhood and makes a commitment, a commitment that he intends to honor even if he has to walk through hell for the rest of his life to get the guy who did this, to get all the bad guys. . . . It's what everyone around the world can relate to: a powerful thing that motivates someone, that drives someone to the brink, that can make someone put on a bat mask, that can get us all to suspend our disbelief and believe in Bruce Wayne and take this journey with him, and it all starts with the origin."

—Michael Uslan, *The Dark Knight Rises*
executive producer[1]

For his first six months of publication, Batman had no origin. He was a shadowy figure who fought crime and solved mysteries for no apparent reason, atypical for early comic book superheroes but consistent with some of the pulp magazine figures that had inspired creators Bob Kane and Bill Finger. The Shadow fought crime in the pulps for years before readers even learned his true identity, much less how he'd come to know what evil lurks in the hearts of men. In November, 1939, *Detective*

Comics #33 opened with "The Legend of the Batman—Who He Is and How He Came to Be!" A father, mother, and son, after a night out at the movies, walk together down a city street. A gunman demands the wife's necklace. The husband moves to protect her. Gunshots. He dies. She dies. Their son stands alone in tears. The narrative tells us, "The boy's eyes are wide with terror and shock as the horrible scene is spread before him." Days later, the boy Bruce kneels at his bedside, hands clasped in prayer by candlelight as he swears by his parents' spirits that he will "avenge their deaths by spending the rest of my life warring on all criminals"—*avenge*, not revenge. Within the fictional biography of Bruce Wayne, this is where Batman begins. Over the years, other details crept in—the father, Thomas Wayne, became a doctor, the unnamed mother became Martha, and their killer became Joe Chill—but six powerful panels out of a tale barely a page and a half long already told readers everything they needed to know to understand what propelled the Wayne son into his crusade against crime. Finger and Kane had contemplated other explanations for what could have turned Bruce Wayne into a costumed vigilante.[2] "Bill and I discussed it," Bob Kane recalled, "and we figured there's nothing more traumatic than having your parents murdered before your eyes."[3]

"Nothing More Traumatic"

Trauma involves (1) experiencing actual or threatened death or serious injury to oneself or others and (2) reacting to this horrific event with intense fear, helplessness, or horror. A tragic event is not necessarily traumatic. The world's three best-known superheroes—Superman, Batman, and Spider-Man—are all orphans, and all their origins include defining moments centered on their parental losses: The infant Kal-El rockets away from his exploding home planet; the boy Bruce Wayne drops to his knees, wide-eyed at his parents' murders; and the teenager Peter Parker, already Spider-Man though not yet a hero, gripping the burglar who has slain Pete's Uncle Ben, realizes with horror that he has seen this man before, that he could have easily prevented the death of the man who raised him.[4] Their respective tragedies traumatize Bruce and Peter, but not so for the Kryptonian tot. Saved from disaster by birth parents who die with their world, Kal-El flies through space, listening to Krypton's version of *Your Baby Can Read*, blissfully unaware of catastrophe. Raised by a loving farm couple who find his rocket in a Kansas field, the child they name Clark Kent grows up without knowing his origin until he's at the brink of manhood, and even when he learns it, Krypton's destruction is remote history, like a story in a book.[5] This disconnect from his homeworld and the fact that he'd been a baby at the time will keep Superman from suffering the kind of *survivor guilt* that might drive Batman and definitely burdens Spider-Man: that feeling of guilt for having survived when others did not and blaming oneself for wanting to see a movie, for letting a burglar get away, for any action great or small on his part, whether realistic or not, that could conceivably have altered the course of events and allowed everyone else to live.[6] Superman gets to feel blessed where Spider-Man feels cursed, and so for different reasons each knows that with great power comes great responsibility. What, then, pushes Bruce, the boy with an inherited fortune and no superpowers, to build himself into a crime-fighter and take on responsibility for protecting others?

Many who research the impact of losing one's parent or parents when old enough to know about it rank that as the single most stressful common life event children can experience.[7] Uncommon traumas like torture or terrorist attacks are not universal experiences, not things most of us anticipate, but sooner or later we all learn that our parents can and will die. Life event stress checklists for children (based on Holmes and Rahe's still-influential stress scale, their Social Readjustment Rating Scale or Schedule of Recent Events)[8] place losing a parent at the very top. Unlike other calamities, losing parents deprives the child of the nurturance, love, and support that might help that child get through other kinds of hard times. For adults, losing a spouse tops that list. Losing your child might upset you more, but losing your spouse upends your life more broadly; among other things, a young child almost certainly didn't help you make ends meet. What's traumatic or stressful for one person might not be for another. That which inflicts *distress* (bad stress) upon one person might bestow *eustress* (good stress) upon another, even in the case of parental death. A sadistic parent's passing might free victimized family members to start a new and better life or, conversely, evil offspring like Superman's archenemy Lex Luthor or Batman's foe Hush might revel in a parent's elimination.[9] Starting a new life is stressful no matter how much you need it. *Change* is stressful. The recurring theme across all the different lists of stress factors (marriage, divorce, a huge win, a huge loss, new employment, unemployment, Christmas) is change.

Children who lose their parents to homicide experience complicated bereavement processes. Many evince debilitating posttraumatic stress symptoms, a difficulty especially common among those who witnessed the homicide.[10] Observers to their parents' murders may display their emotional scarring through tantrums, flashbacks, sleep disturbances, anxiety, dissociation, passiveness, and aggression, or with shocking images, thoughts, and memories, often finding themselves haunted by the murderer's impulsiveness, the victim's suffering, the visible injuries, and their own lack of power.[11]

When you're a child, losing your parents rewrites your world. If you had a loving parent, your everyday life is now absent that love, or had they been unloving, any wish to win their affection and approval during this lifetime goes forever unfulfilled. Indirect losses both emotional and practical will follow. Parental loss likely becomes not one stressor but a series of hassles and pains: loss of parent, loss of resources, loss of old acquaintances, change of residence, increase in responsibilities, and adjustment to either a surviving parent's own changes or a new caregiver's ways.[12] You wonder what will become of you. Losing a sibling, while dreadful, does not endanger your everyday existence. Losing your parents does—and if you witnessed their deaths, you probably feared for your own life at the time. Subsequent fears both rational and irrational can ensue, even the dread, however illogical, that the killer might hunt you down, and so nightmares disturb your peace. Some bereaved children act out,[13] misbehaving out of resentment toward a new caregiver for not being the old or toward the whole unfair world because the parent's death and the consequent life upheaval threaten that child's needs for connection, competence, self-worth, and control.[14] Thinking less abstractly than adults do and less able to articulate their feelings, bereaved children tend to express any anger and anxieties behaviorally.[15] Fortunately that tendency helps them to heal as well because they're also more likely to work out their feelings and concerns through activities like art, games, schoolwork, and stories.[16]

Elisabeth Kübler-Ross derived five stages of grief (denial, anger, bargaining, depression, acceptance) from her interviews with 500 dying patients, originally applying these stages to terminal illness and later to any catastrophic personal loss, including bereavement over losing loved ones.[17] This set of stages lacks consistent confirmation by empirical research,[18] manifests less universally than commonly thought (people can skip stages, get stuck, go back and forth, or follow different processes entirely),[19] and can work differently for young children, who, even if they know what death means, do not understand it the way adults do. A child's mourning process may be incomplete because (1) a grieving child may lose some of his or her self-concept because the child derives much identity through parental modeling and interactions, (2) role conflicts may occur for a bereaved child who makes an effort to replace the dead parent by assuming family roles previously held by that parent, (3) memorializing the dead parent may figure prominently into the child's process of growing up, and (4) the child may interpret the death as abandonment or supernatural punishment for the child's own misdeeds,[20] although treating *maturational grief* (intermittent grief arising from life-cycle milestones) as *incomplete grief* (relatively continuous, acute grief) might be a mistake. Losing parents during childhood is a different kind of milestone than losing them when you're an adult, and it alters other milestones. Childhood loss of a parent commonly leads to surges in grief years after the loss as the individual feels the absence sharply at points peers can still share with their own parents. Bruce Wayne avoids some such experiences by diverging from his peers and creating milestones unique to himself. While his childhood friends finish high school, he studies martial arts on the other side of the world. He never passes through Kübler-Ross's five stages: He never denies what happened—he immediately knows, "They're gone"—and he never dwells in depression. He gets mad, he accepts that this is his new reality, and the only bargain he makes is a vow to stay mad and avenge them, not some plea for their impossible return.

Posttraumatic Stress Disorder

Does Batman have posttraumatic stress disorder (PTSD)? Some people think so.[21] He broods, he's aloof, he's a grown man who dons a mask and regularly replays his parents' murder in his mind decades after they died. These add up to PTSD, right? Maybe not. A person can show some symptoms of a mental disorder without fully qualifying for a clinical diagnosis. Reliving that catastrophic event and letting it rule his life might suggest so. Trauma of human design—rape, torture, terrorism, and certainly a double murder over a pearl necklace—provokes PTSD more easily than disasters or human error.[22] The longer the trauma, the greater its impact tends to be. It wears you down. Even though both his parents die in a flash, young Bruce's time alone with their bodies on that street before help arrives must itself be harrowing, as must hearing the sirens, watching the police gather, answering questions, seeing graphic news footage, and repeatedly experiencing the disappointment of learning that no progress has been made in the case because, in most versions of the story, the Waynes' killer never faces justice for that particular crime.

*Posttraumatic stress disorder,** as its name implies, refers to anxiety suffered long after a traumatic event has occurred—so obviously, in fact, that even some professionals can make the mistake of overlooking the other word in that name: *disorder.* We have to look at whether the trouble is *maladaptive*—does it keep someone from adapting to life? Does it render that person unable to function? Trauma and subsequent stress over it don't prove that a person has the disorder any more than a week spent grieving deeply gets someone diagnosed as having major depression. Whether a given problem counts as a psychiatric disorder, a mental illness, depends on severity, frequency, number, duration, distress, and type of reported symptoms.

Posttraumatic in the American Psychiatric Association's *DSM* or *post-traumatic* in the World Health Organization's *ICD-10.*

You can function poorly in many ways without meeting the criteria for any specific mental disorder.

When is posttraumatic stress pathological? The American Psychiatric Association's *Diagnostic and Statistical Manual of Mental Disorders* (*DSM-IV*[23] or *DSM-IV-TR*[24])* lays out specific criteria.

Criterion A: Trauma. Yes, the event that created Batman (1) involved death or physical danger and (2) horrified the survivor.

Criterion B: Persistent re-experiencing. Yes, Bruce re-experiences his parents' murders through recurrent, vivid recollections and some of his responses when exposed to cues reminiscent of the event. Nightly he seeks out criminals whose actions reflect those of his parents' killer, maybe to make himself face his old fears or maybe to make sure he never stops feeling them. Many individuals suffering survivor guilt report feeling wrong, as if they have betrayed whomever they have lost, when they find they do not feel the old grief and fear as intensely. Many a Batman comic book story begins with him intervening in a mugging. Feelings evoked by these memories and flashbacks, when they come to him normally (i.e., not when he's loopy from exhaustion or hallucinating because of a villain's mind-altering gas), do not enfeeble him. According to one psychologist, the memories "don't usually come to him unbidden; that is, they aren't intrusive, and he usually retrieves the memories in a normal way,"[25] although I'm not so sure. So many cues trigger those memories on his best day, much less every time he's ever feverish, exhausted to the point of confusion, or suffering exposure to hallucinogens (his enemies hit him with those a lot).† Then his mind always trots right back to his

---

*Diagnostic criteria did not change between *DSM-IV* and *DSM-IV-TR*. The *TR* (text revision) part refers to information the APA tweaked in the manual's text (for example, by mentioning new research findings on whether certain disorders are likely to run in families) without reworking the diagnostic system.

†"...lethal Laughing Gas, mind-control lipstick, Fear Dust, toxic aerosols, and 'artificial phobia' pills. Indeed, his career had barely begun before he was heroically inhaling countless bizarre chemical concoctions cooked up by black-market alchemists."—Morrison (2011), 21.

fears, usually his parents' deaths. Most of us would show greater variety in our hallucinatory content. Furthermore, as we'll discuss shortly, intrusive thoughts contribute to some people's posttraumatic *growth*.

Criterion C: Persistent avoidance and emotional numbing. No, he does not avoid reminders of the murders. In fact, his crime-fighting efforts immerse him in reminders. He does not suppress thoughts, avoid feelings, or refuse to have any conversations regarding the trauma. While he eschews the use of guns because they remind him of his parents' deaths, he faces these and other weapons all the time. His active pursuit of situations reminiscent of their murder could, in fact, be *counterphobic* behavior (actions that help combat phobic inclinations by facing feared stimuli instead of trying to escape or avoid them) in that he seeks out the things that most frightened his younger self: criminals and bats. He visits "Crime Alley," as the site of his parents' death becomes known, on every anniversary of when his parents' blood christened it so.*

Numbing of general responsiveness gets complicated. He responds to his environment, but he's guarded. He has feelings even though his general stoicism and frequently inadequate expression of how he really feels might give impressions otherwise. A diagnostician will look at specific symptoms in this area:[26]

Markedly diminished interest or participation in significant activities: During the months after the murders, this might have applied, as may be true of many other symptoms. We don't know that much about his everyday childhood, and when we don't know, we oughtn't guess or judge. No, his devotion to crime-fighting *replaced* many of his previous interests, but putting away childhood interests and activities also happens as part of growing up. His interests and enjoyments changed.

---

*Facing one's fears, however, does not require relentless rumination over them. Batman eventually decides to celebrate their lives more than their deaths by starting a new personal tradition of honoring them on their wedding anniversary instead of "marking the night I watched my father bleed out from his sucking chest wound and my mother from a hole in her throat" (*Batman and Robin* #1, 2011).

He takes great interest in the activities that now mean the most to him, the ones he personally finds most significant. However much Lucius Fox and the Wayne Enterprises board members might like for him to get more involved in the family business, he—much like his father—has never gotten engrossed enough in the business in the first place to call his interest in it diminished. He's no recluse too timid, melancholy, or indifferent to venture out.

Feeling of detachment or estrangement from others: Yes, at one point or another, he estranges everyone in his life.

Restricted range of emotions: Not really. Admittedly, he doesn't laugh much when he's in the mask. His difficulty conveying his feelings often interferes with his relationships with sidekicks and any woman he loves—but he does have those feelings. "Psychic numbing" or "emotional anesthesia" usually starts soon after the traumatic event, when Bruce shows emotion aplenty. He cries when his parents die, he cries later as well, and he summons a mighty anger. "Batman reflects the full spectrum of emotional angst and joy and sorrow that each and every one of us experience in life."[27]

Sense of foreshortened future: No. Children with PTSD may show a sense of foreshortened future, as indicated by a belief that life will be too short to include becoming an adult—a symptom certainly not demonstrated by young Bruce. In point of fact, his sense of future grows.

Criterion D: Persistent symptoms of arousal not present before. Here's a tricky area because a grown man shows many traits he didn't show before age 8. After experiencing the shock of the murders, this boy becomes less fearful, less anxious, less easily startled or surprised than ever before. Bad dreams still disturb his adult sleep sometimes, but otherwise he usually sleeps solidly, especially when the sun's out. "Bats are nocturnal!"[28] Combat veterans who suffer nightmares, often fearing sleep itself[29] or waking in distress even from non-dreaming portions of the night,[30] suffer far worse than he.[31] Bruce Wayne runs on insufficient sleep when he gets too busy—when *current*, not posttraumatic, circumstances intrude. His ability to focus his concentration exceeds that of most people's.

The abundant rage he stores inside him, when it comes out, does so for obvious reasons having to do with what's going on right now—situationally, not randomly, determined—and not in the form of unprovoked outbursts. *Superman on the Couch* author Danny Fingeroth says, "Batman does sit on top of this mountain of anger. I think he's more in control of it than he wants his adversaries to think. He wants his adversaries to think he might lose it at any minute."[32] He dominates his anger. It does not run wild with him. If it did, he'd have gotten himself killed or he'd have beaten the Joker to death long ago. "For years a day hasn't gone by where I haven't envisioned taking him, taking him and spending an entire month putting him through the most horrendous, mind-boggling forms of torture," Batman admits to Jason Todd, previously murdered by the Joker and now resurrected from the dead, a former Robin who can't understand why Batman permits the Joker to live, "but if I do that, if I allow myself to go down into that place, I'll never come back."[33]

His most prominent sign of hyperarousal regarding stimuli reminiscent of the original trauma, his *hypervigilance* (heightened readiness to spot danger), is appropriate to the life he leads. "Like a police officer walking a beat, or a detective taking part in an undercover operation, Batman has his 'antennae' up for possible danger, but hypervigilance is normal in that context. Batman is always on duty, and so it makes sense that he would be preternaturally attuned for possible threats."[34] Note again that his hypervigilance now comes out of his personality, his way of doing everything, not due to feelings of anxiety and stress.

Criterion E: Symptom duration greater than one month. If— repeat, *if*—his adult functioning qualifies him for a posttraumatic mental illness, then yes, the disorder has persisted far beyond one month.

Criterion F: Clinically significant distress or impairment in social, occupational, or other functioning. He does not spend his days mired in a state of distress. He coolly, steadily, sometimes menacingly does the things he needs to do. Given the many traumas he faces almost daily, some distress will arise—that's new stress, not the old.

Not one psychologist or psychiatrist I know who also knows enough about the character would diagnose him with PTSD. "There are symptoms of it, not necessarily the full-blown disorder," says forensic psychiatrist Praveen R. Kambam. "You have to meet all the criteria to make the disorder. I don't think any of us are saying he has that fully. There are some things that he's missing."[35] Does ongoing anxiety over his parents' deaths keep Batman from functioning? As a vigilante crime-fighter, he functions beyond compare. As a philanthropist and socialite, he brings an array of social skills with which he charms the crowd. In interpersonal relationships, short on trust and shorter on intimacy, he has his deficits. His love life is sporadic and often lies dormant. Nobody's perfect. In the areas where he functions worst, he does so because of ingrained personality traits and personal priorities, not because of crippling angst, panic, or anxiety states. "I'd argue that it reflects an exacerbation of previously existing traits," says therapist Jeffrey Kramer. "Given all that he's been through, he probably should have PTSD, but he clearly doesn't."[36] In terms of Batman's chosen life mission, nobody does it better.

The one point in his adult career when Batman shows the most posttraumatic stress follows the death of Jason Todd, the boy who becomes the second Robin after Batman's original sidekick, Dick Grayson, grows up. In the first Batman stories published after Jason dies, Batman does not appear to grieve (due, at least in part, to the fact that writers scripted these before DC knew whether Jason would live or die). On top of the controversy over the death itself, readers grumbled about Batman's blunted response. As one reader noted, "His lack of reaction to Jason's death could destroy him. We all need to grieve, and a failure to do so is catastrophic, emotionally and psychologically, for the grieving person. . . . It isn't easy for the

Batman to show emotion, as it's a human weakness. If he bottles it up, however, it will eventually explode, and he himself will suffer most of all."[37] Batman grows angrier, more aggressive, more reckless, and less effective until Tim Drake, the third Robin, intervenes.[38]

The Search for Meaning: "Why?"

"Why did this happen?" victims will ask, "and why did this happen to me?"

"Why?" is enormous. As any parent answering a child's questions can tell you, answering one "Why?" can lead to another after another until you hit a wall of whys you can't answer. Spectacular tragedy does not require a spectacular explanation—a loner with a grudge really can kill a president, shoot up a schoolyard, or crash a fuel truck into a crowd—and yet we feel like it should. We want cause to transcend effect. A simple truth can leave us feeling cheated. We need to believe in the existence of answers and purpose more powerful than our pain, in reasons and meaning bigger than the results.

When tragedy challenges your worldview, you question your goals and beliefs. To make sense of injustice, we may draw one of three global conclusions: (1) People will get the justice they deserve; (2) there is no justice; or (3) justice happens but it needs our help. The first belief can give us peace. People who believe in a just world suffer less stress and depression, and enjoy life more than people who do not.[39] Many cultures teach their members from childhood to believe the world operates with natural order and justice—the *just-world phenomenon* that psychologist Melvin Lerner says comforts us because most of us, even the worst of us, consider ourselves to be basically good and worthy of fair treatment.[40] Our need to believe the world is just, however, can lead us to make unjust decisions: The crueler the fate, the more harshly we blame its victim.[41] "That girl was asking for trouble with a bullhorn." "He must have done something to deserve that." "That's what those high-society types get for thinking they're better than us. What were they thinking, walking down that street at night?" The people who most need our compassion may instead receive our cruelest critiques.[42] Believing in natural justice makes some people complacent, for they passively count on justice to happen on its own. People who believe we can create justice are more active, take-charge kinds of people, more ready to set aside their short-term self-interests and better able to stay motivated while working hard to satisfy long-term and less self-serving goals.[43] Some of those who most actively pursue justice, not trusting it to happen on their own, feel a need to see it for themselves—thus does Bruce Wayne fight crime with his own fists instead of concentrating on supporting more citywide crime prevention programs for less than the price of a Batplane.

Asking "Why?" does not give victims solace. Answering it might. Searching for meaning can stress the searcher and worsen PTSD symptoms before that person comes out the other side. *Finding* meaning predicts better adjustment.[44] People who report *posttraumatic growth* (positive changes resulting from trauma) experience less depression and greater life satisfaction not by forgetting about the trauma but instead by dwelling on it in constructive ways. Numbing our feelings, refusing to acknowledge or think about bad things that have happened, all the dissociative tricks we play to protect ourselves instead of actively coping will predict more posttraumatic stress, not less.[45] By feeling the negative emotions and recalling the unpleasant events, we might learn from them. Intrusive, unwanted ruminations that run ramshod over other thoughts can evolve into intentional contemplation. Such deliberation, in turn, may help a victim face the pain without drowning in it.[46]

"Why?" goes beyond seeking a direct cause. *Meaning making*, finding value in tragedy or forging our own means to make it have positive repercussions, helps many people cope and may be critical for posttraumatic growth. A shakeup of your worldview can mark the starting point for eventual achievements.[47] "Meaning making is very personal and may involve religion, renewed appreciation for life, or public service."[48] While we don't know much about where the adult Batman stands on formal religion,[49] we do know freshly orphaned Bruce Wayne draws strength from it: He makes meaning from his parents' murders with a bedside prayer in which he vows to wage war on all crime. "He makes meaning of trauma in a few days where it takes the rest of us several years."[50]

Victims dealt life-altering blows to their sense of self, family, and future frequently yearn for retribution.[51] Whereas counterfactual "if only this hadn't happened" fantasies in which the victim wishes for the past to change as if by magic can foster depression, future-oriented revenge plans can bolster the victim, reducing helplessness by empowering the person with a sense that he or she will become capable and take action. "People who have been harmed by another person are goaded into revenge by a brain system that hands them a promissory note certifying that revenge, when it comes, will make them feel good."[52] At his bedside days after his parents die, young Bruce Wayne's promissory prayer trumps any feelings of powerlessness that might crush someone else.

Social Superheroes

Taking up a cause when inspired by a loved one's death and making it one's life's work does not mean the person is mentally ill. Batman channels his grief for his parents into the campaign their deaths inspired, but he's not alone in that regard. Real-world *social superheroes*, individuals whose misfortunes push them to levels of social activism that touch so many lives, find new purpose in life and make their losses meaningful by striving to keep others from suffering the same. They may follow their new purposes by raising public awareness of the problems, pushing for stricter laws and tougher penalties, lobbying for indirect deterrents like alcohol taxes, or even pursuing perpetrators.

Outraged over the lenient sentence leveled against the drunk driver who killed her daughter in a hit-and-run, Candace Lightner made a vow, promising herself "that I would fight to make this needless homicide count for something in the years ahead," and went on to found Mothers Against Drunk Drivers (MADD, later renamed Mothers Against Drunk Driving).[53] The long-unsolved murder and decapitation of his six-year-old son Adam drove John Walsh to advocate for victims and help form the National Center for Missing and Exploited Children.[54] A young man engrossed in his cell phone call ran a red light and killed Linda Doyle, leading her daughter Jennifer Smith to found the group FocusDriven in order to combat distracted driving.[55]

The Holocaust created many activists. Some made meaning by educating others about what happened. Elie Wiesel, after a decade unable to discuss his family's death and his time in the Nazis' Auschwitz concentration and extermination camp, finally wrote his memoirs and then kept writing. More than forty books followed, as did many awards, including a Nobel Peace Prize for speaking out against violence, racism, and oppression. Many scholars credit him for giving the name *Holocaust* to the Nazis' genocidal crimes.[56] Holocaust survivors include Nazi hunters like Simon Wiesenthal, Tuviah Friedman, and Efraim Zuroff dedicating their lives to tracking down war criminals because while evildoers yet live, it's never too late to make them stand trial for their monstrous acts and make the monsters of the future beware.[57]

When developing his realistic take on Batman, Christopher Nolan looked at a figure from earlier in history: "To me, the key to understanding the character is that Bruce Wayne is Teddy Roosevelt."[58] Like Bruce Wayne, Theodore Roosevelt was born into a wealthy urban family with a strong, philanthropic father he looked up to. To compensate for childhood weakness, asthma that kept him sickly and home-schooled, Roosevelt embraced a life of strenuous activity. Also like Bruce Wayne, Roosevelt experienced tragic family loss that drove him to fight injustice. Having already lost his father to a tumor, he lost mother and wife to different illnesses in the same house on the same day. For his diary entry that day, he drew a large X, under which he wrote, "The light has gone out of my life,"[59] followed days later by "For joy or for sorrow my life has now been lived out."[60] He sold his house, left his newborn daughter with his sister, and headed into the Dakota Badlands[61] apparently planning to die, but instead reforged himself and returned to New York to become an activist police commissioner bicycling through the city in the middle of the night, fighting police corruption, and tackling the terrible living conditions suffered by the city's millions of poor immigrants.[62] Before he became the President of the United States, he was the heroic Rough Rider.

Personal tragedy does not drive all comic book superheroes ("Some of them become heroes because it's just the right thing to do," says comic book writer Len Wein),[63] nor is it requisite to becoming a real-world social superhero. Witnessing online chat room participants attempt to groom young girls for sexual victimization prompted Xavier Von Erck to create Perverted-Justice, a computer watchdog agency that works with law enforcement and sometimes *Dateline NBC's* "To Catch a Predator" operation to intercept sexual predators with the help of adult volunteers who pose online as minors.[64]

Why does tragedy crush some people but fortify others? Why do some people fall and stay down while others rise to new heights?

Bouncing Back

The majority of people cope successfully with their traumas.[65] Why some bounce back from adversity despite upbringing, environment, and great hardships,[66] we don't really know. Even though we can identify some factors correlated with *resilience*, the ability to adapt quickly to stress without lasting mental or physical ailments, we haven't ferreted out the causal connections. Highly resilient individuals show greater morale, self-efficacy, self-reliance, perseverance, and purpose in life.[67] Psychologically resilient individuals rebound from dwelling on pain by summoning positive emotions.[68] They invigorate themselves.

Social support helps—quality over quantity. For decades, the comic book stories largely avoided the question of who actually raised this rich orphan. Before *Crisis on Infinite Earths* reshuffled history, Bruce grows up on the estate of his Uncle Philip, a man rarely mentioned before the Crisis and, afterward, never comes up again. Post-Crisis, *Batman: Year One* established instead that the family butler, Alfred Pennyworth, becomes Bruce's guardian. Dr. Leslie Thompkins, a family friend and physician running an inner-city clinic, the first person to notice Bruce at his parents' murder scene and offer him any comfort, involves herself as a parental figure but not as a live-in guardian. It has always seemed like Bruce Wayne raised himself.

In adulthood, Bruce has numerous father figures: Alfred Pennyworth, Commissioner Gordon, Lucius Fox, Henri Ducard. The eco-terrorist Ra's al Ghul wants to squeeze himself into the mix. And his parents, in fractured memory, never leave him. In the comics, Bruce accesses the Batcave not by pole as in the 1966–1968 television series, but either by elevator or via secret passage behind a grandfather clock. He opens the passage by turning the clock's hands to the hour and minute his parents died. Every time he changes from Bruce into Batman, he passes through the moment of their deaths.

The Loss

What exactly did Bruce lose? After all these years, we still know little about Bruce's parents, who die when his story begins, and storytellers who show them via flashbacks depict them inconsistently. Of course, human beings are inconsistent. In presenting Bruce's early memories, writers focus on his life shortly before the murders. Modern interpretations of Dr. Thomas Wayne[69] often depict him as stern and distant at times when dealing with his son and yet unquestionably concerned for the well-being of family and others. Martha is more nurturing, as many mothers will be. Our weak knowledge of them reflects Bruce's limited time in their company. Grown Batman's memories of them come from the boy he'd been before they died. His father's sternest moments could be exceptions that stand out against less memorable everyday affection.

As an only child, young Bruce has no siblings with whom he had to share possessions or affection. His parents' attention and time, he has to share with their social activities, their charitable commitments, his father's work, and some travels they make without him. According to psychologist Alfred Adler, the pioneer researcher of *birth order effects*, an only child enjoys being the center of attention and is likely to have difficulty sharing with peers due to lack of experience sharing with siblings. An only child often prefers adult company and uses more adult language because that it is familiar to them. For the only child's parents, especially parents with resources, the child may be their precious miracle, whether because they have had difficulty previously having a child or because they finally reached the point in life when they actively chose to have one. Under these circumstances, the potential for overprotecting and spoiling the child is great.[70] Adler stressed that he referred only to general tendencies, not universal rules, and that one must consider the entire context and the child's life circumstances. Like Freud, Adler emphasized the importance of early years and experience, not only in terms of what happens but how the child interprets events. Adler felt that three basic childhood circumstances contribute to a faulty family lifestyle: health problems, pampering, or neglect. In Bruce Wayne's case, he may have shifted from experiencing pampering due to his family's sheer wealth even if his parents had handled it well to practical neglect by simply not having parents at all. Adler specifically discussed how orphans, abuse victims, and passively neglected children can experience similar deficits through the lack of a loving parent. Having had parents he loved, Bruce knows the pain and the void of what's missing.

When Bruce loses his parents, he loses milestone experiences his wealthy peers even had in common with children of the working class.

His parents' murder stays in Batman's head. *Detective Comics* #457 cover by Dick Giordano © DC Comics.

Grown, he lacks deep and enduring relationships with any who don't know him as Batman. Bruce Wayne plays the role of a charitable but carefree playboy, perhaps a representation of the kind of man he imagines he might have become. The persona he presents when he is not wearing the mask puts forth a greater deception than his features hide beneath his cowl.

4

Why the Mask?

"But then I found out about your mask."

—Rachel Dawes (Katie Holmes),
Batman Begins (2005 motion picture)

We wear masks. You wear a different set of traits to your grandmother's birthday party than what you'd bring to haggle over the price of a used car. While you're reading this book, you might also be logged on to websites, whether multitasking or awaiting a beep or a tweet that could summon your online persona like the Commissioner on the Batphone calls upon the Dynamic Duo to don those tights. After Bruce decides to combat crime, why does he then decide to fight it wearing a mask?

Wearing a mask is a deliberate choice, not some habit he picks up without realizing it. Bruce Wayne's conscious decision to fight crime as a masked vigilante reflects his cognitive and moral growth, how he develops the kind of logic that deems this path reasonable, and the kind of morality that considers it the right thing to do. Although his origin story shows the moment he chooses to use a bat as his symbol, there is no similarly famous realization that he needs to wear a mask. That decision evolved over the course of more than a decade for him.

Bruce doesn't start off intending to work outside the law. He considers law enforcement and law school until he comes to decide that law itself can impede the pursuit of justice. He attends college, several colleges in fact, only to drop out each time he reaches the point where he feels he has learned as much as he can use. He enters FBI training only to quit after six weeks, frustrated over having learned nothing more than obeying regulations, dressing neatly, analyzing statistics, and writing reports. "The experience confirmed a suspicion he'd long had: He could not operate within a system. People who caused other people to fall did not recognize systems."[1] Traveling the globe, he learns from every instructor, sensei, and expert who can impart the knowledge and cultivate the skills he needs, along with every eminent detective in the world, including French detective Henri Ducard, whose smug amorality appalls the hero-to-be.

Intense physical training elevates him to the pinnacle of human potential, "a perfection reached by few," as artist Neal Adams put it. "He became such a physical specimen as would make a Spartan wonder, and if he entered the Olympics, he would win, place, and show in every event."[2] Neuroscientist, kinesiologist, and martial artist E. Paul Zehr, in meticulously examining the rigorous training and mental discipline necessary to become Batman, concludes that "a person could become Batman (notice I said *a* person, not necessarily you or I). This person would need to have the proper blend of genetic endowment, be driven at a fanatical level by some passionate goal, and have inordinate amounts of time and money to undertake all the extreme privations and training needed. . . . However, the caveat is that it would be enormously difficult to actually be Batman."[3] Repeated physiological stress and frequent injuries incurred bounding across rooftops, pummeling foes, and getting pummeled in return would make a costumed crime-fighting career all too brief. As long as Batman feels to us like someone who could in any way exist in the first place, we as readers will suspend our disbelief regarding much of what follows. This realistic potential lets readers accept Batman as logically possible. We don't scoff at the accumulated effects and logistical impossibility of one man having thousands of adventures as long as we can accept him as the man in the adventure he's having right now and as the boy in the tragedy where it all began.

Cognitive Development: Thinking Batty Thoughts

Long before he makes the crazy-sounding decision to run around dressed like a bat, Bruce Wayne first makes the decision to wage war on all criminals—a goal in some ways crazier than wearing a mask because one person cannot fight all criminals. To understand how the decision to fight crime anonymously evolved somewhere in between those two points, we should look at how his general thinking ability developed. The moment his parents die, he is already Batman even if he has not yet figured that out. He immediately grasps the meaning of what has occurred and quickly forms his life's goal in response.

Unlike a much younger child who thinks death is as reversible as sleep if aware of it at all,[4] Bruce is old enough when his parents die that he can already recognize the concrete and permanent reality of that loss as well as its basic wrongness. His eyes wide with shock and horror as he utters, "Dead. They're d-dead," his lesson is not that death happens but that it happens to people you love. He discovers its universality when it rearranges his universe. Unlike the case of a much older child, however, not so many of the complexities of life have crept their way into his head as to make him feel daunted days later by the magnitude of his avenging oath's intent. His thinking has picked up enough logic to know exactly what happened and too little

Young Bruce immediately understands the horror and makes meaning of it. © DC Comics.

logic to let common sense stop him from tackling a nigh-impossible task. The imagination he hasn't outgrown has picked up some tools to help it create new reality.

Cognition, meaning all mental activities including thinking, knowing, and remembering, develops in stages, according to Swiss psychologist Jean Piaget.[5] An infant in the *sensorimotor* stage takes in the world through sensory and motor interactions, coming to discover how his or her physical movements coordinate with input from vision, touch, and other senses regarding the environment. The infant will grasp, mouth, look, and hear, absorbing information about the chaotic and surprising environment faster than at any other time of life. From about age two until six or seven, during the *preoperational stage,* before picking up better comprehension and reasoning skills (*operations*), the child relies on intuition and imagination rather than logic. The preoperational child has an *egocentric* (self-centered) perspective, not the kind of selfish shortsightedness people mean when they refer to adolescent or adult egocentrism with its difficulty seeing someone else's point of view. The preoperational child generally fails to recognize that others perceive concrete surroundings from an angle other than their own. Ask a four-year-old sitting across the table eating from a bowl of cereal while you read a book, "What's the first thing you see on the table?" The child probably says the cereal. Next ask, "What's the first thing I see on the table?" The child probably repeats, "Cereal." This child has limited ability to think symbolically (i.e., letting one thing, a *symbol*, represent something else) and lacks the concept of *conservation*, the principle that objects don't lose their basic nature—their mass, volume, or number—through superficial changes like moving them around. Pouring water from a tall, thin glass into a short, fat one doesn't reduce the amount of water, nor does cutting a piece of pie in half give the child more pie. Some seven-year-olds get that; some don't. By age eight, most understand these easily.

Before he witnesses the murders and swears his oath, Bruce has already entered the *concrete operational stage* (about age six or seven until puberty), during which he is gaining the reasoning skills that will let him use basic logic to think about events in the physical world.

Because most writers make him eight° when his parents die, he has freshly embarked upon accumulating his *concrete operations*, his simple logic skills for contemplating actual (concrete) objects or events that are not abstract or hypothetical. His fantasy of avenging his parents grows up with his logic. It likely becomes a frame of reference and a focal point about which his mind practices each new reasoning skill, ensconcing the avenging mission in the very way his thoughts function. By the time he reaches the next stage, the mission already defines him like music defined child prodigy Mozart. Preteen reasoning begins to expand beyond actual concrete experience to encompass abstractions and ideals. Some adolescents advance farther into *formal operations* than others.[6] Some adults will distrust cold reason. Regardless of how well they individually fulfill the potential, Piaget believed adolescents have within their grasp the ability to develop *hypotheses* (reasoned guesses about how to solve problems) and systematically deduce a path to each problem's solution—a cognitive ability Piaget called *hypothetico-deductive reasoning*, at which Bruce Wayne becomes a master. Before he goes out solving crimes, he has already become a great detective able to think through complicated sets of clues to generate hypotheses and deduce information regarding crimes that have taken place in the past and those his enemies are planning for the future.

Concrete operations let Bruce consider practical reasons for becoming a masked vigilante, such as the fact that search and seizure laws won't keep him from discovering evidence the police can't obtain. Formal operations let him anticipate ripple effects, as the lives he touches will touch others as well, and see the potential for a symbol to inspire people in many ways. Formal operations also complicate some decisions for him because, instead of the simple good/evil classifications that categorized people early in his concrete operations, he now understands abstractions, complexities, extenuating circumstances, and the fact that people can do bad things for good reasons.

°Most notable exceptions still average out to eight, from authors like Frank Miller depicting him as six years old when the murders occur (*Batman: Year One*, 1987) to some like Geoff Johns placing him at ten (*Justice League* #5, 2012).

Moral Development: Growing a Hero's Conscience

Piaget made observations about how cognitive development shapes morality, setting and then breaking limits on the child's ability to comprehend and utilize moral concepts. The infant starts out in a state of *amorality*, lacking morals, not to be confused with immorality, which involves knowingly violating morals. From about ages four to seven as Piaget perceived children, they're in a state of *heteronymous* (other-defined) morality, when they come to recognize that morals, rules, and laws exist, and conceive of them as properties of reality as immutable as Earth's gravity and fire's heat—so Thomas and Martha Wayne died at a time when Bruce most readily accepted their moral values, when he considered justice to be straightforward and easily defined. Later on, around age 10, children recognize that because people create rules and laws, those rules and laws can change, and thus the child moves into a more independent or *autonomous* (self-defined) moral view, considering intentions, not just consequences, as that individual comes to mature.[7] Bruce establishes his own moral code and decides he can honor his parents' values even through means of which they might have disapproved.

Lawrence Kohlberg expanded on Piaget's writings about morality, refining and building his own theory about *stages of moral development*. Whereas Piaget named the cognitive stages for mental operations, Kohlberg named his theorized moral stages for the person's progression through moral conventions. He saw three levels of morality—preconventional, conventional, and postconventional—with two distinct stages within each for a total of six stages, with not everyone reaching the highest or most advanced. Despite their placement in table 4.1, these do not adhere to a specific timetable as neatly as some aspects of development: People can operate on more than one level at the same time, some morally deficient individuals barely function on any level at all, and moral action may be less dependent on reasoning ability than Kohlberg expected.[8] Before the murders, Bruce has progressed through two stages of *preconventional morality*, that time of life when the person shows no internalization of moral values, when the person's earliest sense of morality was learning to avoid punishment and earn rewards. Stage 1 morality is often tied to punishment. Those in stage 2 pursue their own interests and learn to let others do the same. What is right involves an equal exchange, within the child's skewed perspective of what's equal: Be nice to others so they'll be nice to you. Before age nine, most children reason about moral dilemmas in a preconventional way—most, not all. Bruce is an exceptionally bright child whose philanthropic parents emphasize the importance of looking out for others. Even if the boy has not yet advanced into conventional morality, he is surely ready.

With *conventional morality*, individuals know to abide by standards and internalize those externally determined values, adopting standards set by parental principles, social norms, and society's laws. Early conventional morality (stage 3) views trust, caring, and loyalty to others as the foundations for moral judgments. A child at this point will place great importance on being a "good girl" or "good boy" in the parents' eyes. Those who progress in their conventional morality move from focusing on essential rightness or wrongness as a function of whether specific individuals approve into looking at the bigger picture of society itself (stage 4). Social order, law, justice, and duty become the standards. By most accounts, Bruce grows up expecting to operate within the law even while he also starts cheating the system. To pursue justice unimpeded by well-intentioned adults who want to care either for him or for the orphan's fortune, "He wrote letters that weren't exactly forgeries and weren't exactly anything else—and they enabled him to leave Gotham City at age 14 and begin a global quest for what he wanted to know."[9] When he does so, is he functioning at lower moral reasoning to get what he wants, or has he already started moving into *postconventional morality*, which emphasizes underlying moral principles?

Not everyone achieves postconventional morality. Moral reasoning by social contract (stage 5) recognizes that because people established society's rules by mutual agreement and compromise, society's contract with its members is no longer binding if rules become destructive or if parties to that contract fail to live up to their respective sides of the agreement. When corrupt authorities fail to promote and defend citizens' welfare, when that corruption allows crime to flourish,

TABLE 4.1. THEORIZED EARLY LIFE DEVELOPMENT: COGNITIVE, MORAL, PSYCHOSEXUAL, AND PSYCHOSOCIAL STAGES

Approximate Ages	Cognitive Stage (Piaget)	Moral Stage (Kohlberg)	Psychosexual Stage (Freud)—see chapter 9	Psychosocial Stage (Erikson)
0 until up to 2 years	Sensorimotor		Oral	Basic Trust vs. Mistrust
Nearly 2 until 3 or 4	Preoperational: Symbolic Function Substage	Preconventional Stage 1: Punishment and Obedience	Anal	Autonomy vs. Shame and Doubt
3 or 4 until 6 or 7	Preoperational: Intuitive Thought Substage		Phallic	Initiative vs. Guilt
6 or 7 until Puberty	Concrete Operations	Preconventional Stage 2: Instrumental and Relativist Orientation	Latency	Industry vs. Inferiority*
Puberty until ???	Formal Operations	Conventional Stage 3: Conformity Stage 4: Law and Order	Genital	Identity Achievement vs. Role Confusion[†] —see chapter 10
Adulthood	Postformal: Other theorists have suggested more advanced stages able to synthesize contradictions into a coherent whole.[10]	Postconventional Stage 5: Social contract Stage 6: Universal Ethical Principles	No new stage. By this time, you're either mature or a bundle of neuroses.	See chapter 12 for Adult stages.

*Also known as Industriousness vs. Inferiority.
[†]Also known as Identity Cohesion vs. Confusion.

social contractual reason holds that greater ethical principles must take priority, and a law higher than that of the official lawmakers and law officers should take over. Kohlberg's thoughts on later postconventional morality, focusing on universal ethical principles and mutual respect (stage 6), have not received as much attention by empirical researchers, whether because Kohlberg may have erred or because so few people reach that stage. Bruce Wayne, short on the ability to respect and trust others, lacks the patience to devote himself to achieving ultimate enlightenment through reflection and meditation. After months of martial arts training at Master Kirigi's temple in the Paektu-San Mountains, Bruce chooses not to stay for the additional years he'd need to move beyond his aggression into illumination on the other side.[11]

The Might of a Mask

"I wear a mask. And that mask, it's not to hide who I am,
but to create what I am."
—Batman, *Batman* #624 (2004)

Cognitively, Bruce Wayne reasons that, given his resources and Gotham City's corruption, fighting crime anonymously is a logical thing for him to do. Morally, he has determined that it is the right thing to do. Motivationally, he also may need the mask to overcome any lingering reservations or fears that might hold him back, although he might not anticipate how the anonymity will affect him emotionally.

Costumes are liberating. In the 1919 pulp fiction serial "The Curse of Capistrano," Zorro first rides as a masked vigilante out to defend the oppressed in Spanish colonial California.[12] In 1933, a voice on the radio becomes the vigilante called the Shadow, who wears no literal mask but instead a scarf hides half his face and, more important, he masks himself using the power to cloud men's minds.[13] In 1939, Batman tackles crime in cape and cowl for the first time, perplexing Gotham's police as he operates outside the law like those role models, Zorro and the Shadow, so criminals cannot track him down, invade his home, or take him to court for violating their legal rights. Aside from the utility of the secret identity as protection from others, these disguises must affect how each hero sees himself and how he accordingly acts.

Anonymity makes people act differently or more extremely than usual. It can create *disinhibition*, a lessening of inhibitions, not only by lowering the odds they'll have to face the consequences of their own actions but because anonymity may produce an experience of *deindividuation*, reduced consciousness of oneself as an individual. Disinhibition results from many different causes—e.g., drugs, fatigue, encouragement, party atmosphere, someone else taking responsibility, or getting lost in a crowd—all conditions that can also produce deindividuation. Darkness does both. Onlookers masked by darkness, disinhibited and deindividuated as they watch someone threaten to commit suicide by jumping off a building or bridge, more frequently jeer and yell, "Jump!"[14] Psychologist Phil Zimbardo[15] identified arousal, anonymity, and diffused responsibility all as factors that contribute to deindividuation and therefore make people more likely to engage in impulsive, destructive activities like rioting and vandalism, depending on the nature of the deindividuating circumstances. Although Zimbardo found that women asked to wear pillowcase masks would deliver greater electric shock to helpless "victims" (who didn't really get shocked even though the volunteers believed they were shocking someone), Johnson and Downing[16] pointed out that the Ku Klux Klan–like outfits may have cued participants to behave consistently with the outfits they wore, an unintended sort of role-playing, so these researchers responded with their own study in which volunteers wore nurses' uniforms. When those in the nurses' uniforms were anonymous, they became less aggressive and administered less shock than in *individuation* conditions of heightened self-awareness, when the researchers addressed the volunteers by name, stressing their personal identities. Reduced self-consciousness diminishes the influence of individual traits and heightens responsiveness to situational cues like the costume one is wearing: Dress like a Klansman, become more aggressive; dress like a nurse, become more nurturing.[17]

Reducing self-awareness can have both advantages and disadvantages for the crime-fighter. The mask can make it easier for the hero to lose control. "For superheroes worried about not crossing the line—not being more violent than they need to be to apprehend the villain—wearing a mask can make it harder to monitor that line," psychologist Robin Rosenberg asserts, while also pointing out that diminished self-awareness can help the person feel less pain, less sadness or anger, and less distracted by one's internal experience, thereby enhancing awareness of the external environment.[18]

A mask does not have to deindividuate when it's part of a role or identity that its wearer takes personally. "The reality is that the Batman persona is the true persona," says DC Comics executive editor Dan DiDio, "and that Bruce Wayne is the mask." *The Dark Knight Rises* executive producer Michael Uslan argues, "I think that Bruce Wayne doesn't exist. I think he died that night with his parents, and that form, that boy, that entity who moved on after that was no longer Bruce Wayne. He had at that point in his heart and mind and soul already become Batman. He just had a path, a journey to take."[19] Comic book writer Paul Levitz sees it differently: "The core of his identity always remains Bruce because it's his formative experience as Bruce that fuels both. Batman is a tool he puts on to accomplish what he needs to do." Another comic book writer, Scott Snyder, contends, "It's not like Bruce is some phony thing he wears, but in the scale of the superhero identity, Bruce is deeply tilted towards Batman."[20] *Wisdom from the Batcave* author Cary A. Friedman weighs in: "Which is the real identity—is it Bruce Wayne or is it Batman? The really cool answer, of course, is when we say, 'Oh, it's Batman,' but I think that misses the point. What defines the character is the essential humanity that the character possesses."[21]

We can get lost in our roles, even the roles we consciously design. When psychologist Phil Zimbardo conducted a prison simulation experiment in which he randomly cast volunteers in the roles of either guards or prisoners, the guards got carried away with how harshly they treated prisoners, and many prisoners became dehumanized drones who thought only of escape, survival, and how much they hated the guards.[22] Zimbardo himself lost sight of the project's true purpose and the harsh reality of how guards were treating prisoners, in part because he made the mistake of playing a role as the prison superintendent. It took a heated argument with an outside observer to clear his head before he realized that he and everyone else in the study had gradually "internalized a set of destructive prison values that distanced them from their own humanitarian values."[23]

> Travis Langley: You keep calling it a mistake to have played a role in your own experiment, but don't you understand it all better for having made that mistake?
> Phil Zimbardo: Without a doubt. I also learned things about myself.[24]

Underestimating the importance of his Bruce Wayne identity and learning from that misjudgment similarly helps Batman reassess his priorities and better understand his own nature. When Lex Luthor frames Bruce for murder, Batman decides he doesn't need to be Bruce anyway. "Bruce Wayne is a mask I wear, that I've been wearing since I was a child," he tells his allies, "but it's become a liability, so it's *over*. Bruce Wayne and his troubles aren't my concern anymore. The only thing that matters now is my mission. Nothing will stand in the way anymore."[25] He attempts to quit being Wayne altogether, only to discover that he should not and cannot. A confrontation with Catwoman and the dying wish of a detective who investigated his parents' murder[26] make him realize that in trying to convince himself that he is nothing but the thing he created to scare criminals, he has briefly forgotten the whole point of it all: The people who died once upon a time in Crime Alley were *Bruce Wayne's* parents, not a bat's, and the bat's primary mission is about the innocent more than the guilty.[27] Protect and avenge them. The Batman who remembers this even takes a moment to tend to a criminal as a wounded human being because Thomas Wayne would have.

Batman wears two masks: the Dark Knight's cowl and Bruce Wayne's public façade. Each mask reduces his current consciousness of certain aspects of himself while raising his consciousness and concern about others. We come closest to seeing the "real" Bruce when he's sitting in the Batcave, at the computer with mask and gloves off, drinking coffee while he talks with his father figure, Alfred, and adoptive son, Robin. Maybe on some level he feels he's in the company of Thomas Wayne's ghost and his own eight-year-old self. *Batcave Bruce*, hidden beneath the earth from the worlds in which the masked avenger or bored playboy might circulate, may be our hero at his truest.

5
Why the Bat?

A boy runs where he shouldn't. Ground beneath his feet gives way and he falls. Through the earth he plunges into a cavern dark and damp, a cavity of size undefined in the darkness, silent except for a slow and steady drip, a whisper of wind, and a stir of something else. The darkness moves, "and then they boiled from the blackness, flapping, beating, clawing, a nightmare of leathery wings and gleaming eyes and fangs."[1] Bats screak and they fly, filling the cramped space around him. His terror turns to despair before an arm curls around him, his father having descended to lift him back up into the day. Bruce wonders if he'd fallen into hell. The world has now changed. All its shadows seem to be reaching his way. He never escapes the shadows. After a man with "frightened, hollow eyes"[2] later comes out of the shadows and Bruce's parents fall to the man's gunfire, Bruce finds his own place in the darkness. Instead of running from shadows and fears, he cloaks himself with them.

Alfred (Michael Caine): Why bats, Master Wayne?
Bruce (Christian Bale): Bats frighten me. It's time my enemies shared my dread.[3]

Facing Our Fears

We all have things that bother us or situations we just don't like. Some
of them we might sharply fear, but that doesn't mean we're phobic.
Many people who say they have phobias are wrong. Discomforts and
dislikes that fall short of pathological fears are *aversions*, which disturb us without overpowering us. A *phobia* is a persistently intense
and unrealistic fear that causes such distress or so significantly impairs
function that it counts as a mental illness. Degrees of fear that fall
within the normal variety of human experience do not qualify. People with *agoraphobia* have a fear of open spaces, an often crippling
dread that renders its sufferers unable to go outside. Those with *social
phobia* fear social situations. They want friends. They wish they could
leap into social interactions, but they become so embarrassed and
afraid that they end up avoiding the very thing they want most. All
other phobias, with thousands of different names, in the *DSM* get
lumped together under the collective term *specific phobias*. Agoraphobia and social phobia, by keeping the individuals environmentally or socially trapped, interfere with life more broadly than other
phobias. Even *claustrophobia*, a specific phobia of closed spaces that
can make riding an elevator as terrifying to a claustrophobic person
as stepping out the front door would be to an agoraphobe, does not
keep that person trapped. The claustrophobe can travel the earth. If
young Bruce's dread of the bats in the shadows and beneath his family's property begins intruding frequently into his thoughts and makes
him ready to cry at the thought of playing in his own yard, he might
qualify for *chiroptophobia*, the specific phobia toward bats, or maybe
sciophobia, a pathological fear of shadows.

Other phobias that would directly impede Batman's effectiveness—
so it's a good thing he doesn't have them—include *acrophobia* (fear
of heights), *achluophobia* or *lygophobia* (darkness), *noctiphobia* or
nyctophobia (night), and *maskophobia* (masks). Fears that would

impede anybody's ability to face Gotham's criminal population include *agateophobia* (fear of insanity), *agliophobia* (pain), *hoplophobia* (firearms), *icophobia* (poison), *Samhainophobia* (Halloween), *scelerophobia* (burglars), *traumatophobia* (injury), and *zoophobia* (animals—cats, bats, rats, birds, hyenas, all). Conversely, *kleptophobia* (fear of stealing) would interfere with committing theft. Here are a few more examples of the many phobias that would inconvenience those who must face specific Bat-foes:

- *Ailurophobia (felinophobia)*—cats (Catwoman, Catman)
- *Automatonophobia*—fear of ventriloquist dummies (the Ventriloquist's dummy Scarface)
- *Bibliophobia*—fear of books (Bookworm, Scarecrow)
- *Botanophobia*—fear of plants (Poison Ivy)
- *Caligynephobia*—fear of beautiful women (Talia, Catwoman, and many others)
- *Chiroptophobia*—fear of bats (Man-Bat)
- *Chronomentrophobia*—fear of clocks (Clock King)
- *Cocklaphobia*—fear of hats (Mad Hatter)
- *Coulrophobia*—fear of clowns (Joker, Harley Quinn)
- *Cryophobia (frigophobia, pagophobia)*—fear of extreme cold, ice, or frost (Mr. Freeze, Penguin)
- *Egyptophobia*—fear of Egypt or Egyptian culture, artifacts, etc. (King Tut)
- *Electrophobia*—fear of electricity (Maxie Zeus)
- *Geminiphobia*—fear of twins (Tweedledum and Tweedledee, cousins who look like twins)
- *Herpetophobia*—fear of reptiles (Killer Croc)
- *Hypnophobia*—fear of hypnosis (Mad Hatter)
- *Iatrophobia*—fear of doctors (Crime Doctor, Dr. Death, Hush)
- *Leporiphobia*—fear of rabbits (White Rabbit)
- *Logizomechanophobia*—fear of computers (Anarky)
- *Mottephobia*—fear of moths (Killer Moth)
- *Ophidophobia*—fear of snakes (Copperhead)
- *Ornithophobia*—fear of birds (Penguin, Court of Owls)
- *Ovophobia*—fear of eggs (Egghead, Humphrey Dumpler)

- *Phobophobia*—fear of fear itself (Scarecrow)
- *Pogonophobia*—fear of beards (Hugo Strange, Maxie Zeus)
- *Pyrophobia (arsonphobia)*—fear of fire (Firebug, Firefly)
- *Radiophobia*—fear of radiation (Dr. Phorphorous)
- *Selachophobia*—fear of sharks (Great White Shark)
- *Sinistrophobia*—fear of things to the left (Two-Face)
- *Tatouazophobia*—fear of tattoos (Mr. Zsasz)
- *Zeusophobia*—fear of gods (Maxie Zeus)

Medication works with the brain's chemistry to relax the individual and help alleviate symptoms of fearfulness, especially for those who suffer panic attacks as part of their phobic response, but medication alone will not teach the person a new way to think. Some phobias require specific methods. *Social skills training* can help those with social phobia learn new ways to interact with others, and group therapy might prove particularly useful in their case; after all, it's a form of social interaction in which their social fear already unites them. With some tweaking to adjust for logistical issues like working with a specific visual stimulus as opposed to a complicated situation a person fears, therapists can apply most phobia treatments to any specific phobia. Various therapies for treating phobias amount to different ways of doing one thing: facing the fear.

We can face our fears in blunt confrontation or in a roundabout manner, rapidly or gradually, directly or indirectly, in our actions or in our heads. Where older approaches like Freudian psychoanalysis would take months or years, however long the analyst might persist in exploring the origins of a client's fear, behavioral and cognitive-behavioral therapies instead identify symptoms and work efficiently to change the phobic reactions in a limited number of therapeutic sessions. With *systematic desensitization*, the person approaches the fear by degrees, first learning to relax around something resembling or reminiscent of the feared stimulus, like practicing relaxation exercises in the presence of a happy-faced cartoon bat on a Halloween decoration in early sessions, a more realistic rubber bat in subsequent sessions, and so on until reaching the point of being more relaxed that most people would be in the presence of a live bat. *Flooding* skips those little steps and cuts to the chase: Instead of relaxing the client, immerse that individual in anxiety, keeping him or her surrounded in the feared stimulus until the body naturally tires of feeling such strong fear symptoms. An elevated heart rate eventually slows down. *In vivo* ("in life") flooding, probably the most stressful of these techniques, can backfire. Because it has a high dropout rate,[4] those who give up by escaping the situation before the anxiety has time to lessen wind up with another bad experience, another bad chapter in their histories with the feared stimuli. Like flooding, *graduated exposure* provokes anxiety, but, like systematic desensitization, does so by degrees. Where flooding immerses the client in the worst of the fear, graduated exposure plants the client in situations that cause only minor anxiety before moving on to confront greater stressors.

In the film *Batman Begins*, the adult Bruce returns to the site where some of his childhood fears first began. After climbing down through an old well, he pauses to stare into a gap in the earth, an ugly mouth of gaping rock that opens to darkness below, dripping water as if salivating at the chance to devour him. In that pause, he confronts the tension he feels there before descending anyway. Down in the cave, he stands, he steps around, he looks for the bats. When he shines a light their way, they fly out. Surrounded, he drops to one knee for only a moment before rising, while the cloud flies around. As he stands there, tall and stalagmite-still, his racing heart does not deter him from learning to bask in the bats. "He stays with the fear until he calms down and sees that he's okay."[5] For however long it takes, he stays planted right there.

The Roots of Fear

As long as a fear's original cause is not presently a factor in a person's life, behavioral therapy does not require the therapist and client to unearth that source. They should identify situations and cues that the client associates with the feared stimulus and any reinforcements or rewards the person receives for escaping or avoiding the stimulus, in order to reduce the likelihood that any of these might trigger a phobia's resurgence. Batman and many of his enemies, especially the Scarecrow, Dr. Jonathan Crane, have additional reasons to understand where fear comes from: They like to instill it.

Phobias often get started through *respondent conditioning*, known more commonly as *classical conditioning* simply because Ivan Pavlov discovered it before Edward Thorndike made another kind of conditioning well known. Bruce Wayne does not have to learn to find a fall into a cave frightening. His initial fear is a natural, unlearned reaction—an *unconditioned response* to an unlearned, *unconditioned stimulus*. The bats naturally startle Bruce when they fly out. The sight of a bat or the shadows around the estate had never previously scared him to this degree, but through association with unconditioned stimulus and response (the fall and the fear), anything reminiscent of a bat (like a performer's mask during a play the family sees in *Batman Begins'* version of his origin) becomes a *conditioned stimulus*, a learned trigger, with a *conditioned response* of learned fear. Gotham's criminals later learn to fear anything associated with Batman, like the Bat-Signal Commissioner Gordon shines at times to give honest citizens comfort by reassuring them a hero roams the night. While that light on the clouds can't break the crooks' jaws or send them to jail, the masked man it heralds just might. The signal meant to summon Batman, comfort citizens, and discomfort criminals can dishearten the city's police,[6] though, because it says they're not good enough, it says they can't handle Gotham's crime.

Many behaviors intentionally or inadvertently learned via classical conditioning might die out if the conditioned stimulus no longer precedes the unconditioned stimulus. If food no longer follows Pavlov's bell as it did when he trained dogs to salivate at the sound of the bell, the cessation of the food will lead to *extinction*, an elimination of the learned behavior, in this case no more drooling upon hearing that bell ring. Unlike many other behaviors, phobias tend not to undergo normal extinction because phobias reinforce themselves via the relief that rewards avoidance or escape. Classical conditioning might cause many phobias, but another kind of conditioning perpetuates them.

Without disagreeing with Pavlov's main ideas, Thorndike noted that they were incomplete. Classical conditioning, in which stimulus precedes response, failed to explain the effects of reward and punishment, which follow an action. Thorndike called learning from consequences *instrumental conditioning* because the behavior is instrumental in determining which consequence will follow, whether the action gets rewarded or punished. B. F. Skinner later preferred to think of this as *operant conditioning* and referred to reward as *reinforcement* because some consequences strengthen (reinforce) behavior even when no reward was intended. A grandparent who gives a child a piece of candy to shush a tantrum in the grocery store doesn't mean to convey, "Oh, that's so cute—yes, it is—let's just reward you for tossing that big ole fit," but that grandparent has reinforced the behavior nonetheless, skyrocketing the odds that the grandchild will throw another tantrum the next time they go shopping. In addition to fortifying the phobias that classical conditioning creates, operant conditioning can conjure phobias on its own by reinforcing milder fears until they grow massive.

Reinforcement can be positive or negative. Punishment can be positive or negative too. People confuse punishment with negative reinforcement so often that if you ever hear the term *negative reinforcement* on television, you almost certainly hear it used incorrectly. They're not positive and negative in the sense of good and bad, pleasant or unpleasant. They're positive and negative in terms of math: Something gets added or taken away. *Positive reinforcement* rewards the individual by adding something; a parent's hug may reinforce a child's fearfulness if hugs don't come easily enough otherwise. *Negative reinforcement* also rewards the person but by taking something away; covering your eyes keeps you from seeing a feared stimulus and raises the odds that you'll cover your eyes at other times. *Positive punishment* delivers an adverse consequence by adding something unpleasant; approaching the thing you fear makes your heart race and your body shake until you can't stand it. *Negative punishment* hurts you by taking something away; after going to the movies, you lose your parents to a mugger's bullets, so you might not visit the theater again real soon. Even if a consequent stimulus is coincidental, emotionally we can still feel reinforced or punished. Any of these can make us fearful or—given different combinations of actions and consequences—promote or reduce any behavior we're capable of performing.

Learning alone does not explain every phobia. Heredity invests us with a natural preparedness to learn some fears over others.[7] We require less learning from experience to develop fears toward animals or heights, stimuli naturally associated with certain risks, than toward flowers or many other animals naturally unlikely to hurt us. This natural preparedness shows up more clearly early in life. For example, fears of animals (snakes, wolves, cats, bats) or natural environment (storms, heights, water, night) tend to have a childhood onset.[8] Batman preys on those fears.

The Intimidation Game

What's the practical value in making Batman's foes feel fear? Making criminals afraid may (1) deter them from committing crimes in the first place; (2) impede their ability to fight him by making them jumpy, reckless, too scared to shoot straight, perhaps paralyzed with fear; (3) make them panic and abandon each other; (4) drive some out of town (what idiot brings drug trade to Gotham?); (5) extract information; (6) punish them; and (7) make Batman feel big. He's a bit of a bully—for a good cause. In his head, he's out to stop crime. In his heart, he's also out to hurt criminals. Fear hurts.

Fear is often a less effective motivator than pleasant emotion. As a method of influence, fear arousal more strongly affects changes in attitude than in subsequent actions or intentions.[9] We change attitudes more easily than we change our actions. When motivated to reevaluate our actions, we're more likely to alter our attitudes to justify the way we do things,[10] so the frightened criminal may simply come up with additional reasons for committing the same crimes. *Protection-motivation theory*[11] holds that fear induces a motivation to protect oneself (regardless of whether that means protecting via fight or flight), affecting how we appraise fear-arousing threat, and that fear will influence us most when we believe (1) that we should change our behavior because the dangers look serious and probable and (2) that we can change because we have effective-seeming options that we believe ourselves capable of fulfilling. Changing our attitudes regarding any piece of those beliefs (e.g., downplaying the odds of getting cancer or the likelihood of crossing paths with Batman) comes to us more easily than learning new behaviors.

Fear as a motivator runs into some of the same problems punishment does: Strong deterrents work faster, but mild deterrents last longer. The crook who's scared of Batman hasn't learned what's wrong with crime itself. Strong coercion doesn't teach people to internalize values.[12] Authoritarian parents who focus heavily on fear and punishment as instructional methods foster their children's *extrinsic motivation* for staying out of trouble, motivation to do one action or not do another solely to get an external reward or avoid punishment, but fail to help them build *intrinsic motivation*, the desire to perform an action for its own sake.[13] One problem with fear-based training is that these aversive consequences need to follow an action every single time to be effective, which may be impossible to achieve. Every time you break into a store and neither Batman nor the police show up, the thrill of "getting away with it" becomes its own reward, adding an intrinsic thrill on top of the extrinsic reward, whatever loot you took away from the scene. Another problem with focusing heavily on what a person shouldn't do is that you fail to teach them alternatives as to what they should do instead. Punished behavior is suppressed, not forgotten.[14] Plenty of criminals upon release from jail go right back to crime because that's what they know. Fear-based training and persuasion depend on the target's proclivity to feel fear,[15] a proclivity not everyone shares to the same degree.

When Batman needs information quickly, like where a kidnapper is holding a victim, and his other methods of gathering and analyzing information have failed him, the pressure of that ticking clock typically drives him to the seedier side of town, where he rattles the lowlifes until somebody surrenders an answer. Growling, "Where's the Joker?" doesn't help if nobody knows. Torture victims, interrogation subjects, and others pressed hard enough for information they don't know may in desperation spit out bogus answers to get a moment's relief. Knowing Batman might come back for you later may not override the panicked feeling that you need to get him off you right now. How does Batman know they're telling the truth? He's like many police interrogators, convinced they can spot a lie despite poor evidence that they really can,[16] although Batman doesn't even read Miranda rights before wresting information out of people. The predominant model of police interrogation used across the United States,[17] the Reid method,[18] is confrontational and controversial, aimed at intimidating and stressing the suspect into confessing, as opposed to Western European countries, where interrogation is more of a rational, information-gathering process.[19] The Reid method starts out like that, beginning as an interview and, after deriving enough information to consider the subject a suspect, progressing into accusatory interrogation. No one can accurately estimate the false confession rate or number of convictions based on *false confessions*,[20] admissions to crimes the defendants did not really commit, but DNA exonerations that have come rolling in reveal that a frightening number of people have admitted to crimes they never committed. "Many of these stories recount horrific tales of psychologically—and, in some cases, physically—abusive interrogations of children and adults, including many who were cognitively impaired."[21] Even after training in deception detection, despite some claims of success rates as high as 85%, the majority of research finds that police investigators and other professionals perform only marginally better than chance when it comes to spotting who's telling the truth.[22]

The polygraph, the so-called lie detector ("lie indicator" would be more accurate), which records physiological signs of stress like changes in heart rate, respiration, and perspiration, is something of an intimidation device itself. Psychologist William Moulton Marston—who, under his Charles Moulton pseudonym, created the superheroine character Wonder Woman with her magic Lasso of Truth—helped pioneer the use of physiological measures to detect deception back in the 1920s, and yet even after all this time no method of lie detection is foolproof. Despite millions spent on the use of polygraphs for spybusting attempts, polygraphs do not catch spies.[23] Despite some polygraph promoters' claims of 90–100% accuracy, laboratory tests show polygraph accuracy rates more consistently around 60%,[24] little better than chance, with an error rate where false positives outnumber false negatives by as much as 2 to 1—in other words, experts who make errors are twice as likely to say innocent people are lying than to say the guilty are telling the truth.[25] Physiological and emotional stress, especially when you're suspected of wrongdoing, does not prove you're lying;[26] in fact, many inveterate liars spin lies more easily than they tell the truth, and psychopaths may feel unstressed telling either. The polygraph is a useful prop. It may deter wrongdoing by those who believe it works[27] and it can provide a polygrapher with a theatrical tool to help elicit admissions during *post*-polygraph interviews.[28] For reasons such as these, polygraphs are generally not admissible as evidence in courts.

Torture interrogation (physically or psychologically abusive questioning) does not yield reliable information[29]—despite which, people generally believe that it works well[30] and that it is, therefore, in some cases justified. It produces behavioral effects, certainly, but in the areas of instilling terror and stifling opposition.[31] Elicitation of accurate information was rarely the witch hunter or inquisitor's goal. "When accuracy is the goal of interrogation, as it is in intelligence collection, the coercive power of torture is likely to result in proffered misinformation, misdirection, and lies—ineffective outcomes by any measure."[32] Based on evidence from experienced interrogators, the FBI (in contrast to the CIA) has objected to torture, regarding it as unreliable and ineffective.[33] Successful interrogators establish rapport between interrogator and source, applying powerful persuasion techniques that have been tested and retested for their efficacy based on understanding the subject's needs, motives, and self-perceptions.[34] Non-abusive interrogation methods require greater talent and skill. Why thrust poorly trained soldiers with random social skills into the position of administering torture protocols? Fear evokes urgency. When fight-or-flight kicks in, desperation urges us, "Do something now!" Using torture makes its users feel stronger and their supporters vicariously so. In the wake of horrifying tragedies like the 9/11 attacks, people yearn for any means by which they might restore a sense of order and control. Many yearn simply to make somebody else hurt and so they concoct rational-seeming excuses to inflict retaliatory pain even if it means turning a blind eye to abstract ethical dilemmas or concrete evidence that painless methods should prove more effective. To extract information from *allegedly* mean, cruel enemies, people want mean, cruel methods to work. Making nice with a monster repulses us. In *The Dark Knight*, the Joker points out to Batman the pointlessness in banging the clown around in a police interrogation room. Using ineffective truth extraction techniques to satisfy a desire for retributional justice[35] gets in the way of effective persuasion. Interrogators rarely find themselves facing the "ticking bomb" scenarios used to rationalize torture, so rarely that most experts have never faced one at all. Moreover, numerous experienced interrogation experts say that were they to face such a dire emergency where someone's life depended on rapid extraction of information, they'd stick with *non*-abusive methods proven to work better.[36] When a Gotham crime lord called Black Mask tortures a young heroine nearly to death, trying to extract secrets she knows about Batman, he learns little.[37] Why doesn't he issue threats he doesn't have to carry out? Why doesn't he try a truth serum, have a flunky dressed like Batman talk to her while she's delirious from fatigue, or paint the picture that she might improve the heroes' odds for survival if she'd only share what she knows? Those tricks take finesse. Mainly, Black Mask likes to hurt people. He enjoys wielding brutal power.

Terrorism, illegal violent or otherwise dangerous actions committed in order to intimidate or coerce in furtherance of political or social objectives,[38] "the systematic use of terror, especially as a means of coercion,"[39] is a theatrical crime against persons or property, a crime in which its greatest gains are symbolic or psychological satisfaction for its perpetrators.[40] Terrorists' motives are diverse. Some of their goals are straightforward: express outrage, get an imprisoned leader released, drive the U.S. military out of a territory. Some terrorist ideals get more abstract or complicated. Serial bomber Ted Kaczynski filled more than 50 pages with his "Unabomber Manifesto," 35,000 words meant to incite an anti-technology revolution.[41] Technology scared him, so he tried to scare people into sharing his fear.

The Joker in the movie *The Dark Knight*, a post-9/11 allegory for how terror breaks down reassuring moral categories, is out to scare everybody into dismantling their moral compasses. He doesn't understand the world and its people much better than Kaczynski but similarly wants to believe he does. If he were confident in that belief, he wouldn't feel quite so driven to confirm it. Like Kaczynski, he thinks he can get people to reveal how they're like himself: Kaczynski expected people to take up the anti-technology cause; the Joker expects people to reveal how easily they'll turn against each other. He gets his bank robbing flunkies to eliminate each other, makes two thugs fight to the death with a broken cue stick, drives Harvey Dent into turning killer, goads a detective into an attack that gives the Joker his opening to break out of jail, and contrives for Batman to break his one rule. "I'll show you," he tells Batman. "When the chips are down, these, uh, these 'civilized' people, they'll eat each other."

Having seen Batman use terror to get what he wants, the Joker sees—or wants to see—a kindred spirit and wants Batman to see that too. The Joker tells mobsters meeting in the back of a restaurant, "I know why you choose to have your little group therapy sessions in broad daylight. I know why you're afraid to go out at night: the Batman. See, Batman has shown Gotham your true colors, unfortunately." The Joker means to make the good citizens of Gotham show their "true colors" as well. Repeatedly he panics the populace into providing him with exactly the opportunities he wants, like when he drives a judge straight to a car bomb, scares people into evacuating the hospitals so he can reach Dent and snatch a busload of hostages, or makes police sharpshooters so frantic they nearly shoot those hostages themselves. "You crossed a line first, sir. You squeezed them, you hammered them to the point of desperation, and in their desperation, they turned to a man they didn't fully understand," Alfred tells Bruce, before suggesting that Bruce doesn't fully understand the Joker either. "Some men aren't looking for anything logical like money. They can't be bought, bullied, reasoned, or negotiated with. Some men just want to watch the world burn." Batman scares the mob into turning to the Joker. The Joker wants to scare everybody into turning *into* the Joker, like the 9/11 terrorists scared Americans into becoming torturers.

The Joker's wrong, though—not completely, but enough that two boatloads of people terrified for their lives refrain from blowing each other up. People can be better. Resisting impulses to turn on one another, giving others the benefit of the doubt, is often the best strategy for everyone in both the short term and long. Suspects facing the *Prisoner's Dilemma*, the opportunity to earn freedom by turning against each other, more frequently come out ahead by staying quiet and gambling that their accomplices will zip it as well.[42] Batman trusts correctly that the Joker will see no explosions from those two ships. We gamble on each other's better nature all the time. Sometimes we're wrong, but living without taking those gambles means living gripped by paranoia, which isn't living fully. The human race continues because we haven't all killed each other off.

Fright characterizes Batman's rogues gallery unlike any other. His enemies dress as if en route to a Halloween masquerade party full of trick-or-treat tricksters, evoking chills and thrills. The Waynes' uncostumed killer, Joe Chill, reflects the fears that give birth to Batman. People grow resistant to fear, though. Graduated exposure to Batman may inoculate Gotham's criminal element against him. He's a vaccine whose active ingredient is intimidation. Vaccine-resistant strains, the less easily intimidated criminals, survive and thrive by seizing opportunities previously enjoyed by more fearful felons. Despite Bruce Wayne's contention that criminals are "a superstitious, cowardly lot," the most dangerous monsters often feel too little fear to hold themselves back: the psychopaths.

CASE FILE 5–1 Scarecrow

Real name: Dr. Jonathan Crane

First appearance: *World's Finest Comics* #3 (Fall, 1941)

Origin: A gangly bookworm victimized by school bullies and raised by a grandmother who regularly punishes him by leaving him alone in a dilapidated chapel where flocks of birds might peck, harangue, and torment him, Jonathan Crane masters his fears by growing up to become a master of fear itself, a psychology professor whose unorthodox methods include firing a gun in class while demonstrating the acquisition of fear. The standoffish, shabbily dressed psychologist never fits in with other faculty. Why buy nicer clothes when that money could go into his book collection? After lecturing on how protection rackets make money by making people afraid, Crane decides to become the symbol he already resembles, "a symbol of poverty and fear combined! The perfect symbol—the Scarecrow."[1] Going into business as a one-man protection racket, he gets unethical businessmen to hire him to drive their rivals away through his use of violent scare tactics, even murder. Unfazed after the university fires him for inappropriate teaching methods like shooting that gun in class, the Scarecrow steps up his reign of terror, striking again and again until Batman and Robin bring him down.

> *"Guy dresses up as something horrific, goes out into the night and terrifies his enemies. He's acting out from deep, visceral trauma—probably childhood. Sound like anyone you know?"*
> —Batman, discussing the Scarecrow with Robin, *Year One: Batman Scarecrow* #1 (July, 2005)

❅   ❅   ❅

Where Bruce Wayne dresses like Dracula to scare the guilty, Jonathan Crane—yet another villain who inverts key aspects of the hero—dresses like a scarecrow to panic the innocent. At first, the Scarecrow fails to secure his place in Batman's rogues gallery. Appearing only twice in the early 1940s, he doesn't become a recurring enemy until after he reappears in 1967. Readers found him more interesting once he moved beyond terroristic scare tactics and into the realm of psychophysiological manipulation. When he returns, he uses a chemical spray to overwhelm victims and crime-fighters with the most primal human fears: heights, animals, darkness.[2] Over the years, he develops variants of his fear toxin, typically administering it as a gas to prey on individuals' personal fears (like Batman's dread of losing those closest to him)[3] with *hallucinogenic* effects inducing vivid visual and auditory hallucinations of whatever stimulus or situation frightens each of them most. Sometimes, instead of inducing fear, the Scarecrow unleashes drugs that eliminate fear in order to make the exposed recipients reckless to the point of endangering their own lives[4] or, among those for whom only the fear of consequences restrains their darkest impulses, hazardous to the lives of other people.[5]

Are any of ex-Professor Crane's toxic techniques plausible? Yes.

Psychoactive substances (psychologically active, altering perception and mood, a.k.a. *psychotropic* as Batman refers to Crane's toxin in *Batman Begins*), including both approved medications and recreational drugs, generally operate by boosting, blocking, or mimicking the body's natural hormones and *neurotransmitters* (the chemicals that regulate nerve cells' activity and relay signals throughout the nervous system). *Nerve gases* produce their effects by increasing the activity of the body's most prevalent neurotransmitter, *acetylcholine*, which enables learning, memory, and muscle contraction. A rapid burst in acetylcholine activity can produce lasting damage by exciting an eruption of muscle contractions, including respiratory seizures that can kill within a minute. If Crane could create a drug that operates on other neural systems, targeting the ones related to fear, and then release that drug in gaseous form, he would essentially invent a different kind of nerve gas.

Our natural stimulants, the neurotransmitters known as the *catecholamines*, fire up the nervous system to increase heart rate, blood flow, and the brain's oxygen supply. Specific catecholamines are *epinephrine* (a.k.a. *adrenaline*) and *norepinephrine* (a.k.a. *noradrenaline*). Catecholamine deficits correlate with depression, and excesses predict stress, anxiety, and physical reactions that resemble our responses to danger: racing heart, palpitations, tremors, hyperventilation. Elevating these physical reactions can heighten a fear response but might also intensify anger or positive emotions as well, just as stimulant substances like caffeine, cocaine, and amphetamines can enhance either unpleasant feelings like anxiety and paranoia or pleasant feelings of euphoria and well-being.[6] Both activate systems as part of the innate *fight-or-flight* response: reacting to danger with readiness to attack or run and hide.[7] Fun physical activities, for example, outdoor adventure tasks like canoeing and climbing rocks, can elevate catecholamine levels as well.[8]

To instill fear specifically, Crane's toxins must target neural areas associated with the fear side of that equation. Increasing motor responses associated with fear, like rapid heart rate or respiration, could help, but he can't rely on that alone because his victims might interpret those sensations as enhanced excitement or anger. The antidepressants known as *serotonin-norepinephrine reuptake inhibitors (SNRIs)* operate much like the more widely used *selective serotonin reuptake inhibitors (SSRIs)*. SSRIs combat some forms of depression, anxiety, and obsessive thinking by making the brain use its *serotonin* (a calming neurotransmitter) more efficiently, *selectively* increasing effectiveness in some neural regions more than others so that different SSRIs will work better with different problems: Some will work better on social anxiety,[9] while others might better treat eating disorders.[10] SNRIs provide an added kick with norepinephrine stimulation.[11] Although clinicians have used SNRIs to make anxiety sufferers feel better,[12] a villain like Crane could selectively target different arousal systems conceivably to make anxieties worse. Crane doesn't want to calm them down, though, so he wouldn't increase serotonin's effectiveness too. In fact, he'd likely include a selective serotonin blocker in his recipe. Some SNRIs also enhance *dopamine*,[13] an important neurotransmitter of which Parkinson's patients have too little and schizophrenic individuals generally have too much, which might figure into his toxins' hallucinogenic effects.

Within the brain, Crane would hit the *limbic system*, the so-called animal brain,[14] a doughnut-shaped collection of brain parts at the border between the *brainstem* (controlling basic life support deep down in the brain, atop the spinal cord) and *cerebral cortex* (where conscious thought and more advanced functions take place across the brain's surface). The limbic system includes the *hippocampus,* which processes explicit memories for long-term storage; a cluster of parts collectively known as the *hypothalamus*, which governs some motivation (hunger, thirst, caring whether we freeze or overheat) and emotion (sex drive and the flight-or-flight response to danger); and the *amygdala*, which links our motivations and emotions to the stimuli that set them off (actually *amygdalae*, plural, since there's one on each side of the brain). Electrical or chemical stimulation to the hypothalamus or amygdala can make an animal leap to attack[15] or, with only a slight difference in target location, cower in fear.[16] Crane might also target the brainstem's *locus coeruleus* and other structures involved in the central stress circuitry,[17] giving this psychology professor gone bad many options as he induces stress, anxiety, and outright panic in his victims.

There's more to us than automatic stimulus/response, though, just as there's more to fear itself than arousal activation. Both physiology and cognitions—our perceptions, memories, and interpretations—together can create our feelings. According to Schachter and Singer's *two-factor theory*, whenever we experience forms of general autonomic arousal (e.g., elevated heart rate) similarly associated with different emotions like fear, joy, and anger that involve similar general autonomic arousal, we interpret our own feelings and label them according to available cues. Arousal from one source like a shot of epinephrine could become happiness when exposed to someone else who acts euphoric or testiness around a person who acts irritated,[18] a process known as *excitation transfer.*[19] "Arousal fuels emotion; cognition channels it."[20] We can often think our way through our feelings. The Scarecrow once uses a device that sends vibrations to *the parasympathetic nervous system*, the division of the autonomic nervous system that normally calms the body. Batman works his way around its effects by asking himself how Crane stays calm and realizes it's simply because the psychologist knows there's no reason for fear. "Since it was your gadget, it was logical to understand that I had nothing to fear, either! Simple mind over matter, Scarecrow!"[21] He successfully tells himself not to interpret those physiological sensations as fear.

This happens long before the Scarecrow, through repeated exposure to his own toxins, loses his capacity for fear. Complete loss of fear by someone who grew up fully able to experience it is so rare that the phenomenon lacks systematic research and classification, but it does happen, as in the real-life case of "patient SM," whose specific amygdala damage left her unafraid even when held at gunpoint.[22] Like her or the research animals who no longer frighten due to experimental cuts to their fear centers, Crane no longer feels afraid of anything—and he misses that sensation.[23] The master of fear grew up wanting to accept his fears and control them, not eliminate them altogether. His own toxins won't induce fear in him either, whether because he has developed a *tolerance* (resistance to their effects) or damaged his fear centers so severely. A victim of his own devices, the boy who grew to cook up some fear for others now desperately seeks new ways to serve it to himself.

CASE FILE 5–2 Hugo Strange

Real name: Dr. Hugo Strange

First appearance: *Detective Comics* #36 (February, 1940)

Origin: Debuting in the comics as a mad scientist who fights Batman months before the more colorful Joker and Catwoman come along, back in the days when readers could accept a villain using a fog-and-lightning machine to cover a bank robbery instead of making a fortune off the fact that he has invented a fog-and-lightning machine, he's the first candidate to become a Moriarty to Batman's Holmes, ahead of the curve in many ways only to get supplanted in every way as Bob Kane and crew kept creating flashier foes. Strange, for example, spreads "fear dust" around the city[1] months before the Scarecrow appears. He dies a lot. Many appearances end with Strange presumed dead, only to survive somehow and later return to vex the Dark Knight yet again. In his Bronze Age appearances, he discovers Bruce Wayne's big secret[2] and makes several attempts to take his place in the Batman costume.[3]

"I can know what it feels to be the Bat-Man psychologically but not—not physically. God, h-how I envy him—how I hate him."

—Hugo Strange in *Batman: Legends of the Dark Knight* #11
(November, 1990)

❖   ❖   ❖

Rebooted after *Crisis on Infinite Earths*, Strange reenters comics as a prominent psychiatrist whom Gotham's mayor hires to develop a forensic profile on the city's new bat-clad vigilante and to form a strategy for turning public sentiment against the Batman. Strange articulates his thoughts to a lingerie-clad mannequin. Donning his own version of a Batman costume helps him understand his target's point of view—not the worst of strategies, as it helps him recognize the compulsion, the symbolism, and the disinhibiting empowerment that comes with the costume, except that Strange quickly envies Batman's freedom to run rampant through the night in that outfit and escalates his own actions to kidnapping the mayor's daughter in order to frame Batman. Strange deduces Batman's identity. The secret seemingly dies with him when he gets shot by police and falls into the river after Batman clears himself of Strange's frame.[4] Reminiscent of the original Strange's use of fear dust, this Strange soon teams up with Scarecrow Jonathan Crane to strike terror into Gotham, though the two quickly turn against each other and Crane impales Strange on a weather vane.[5] Later posing as a psychiatrist running standard stress evaluations on Wayne Enterprises employees, Strange tries but fails to coax a drugged Wayne into admitting he's Batman. Concluding that he erred in ever thinking Wayne was Batman, Strange breaks down and finally goes to Arkham Asylum instead of faking another death, not without dressing like Batman again in this course of this story[6] because keeping Hugo Strange out of a Bat costume would be like keeping cross-dressing filmmaker Ed Wood out of a skirt.[7]

As a psychiatrist writing a forensic profile, Strange is not formally a *forensic psychiatrist* whose main criminological responsibility would be to evaluate competency to stand trial or claims of mental illness in insanity defense cases, nor does he regularly work as an *offender profiler.* Offender or *criminal profiling*, known by many names, involves identifying an offender's demographic and individual characteristics, including signs of specific mental illness, from crime scene evidence and behavior reported by witnesses. Profiling had a long history before it had a name, as early as George Bagster Phillips and Thomas Bond's efforts to profile Jack the Ripper.[8] Since the FBI built its profiling program in the 1970s, a wide range of techniques have emerged, with five main approaches that vary in the manner and degree of emphasis on statistical probability, scientific method, deductive versus inductive reasoning, perspective-taking, training, and guesswork:

Criminologists, psychologists, and psychiatrists like Strange (well, psychiatrists—nobody's just like Hugo Strange) use *personality profiling* to construct a picture of the offender's likely personality traits and personal history. With *criminal investigative analysis*, the FBI's method, law enforcement officers trained in profiling review crime scene patterns and indicators and draw from interviews with past offenders to estimate the type of organized or disorganized offender likely to have committed the crime. *Investigative psychology*, conducted primarily by academic psychologists and criminologists with no investigative training, provides a fresh perspective by using typologies and past empirical studies to construct profiles. *Behavioral evidence analysis* emphasizes deduction and critical thinking, integrating more forensic psychology and scientific hypothesis testing into the process. *Geographic profiling* analyzes neighborhood characteristics and crime scene locations on the map to identify travel routes and determine where the offender is likely to recreate, live, and work.[9]

Criminal profiling depends on fundamental assumptions that (1) the crime scene reflects the perpetrator's personality, (2) the *modus operandi* stays noticeably similar over time, (3) so does the signature, and (4) so does the personality. The instrumental *modus operandi* (meaning method or mode of operation, *M.O.*) is the criminal's standard method of committing a crime, the actions the person uses in order to make that crime happen. As part of his M.O., the serial killer Ted Bundy often wore a cast or sling to look like he was harmless and in need of assistance before he would force a woman into his car. A noninstrumental *signature*, actions not necessary for committing the main crime, puts the offender's "own personal stamp"[10] on the crime.[11] Leaving a playing card after committing a murder does not help the Joker commit or try to get away with that misdeed. It boldly declares his ownership of the crime. Repeat offenders, especially serial and spree offenders whose crimes serve emotional more than instrumental needs, produce patterns in their actions most suitable for profiling because their cases seem to reflect the offenders' psychopathology.[12]

Criminal profiling has grown as a profession, and critics of criminal profiling have grown loud. Like some stockbrokers, sportswriters, and professional psychics, profilers may point to their hits, their accurate predictions, while failing to note the frequency of their misses. They may defuse criticism by saying, "I'm not always right," without confirming how often they are right. *Retrofitting* can occur, retroactively interpreting new facts and selectively remembering or misremembering details of a prior prediction to say these new facts prove the prediction.[13] *Inter-rater reliability rates* would be helpful: Will two different profilers looking at the same crime scene information without consulting with each other develop similar profiles? Individual criminals do not fall into neat typologies where those who show one set of behaviors consistently match each other on other behaviors.[14] Actions do not necessarily reveal specific motivations. "The fact is that different offenders can exhibit the same behaviors for completely different reasons," says Brent Turvey, a forensic scientist critical of the FBI's approach.[15] Many forensic psychologists and psychiatrists express skepticism, calling for more empirical validation,[16] with the majority in one survey believing it's simply not scientifically reliable or valid.[17] The profilers themselves cannot see eye to eye with their field, riddled as it is with contradictions and disputes.[18]

Locking onto an innocent suspect who fits a profile (a *false positive*) upends that person's life and delays identification of the true culprit. In contrast, investigators can overlook a guilty person erroneously when that offender does not match the profile (a *false negative*). Jumping to conclusions locks the expectations of investigators in a way that can be difficult to overcome. Because discovering that we have erred jostles our worldview, we do not easily give up our beliefs even in the fact of contradictory evidence (*belief perseverance*), a fact that saves Bruce Wayne for a time while Strange sticks to his assumption that a *wife*'s murder must be what drives Batman but, once Strange discovers that it had instead been Batman's parents who died, means that Strange hangs onto his belief that Bruce is Batman for a long time. Giving up that belief comes so hard for him that doing so contributes to Strange's mental breakdown.

6

The "Superstitious, Cowardly Lot"

Criminal Nature

"Criminals are a superstitious, cowardly lot. So my disguise must be able to strike terror into their hearts! I must be a creature of the night, black, terrible."

—Bruce Wayne, *Detective Comics* #33
(November, 1939)

 re criminals really a "superstitious, cowardly lot"? When the main person who can say what's going on inside a criminal's head is that same criminal, who may mislead out of sheer habit, who might not even understand his or her own thoughts and motivations well enough to share them, and who will say whatever it takes to shirk responsibility, we should be wary of trusting even our best source, much less our own guesses. From observations of their behavior and the skills they demonstrate in specific situations, including the errors that lead to their arrests, we know that many criminals demonstrate poor problem-solving skills and difficulty applying logic. For example, delinquent youth favor ineffective solutions when evaluating problems in social situations.[1]

The kinds of cognitive weaknesses Batman hopes to exploit when he decides to prey on their superstitions have already impaired their ability to generate nonaggressive solutions, conceive of legal ways to get the things they want and need, and then keep themselves from getting caught.

But cowardly? Which requires greater fearlessness, doing the right thing or breaking the law? Nervous, fearful individuals on average commit fewer crimes. Low fear of punishment reduces the effectiveness of some deterrents against crime—not only potential incarceration but the risks involved along the way—and may therefore predispose fearless individuals like extraverts and psychopaths to take risks and seek thrills the fearful might not pursue.[2] *Batman Begins'* Scarecrow might succumb to his own fear toxin, but *The Dark Knight's* Joker and *The Dark Knight Rises'* Bane each demonstrate abnormal deficiencies in ability to feel fear.

Cowardice and superstition aside, is Batman's assumption that criminals share common traits right? What *is* a criminal personality?

Out of the different personality factors most thoroughly examined over thousands of studies, *extraversion* (the personality dimension that includes outgoing, assertive behavior and social fearlessness) correlates most strongly with lawbreaking actions. "Because extraverts have higher needs for excitement and stimulation to break the daily boredom, they are also most likely to run counter to the law."[3] *Extraverts* (people high in extraversion) are less afraid in general than are the more reserved, less outgoing, and less sociable *introverts*. Fearlessness should give extraverts greater capacity for both criminal and heroic behavior. Lack of inhibition characterizes both extraversion and psychopathy,[4] which we'll look at shortly, but extraversion and psychopathy are different personality dimensions.[5] Introverts as easily as extraverts can have shortcomings or strengths in the areas of empathy and moral concerns,[6] even if extraverts more easily act out the riskiest impulses or those most likely to impact others. Attending more to the external environment than their own inner experience, extraverts predominantly seek gratification from outside themselves. Introverts occupy themselves and stay out of other people's way. Introverted fiends exist, of course. Serial killers Ted Bundy and John

Wayne Gacy may have been charming, outgoing fellows, but think how often a serial or mass murderer's neighbors say, "He was a quiet sort, kept to himself."

Extraversion and sociability are separate dimensions. Extraverts include likable social butterflies as well as sadistic social predators. For the Joker and Penguin, committing a crime with no audience would be pointless. They don't always understand people as well as they think they do, especially not the better part of human nature, nor do they generally care about anybody else's welfare aside from the Penguin's devotion to his mother,[7] and yet they love social gatherings and public demonstrations, habitually seeking gratification from others, as is typical of extraverts. The Riddler, who also loves attention and can be quite the showman onstage, lives to beat others, but takes less interest in other people's activities and lives. Fearlessness and consciousness of others can help the shapeshifter Clayface impersonate others where nervousness and lack of extrapersonal awareness would interfere with even the most conscientious introvert's performances.

Introverted loners like the more reclusive Mr. Freeze, Mad Hatter, and Poison Ivy dislike crowds and avoid social interactions for long periods of time. Until a beautiful woman named Nora tries with limited success to bring him out of his shell, Victor Fries contents himself with his studies during the years before he becomes Mr. Freeze. The Mad Hatter shows less interest in people than in their hats. Likewise, Poison Ivy grows up compensating for her social paralysis by occupying herself with non-human, nonjudgmental plants that can't reject her. Unable to relate to others and uninterested in developing better social skills, both the Hatter and Ivy resort to manipulating others via mind control to get what they want.

The extraversion-introversion factor, instead of presenting a strict dichotomy where a person is clearly one or the other in every single situation, presents a broad range of qualities with most people showing a mixture of extraverted and introverted traits, even if one main pattern dominates. Extraverted Harvey Dent is an outgoing district attorney until tragedy makes him resent his own basic nature and he tries to withdraw from everything he previously valued. One might argue that many of Batman's other foes are introverts who overcompensate for their social shortcomings by attacking the society they never fit into. Regardless of individual designations as extraverts and introverts, the villainy of all the major Bat-foes grows out of their respective social interests and resentments. Why else would they commit their crimes wearing outrageous outfits?

The Roots of All Evil: Some Theories on Crime

The optimistic *conformity perspective* on crime assumes human beings are creatures of conformity, ready to do right so we can fit in with others. Conformist theories hold that the desire to fit in motivates us to follow social conventions and laws when we can, but we might also break laws when lawbreaking strikes us as the way to get the things that can help us live up to society's materialistic expectations. *Humanistic psychology*, a branch that views the individual human being (not some therapist) as the best determinant of his or her own abilities and needs, is one example of a conformist perspective. Humanists focus on our better nature, emphasizing healthy people's personal growth instead of dwelling heavily on our worst qualities. According to humanistic psychology founder Abraham Maslow, nature gave us an inborn drive to become better people and to pursue our potential as human beings, and whether the many challenges we face along the way help us advance or hold us back is up to us. Aside from the innate drive to fulfill one's potential, humanistic psychologists believe strongly in free will and therefore hold individuals responsible for their own actions. Maslow said we must meet our most basic physiological needs before we can progress into higher levels of personal growth, working our way up through a *hierarchy of needs*, Maslow's stratified pyramid.[8]

Maslow said we work our way up from the most basic needs and that deficiencies in the lower levels will require too much of our time, attention, and effort for us to progress smoothly into higher levels with more advanced psychological functioning. People stuck in the lower levels fixate on their deficits even after meeting basic needs, choosing to focus on whatever they still don't have instead of

Maslow's Hierarchy of Needs.

appreciating what they do have so they can flourish as human beings. Selina Kyle's poverty and homelessness,[9] Pamela Isley's timidity and familial neglect,[10] and Oswald Cobblepot's physical deformity and victimization by bullies[11] during their respective childhoods get them each in the habit of focusing on their deficits and later lead them each to seek fulfillment with things and thrills as the adult Catwoman, Poison Ivy, and Penguin, habits that continue long after they meet their basic needs. "Mother, father, child, and cat-goddess guardian— everything I never had," Selina remarks while reflecting on the goods that fill her residence, "and now it's mine. A home of stolen happiness."[12]

Criminal behavior can emerge among those who have grown frustrated over unmet needs or among those who choose to stay mired in a lower level, simply wanting more and more. Psychopaths hunger for baser needs so thoroughly that Maslow felt they could understand love no better than a person blind from birth comprehends the color red.[13] The hierarchy of needs provides a useful construct, a popular model with both uses and limitations. Where might Batman himself fall in this hypothesized hierarchy? In seeking to reach peak efficiency as a crime-fighter, he actively decides against pursuing *self-actualization*, the fulfillment of his potential as a human being. One criticism of Maslow's theory is that his definition of self-actualization overemphasizes individual development.[14] Rather than spend another twenty years studying under Master Kirigi to attain illumination, Bruce Wayne chooses to forego his personal growth so that he may combat evil right away.[15]

The more pessimistic *nonconformist perspective* views humans as undisciplined creatures not inherently motivated to conform, beasts itching to flout social norms and wantonly commit crimes—born to be bad but held back by society. As the Joker argues in *The Dark Knight*, "all it takes is a little push" to bring out the beast in anyone. For example, Sigmund Freud's *psychodynamic* approach (see chapter 9) and later *neo-Freudian* views ("new Freuds" subscribing to modified versions of his position) explain behavior in terms of unconscious motives and drives, viewing human nature as essentially antisocial, biologically driven by the id's pleasure principle to get what they want when they want it. When the Joker gets an impulse to kill or steal, he acts on it without hesitation.

Both of these larger perspectives, conformist and nonconformist, in attributing our basic inclinations to inborn nature, take the nature side of the long-running *nature versus nurture* debate: a philosophical exchange over whether we act as we do because of how we're born (nature) or because of how life treats us (nurture). Humanistic psychologists criticize both sides of the nature versus nurture debate for being too *deterministic* (saying something other than free will determines everything we do), and yet their view includes some determinism by saying we're innately motivated to become better people. *Existentialist psychology*, a more philosophical approach, winds up being less optimistic by shucking that bit of determinism to stress the importance of free will as we each find meaning in our own existence.[16]

Anti-Batman tales, stories of villains whose backgrounds and characteristics mirror Batman's, depict the power of nurture in determining whether a person becomes a hero or a villain by rearranging the circumstances of the Dark Knight's origin. Whereas Bruce Wayne sees a mugger kill his parents and grows up to fight criminals as Batman, other boys who separately see police officers kill their criminal parents grow up to become costumed cop killers, the Wrath[17] and Prometheus.[18] In an alternate universe, the hoodlum Joe Chill raises Thomas Wayne Jr.

to become the supervillain Owlman after a police officer kills Thomas's mother and brother Bruce.[19] In the nurture argument's corner, the *learning perspective* assumes all these boys started out with neither innate goodness nor evil, no inherent readiness to conform or rebel. This perspective instead declares that we all learn our actions from how circumstances reinforce or punish our behavior or by witnessing how other people act. The branch of psychology known as *behaviorism* espouses the learning perspective, arguing that psychology should focus on measureable actions when trying to explain humans and nonhumans alike[20]—not Freud's unconscious mind, not other psychologists' conscious processes, not even an individual's heredity. John B. Watson, behaviorism's founder—who posited that classical and instrumental conditioning (explained in chapter 5) could influence everything a person does—once said, "Give me a dozen healthy infants, well-formed, and my own specified world to bring them up in and I'll guarantee to take any one at random and train him to become any type of specialist I might select—doctor, lawyer, artist, merchant-chief and, yes, even beggar-man and thief, regardless of his talents, penchants, tendencies, abilities, vocations, and race of his ancestors."* Albert Bandura expanded on this to include *observational learning*, a.k.a. *imitational learning*, to account for how we acquire actions we see others perform, behaviors we pick up from personally having been reinforced or punished.[21] Watson demonstrated how both classical and instrumental conditioning could cause phobias, Bandura showed how easily people imitate aggressive actions modeled by others, and many effective therapeutic techniques have evolved from their methods. Behaviorism and its variants like Bandura's social behaviorism remain influential to this day, even though other views like *cognitive psychology*, a modern branch of psychology using the scientific method to explore internal mental processes (memories, attitudes, beliefs, problem-solving, information-processing—our *cognitions*[22]), have in some professionals' minds eclipsed it. Although *cognitive behaviorists* apply behaviorism's

---

*At the end of which, he added, "I am going beyond my facts and I admit it, but so have the advocates of the contrary and they have been doing it for many thousands of years," so his beliefs were a little less radical than he often sounded (Watson, 1930, 104).

principles to cognitive processes, the strictest behaviorists scoff at the term *cognitive behaviorism* as an oxymoron[23] that contradicts itself.

Bruce's parents alert him to the need to help others. Teaching him through both word and deed, they strive to reinforce his better qualities, they discuss the reasons for putting others first, and they model altruistic behavior in both life and death. As Bruce grows, he keeps learning more about how his parents lived their lives. Their lives, not just their murders, have taught him to be heroic—which seems to make a strong case for nurture except that he also inherited their nature in his genes. So which is right—learning perspectives that emphasize nature or biological perspectives and others that stress nature? Both. Few who seriously research these issues will argue 100% for either side. Winning the debate, the *interactionist perspective* asserts that nature and nurture interact to make us who we are.[24] Heredity provides a natural potential that life experience may or may not bring out. If your identical twin develops schizophrenia, you have about a 50–50 chance of developing it yourself, only a little lower if separated at birth.[25] With no hereditary influence, your odds would be no higher than anyone else's, but if heredity controlled it completely, every person with a schizophrenic identical twin would develop schizophrenia, too. Nature plays the greater role in some things and nurture exerts more power over others.

Bad Seeds and Early Misdeeds: Juvenile Delinquency

A *socialized offender* routinely breaks laws because of having picked up criminal behaviors from his or her environment, the product of learning through conditioning and observation, in contrast to the *nonsocialized offender* (which psychologist Leonard Berkowitz called the *individual offender*)[26] whose offenses arise from a long series of frustrations over unmet needs. Instead of learning criminal patterns from others, the individual offender comes up with some independently. A nonsocialized juvenile delinquent tends to become much scarier than a socialized one and is more likely to stay that way. Despite spending time as Batman's sidekick, the juvenile delinquent who becomes the second Robin never outgrows his antisocial inclinations and eventually becomes Batman's enemy, a deadly antihero and sometimes crime lord.

Conduct disorder refers to a disruptive, repetitive, and persistent pattern of antisocial behavior during childhood or adolescence in which the youth keeps violating the rights of others or major age-appropriate rules and social norms. These behaviors fall into four groups: (1) aggression to people and animals, (2) property destruction, (3) deceitfulness or theft, and (4) serious rule violations (truancy, running away, staying out at night without permission starting before age 13).[27] Juvenile socialized offenders who commit antisocial acts as part of group activity usually have age-appropriate friendships, show concern for the welfare of their friends or gang members, and are unlikely to betray friends by informing on them.[28] Few youngsters of the group type remain delinquent past adolescence. For all the trouble they may get into, they're still learning social skills through peer interactions, such as they may be ("I wanna break this window; you got the last house"). Nonsocialized juvenile offenders with conduct disorder exhibit more bullying, physical aggression, and other cruelty toward peers and may be hostile and abusive toward adults as well. Sheer callousness, flat disregard for others' feelings or well-being, is their most striking feature.[29] Rejected and unpopular, they lack close, confiding relationships.[30] If they do connect with someone else who shares their antisocial interests, the person will usually be distinctly older or younger, not an immediate peer, and their interactions stay superficial. The earlier their antisocial actions begin, the more likely it is that the problems will persist for life, albeit transformed into "adult" manifestations. Those with *childhood onset* have symptoms of conduct disorder before age 10 and those with *adolescent onset* do not, although concealment of the misbehavior may cause caregivers to underreport problems and overestimate age of onset.[31] Juvenile delinquents who do not start engaging in antisocial actions until adolescence tend to outgrow that behavior, whereas those who engage in pre-adolescent antisocial actions frequently do not.[32]

Commissioner Gordon's son James Jr.—an infant born in *Batman: Year One* and the cute kid Two-Face threatens to shoot in the movie *The Dark Knight*—during his childhood kills animals out of curiosity, dresses like a homicidal maniac for Halloween,* and apparently murders one of his sister's friends.[33] A doctor who's certain the boy's problems do not indicate autism wants to give him a PCL, the Psychopathy Checklist,[34] to the surprise of James Sr., who knows "they give that out at Arkham."[35] Gordon says the test measures *psychopathology*, which means the study of mental illness, although many people, even professionals, use the term to refer to mental illness itself. He's technically right, if imprecise, since psychopathy falls within psychopathology. Can good people raise a monster? Family situations where solitary aggressive and childhood-onset conduct disorder appear reveal parents with severe marital disharmony, instability, alcoholism, mental illness, antisocial behaviors, and other problems—frequently *but not consistently*. Twin and adoption studies provide evidence that both genetic and environmental factors influence the emergence of conduct disorder.[36] Differences in brain activity among youths who lack empathy are correlational: Maybe the fact that aggressive adolescents show strong activation in the *amygdala* (the brain structure linking emotions to the stimuli that evoke them) and *ventral striatum* (an area that responds to feelings of reward) when watching others get pain inflicted upon them means that their brain differences make them enjoy watching pain, but it may be the other way around. Maybe their enjoyment at seeing pain causes those areas to fire up, so that does not prove the neural circuitry created the psychopathic tendencies.[37]

Where does evil come from? We don't exactly know. James Gordon Jr. is a product of more than genes, upbringing, and head injury. He's a child of Gotham City, the city that killed the Waynes and gives rise to a never-ending line of hoodlums and freaks. At age 17, he enters a drug trial for a medication called Diaxamene, designed to "stimulate peptide production in the part of the brain that controls human emotions. It helps people with severe

---

*The Joker, who later cripples Junior's sister and murders his stepmother.

antisocial neurological function experience empathy."[38] (The drug is fictitious, so do not ask your doctor if Diaxamene might be right for you.) No medication can create empathy in someone who has never felt it.[39] None. However, superhero comic book stories are science fiction, even the non-super-powered Batman's stories in everything from his gadgets to the Joker and Scarecrow's specialized toxins.* Even within the story, the drug does not work as intended. Prodding Junior to contemplate the differences between himself and others, this newfound perspective simply makes him decide normal people are weak and dysfunctional while men in the drug trial like himself are stronger and more highly evolved. He refigures the medication's formula to create a drug that can suppress empathy rather than stimulate it. The story does not reveal whether his attempt to taint baby formula with the inverted medicine has succeeded, ending instead with Dick Grayson and Gordon Sr. wondering if James Jr. has infected "thousands of infants with a drug that could help them grow up to be sociopaths."[40] Again, this seems unlikely, but we can't rule out the possibility. The brain is a tricky thing. Experimental *lesioning* (inflicting damage) to specific brain parts like the amygdala can change which emotions we feel in reaction to particular stimuli.[41] A chemical capable of damaging the amygdala and other neural regions that process how we feel about others could conceivably lower its recipient's empathy and, among individuals with either inherited or environmentally created psychopathic potential, raise the odds they grow up evil.

Integral to the definition of conduct disorder is that the individual is violating age-appropriate societal norms and rules. The child who grows up in an environment where truancy and violence are the norms, where adults all around him or her actively train and encourage such behavior, whether in a war-torn Third World nation or a

---

*Seriously, science fiction. For more on where Batman's toys do and don't stand up to real science, read *The Science of Superheroes* (Gresh & Weinberg, 2002) or *The Physics of Superheroes: Spectacular Second Edition* (Kakalios, 2009) or watch the Discovery Channel TV series *MythBusters*, season 5, episode 17, "Superhero Hour."

Mafia-dominated part of uptown, might not qualify for any mental disorder. *Adaptive delinquency*, in which the behavior is an attempt to adjust to the manifold disadvantages of poverty and inner-city living,[42] not a mental illness, might better describe the thievery committed by orphans Selina Kyle and Jason Todd, both of whom have practical reasons for dodging the foster care system (especially Selina, after an orphanage director tries to drown her)[43] even though that means scraping to survive before they become, respectively, Catwoman and Batman's second Robin.

Evil by Many Names

Commissioner Gordon worries that his son's a sociopath. James Jr. calls himself a psychopath. Which one has it right? They both do. The words—synonymous according to some writers; not synonymous but overlapping according to others—each suit James Gordon Jr., along with most of Batman's foes. *Psychopathy, sociopathy, antisocial personality disorder, dyssocial (dissocial) personality disorder, sadism, adult antisocial behavior . . .* these terms and more amount to psychological professionals' attempts to pathologize a non-psychological term: *evil*.

Psychotic does not mean psychopathic, nor does *antisocial* mean unsociable, no matter how many fictional characters or even real-life experts you've heard confuse the terms. Conditions like schizophrenia and senile dementia can turn good people psychotic as easily as bad ones. *Psychotic* individuals have lost touch with the real world as indicated by gross reality distortions, notably hallucinations and delusions (see chapter 8). The world's most dangerous people tend to be coldly sane. They may think and feel differently from most people, but they know enough of what's really going on to use it against others. A psychopath who also happens to be psychotic is still heartless even at times when the hallucinations and delusions go away, as when the schizophrenic Mad Hatter uses a "thinking hat" to help himself think more clearly. Schizophrenic Maxie Zeus, cured of his delusional belief that he is the Greek god Zeus, nevertheless sells the Joker venom mixed with Ecstasy as a recreational drug, dangerous despite his nobler intentions.[44] More antisocial than psychopathic, Maxie enjoys greater freedom at Arkham, staying out of the maximum-security area where asylum administrators store more dangerous criminals.[45] *Antisocial* means antithetical to social norms, in opposition to society's rules and expectations for how civilized people act. Antisocial behavior violates people's rights in big ways. An antisocial individual may be unsociable or sociable, either one—it's a separate issue. Some can be quite charming, at least superficially, while they go about manipulating others, like the Joker charming his way into psychiatrist Harleen Quinzel's heart.[46]

The first edition of the American Psychiatric Association's *Diagnostic and Statistical Manual of Mental Disorders* treated *sociopathy* as a whole category of different mental illnesses for people "ill primarily in terms of society and of conformity with the prevailing cultural milieu,"[47] a category that included antisocial reaction, dyssocial reaction, addiction, and sexual deviation—not the contemporary view. A non-sociopath can have some addictions and *paraphilias* (the modern psychiatric term for sexual deviations, conditions in which the person is unable either to experience or enjoy the normal sexual response cycle without actions or imagery most people consider bizarre) without being a criminal. As long as you and your consenting adult partner have fun with your whips, chains, stilettos, balloons, pastries, puppets, garden tools, or whatnot together in the privacy of your own home, there's nothing antisocial about that. Even if it interferes with your ability to enjoy mature relationships to the point that it qualifies as a mental disorder, you haven't necessarily violated anybody else's rights. Modern writers tend to use the poorly defined term *sociopath* interchangeably with *psychopath*. "The purist, however, considers the sociopath a habitual criminal offender who has not been properly socialized."[48] Those who make distinctions may treat sociopathy as a product of environment, less deeply rooted than psychopathy, or view the sociopath as being more capable of interpersonal bonds like loyalty even as they hurt outsiders. Ra's al Ghul sometimes calls Batman a sociopath. "He will be grieving,

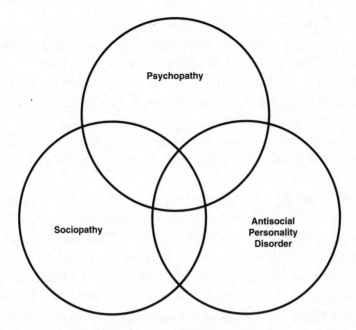

Venn Diagram of the Evil Disorders. The figure reflects how psychopathy, sociopathy, and antisocial personality disorder overlap in their definitions, not in terms of population distribution.

but he will most likely lean on his sociopathic nature,"[49] al Ghul says, a remark that fits some meanings of sociopath but not others. Keep in mind, the 500-year-old eco-terrorist may not have read a *DSM* since 1952.

These days, the greater issue diagnostically is distinguishing antisocial personality disorder (APD) from psychopathy. APD is a *DSM* diagnosis, psychopathy is not, and yet many therapists and criminologists concentrate on psychopathy as the more meaningful construct when trying to understand evil. An *antisocial personality disorder* diagnosis focuses more on objectively assessable actions* (lawbreaking, deceitfulness, impulsivity, aggressiveness, recklessness, irresponsibility), with the specific trait of remorselessness as just one of the possible symptoms. *Psychopathy* places greater emphasis on

---

*Which seems ironic for a *personality* disorder.

internal qualities, specific emotional and interpersonal qualities like grandiose self-concept, lack of empathy, and rejection of responsibility for one's own behavior. Psychopathy's essential quality is lack of conscience: They should know the difference between right and wrong, but at heart they don't understand it and they don't care. The *criminal psychopath* regularly breaks laws, as opposed to other psychopaths who, despite their lack of empathy or moral concerns, might have other reasons for not committing numerous criminal or antisocial acts.

Because the *DSM* defines APD in terms of antisocial actions, based largely on earlier studies of prison inmates' characteristics, the majority of inmates meet its criteria.[50] This should come as no surprise. Test developers who create assessment tools based on thousands of previous criminals' answers should find it no more shocking or impressive when later criminals produce high scores than if most mimes nod *yes* a lot while completing an *Are You a Mime?* questionnaire. Criminality is not an essential component of psychopathy,[51] even though Hervey Cleckley interviewed incarcerated psychopaths for *The Mask of Sanity*, his landmark book that laid the groundwork for defining and studying psychopathy.[52] The title refers to the social "mask" that conceals the true nature of psychopaths who outwardly mimic normally functioning persons. Cleckley identified numerous traits common among psychopaths, including superficial charm; absence of nervousness; unreliability; untruthfulness and insincerity; lack of insight; lack of remorse or shame; inadequately motivated antisocial behavior (as opposed to non-psychopaths, who might commit antisocial acts out of desperation or for other clear reasons); poor judgment and failure to learn from experience; pathologic egocentricity and incapacity for love; poverty in major affective (emotional) reactions; interpersonal unresponsiveness; impersonal, trivial sex life; and failure to follow any life plan.[53] Batman's foes broadly demonstrate most of these qualities. Some, like the Joker, show signs of them all.

A person could have many of these qualities without having them all. *Snakes in Suits: When Psychopaths Go to Work*[54] laid out core deficits that might produce psychopaths who are not physically aggressive. Some fail and get imprisoned for white collar crimes while others successfully avoid criminal sanction yet cause interpersonal problems for everyone who works around them.[55] Layfolk and the media bandy the term *psychopath* about so commonly in connection with serial killers and other clear-cut fiends that people popularly overestimate the criminality, severity, and sheer twistedness of most psychopaths. The person with no conscience, no empathy anywhere in his or her soul, might or might not take an interest in violence or sadistic cruelty. Consider the stockbroker who misappropriates millions, gutting retirement funds and fleecing so many who entrust their savings to him, indifferent to lives wrecked along the way and even resentful toward those darn complainers.

Prognosis: Do Psychopaths Get Better?

Diagnosis involves naming a person's condition, identifying what's wrong whether that means determining physical ailments like measles and malaria, mental illnesses like PTSD and major depression, or personality issues and disorders that not everyone considers to be mental illnesses. A *prognosis* is a forecast, the clinician's estimate (best guess) about a condition's probable course, duration, and eventual outcome. Prognosis for psychopathy and various personality disorders is poor. Criminals without ingrained personality problems such as psychopathy and APD are more likely to reform.

No medication can make a psychopath grow a conscience, and they do not respond well to therapy. Doctors typically prescribe medication to those with antisocial personality disorder only when they exhibit *comorbid conditions* (any additional disorders they also happen to have) like addiction or depression,[56] although psychopaths "usually do not exhibit mental disorders, either mild or severe,"[57] so therapists often don't even have that much to work on. Psychopaths lack insight, drive, and incentive to change. "Because they aren't disturbed by their behavior, they are rarely genuinely motivated to change, which makes any real collaboration between therapist and patient unlikely."[58] In fact, some forms of therapy seem to make them worse by allowing them to hone their skills at manipulating others.[59]

Treatment for antisocial non-psychopaths nets better results by fostering impulse control, teaching them to recognize triggers that set off their problematic behaviors, and helping them improve problem-solving skills.[60] *Cognitive skills training* seeks to modify *how* an offender thinks, targeting problem-solving and perspective-taking skills, while *cognitive restructuring* works on *what* the criminals think (specific values, attitudes, not blaming others, ways to minimize harm).[61]

Antisocial personality disorder, the diagnosis that focuses on antisocial actions, does not often appear in old age. Age-related reductions in impulsivity, social deviance, and antisocial behavior do not prove time has warmed up antisocial individuals' cold hearts. Older psychopaths, while exhibiting fewer of the impulsive, antisocial actions that might get them arrested or diagnosed with antisocial personality disorder,[62] nevertheless remain frequently selfish, callous, deceitful, manipulative, and deficient in empathy toward others.[63] Losing the ability to stir up as much mayhem as they may have in younger days does not necessarily turn them into warm, caring human beings.

Meet Joe Chill

Which kind of crook killed the Waynes? We don't know much about their killer, the mugger Joe Chill. Much as we might like to demonize the man whose sins launched a billionaire vigilante's war on crime, he seems to be a small-time thug who panics when Thomas Wayne stands up for Martha and then she screams. The few stories that depict confrontations between Chill and the grown Batman show him to have become a career criminal, maybe becoming a hard-nosed mob hitman[64] or maybe a mid-level crime boss whom Batman terrifies.[65] Either way, antisocial personality disorder seems likely. The hitman version, while seeming more coldly psychopathic than the terrified crime boss incarnation, comes across as more human and more interested in other people than many of Batman's foes.[66]

Earthy Joe Chill would seem out of place in a gathering of Batman's flamboyant, most malevolent foes. Neither does he belong among the lunatics crazy enough or idiots dumb enough to take jobs as supervillains' henchmen. Batman may spend more time taking down everyday criminals reminiscent of Chill, but he more famously fights freaks, among whom the distinctions between the different evil disorders matter little because most of them fit the whole lot.

CASE FILE 6–1 Bane

Real name: Unknown

First appearance: *Batman: Vengeance of Bane* #1 (January, 1993).

Origin: A corrupt court system imprisons a woman in a hellish South American prison, Peña Dura, for the crimes of her lover, a revolutionary who evades capture. After she dies, their son has to serve out their sentence in that prison where he was born.[1] He grows up among killers and madmen. He plays with the rats. Bane, this child of two fierce warriors, learns from hardened criminals and a visiting Jesuit priest, whose books provide the boy a classical education and whose gifts of toys give him some solace—especially his teddy bear, Osito, which the boy considers his only friend. A hole in Osito's back conceals a knife that Bane uses against those who bully him. Bruce Wayne at age 8 sees his parents murdered; Bane at 8 commits his first murder. Bane pushes himself to become harder, stronger, deadlier every day, to do more than survive there. He means to thrive. Killing dozens of other inmates along the way, Bane establishes himself as king of the convicts. An experimental drug called Venom, expected to kill him like previous test subjects, instead gives him monstrous strength. He engineers a jailbreak and heads for Gotham City, attracted by the challenge of beating Gotham's Dark Knight. After exhausting Batman by freeing all of Arkham Asylum's villains, Bane attacks him at Wayne Manor and breaks the hero's back, earning Bane his reputation as "the man who broke the Bat" and forcing a recuperating Bruce to enlist a hero called Azrael to take his place temporarily as Gotham's guardian.

"I've known you since I lived in the hell of a dark hole thousands of miles from here. I've known you in my dreams. And I escaped from that hell—escaped from my dreams—for one reason only. To find you—and to break you."

—Bane to Batman in *Batman* #496 (July, 1993)

✿   ✿   ✿

Bane is to Batman what a juggernaut called Doomsday is to Superman: a brand-new Big Bad who comes out of nowhere, causes chaos all around, and then delivers the hero his greatest defeat. Bane's drive to beat Batman for the sheer sake of beating Batman illustrates his strong achievement motivation, *Need for Achievement*: the need to overcome obstacles, to attain a lofty standard, and to rival and surpass others. Biochemist Henry Murray, who turned toward a career in psychology after psychiatrist Carl Jung guided him through his personal dilemmas, identified a variety of needs that motivate and direct human behavior.[2] Not everyone has every need. Over the course of a lifetime, a person might or might not experience them all. Needs can influence particular individuals so regularly that the possession of a consistent need becomes part of those individuals' personalities. Following up on this, psychologist David McClelland asserted that three dominant needs comprise human motivation: Need for Achievement (NAch), Need for Power (NPow), and Need for Affiliation (NAffil).[3] A person could feel driven toward achievements unrelated to power and affiliation. Bane yearns for power, too, but belittles affiliation.

"It is the nature of plans involving others. They are flawed because humans are flawed. I will miss the antics of my foolish associates, especially the girl. But I cannot be Bane with them attached to me. The authorities think they have won. But my plan left no room for error. Either I conquered my enemy or I was set free of all encumbrances, even the girl. It was caring. It was emotion that made me weak. And now I am free of it. As I planned all along."

—Bane in *Secret Six* #36 (October, 2011)[4]

He understands strength in numbers and can enjoy a few people's company, but as he lacks incentive to maintain that enjoyment, he demonstrates low *Need for Affiliation*, the need to belong with others. Those who value affiliation most, requiring approval and interpersonal connection, make good team members but poor leaders. Reflecting on his few tentative attachments makes Bane decide they put him at risk because enemies could use those bonds against him, so he parts ways with a group called the Secret Six.

Subsidiation refers to situations in which one need activates to satisfy another. Bane's *Need for Power*, secondary to his Need for Achievement, supplements that greater motivation. Power helps him achieve. Personal power, power over himself, he believes helps him attain power over others. The everyday management of any criminal organization would leave him dissatisfied if that power posed insufficient challenge. He weans himself off Venom, a source of physical might, when he decides addiction to Venom would be weakness, and yet he risks addiction again at times when the Venom offers him an advantage in pursuing a valued goal.

> *"It doesn't matter who we are. What matters is our plan. No one cared who I was until I put on the mask."*
> —Bane (Tom Hardy) in *The Dark Knight Rises* (2012 motion picture)

7

The Halloween Party
Why All the Costumed Crooks?

After the arrival of its costumed hero, Gotham City sees a proliferation of costumed characters, most of them criminals whose theatrics and preoccupations rival the Dark Knight's. Does Batman inspire their histrionics no less than he inspires new heroes, does he attract creative crooks to Gotham, or does Gotham itself create them all, vigilantes and villains? These villains are not simply out to steal. They seek excitement, they need challenges, and they want attention. Quietly stealing a fortune and getting away with it won't feed their other needs. On top of the psychopathy and antisocial personality disorder that the previous chapter covered, the most famous felons in Batman's rogues gallery show extreme behaviors that transcend those of everyday criminals.

Serial Crime

A *serial criminal* (e.g., serial killer, rapist, or arsonist) commits a series of three or more crimes of a specific type with a "cooling-down" time—a varying interval of weeks, months, or more—between separate lawbreaking incidents. Some seek attention, others do not. How does a serial criminal differ from any other repeat offender? The lack of ulterior purpose plays a role. Whether a hired assassin like Batman's enemy Deadshot[1] kills cold-bloodedly or gains personal satisfaction from the act, the main thing that contract killer gets from each specific kill is a fee or other clear external benefit. A terrorist kills and destroys in order to instill terror and advance an agenda, however sensible or insensible that agenda may be, as the Joker does throughout the 2008 motion picture *The Dark Knight.* The *serial murderer* kills for killing's sake, satisfying an emotional drive. Gotham's nihilistic serial killer Victor Zsasz—who cuts hundreds of tally marks on his body, one for each person he claims to have murdered—keeps himself from feeling depressed about the meaninglessness of life by "liberating" others from the burden of breathing.[2] So why don't we say "serial vandal"? Why don't we call a kleptomaniac who repeatedly steals for thrills and then loses interest in the stolen items a "serial shoplifter"? As popularly used, the *serial* terminology clearly denotes heinous violation of the rights of others.

A criminal on a *crime spree* commits the crime at three or more locations over the course of hours or days without cooling down. In 1958, 19-year-old Charles Starkweather and his 14-year-old girlfriend Caril Ann Fugate murdered 10 people, including Fugate's parents, during their eight-day killing spree across Nebraska. *Spree murder's* swift nature and the frequency with which these killers end up dead make this phenomenon, already hard to understand, even harder to study. Few criminals get to go on more than one crime spree, much less an entire series of repeated sprees, in real life. Gotham's criminals combine elements of series and spree with a bit of mass murder mixed in, as befits comic book series' need for recurring villains and Bill Finger's classic formula of pitting Batman against each foe three times per story: First Batman loses; next time's a draw; and finally Batman wins. Whereas serial murder includes breaks over time and spree murder involves changing locations, *mass murder* involves killing three or more people in the same location without cooling off in between. Several of Batman's enemies, not just the Joker,[3] have slain entire families.[4]

Batman's enemies range in the degree to which their crimes are instrumental in nature. They do steal for money. They kill, extort, and give fish clown-faces thinking to make money. There are better ways to make money, more effective methods that draw less of the authorities' attention. Arguably the most instrumentally driven Bat-foes are the eco-terrorists Ra's al Ghul and Poison Ivy, both out to protect nature from humankind. Both think globally, Ra's more so than Ivy who can also be content for a time with the flora of an island[5] or local park.[6]

Personality Disorders

The criminal nature of Batman's foes seems so deep-seated in most of them that they often appear to have personality disorders. Your *personality* is your characteristic pattern of behavior, your set of dis-positions and tendencies to act and feel certain ways—*characteristic* in that it characterizes you, it distinguishes you from other people; *pattern* in that it refers to your qualities that have greater consistency over time; and *behavior* broadly meaning both overt actions and covert mental processes like thoughts, feelings, attitudes, and beliefs. Some-one with a *personality disorder* has difficulties so deeply ingrained in who she or he is as a human being that the central problem defines that person. This is not something that comes and goes simply based on circumstances. Medication, which may alleviate some resultant difficulties like depression over life's complications, cannot cure the core problem—a pill does not give you a personality. People with per-sonality disorders have never been enough like other people to grasp fully the depths of their own problems and how very different they are from everyone else. Rather than recognizing themselves as the true source of their own unhappiness, if they're unhappy, they can mope, feel unhappy about how life isn't working out like they desire, and get frustrated when everybody *else* fails to arrange the world to suit their tastes. They lack the insight and motivation needed to change. Personality disorders are also known as *trait disorders* because the person's essential problems are their own traits, not simply transitory shifts in mood or coping ability like PTSD and major depression.

Clinicians do not diagnose children with personality disorders because, for one thing, no matter how clearly some people under 18 appear to be developing personality disorders, a few will surprise everyone and mature into healthier human beings. Symptoms do show up early. The most callous antisocial adult would have been a cruel child. In some cases, knowing a person's childhood experiences may shed light on a personality disorder's origins. A lot of Batman's foes face ostracism in childhood—the Penguin for both physical and social oddity, the Riddler for being a smarty-pants—experiences that can lead to withdrawal, anxiety, resentment, paranoia, or aggression,[7] though why one child in such a situation develops one way and a different child grows another remains a bit of a mystery.

The person with antisocial personality disorder isn't the only one short on empathy. The four most dramatic or volatile personality disorders, grouped together as the *DSM*'s "Cluster B"[8] personality disorders—antisocial (see chapter 6), borderline (chapter 2), narcissistic, and histrionic—all show psychopathic qualities.[9] Lack of empathy, a pervasive pattern of grandiosity, an inflated sense of importance, and a need for admiration all figure into *narcissistic personality disorder*, that is, super-egotistical disorder. They know they're great. "They possess excessive aspirations for their own lives and intense resentment for others whom they perceive as more successful, beautiful, or brilliant. They are preoccupied with and driven to achieve their own goals and think nothing of exploiting others in order to do so. Despite their show of grand self-importance, they are often troubled by self-doubt. Relationships with others, whether social, occupational, or romantic, are often distorted by the perception of others as tools for self-gratification."[10] Noting differences among narcissists, some personality psychologists[11] proposed subtypes: *amorous* (sexually preoccupied and seductive while avoiding intimacy), *elitist* (upwardly mobile, flaunting accomplishments and status), and *unprincipled* (lacking standards for acceptable behavior). Any of these can exploit others, in different ways, for different reasons. The unprincipled narcissist shows antisocial tendencies. Unscrupulous, unremorseful, and untruthful, this arrogant individual, when caught breaking laws, blames victims for the fact that the narcissist got caught. A narcissist breaking laws and violating others' rights often enough can also qualify for antisocial personality disorder; a person can qualify for more than one personality disorder. Nobody follows a cookbook when developing a personality, healthy or otherwise. These disorders are labels professionals made up to simplify the act of studying, discussing, and trying to predict patterns of behavior observed in different individuals. The Penguin is quite elitist. In most depictions, he has been a potbellied man, odd-looking with a beaklike nose, shorter than average but not abnormally so, and never with flipper hands until Tim Burton turned him into a circus freak for the film *Batman Returns*. Since then, depictions have gone back and forth in whether he's "funny-looking" or freakish, his manner becoming more compensatory than in earlier days. He "compensates for his short stance and horrible appearance with an active sense of panache. He is constantly seeking attention to his small self, exhibiting histrionic personality tendencies as well as narcissistic tendencies."[12]

The defining quality of *histrionic personality disorder* is constant attention-seeking behavior. This "drama llama" far exceeds the normal human need for attention. *Histrionic* essentially means theatrical, melodramatic. Many people who try too hard to get attention don't qualify for this disorder because that yearning does not fully rule their lives. The histrionic person does whatever it takes to be the center of attention at any time. They make great shows of emotion, like wailing at the funeral of people to whom they weren't particularly attached, only to switch readily to another expression if it gets more reaction. Those emotional displays are fleeting and shallow. Unlike the narcissist, even the compensatory narcissist, the histrionic person feels altogether inadequate and unworthy.[13] While the narcissist expects to be the center of everyone's world, the histrionic person does not expect attention and therefore frantically, perpetually strives to get it. Some histrionic individuals habitually tell lies, a symptom called *mythomania*, compulsively lying even when honesty seems advantageous, because the truth makes them uncomfortable. Lies protect them. If you don't like the histrionic person's lie, he or she doesn't have to take that dislike personally because it's not about anything real, whereas a scowl at something truthful could hurt deeply. Even those histrionic persons who don't lie all the time exaggerate, inflate, and tell every story theatrically. They so desperately want you to find them interesting, it's ironic that they fail to follow the number-one rule for getting others to find you interesting: You must show interest in *them*. Batman's enemies may sometimes seem more narcissistic than histrionic at heart, but their outlandish antics scream for attention. As the Penguin once put it, "Where's the thrill in committing the perfect crime if nobody knows it was you?"[14]

With few exceptions, Batman's enemies know what they are doing. They know who they hurt and they know it's wrong. For some of them, that's what makes it fun. Roman Sionis, the first Gotham crime lord to call himself Black Mask (not to be confused with the second Black Mask, Dr. Jeremiah Arkham, who suffers psychotic episodes with hallucinations and delusions), applies cutthroat business practices in his efforts to take control of the underworld. When Batman finally captures him, Sionis goes to Blackgate Penitentiary, not Arkham Asylum—until, of course, his inevitable escape. The man likes torture. When he tortures Stephanie Brown, a.k.a. Spoiler, trying to extract information about Batman, this would seem to be an instrumental act driven by *extrinsic motivation* (drive to do one thing to achieve something else) because he is putatively torturing her in order to achieve another purpose.[15] When he tortures Catwoman's sister Maggie and brother-in-law, kills the brother-in-law, and forces Maggie to eat her husband's eyes, this is an *expressive* act driven by *intrinsic motivation*, an expression of his own feelings, something he enjoys. This degree of torture serves no clear purpose. Catwoman doesn't even know about the eyes until after she has already surrendered to Black Mask.[16] Cruelty so deeply ingrained in Sionis's personality might indicate *sadistic personality disorder*[17] if his craving to hurt others, physically or psychologically, permeates most aspects of his life—not to be confused with *sexual sadism*, in which the person hurts others specifically to achieve a sexual thrill. More likely, he is a sadistic psychopath, demeaning and aggressive with no conscience but not always ruled by his sadism, however extreme it may be.

Personality disorders may be less permanent than clinicians have traditionally thought. The previous chapter pointed out that the elderly exhibit lower rates of antisocial personality disorder. In fact, all the Cluster B personality disorders become less prevalent in old age. They "have traditionally been viewed as disorders of immaturity, consistent with the relative rarity in the geriatric population of either the prototypical manipulative, self-injurious borderline woman or the criminally sociopathic man."[18] It is possible that these individuals suffer personality retardation, a developmental delay by which their personalities mature more slowly than other individuals', thereby taking decades longer to learn to care about people, to become more comfortable with others and themselves, to establish more stable traits, or even to grow a conscience. The *maturation hypothesis* proposes that many individuals with Cluster B personality disorders become better able to manage their behaviors over the course of their lives.[19] Then again, because these individuals are more prone to engage in dangerous activities, recklessness can get them killed. Threats, manipulation, and violence can push others into fighting back. Police kill more of them, as do other criminals, would-be victims, and Good Samaritans coming to someone else's defense. Attention-seeking behavior might include suicide attempts that inadvertently succeed. Narcissistic or histrionic individuals feeling frustrated or underappreciated may choose to say good-bye to this cruel world that won't show them enough attention. Alternately, the lower prevalence among the elderly may be an illusion created by weariness with life or reduced ability to act out the rotten things they'd love to do if only they still could.

Sensation Seeking

Some do it for thrills. Sensation seeking, "the need for varied, novel, and complex sensations and experiences, and the willingness to take physical and social risks for the sake of such experiences,"[20] has emerged as one explanatory construct for the lengths to which some people will go in their pursuit of excitement. Why do some engage in legal, socially accepted kicks and adventures (*non-impulsive social-ized sensation seeking*) while others might abuse drugs, break laws, gamble out of control, and endanger themselves or others (*impulsive unsocialized sensation-seeking*)? People are complicated. While Batman is not impulsive, his social acceptability remains arguable, and those norm-violating, lawbreaking villains aren't all so impulsive. Some are quite meticulous, even patient, in forming their plans. Jet pilots (e.g., Batman's Justice League colleague Hal Jordan, a.k.a. Green Lantern), skydivers, firefighters, riot control police officers, and race car drivers score high on sensation, but in different ways from drug addicts, juvenile delinquents, and other criminals.[21]

Psychologist Marvin Zuckerman identified four major components to this variable: (1) *thrill and adventure seeking* (physical activities involving danger, speed); (2) *experience seeking* (novelty—e.g., travel, art, noncomformist lifestyle); (3) *disinhibition* (seeking release through uninhibited social activities like wild parties or methods of identity concealment like wearing a mask); and (4) *boredom susceptibility* (restless discontent and aversion to repetition and routine).[22] These qualities overlap with the impulsive, antisocial, or unstable lifestyle seen among many psychopaths, but are separate issues from psychopathy's callous, egocentric, unremorseful side.[23] Batman's flamboyant, thrill-seeking foes have both those subfactors covered well, as when the Joker both impulsively and remorselessly shoves a henchman into ongoing traffic for not laughing[24] or hurls girlfriend Harley Quinn out a window without bothering to see if she survives.[25]

Sensation-seeking men score higher on thrill- and adventure-seeking, disinhibition, and boredom susceptibility; sensation-seeking women score higher in experience seeking—in general, not universally. A sensation-seeker himself, Zuckerman's reflections on his own life take us back to the question of whether people with these ingrained traits really outgrow them. In his college days, he "reached my full sensation-seeking potential through drinking, sex, and hitch-hiking around the country," and had imagined that upon retirement, he would spend his days hang-gliding, parachute-jumping, and doing many more adventurous things. Toward age 74, the need for physical adventure declined, but the need for new experience never changed.[26] In the comics, the original Batwoman eventually trades in her costumed nightlife for the thrills of running her own circus.[27] The Golden Age Batman retires from administering justice with his fists to take on procedural challenges by becoming Police Commissioner Bruce Wayne and marital challenges by becoming husband to the Catwoman of Earth-Two[28]—his life still revolving around crime and at least one criminal, still pursuing his passions even as he changes his methods of doing so.

Obsession

Obsessions, "persistent ideas, thoughts, impulses, or images that are experienced as intrusive and inappropriate and that cause marked anxiety or distress,"[29] abound in the lives of Batman and his foes (e.g., how he dwells on his parents' deaths or how his enemies obsess over him). Unlike many obsessed individuals, these characters give into their preoccupations, rarely attempting to ignore, suppress, or otherwise neutralize those recurring thoughts or resultant *compulsions* (clearly excessive, repetitive actions or even mental rituals like counting that the person feels compelled to perform) and experiencing discomfort whenever circumstances force them to resist. Because the preoccupations are technically obsessions only if "experienced as intrusive and inappropriate," most of these characters are not actually obsessed. Because these time-consuming themes and habits do not distress most of these characters, who live without interest in resisting, few of them will ever qualify as having obsessive-compulsive disorder (OCD). The *DSM* specifies that adults with OCD, by definition, "have at some point recognized that the obsessions or compulsions are excessive or unreasonable,"[30] though insight into the unreasonableness of the obsessions and compulsions ranges widely. OCD is an *anxiety* disorder; the obsessions and compulsions, one way or another, bother the sufferer. Some obsessive-compulsives are uncertain; others know fully what's wrong. Insight can vary across times and situations, such as when a person sees a problem for what it is while discussing it with a therapist but sets all that insight aside outside the therapist's office. Through most of the Riddler's history, he relishes the challenge of creating puzzling crimes, freely sending riddles that give Batman and the police clues to those crimes even though giving such clues might help the crime-fighters foil and capture him, but sometimes he tries not to send those clues. Sometimes he resists. He's saner than many of Gotham's ghouls.

Celebrities of Crime

Like common criminals, Gotham's costumed crooks indulge themselves, satisfying their whims, desires, obsessions, and compulsions at the expense of others. Unlike everyday repeat offenders, however, they transform themselves into surreal entities, dangerous celebrities who transform the world itself into their playground and its people into toys over and over again. To a great extent, they're living the dreams that starry-eyed individuals like the disturbed young man who shot President Reagan in hopes of turning himself into a celebrity[31] spin through their heads. In masks, makeup, tally marks, and more, they enrobe themselves in nightmares in order to transcend mundane reality and enter a world of living legends at any cost. Most of them, who know exactly what they're doing, are no less sane in their world than professional singers Madonna, Lady Gaga, or KISS, who re-create themselves into spectacular stage personas to become different generations' stars. Elvis Presley gyrated in sequins and cape before Las Vegas crowds, Carmen Miranda wore a bowl of fruit on her head, and the Riddler wears question marks wherever he stages his show.

CASE FILE 7–1   The Riddler

Real name: Edward "Eddie" Nigma, Nygma (*Batman Forever*), or Nashton. Comics go back and forth on which is his birth name, which is an alias, and which is a misspelling.

First appearance: *Detective Comics* #140 (October, 1948).

Origin: Unlike the Joker, Penguin, and Two-Face, the Riddler has no abnormal physical qualities and can walk freely through a crowd. He has no particularly dramatic origin story. Obsessive-compulsive disorders usually don't. Gifted with great deductive ability, he grows up as a child who loves solving puzzles. Finding ways to cheat others is a kind of puzzle he likes. Instead of

The Riddler studies psychiatric literature in hopes of curing his compulsions in *Batman* #179 (1966). © DC Comics.

punishing young Eddie when he discovers the boy has been stealing from Dad's pockets, his father begins hiding money in increasingly creative locations. "He wanted to see exactly how far I would go. Said if I was going to be such a stubborn little thief, I was going to have to earn it."[1] As a child, his "love for brain-teasers was exceeded only by his overwhelming desire to win at any cost,"[2] which over time creates a problem that feeds itself: He enjoys solving and creating puzzles, too few people are bright enough to keep the task of creating puzzles challenging for him, and yet his need to win won't let him enjoy seeing his creations get solved.

> "Life's full of questions, isn't it, Batman? Though, naturally, I prefer to think of them as riddles."
>
> —Riddler in *Batman* #452 (August, 1990)

❖   ❖   ❖

At one point, Nigma recovers memories of how his father's abuse drove him to his convoluted truthfulness, but extensive empirical investigations by psychologist Elizabeth Loftus and others suggest that we need to be wary of trusting memory,[3] much less "recovered" memories,[4] emotion-laden memories,[5] or Freud's view of repression itself.[6] Yes, the abuse may have occurred. Then again, Eddie's unhealthy mind and the circumstances under which the memories come to him could easily conjure a *pseudomemory*, a bogus remembrance that makes a dream, daydream, suggestion, fantasy, or dread seem vividly real.

The Riddler first appears as a sideshow carny who cheats customers with rigged puzzles and games. Aching for greater thrills, he heads to Gotham and dons a costume specifically so he can challenge Batman, whom he sees as a potentially worthy adversary. Gotham's Caped Crusader and costumed crooks directly inspire this man to become an archcriminal.

> Riddler: First, I must call Commissioner Gordon . . . and then confound him with a little riddle.
> Girlfriend: Oh, why take time for that?
> Riddler: Crime is no fun without riddles. I'll have you know that's the main reason I took up this crime game.[7]

He loves the limelight. Attention feeds him. His riddles and death traps, while ostentatious in nature, aren't just about seeking attention, or he wouldn't create traps that always have a way out. There's a kind of honesty in everything the Riddler does. He'd rather tell the truth creatively than lie outright—hence, the riddles. The attention he could get by killing Batman or by outing his enemy as Bruce Wayne pales in comparison to his love of the riddle itself. Having deduced Batman's secret identity, the Riddler taunts him with possible exposure until Batman calls his bluff: "Riddles are your compulsion. Your addiction. And a riddle that everyone knows the answer to is worthless."[8]

However much he sometimes wants to commit a crime without sending a riddle when the caper itself already challenges him, he cannot. When he tries to commit a series of robberies without telegraphing his plans to Batman via his trademark riddles, he subconsciously leaves clues anyway.[9] His attempts at fighting the compulsion show that he recognizes it's not healthy. "You don't understand," he says after one failure. "I really didn't want to leave you any clues. I really planned never to go back to Arkham. But I left you a clue anyway. So I…I have to go back there. Because I might need help. I…I might actually be crazy."[10] Irresistible impulse, although part of some legal standards for insanity, by itself is generally insufficient as a legal defense. Otherwise, kleptomaniacs and addicts of many kinds would be unconvictable. Addictive behaviors continue long after they stop being fun because failing to act on them stresses the addict, pushing that person to seek release from the internal pressure.

Physician Rakul K. Parikh[11] diagnoses the Riddler with *obsessive compulsive disorder* (OCD), which is not a psychotic disorder. The Riddler knows his obsessions and compulsions originate from within himself, not from anybody else beaming them into his head. *DSM* criteria for OCD specify that at some point "during the course of the disorder, the person has recognized that the obsessions or compulsions are excessive or unreasonable,"[12] so the Riddler's doubt and fear that these symptoms mean he's psychotic actually suggest that he is not.

> Riddler: You dimwits think I create my riddles because I want to be caught. What naïve, pedestrian thinking. To me, crime is performance art! And that's what you psychobabblers share with the rest of the world. Lack of vision.[13]

The Riddler has gone through spells without the overwhelming need to commit riddling robberies. Retaining his interest in puzzles and crimes during the lengthiest of his OCD remissions, after emerging from a coma missing many memories including his knowledge of Batman's identity, he becomes a private detective solving crimes out of self-interest[14]—for stipends, rewards, publicity, and sometimes to clear his name when crimes looks like his.[15] Even without his compulsion to create conundrums, he's a self-centered jerk. His lack of empathy and regret still indicate psychopathy.

Without a hint of remorse, he ignores a plea to help a friend in danger because a good mystery occupies his thoughts.[16] His relationships are shallow. Despite showing features of both psychopathy and *narcissistic personality disorder* with his massive ego, he is no sadist, he's not the most malicious of Batman's enemies, and so he does not easily fit the severe antisocial/narcissistic blend that Erich Fromm first called *malignant narcissism.* He is not "the quintessence of evil."[17]

People interest the Riddler. He doesn't seriously care about specific individuals, but he wants attention and enjoys adoration. He's attracted to women and often has one at his side during a crime spree. Except for a pair of biker women who become henchwomen called Query and Echo, we rarely see any of these girls more than once, and he'll abandon those two when leaving them behind helps him cover his escape from Batman.[18] Romantically he shows interest in women, though only while they're new and unknown. When they lose their mystery, they lose their appeal. "He wasn't in love with her. He was in love with the riddle!"[19]

Unsettled when a bomb goes off in his face, Eddie grows disillusioned with clean living. Old impulses start nagging once again. When Edward Nigma's OCD rears its head, he plans crimes. Lacking any strong connection to non-criminals, he has no one to ground him, no reason beyond self-interest to stay out of crime. His return to crime is confirmed when he shows up with a spunky teenaged partner he calls his daughter, Enigma. If she is his daughter and they maintain a relationship, that one thing could help him become less full of himself. While some narcissistic individuals put themselves even before their own children, some other narcissists can adore their children as extensions of themselves, which then teaches some of them to care and think outside themselves. Father and daughter bond by ambushing Batman.[20]

Periodically, writers who miss either the point or the value of this character send him down the mirth, mayhem, and murder route. These attempts to make him edgier never stick, and then later writers who want to write real Riddler stories chalk the previous aberrations up to insanity, mind control, or demonic possession.[21] This kind of cognitively driven robber, motivated by intellectual and artistic challenge, simply does not have a multiple murderer's background, motivation, personality, or sadistic passion.

> *"I am nothing like the Joker! Why does everybody keep saying that?! That clown is only interested in mirth, mayhem, and murder! I, on the other hand, live for mental challenges! Games of wit! The chance to outsmart worthy opponents!"*
> —Riddler in *Harley Quinn* #6 (October, 2001)

CASE FILE 7–2 The Penguin

Real name: Oswald Chesterfield Cobblepot

First appearance: *Detective Comics* #58 (December, 1941)

Origin: Teased and bullied by other children who nicknamed him "Penguin" for his squat body and beaklike nose, lonely little Oswald Cobblepot turns to his mother's pet birds, calling them "my only friends"[1] because they wouldn't judge or reject him. He wants human friends. He wants a girlfriend. Strange-looking and socially awkward, he never fits in, a misfit mocked at school and in his family's wealthy circle. His overbearing and overprotective mother, convinced he might catch pneumonia and die like his father, makes him carry an umbrella everywhere he goes.[2] When she, too, dies (or, in a later version, becomes invalid),[3] leaving behind debts that send their holdings into foreclosure, he loses everything he has ever clung to for security: the person, the prosperity, the pets. Even the birds get repossessed. Having always ached to fit in among the social elite, he decides to buy his way into high society. Outcast Oswald turns to crime—with flair.

❖   ❖   ❖

Despite his integration of bird motifs and trick umbrellas, the Penguin is not pathologically obsessed with either. Unlike the Riddler, who must send riddles, or Two-Face, who becomes crippled with indecision when he can't toss his special coin, Oswald can function without his signature accoutrements. A museum curator putting a jeweled bird on display can count on Cobblepot to come steal it, of course, but passionate collecting does not necessarily equal utter obsession. In the Penguin's first appearance, the umbrella is his instrument of theft (hiding a rolled-up painting in its handle) and attack (firing bullets, acid, and strangling gas), thus making it part of his *modus operandi*. Unlike most other prominent Bat-foes, the Penguin when incarcerated goes to prison, not Arkham Asylum. Even by Gotham's ambiguous standards for criminal insanity, the Penguin is sane. For all his ruthlessness, the Penguin shows greater rationality than the Joker, more moments of sympathy than the Riddler, and a stronger need for superficial social acceptance than most of Batman's other foes.

> *"The way you were being treated was beyond savage, and I simply couldn't stand for it. Not even caged animals should be treated that way."*
>
> —Penguin to woman he saves from black-market slavery, *Joker's Asylum: The Penguin* #1 (2008)

> *"Careful, careful—wauck wauck. Every one of them has a mother."*
>
> —Penguin to Catwoman, sweeping up dehydrated pirates in *Batman: The Movie* (1966)

This little man who needs to be larger than life fits what's informally and stereotypically known as a *Napoleon complex*, driven by his perceived social and physical handicaps to inflate himself in other areas of his life.[4] With the stature of Napoleon and the nose of Cyrano de Bergerac (each of which range from slightly odd to freakishly unnatural, depending on who's drawing him at the time), Oswald overcompensates for feelings of inferiority by becoming self-centered, disdainful, and domineering toward others, a pattern that Alfred Adler called a *superiority complex*—as opposed to the *inferiority complex*, in which the person with poor self-esteem feels helpless, incapable of coping with life's demands, and unable to compensate for those inferior feelings. Physically different, maternally overprotected, and socially ostracized, Oswald Cobblepot hits the trifecta of what Adler considered the childhood sources for pathologically extreme feelings of inferiority: organic inferiority, spoiling, and neglect. Adler saw the motivation to become better, *striving for superiority* as he called it, as the fundamental fact of human life.[5] We grow and move forward in life. The eight-year-old becomes more capable than he was at seven. One with healthy self-esteem feels good about that growth, whereas one forming an inferiority complex fails to value his own achievements and another who's constructing a superiority complex *over*values his strengths so he can try blinding himself to his shortcomings. Reality does not always let us ignore the things we dislike. Still sensitive to being mocked, the Penguin might destroy someone's life or career over an insult, whether genuine or misinterpreted, and no matter how old the insult, because doing so makes him feel bigger.

His hat adds height. So does his umbrella when it's up. Attired in monocle, tuxedo, and top hat, wearing no costume per se, the Penguin dresses the same to rob a bank as he does to host a lavish party or run for mayor. Does he truly fancy himself to be a refined gentleman, or is he a high-society wannabe? In older stories when he consistently looks fully human, albeit caricaturish, it's harder to tell. In some post–*Batman Returns* comic book stories—not all, but those in which he looks the most deformed—he thinks of the Penguin, his darkest, most animal nature, as his true self and Oswald Cobblepot as a pretense, a ruse, and in those instances, yes, the suit, the hat, everything about him that says, "Here's a gentleman," is all part of his Halloween costume.

Many stories over the years have shown the Penguin's attempts to go straight (or pretend to) after legal releases from prison. When he breaks out of prison, he's a gimmick criminal, but whenever he walks free, we get to watch his attempts to move upward in business, in the underworld, and in the social scene. From as early as the first story in which he ever appears, he has always wanted to be a crime boss. Mob bosses operate less effectively when they have to hide from the law. So do con artists. "Aren't you people forgetting the facts?" Batman cautions a parole board against releasing Cobblepot. "The Penguin is not only a master thief, he's a con man—don't let him fool you!"[6] Sometimes the Penguin lies about walking the straight and narrow; sometimes he tries to keep his dealings legal. Tiring of incarceration, he seemingly goes legit and opens a trendy nightclub, the posh Iceberg Lounge, where he makes a bundle off overpriced merchandise, all the while hosting Gotham's criminals in the club's back rooms. For years he walks a fine line, playing informant to costumed heroes often enough that they leave him right there even while he works on building his underworld clout—until, as with all such attempts, his insecurities make him go too far and hurt too many people, including one woman ready to love him, and he returns to prison in the end.[7]

> *"A perfect crime is a work of art, a thing of beauty, and a joy forever, to paraphrase the Bard!"*
> —Penguin, *Detective Comics* #611 (February, 1990)

CASE FILE 7–3 Poison Ivy

Real name: Pamela Lillian Isley (Dr. in some versions)

First appearance: *Batman* #181 (June, 1966)

Origin: A botany/biochemistry student writing her thesis on plant-animal hybridization, shy, timid Pamela Isley gets seduced and betrayed by a man who poisons her, altering her biochemistry in a way that renders her body immune to all toxins, her kiss toxic to others, and her mood subject to violent swings. Unable to bear children, she experiments with creating plant-based life forms she calls her "children." Robbing and killing to fund her research, she becomes an *eco-terrorist*, an environmentally motivated terrorist dedicated to preserving plant life at all costs. She creates pheromonal scents that make others, especially men, susceptible to her influence. Over time, she becomes more plantlike herself—her skin turns green; she develops an empathic link with plants and then the *florakinetic* ability to control them through sheer will—and Poison Ivy evolves into a formidable foe.

❖   ❖   ❖

The greener she grows, the less human she becomes. Despite some attraction to Batman and others, more apparent earlier in her criminal career, Ivy grows detached from humanity and less interested in people over time. Her best and sometimes only friend is the Joker's moll, Harley Quinn, whose friendship helps ground Ivy not only by reconnecting Ivy to the human race but because Ivy tends to think more sensibly when faced with Harley's irrationality. Unlike fellow eco-terrorist Ra's al Ghul, who wants to reduce the human population and would destroy all civilization if he thought it necessary to keep people from destroying the planet, Ivy's ecological efforts concentrate on preserving and promoting plant life—more positive than Ra's, albeit twistedly so, since she'll kill individual guards who might keep her from stealing what she needs and she periodically hunts down corporate bigwigs whose companies have destroyed forests and her floral "children."

A plant-human hybrid with chlorophyll in her blood, she has no interest in destroying humankind, nor in saving it, but she still knows she's more than a vegetable. "I can't deny I'm a creation of both the plant and human worlds. I can't stay in one too long before I begin to miss the other."[1] When she feels both sides of her nature in balance, she takes a *biocentrist* ("life-centered") perspective, an ethical viewpoint extending value to all species, ecosystems, and natural processes, regardless of sentience. During her biocentrist spells, she helps feed fruit to the homeless and underprivileged instead of feeding people to her plants, not that these periods last. Her empathy for plant life, a kind of psychic link to vegetation, intrudes on her already limited ability to feel for non-plant life. A child of wealthy but distant parents, she never learns how to get close to others. Receiving no empathy growing up, she never develops any of her own. The fascination she feels for plants while growing up may come about in compensation. Loving plants is safe because they will not reject, chide, or abandon her. Empathy, the capacity to recognize and share others' feelings, eludes her until mutagenic changes force her to feel what the plants around her experience—just plants, not people. Still not attuned to other people's feelings and never having learned outgoing social skills, she relishes her biochemical power over others instead. When she ponders why she doesn't move into a jungle and stay, she considers, "Perhaps it's the power I exert over others that keeps driving me back. I like a challenge and I can't rest when I feel I haven't won."

The comic books keep referring to her power over other people as pheromonal, but is it really? A *pheromone* is a social scent, a chemical that triggers a natural behavioral response by members of the *same species*. Our bodies detect pheromones through our sense of smell, affecting us through our olfactory system even if we don't consciously realize it at the time. *Sex pheromones* attract mates, typically the female of the species emitting pheromones that indicate her sexual receptivity, as opposed to *releaser pheromones*, which can attract mates from miles away without eliciting a direct sexual response. While Ivy has greater power over men, she can influence women as well, like when she makes Catwoman deliver a case of money to her.[2] Organisms can release some types of pheromones that will affect members of the same sex, like *aggregation pheromones*, which will bring members of the same species together regardless of gender. If she gave more thought to the range of people's feelings, Ivy might try using *alarm pheromones* to trigger fight-or-flight responses, thereby making people turn violent or fearful. To the extent that Ivy's influence is plant-based, the power is *not* pheromonal because humans and plants are different species. Botanical biochemist that she is, Ivy evidently realizes that. When she attempts unsuccessfully to make Catwoman disclose Batman's identity, Ivy calls the particular chemical she releases a toxin, not a pheromone.[3]

> "I am not insane. I've just been pushed too far."
> —Poison Ivy, *Batman: Poison Ivy* (1997)

8

The Madhouse
What Insanity?

"Sometimes I question the rationality of my actions. And I'm afraid that when I walk through those asylum gates, when I walk into Arkham and the doors close behind me, it'll be just like coming home."

—Batman in *Arkham Asylum: A Serious House on Serious Earth* (1989)

Arkham Asylum, full name The Elizabeth Arkham Asylum for the Criminally Insane, Arkham Hospital when first mentioned in print[1] and occasionally Arkham Sanitarium, houses the criminals whom Gotham City's legal system deems insane. Fittingly named after horror master H. P. Lovecraft's fictional "ancient, mouldering, and subtly fearsome town," the "witch-cursed, legend-haunted" Arkham, Massachusetts,[2] this facility faces more escapes, infiltrations, riots, assaults, and impersonations during Batman's career than some nations' entire penal systems see in a century.

Comics scholar Paul Lytle lists Arkham's major problems: The inmates run the asylum; the inmates run away from the asylum; and the people hired to run the asylum should be inmates.[3] It's a horrible place where a white-collar criminal like Warren White can enter sane, simply faking mental illness to dodge a prison sentence,[4] only to find himself mutilated by other residents, then lose his mind and become a freakish villain himself, the Great White Shark. "White went inside a criminal, but a sane one—greedy and immoral, but sane. Arkham made him into an insane supervillain. Arkham took a normal, white-collar criminal, and turned him into something more akin to the Riddler or Penguin."[5]

Insane Places

The earliest asylums emerged during the Renaissance, originally founded by religious orders to care for and shelter those afflicted with mental illness, to give them refuge—i.e., *asylum*—from a world where they did not fit. These facilities began to pop up throughout Europe and, too quickly, problems set in. Overcrowding and budgetary problems created less humane conditions, and the patients became more like inmates, shackled and locked away where the world outside might forget them, problems that escalated for over 300 years. In 1793, a French asylum's new administrator, the young physician Philippe Pinel, removed patients' chains, let them come out to see sunlight, and ordered an end to physically brutal "treatments" that involved beatings and bloodletting.[6] Benjamin Rush, a signer of the Declaration of Independence who would become known as the "Father of American psychiatry," during this time campaigned for more humane housing for the mentally ill. Although he remained uncertain what to do with the mentally ill, he knew chains and dungeons couldn't heal them. Rush decided patients needed to be treated like human beings, shown basic compassion and morality, an approach known as *moral therapy*, despite which his moral methods included bloodletting,[7] enclosing patients in coffin-like boxes, and swinging them around to shake the madness out.[8] Good intentions, right? Progress happened slowly. Dorothea Dix and many others later campaigned for more humane conditions in the mental hospitals, penitentiaries, jails, and almshouses that housed mentally ill individuals. Asylums for the criminally insane did not yet exist because, technically, neither did insanity.

Insanity is a legal standard, not a medical classification or psychiatric diagnosis, one that excuses individual responsibility for committing criminal offenses on the grounds that those who lack rational awareness of what they're doing need treatment, not punishment. The modern insanity defense began in 1843 with one Daniel M'Naghten,* who, driven by persecutory delusions that the British prime minister Sir Robert Peel had personally caused M'Naghten's hardships, attempted to shoot Peel but instead killed Peel's secretary. After the jury found M'Naghten not guilty by reason of insanity, ensuing controversy led to the M'Naghten Rule, the so-called "right/wrong" test, which required evidence that, due to mental disease or defect at the time of the crime, the defendant lacked the ability to understand the nature and quality—and therefore the wrongness—of his or her own actions. The M'Naghten Rule became the foundation for the insanity defense in Great Britain and America. Other standards that followed built from it, and U.S. states would vary on which standard they follow, particularly with regard to whether the defendant's actions resulted from an *irresistible impulse* (inability to restrain one's own actions due to mental defect), all of which changed with the Insanity Reform Act of 1984. Public outrage over a jury finding President Ronald Reagan's would-be assassin John Hinckley not guilty by reason of insanity prompted changes in federal and many state laws. Some states began allowing courts the option of finding defendants *guilty but mentally ill* so that a defendant deemed to have been mentally ill at the time of the crime would receive treatment in a psychiatric facility until no longer mentally ill, then would go to a correctional facility to serve out the remainder of the sentence. The fact that Arkham residents like Two-Face may walk free during periods of sanity[9] regardless of however many crimes they've committed, no matter how many people they've killed, indicates that the Gotham legal system found them not guilty by reason of insanity. Julian Day, a.k.a. the non-lethal criminal Calendar Man, appears to be one exception, as attorney James

---

*Also spelled M'Naughten or McNaghton, depending on the source.

Daily notes at *Law and the Multiverse.*[10] In *The Long Halloween*, authorities offer to commute Day's sentence to time served if he'll help stop an enigmatic serial killer called Holiday, an offer that makes sense only if Day is guilty but mentally ill.[11] Had Day been found not guilty by reason of insanity, he'd have had no sentence to commute.

Criminal commitment, committing someone involuntarily to a mental health facility when charged with a crime, is not limited to those who have already stood trial. Defendants who have yet to go to trial may get sent there for evaluation or to receive treatment when the trial cannot proceed until the defendant becomes *competent to stand trial*, able to understand what's going on well enough to participate in his or her own defense. Some cases never go to trial if they involve defendants who never reach states of competence. Defendants who do not become competent may eventually be released without trial unless they're considered dangerous—in which case *civil commitment* becomes necessary, the involuntary commitment to a mental health facility of persons deemed to be at significant risk of harming themselves or specific other persons.

In the real world, would Batman's enemies be found criminally insane? In most cases, no, experts agree they would not.[12] Outlandish, difficult, even dangerous behaviors, actions so bizarre that any layperson would readily say, "That's just crazy," do not inherently mean the person has suffered a full-fledged break from reality. Jeffrey Dahmer ate people. His ways of thinking and feeling were out of sync with nearly everybody else's. Wild ideas filled his head and dark desires drove him, but he knew what he was doing, he knew it was wrong, and he knew to conceal his evil deeds. While his personality test scores indicated emotional abnormalities, the tests did not indicate that he was psychotic.[13] Thus a jury found Dahmer legally sane, criminally responsible for his actions, and he therefore went to prison, not any mental hospital, there to remain until a mentally ill inmate beat him to death with a broom handle. In Gotham City, he might have lived and escaped Arkham to kill again. However much some Gotham authorities might like to haul villains such as the Joker to prison[14] like Dahmer instead of admitting him into a mental hospital like Hinckley, they don't have that option because their courts have found the Joker insane.

A psychotic person could be sane, contradictory as that might sound. To acquit by reason of insanity, the jury would have to believe defendants so mentally ill that they didn't understand the nature of their actions or didn't know that those actions were wrong. If your friend tells you to shoot your next-door neighbor, you know that it's wrong, you shouldn't do it, and you need some better friends. If a hallucinatory elephant tells you to shoot your neighbor, you might still know that it's wrong, you shouldn't do it, and you need some better elephants. Friend or elephant, you're still sane. If, on the other hand, you shoot the neighbor because you're convinced he's an extraterrestrial creature coming to suck out your brain, then in that case, you are unable to recognize the real-world meaning and wrongfulness of your actions, it's a desperate act of self-defense insofar as you knew, and you should therefore be found insane. The villain Maxie Zeus thinks he is the king of the Greek gods. Having become increasingly delusional over time, he stops getting sentenced to Blackgate Penitentiary and starts winding up in Arkham Asylum instead.

Psychologist Bradley Daniels suggests that in Gotham City, the decision to commit a criminal in Arkham rather than sentence to prison apparently goes like this:

> Question 1. Did the defendant wear a costume when committing the crime? If yes, move on to Question 2.
> Question 2. Were the crimes centered around some compulsion or theme, such as the number two (Two-Face), plants (Poison Ivy), or riddles (The Riddler)? If yes, refer to Arkham.
> Question 3. Could you easily imagine this type of criminal living in and committing this type of crime in the real world? If yes, sentence to Blackgate Penitentiary.[15]

As Daniels notes, neither this process nor Arkham itself resembles how involuntary civil commitment and mental health treatment really operate. That said, though, Gotham's court system and its forensic mental hospital each struggle to cope with the management of criminal types that do not themselves exist in the real world.

Lunatics in Charge

"If you think Arkham's scary as a doctor, you should try it as a patient."
—Harley Quinn, *Detective Comics* #831 (June, 2007)

The number of Arkham therapists who go mad and get committed to their own asylum may seem ridiculously high and its guards may strike you as unrealistically callous, cruel, or downright dumb, but honestly, who else would work there? Killer Croc bites off guard Aaron Cash's hand[16] and the Joker murders Cash's infant son by giving him tetanus with a rusty nail.[17] The Joker alone has killed more Arkham staffers than the number of victims a typical serial killer takes in an entire career. To survive your employment at Arkham, your best hope may be to become a master villain yourself. The asylum's founder, Amadeus Arkham, lives out his days as one of its residents; a later Arkham family member who runs the asylum, Jeremiah Arkham, becomes a supervillain; so does psychiatrist Harleen Quinzel after she falls in love with the Joker; delusional administrator Charles Cavendish lets the prisoners take staff hostage; and administrator Alyce Sinner has committed mass murder before she ever goes to work there. While they all violate ethical standards, Amadeus Arkham and Harleen Quinzel, a.k.a. Harley Quinn, illustrate particular problems with conflict of interest.

Dual relationships or *multiple relationships* in psychotherapy exist when a therapist has more roles in the client's life outside the therapeutic relationship. If your suicidal cousin up on a ledge refuses to speak to anyone but you or your former student wants your recommendation for the best therapist for that student's specific problem, refusing to apply your training as a therapist in the situation might be less ethical than creating that dual relationship would be. You've been seeing a client for months before you discover during a family reunion that he's your wife's cousin, but promptly terminating therapy will not make the dual relationship go away—you have obligations even to former clients.[18]

Arkham Asylum's founder, Dr. Amadeus Arkham, converts his newly inherited family home into a facility for the treatment of the mentally ill, inspired by Martin "Mad Dog" Hawkins, a mentally ill killer likely to become "trapped in the penal system with no hope of treatment." One night, sometime before the home's conversion into asylum is complete, Hawkins murders the doctor's wife and daughter. When the asylum opens on schedule, one of its first residents is Hawkins. For months, Amadeus listens to Hawkins recount the atrocity. One year to the day his family died, Amadeus straps his family's killer to an electroshock couch and electrocutes the man. He subsequently develops auditory hallucinations, disorientation, distorted sense of time, paranoia, delusions. Not until Amadeus tries to kill his stockbroker does he receive treatment, in the form of commitment to his own asylum. "I'm home. Where I belong."[19] For legal, ethical, and logical reasons, no one should ever have placed Hawkins in the care of his victims' family member.

Jeremiah Arkham turns out worse. Amadeus hurts his family's killer; Jeremiah hurts many more. He becomes a crime boss, the new Black Mask. Jeremiah is sometimes psychotic. He hallucinates whole conversations with patients who don't exist.[20] Comic book stories featuring him mix and match symptoms of paranoid schizophrenia and dissociative identity disorder in ways that defy real-world analysis. "He's a genuine schizophrenic," says his successor Alyce Sinner. "While he's Jeremiah Arkham, he has no recollection of his other existence as Black Mask."[21] Alyce, a deranged mass murderer herself, is an unreliable diagnostician, although she's not the only one to muddle the terms when discussing Jeremiah's state of mind. Schizophrenia is not multiple personality, and fully schizophrenic individuals likely lack the focus to develop distinct and consistent sets of alter personalities. Schizophrenia involves a broad loss of contact with reality, with symptoms like disorganized thinking, delusions, and hallucinations. Jeremiah's extensive interactions with hallucinatory patients and delusions regarding them do suggest schizophrenia, specifically paranoid schizophrenia, but the behavior Sinner cites, his periods of dissociating into a distinctly different alter personality as the second Black Mask, would not. After *Flashpoint* alters history, Dr. Jeremiah Arkham, with his questionable methods, winds up running the asylum again.[22]

Treatment Issues

*"You must admit it's hard to imagine this place being conducive
to anyone's mental health."*
—Batman in *Arkham Asylum: A Serious House on Serious Earth* (1989)

Some of Arkham's therapists and administrators are *psychologists*, professionals with doctorates in psychology. Clinicians with Master's degrees don't tend to call themselves "Master's-level psychologists" anymore, at least in part due to licensure requirements. Psychologists employed by Arkham appear to be *clinical psychologists*, who must have specialized clinical training and years of supervised experience treating clients. Psychologists come in many kinds. Despite the popular view of what psychologists do, only about half work in therapeutic occupations. Others work in a variety of fields, including academics (like the Scarecrow, Dr. Jonathan Crane), research, industry, business, government, forensic investigation, and more. Also despite popular views, therapists usually are not *psychoanalysts* (meaning Freudian or neo-Freudian psychologists or psychiatrists). Arkham also employs *psychiatrists*, mental health professionals who graduated from medical school, *not* the same thing as psychologists even though the writers often confuse these terms. Psychologists completed many psychology courses and earned doctorates in psychology, usually a Ph.D. Psychiatrists did not have to take any psychology classes but instead took some psychiatry coursework (medical school classes on prevention, assessment, diagnosis, and treatment of mental illness without requiring broader knowledge of other areas of psychology) and later received specialized psychiatric training during medical residency. Unlike psychologists, psychiatrists can prescribe medication as needed for a range of conditions including obsessions, compulsions, depression, and psychosis, along with many more. Many people get their psychiatric medications from their family doctors or general practitioners even though those individuals have not studied psychiatry as intensively and psychiatrists tend to treat mental illness more effectively.[23] Psychiatric nurses, social workers, counselors, and a number of other professionals can qualify to administer psychotherapy depending on educational background, test scores, and state licensure requirements.

Most important, when it comes to understanding how treatment at Arkham Asylum in any way resembles the real world, we must ask: *Where are their meds?* Psychiatric hospitalization generally includes medication, a lot of it—the sooner, the better.[24] The most immediate concern for therapists other than Jeremiah Arkham would be to reduce the residents' dangerousness. "They'd be heavily sedated, heavily medicated. They'd be walking zombies. People like the Joker would get doped up on Thorazine all the time or other old school antipsychotics where they'll just sit and be passive."[25] Traditional antipsychotic medications like Thorazine block a neurotransmitter called dopamine, reducing positive symptoms (active hallucinations and delusions) in the majority of schizophrenic recipients.[26] They also have fast-acting sedating effects. So why is it that almost every time Batman makes the walk into the asylum, all his enemies are alert in their cells, ready as ever for the next breakout or riot? Arkham's psychiatric pill-pushers may be administering *atypical antipsychotic* medications, which are less sedating, show lower rates of relapse, and have different side effects (e.g., possible heart problems instead of involuntary tremors or facial contortions).[27] Batman's enemies don't show the weight gain that might occur with either type of antipsychotic, so maybe incompetent Arkham staffers fail to make certain the residents swallow their pills.

Arkham's therapists talk a lot. Usually without following any obvious therapeutic model, they encourage the patients to discuss their lives, thoughts, and desires. To be fair, we see limited examples from the hundreds of hours they spend struggling to manage these difficult clients. Dr. Ruth Adams in *Arkham Asylum: A Serious House on Serious Earth* likes *word association*, asking the client to respond with the first word that comes to mind when presented with each item from a word list. Clinicians pay attention to response time, nonverbal reactions, and how unusual the responses are. Individuals with psychosis or other cognitive deficits may show *loosening of associations,* in which responses unrelated to the stimulus words reflect disorganized thinking, which will also manifest in disorganized conversation. Several Arkham therapists like the approaches employed by Freud and Jung—Amadeus Arkham is said to have spent time with Jung—

even though numerous professionals question the effectiveness of Freudian and other talk therapy methods for treating psychotic individuals.[28]

> Dr. Edwards (to Batman): Group therapy—that was Dr. Buscaglia's suggestion—was one big disaster. The Riddler answered everything with another question. Harvey Dent objected to everything anyone said—including himself. All Maxie Zeus talked about was the women he claimed he seduced in the form of a swan. It was chaos. They couldn't even agree on how much they hated you.[29]

More clinicians use *group therapy* with psychotic individuals than you might expect[30]—which at Arkham could be tremendously dangerous or potentially hilarious. ("Now, Joker, how do you think that makes Mad Hatter feel?") Treatment of psychotic individuals tends to include a lot of psychoeducation, teaching clients about themselves and their world, often starting with *skills training* because cognitive impairments have eroded social skills, problem-solving, basic self-care (like hygiene), coping strategies, and stress management. *Symptom management* becomes important, teaching clients to notice the symptoms that predict relapse. Through *cognitive-behaviorial therapy* (CBT), therapists address patients' symptoms and the distress they cause. *Insight training* normally involves getting them to understand how their actions hurt others, but psychopathic patients are unlikely to care and the sadistic ones would love finding out that they've hurt people even worse than they'd known. When dealing with psychopaths, teaching them to recognize how their behavior hurts themselves can be most useful. The Penguin makes a better counselor for the Riddler than any professional at Arkham when he congratulates the king of clues for discovering the value in operating on the right side of the law (advantages like staying out of jail).[31] A therapist, unable to hand the psychopath a conscience, may at least teach that client practical, logical reasons for doing right instead of wrong— admittedly, what might be a hopeless task when the psychopath is also psychotic.

In order to break Harvey "Two-Face" Dent from his obsession with duality and tendency to view everything in black and white (a defense mechanism called *splitting*), Ruth Adams uses a form of shaping to wean Two-Face away from tossing a coin to make decisions. Getting him to use a six-sided die instead makes him view every choice as having six alternatives instead of two.

> Adams: He did so well with the die that we've been able to move him onto a deck of Tarot cards. That's seventy-eight options open to him now, Batman. Next, we plan to introduce him to the I Ching. Soon he'll have a completely functional judgmental facility that doesn't rely so much on black and white absolutes.
>
> Batman: But right now, he can't even make a simple decision like going to the bathroom without consulting cards? Seems to me you've effectively destroyed the man's personality, doctor.
>
> Adams: Sometimes we have to pull down in order to rebuild, Batman. Psychiatry's like that.

Shaping is the process of training by rewarding successive approximations of a target behavior, as mentioned in an earlier chapter's look at how systematic desensitization, a shaping technique, can treat phobias. In Harvey's case, the *target behavior*—the goal, whatever it is that therapy is supposed to help the client progress into doing—is to make decisions for himself. His method of making choices has changed shape and become more like the target, but does not reach that target because Batman returns Harvey's coin to him in order to end an asylum takeover. "You're going to undo all my work," says Adams. The Joker agrees to let Two-Face decide for them all. Harvey says that if the coin's scarred side comes up, Batman dies. He tosses the coin, catches it, and announces, "He goes free." The takeover ends. Harvey appears to have regressed completely, and yet the story's final pages show him alone, looking at the coin, which actually landed scarred side up. Harvey has lied about the outcome. He has made a choice for himself and for the better.

"Still, you can't say we didn't show you a good time. Enjoy yourself out there. In the asylum. Just don't forget—if it ever gets too tough—there's always a place for you here."
—Joker as Batman exits Arkham, *Arkham Asylum: A Serious House on Serious Earth*

CASE FILE 8–1 The Mad Hatter

Real name: Jervis Tetch

First appearance: *Batman* #49 (October–November, 1948)

Origin: Arguably the maddest of the madmen to earn a spot in Batman's rogues gallery, Jervis Tetch, the Mad Hatter, is a diminutive man with prominent upper teeth and *macrocephaly*, an oversized head. In his childhood days, boys and girls shied away from the misshapen Tetch. Having no friends, "none that I didn't hypnotize,"[1] he grows up fervently wishing he could escape into Lewis Carroll's Wonderland. Growing up with parents and siblings of normal stature[2] likely compounded his *inferiority complex*, although his physical abnormality is insufficient to explain his psychosis. We know almost nothing else about the late Tetches.* Their methods of upbringing may have steered Jervis wrong. Then again, other biological factors beyond their knowing or control may have caused this son's *paranoid schizophrenia*, the type of schizophrenia that most prominently features systematic delusions with persecutory or grandiose content.

"You're mighty in Gotham, Batman, but in Wonderland, the Mad Hatter reigns supreme."
—Mad Hatter in "Mad as a Hatter," *Batman: The Animated Series* ep. 27 (October 12, 1992)

---

*The White Knight, a mission-oriented psychotic villain, kills the Tetches as part of his campaign to remove all the Arkham Asylum villains' relatives from this world in case they, too, might turn evil (*Batman and Robin* #1, 2011).

❊   ❊   ❊

Dr. Blakloch of Arkham Asylum: "Jervis is a paranoid schizophrenic. And he's obsessive-compulsive, and highly delusional. He's got an immature self-image, so he identifies more with children than adults. Oh, and he's a genius too."[3]

Blakloch also notes that Tetch sometimes starts rhyming when stressed. Some psychotic individuals will *clang*, stringing words together meaninglessly for their rhyming sound—for example, "The bed said it's led red dead." Tetch makes more sense than that, but if his psychosis progresses to a point where he suffers greater detachment from logical processes, clang associations seem likely given his existing inclination to rhyme. The rhyming may simply reflect his fascination with Lewis Carroll's best-known works, *Alice's Adventures in Wonderland* and its sequel, *Through the Looking-Glass*, particularly the first book's "A Mad Tea Party" chapter. Carroll's Hatter character becomes Tetch's own identity.

The Mad Hatter's debut as a thief on a crime spree, robbing high society like he has a vendetta against the upper class, marks his only Golden Age appearance. A different Mad Hatter appears in the comics from 1956 until 1981, when the original comes back. In his later appearances, Tetch designs mind-control devices that he hides in people's hats. Even though his prowess with neurotechnology should make him one of either the most successful inventors or the most formidable criminal masterminds on earth, he lacks the necessary vision, talent, charisma, and soundness of mind that might elevate him to either the Forbes 500 or the supervillain A-list.

As a form of self-regulation, Tetch keeps a mind-control device in his own hat so he can change its setting to *blissful* when he wants to lie naked and drooling, surrounded by hats with one planted across his lap.[4] That scene might suggest that his sexual preference involves one of the *paraphilias*, the group of sexual disorders for individuals who either cannot experience the sexual response cycle or cannot enjoy it without engaging in a specific form of behavior that most of us consider bizarre, and specifically would indicate the paraphilia called *fetishism*, a need to reach sexual gratification through the use of nonliving, normally nonsexual* objects, a need so persistent that it creates problems such as clinically significant distress, sexual dysfunction, occupational or social impairment, or violations of others' rights.[5] Without a hat, Tetch is not interested. He ignores a tall, beautiful woman who walks by naked during breakfast: "Talk to me again when she's properly clad."[6] Tetch's psychosis complicates this diagnosis, though, because we do not know how he would act and feel were he to attain a nonpsychotic state. If he could turn sane, would he want to date a woman who wore no hat? Fetishism, if his attachment to hats is sexual at all, is insufficient to account for the breadth of his interest in them.

Tetch thinks of hats as living things. Betrayed by a supposed ally, the villain Ragdoll, Tetch murmurs, "That's what friendship is, this side of the Looking Glass," and clutches his big, battered hat, calling it, "My friend. My only friend." By attributing traits such as friendship to a hat, Tetch evinces *animism*, the belief that inanimate objects have living qualities like intention and feelings, a belief typical of preschool children. A child may cry out of fear that a plush toy is suffering pain or stamp on the sidewalk out of anger at that sidewalk for making the child fall down. For Tetch, it exceeds childlike belief. He hallucinates. In his head, he hears hats. "I'm sorry, child. It's the hats. They tease and betray me."[7] Believing that hats can seize power over his mind and actions for both good and bad purposes, even hats without his mind control devices in them, exemplifies a *delusion of control*.

The small man who wants to live in Wonderland—and in his mind sometimes does—feels more comfortable in the company of children than adults. Some stories have indicated, without confirming, that Tetch may be a *pedophile*, someone whose primary sexual focus is on children.[8] He has stood up for children and protected them from others who might do them harm. He also been known to kidnap

---

*In other words, not devices used for tactile sexual stimulation.

children and drug them to make them act out his Mad Tea Party fantasy.[9] Psychiatrically speaking, not all child molesters are pedophiles. Some molest children as sadistic or antisocial acts with no specific sexual preference for children over adults.

Tetch's interest in children could be one aspect of his psychosis coupled with childlike self-image, in which case his fellow Gotham villains would insinuate pedophilia anyway. If his unhealthy fixation on children over adults includes sexual fantasies and urges (remember, Tetch does not fare well at distinguishing fantasy from reality), he would be, in the typology of pedophiles, a child molester of either the inadequate or fixated type, the particularly immature types. The *inadequate type* of child molester, usually because of a mental defect like mental retardation, senility, or psychosis, cannot recognize the wrongness of his or her behavior. Known for being strange or bizarre, this is a loner—not by choice but due to inability to establish relations with others. This person prefers children over adults because they seem less intimidating than adults. Not one to inflict injury upon children or have sexual intercourse with them, the inadequate molester instead kisses, holds, or fondles. Were Tetch sexually focused on children even when sane (perhaps while wearing the "thinking hat" that helps him focus his thoughts), then he would be a preferential type of molester known as *fixated*. Immature, uncomfortable around adults, and childlike in lifestyle and manner, the fixated offender "loves" children, does not want to harm them like a sadistic molester would, and does not recognize how harmful his actions toward them nonetheless are. This one courts children, gives them gifts and attention, and slowly becomes more intimate, moving toward sexual activity but only after a long progression.[10] Tetch's mental defects suggest the inadequate type *if* he qualifies at all. This particular man who draws children into his escapist Wonderland fantasy without developing a lasting connection to any one of them probably does *not* have sexual intercourse with those girls and boys— but he might get too personal with their headwear.

> *"I would say I'm very much cleverer than any of the people who put me here. As a matter of fact, I could leave any time I wanted. It's only a doll's house after all.*

"Anyway, I don't mind. I like dolls, particularly the live ones."

—Mad Hatter in *Arkham Asylum: A Serious House on Serious Earth*
(1989)

CASE FILE 8–2   Harley Quinn

Real name: Dr. Harleen Frances Quinzel

First appearance: *Batman: The Animated Series*, episode 22, "Joker's Favor" (September 11, 1992). Originally voiced by Arleen Sorkin.

Origin: Brooklyn girl Harleen Quinzel grows up, like several of the Robins, with one non-criminal parent and one lawbreaker, that being her con-artist father, whose *modus operandi* is to charm older women and fleece them out of their fortunes. Even from behind jailhouse glass, her father tries conning his own daughter out of whatever loot she has stashed away. "Y'know, Pop," Harley remarks when visiting her father in jail, "the main reason I became a psychiatrist was so I could understand why you did the things you did to our family."[1] It's a family so full of contradictions, the Christmas tree in the corner near the menorah seems fitting. Her mother's pattern is to express frustration by slamming the door in Harley's face or blowing up, shouting, "I should throw you all out! Force you to fend for yourselves for once! Then maybe you'd all finally grow up," then immediately apologize for her own aggravation. Young Dr. Quinzel interns* at Arkham Asylum because "I've always had an attraction for extreme personalities. They're more exciting,

---

*Point of contention: Psychiatrists have completed their psychiatric residencies. Medical school comes before internship; internship comes before residency, although the internship year could possibly be the first year of residency. Let's chalk this one up to Harley arriving at Arkham as an intern, maybe also working at a regular hospital during that first year, and then completing her psychiatric residency there before turning outlaw.

more challenging. . . . You can't deny there's an element of glamour to these super-criminals."[2] The Joker plays on her interests and insecurities. He charms her with a wink, tempts her with his secrets, earns her sympathy with lies about his father, and wins her heart by making her laugh.

Harley: It soon became clear to me the Joker, so often described as a raving, homicidal madman, was actually a tortured soul crying out for love and acceptance, a lost, injured child trying to make the world laugh at his antics. ...Yes, I admit it. As unprofessional as it sounds, I had fallen in love with my patients. Pretty crazy, huh?

Joker (*now sitting in the therapist's chair, listening to Harley on the sofa*): Not at all. As a dedicated, career-oriented young woman, you felt the need to abstain from all amusement and fun. It's only natural you'd be attracted to a man who could make you laugh again.

Harley: I knew you'd understand.

Joker: Any time.

✿   ✿   ✿

Donning a harlequin outfit and accepting the Joker's play on her own name, Harley Quinn helps him escape and commit crimes, willfully overlooking the worst of what he's doing and rationalizing the things she can't ignore. In *Batman: The Animated Series*, she regularly serves as his moll and accomplice. Her stories in DC Comics publications mostly take place after she has already struck out on her own without him. No matter how often he hurts her, no matter how many times she says she's through with him forever, she follows those remarks by showing the hopes she holds for him.

Harley: Not this time.

Catwoman: Oh, please. He'll be calling for your money the second he hears about it.

Poison Ivy: Then you'll be skipping out the door for another round of abuse, humiliation, and regret.

Harley: *Has* he called?![3]

Fortunately for her, Ivy made Harley immune to all toxins, thus protecting her from some of the Joker's favorite methods of bumping people off.[4]

Dependent Personality Disorder

An individual with *dependent personality disorder* defines his or, as in this case, her own self-concept in terms of some other person. Beginning before adulthood, the consistently and severely dependent person fears separation, lacks self-confidence, clings and submits, passively lets others lead her through life, and easily finds herself crippled with indecision, all in the hope that she might receive caregiving, comfort, and security. Because she fears losing support or approval, the dependent person does not easily disagree with anyone, especially not the one upon whom she depends most. She may make outlandish self-sacrifices and tolerate verbal, physical, or sexual abuse. Even though this can be a person full of strengths and abilities, she feels so unable to function alone that she will go along with almost anything rather than risk having the other person leave her. She does not trust her own abilities. She's afraid to trust them. Recognizing her own strengths scares her, as though being able to live alone might increase the chances she'll wind up all alone.[5] The basic human need for affiliation has twisted and swollen into something that rules this individual. When a dependent person attaches to a narcissist, it might work for a time because they're both in love with the same person, but the dependent's clinginess wearies the narcissist, who wants much from others but gives little in return.

Harley Quinn re-creates herself in the Joker's image.[6] Having only tolerated the "harlequin" play on her name after hearing it her whole life, she finally accepts it from the Joker, dons a harlequin costume to break him out of Arkham, and tosses away every professional achievement she has spent her life building. She takes heaping abuse from the man, including multiple attempts on her life. Lying battered and broken in an alley after the Joker hurls her out of a window, Harley blames only herself: "My fault. I didn't get the joke."[7]

Lost, vulnerable without the Joker, and easily manipulated despite her intelligence and other strengths, she follows her friend Poison Ivy into assorted misadventures, bringing out Ivy's more human side until Harley sees the Joker. A *social chameleon*, Harley molds her personality to suit Ivy, then snaps into ruthlessness around him and betrays her best friend when she's in Joker moll mode.[8]

Folie à Deux

A person suffering *shared psychotic disorder*, a.k.a. *shared psychosis* and originally known as *folie à deux* ("folly of two"), buys into someone else's psychosis and takes on, in part or even in whole, the other's delusional thinking.[9] With nothing in Harley's history to suggest that she was psychotic before those months in Arkham while the Joker manipulated her, this diagnosis seems possible *if she's really psychotic*. She does not hallucinate or show any other strong symptoms that might suggest she has become schizophrenic. Note, though, that a distorted point of view and willful blindness to some things that should be obvious to anyone do not in and of themselves mean she's psychotic. It's a matter of severity. The fact that she eventually earns a death sentence after killing someone over the Joker indicates that the law finally deems her sane enough to die—even if she gets to work off that sentence as a member of the government's Suicide Squad.[10]

Coping Strategies

Whether Harley suffers dependent personality disorder, shared psychosis, neither, or both, how does anyone smart enough to get through medical school become so desperate for affection and approval in the first place? Her susceptibility to manipulation has governed her. Professional opinions are mixed as to what causes such extreme dependence and suggestibility. Maybe a cruel parent who made the child feel worthless nevertheless showed enough inconsistent affection and attention to give that child false hope. Maybe an overprotective parent makes life so easy that a child fails to develop adequate coping skills or makes it too easy for them to stay under someone else's wing. Harley's loser of a brother still hasn't gotten off the couch, found a grownup job, bought a home, or married the mother of either of his children. Even after Harley gives him enough money, he finds it too easy to stay in their mom's home.

Harley's father, as he first appears, is a con artist. He lies to everyone, including family. Growing up with a parent who's an inveterate liar tends to make a child either gullible or cynical, one extreme or another, ready to trust everything or nothing. Harley went for gullible. Her intelligence makes it a challenge to stay so gullible, so she shuts off part of her smarts. She protects herself with reality-distorting defense mechanisms, neurotic defense mechanisms Freud felt could turn psychotic if taken to an extreme: *denial*, refusing to believe stressful truths; *suppression*, refusing to think about stressful truths that have entered her memory; and *rationalization*, making up excuses like blaming Batman for the Joker's behavior. These let her hold onto her hope.

> Harley: Well, no more. That pasty-faced creep has threatened my friends for the last time. I'm through with him.
> Catwoman: Glad to hear it.
> Harley: Of course . . . if the real Mr. J. shows up again, who's to say he won't have changed for the better? After all, it's not impossible . . .
> (*Poison Ivy wraps a vine around Harley's mouth.*)[11]

Fans debate the nature of the Joker's relationship with Harley. Clearly he's using her and doesn't care if she dies—more than once, he has tried to kill her—but exactly what does he use her for?

> Travis Langley: Would you ever have imagined the Joker having a girlfriend?
> Jerry Robinson: I would.
> Michael Uslan: I'm less concerned or worried or terrified about what the Joker could do with a woman as opposed to what the Joker could do with a pencil.
> Adam West: I think that *Batman* generally is a little island in time, spinning around forever, and it can take so many

Harley Quinn cosplayer (a real-life mental health worker) at New York Comic Con. Photo by Travis Langley.

different levels and forms that one could do anything with it. Joker could have the mansion at Hefner's place and his own show. Of course he could have a girlfriend. It might be very interesting.[12]

The details of any sex life between Harley and the Joker remain the stuff of fan fiction and nightmares. Frank Miller's Joker wouldn't have sex;* Alan Moore's might. When Harley's creators Paul Dini and Bruce Timm first unveiled her origin in *Mad Love*, a special issue of *Batman Adventures*, the comic book series modeled after their program *Batman: The Animated Series*,[13] they showed her as an undergraduate psychology student who'd rather apply her feminine wiles on professors than study to earn her grades, and left us to wonder if that's how she later gets her high medical school grades as well. Harley spends seven pages of that story in a skimpy red nightgown trying to entice the Joker.

---

*Miller: "Bruno was a woman, a cohort of the Joker. He never had sex with her because sex is death to him. Put more accurately, death is sex." (Sharrett, 1991, p. 37)

"Aw, c'mon, puddin', don't you wanna rev up your Harley?" His indifference gives way to anger over her distracting him from designing the ultimate death trap—a common occurrence between them, it seems. "Another night I get all dolled up, and another night I get the boot."* If the Joker has no iota of interest in sexual activity, wouldn't Harley have learned long ago that any attempt to seduce him would be a waste of time? Keep in mind that we're talking about the woman who regularly fails to get a clue when it comes to her man. Harley wants the Joker, however she can get him, but what on earth does he want?

CASE FILE 8–3 The Joker

Real name: Unknown, possibly Jack

First appearance: *Batman* #1 (Spring, 1940)

Origin: A robber known as the Red Hood plunges into a chemical waste catch basin while escaping from Batman. The chemicals turn his hair green, his lips rouge-red, and his skin chalk-white. He becomes the Joker.[1] That's all we know—maybe more than we need to know. Beyond that, we can't trust anything the Joker tells us about his background because the Joker lies. In the comics and movies, he describes his backstory differently every time, even to himself. As he says in the game-changing graphic novel *The Killing Joke*,[2] "I'm not exactly sure what it was. Sometimes I remember it one way, sometimes another. If I'm going to have a past, I prefer it to be multiple choice!"

> *"They've given many origins of the Joker, how he came to be. That doesn't seem to matter—just how he is now. I never intended to give a reason for his appearance. We discussed that and Bill [Finger] and I never wanted to change it at that*

---

*An Easter egg (hidden surprise) image of Harley's positive pregnancy test stick in the 2011 video game *Batman: Arkham City* confirms nothing but certainly keeps the topic stirred up.

> *time. I thought—and he agreed—that it takes away some of the essential mystery."*
>
> —Jerry Robinson, the Joker's co-creator°

✿   ✿   ✿

The Joker defies diagnosis. His behavior doesn't neatly fit any specific mental illness beyond his obvious psychopathy. He has no conscience, no empathy, no personal concern over right and wrong. Antisocial personality disorder describes him in many ways but is inadequate, failing to distinguish him from many petty thieves. There's so much more to the Joker. We just don't know what's going on inside his head and for storytelling purposes, it's best that we don't. Knowing he had a specific mental illness might engender our sympathy.

> *"Unlike you and I, the Joker seems to have no control over the sensory information he's receiving from the outside world. He can only cope with that chaotic barrage of input by going with the flow. That's why some days he's a mischievous clown, others a psychopathic killer. He has no real personality. He creates himself every day. He sees himself as the Lord of Misrule, and the world as a theatre of the absurd."*
>
> —Dr. Ruth Adams in *Arkham Asylum: A Serious House on Serious Earth* (1989)

The fictional Dr. Adams, although one of Arkham's better clinicians, also gets a number of things wrong, so take that with a grain of salt. If we cannot diagnose him more specifically, whether because he's Adams's Lord of Misrule or because we lack solid information, can we at least determine whether he's really insane? The Joker has murdered many, including Commissioner Gordon's second wife and Batman's second Robin, and can continue creating tragedy because in Gotham, as in real life, the criminally insane

---

° "The concept was mine. Bill finished that first script from my outline of the persona and what should happen in the first story . . . so he really was co-creator. And Bob and I did the visuals, so Bob was also."—Jerry Robinson, personal communication, June 23, 2009.

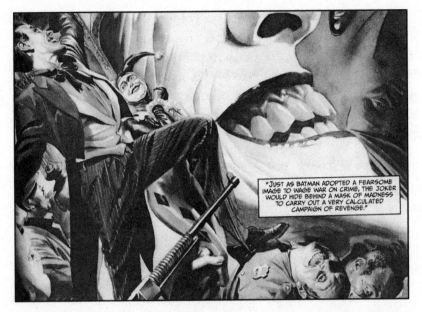

One Arkham therapist argues that the Joker's actions, however bizarre, reveal "a sane man who willfully causes anguish and clearly enjoys it." From "Case Study" by Paul Dini and Alex Ross.[4] © DC Comics.

evade execution. The Joker himself asserts, "I'm not mad at all. I'm just differently sane,"[3] but how would he know? Insane individuals have limited, if any, ability to recognize their own shortcomings. When Jason Todd tells the Joker, "You're not nearly as crazy as you'd like us all to believe. Or even as crazy as you'd like to believe. It just makes it easier to justify every sick, monstrous thing you've ever done when you play the part of the mad clown. You're crazy, bubba—but you ain't that crazy," the clown loses his smile.[5]

Between his criminal rampages, the Joker sometimes experiences melancholy spells when he either grows bored or feels frustrated by his own failures—*ergo* consequences of circumstances and not because he's cycling between the extremes of *bipolar disorder* (still known to many by its old name, *manic depression*). Bipolar individuals alternate between depression and the extremely energized, elated state known as *mania* in cycles due to brain chemistry, not randomly up and down from one day to the next, not due to a psychotic disorder, and not due to the individual's ingrained personality traits. The Joker is more maniacal than manic. When the Joker occasionally goes off to sulk on his own for a while, he does so in response to specific circumstances. He doesn't have as much fun as he did in his earlier days. As a former henchman put it, the Joker has "become a sullen, psychotic creep."[6] Though not cycles, the Joker's history has gone through four distinct stages:

1. Ace of Knaves (sane killer)—early in the Golden Age of Comics: During his first two years in print (1940–1942), the Joker murders many victims. In 1942, DC Comics creators sensitive to mounting public concern over comic book violence ended the Joker's killing spree with "The Joker Walks the Last Mile," a tale that sees the Joker executed for all his previous crimes. Quickly revived by henchmen after his electrocution while having paid the penalty for past offenses, the Joker walks free until apprehended for new robberies by the story's end.[7]

2. Clown Prince of Crime (kooky crook)—later Golden Age and all of the Silver Age (1956 until about 1970): For more than three decades, the Joker restricts himself to committing wacky crimes. Rather than murder people, he would instead resort "to pulling off astonishing crimes in ludicrous situations, often with preposterous gadgets."[8] Regardless of his antics, writers depicted him as legally sane, as illustrated by one story in which he briefly fakes insanity so he can go to a less restrictive insane asylum instead of the state prison.[9,*]

3. King of Arkham Asylum (insane killer)—Bronze Age (about 1970 to 1986): After a four-year absence from the Batman titles, 1973's "The Joker's Five-Way Revenge!"[10] brought him into the post-Vietnam era as a killer deemed legally insane,

---

*That story's court-appointed diagnostician, fooled by the Joker, diagnoses him as having "hebeophrenic schizophrenia." *Hebephrenia* is an alternate name for what the *DSM-IV-TR* calls *disorganized schizophrenia*, a type of schizophrenia marked by inappropriate emotions and disorganized behavior and speech rather than hallucinations and delusions. The *hebe*-prefix refers to youth because this condition tends to start earlier in life than do other forms of schizophrenia.

now escaping from an asylum instead of prison. A Joker crazier than ever resumes killing while now facing a Batman darker than he has been since 1939.

4. Harlequin of Hate (personal killer)—Modern Age: After decades of doing our heroes no real harm, the Joker begins maiming and killing some of the people closest to Batman and Commissioner Gordon: He cripples Gordon's daughter, Barbara;[11] kills Batman's second Robin, Jason;[12] and kills the Commissioner's second wife, Sarah.[13]

When he starts killing again in the 1970s, the Joker also starts trying to teach the world some deadly lessons. Those lessons grow more abstract over time, from killing a family to make Gotham's citizens afraid to testify against criminals[14] early in that third stage to crippling Barbara Gordon in order to make a point about human nature. Because the world makes no sense to the Joker, the fact that anyone else believes it does bothers him. After he shoots Barbara as part of an effort to drive her father insane, he assumes—wrongly—that he has demonstrated that there's no difference between himself and everyone else. "All it takes is one bad day to reduce the sanest man alive to lunacy. That's how far the world is from where I am. Just one bad day."

> Joker: When I saw what a black, awful joke the world was, I went crazy as a coot! I admit it! Why can't you? I mean, you're not unintelligent! You must see the reality of the situation…. It's all a joke! Everything anybody ever valued or struggled for—it's all a monstrous, demented gag. So why can't you see the funny side? Why aren't you laughing?
>
> Batman: Because I've heard it before—and it wasn't funny the first time.[15]

The Joker has always tried to reshape reality to fit himself, starting with the first crime he ever commits in the comics, when his Joker-toxin leaves a rictus grin on the dead millionaire he just robbed. "He wants to permanently stamp his unique face on nature,

Do those fish prove the Joker really is insane after all? From *Detective Comics* #475, cover by Marshall Rogers & Terry Austin. © DC Comics.

to transform the world in his image," writes comics scholar Peter Coogan. "He seeks to make the world comprehensible by transforming it into a twisted parody of himself,"[16] like the time he gives his face to Gotham's fish in "The Laughing Fish,"[17] a story often cited as the proof that the Joker truly is out of touch with reality.[18] Expecting to reap millions by copyrighting fish disfigured with hideous clown faces after he dumps toxins in the local waters, the Joker simply does not understand why he cannot copyright fish, nor the fact that threatening to kill the copyright clerk cannot get him what he wants. "'The Laughing Fish' was my attempt to try to show that this guy just wasn't logical," said author Steve Englehart. "I really wanted to come up with some concept that was just insane on the face of it. I mean, the whole idea of copyrighting fish based on dumping chemicals into the ocean and trying to get the government to go along with it, anybody else would look at this and go, 'That's clearly not sane.'"[19] Psychologist Robin Rosenberg has wondered, though, whether this proves insanity or simply failure to understand copyright law.[20]

> *"I took Gotham's White Knight and I brought him down to our level. Madness, as you know, is a lot like gravity: All it takes is a little push."*
> —The Joker (Heath Ledger) in *The Dark Knight* (2008 motion picture)

9
The Psychodynamic Duo
Freud and Jung on Batman and Robin

Sigmund Freud (1856–1939) died the year Batman debuted, the month before the character's origin saw print. While the founder of psychoanalysis never commented on our hero's background, he wrote a great deal on related topics, from which we might infer what he'd have had to say about the character. The role of early childhood experience and the power of trauma to route the course of personality, the very things that created Batman, fascinated Freud. To him, early experiences create conflicts and unconscious turmoil we wrestle with throughout our lives. Conscious of the circumstances that drive him, Batman in many ways is ahead of most people.

Freud, perhaps the most famous figure in the history of psychiatry and psychology, developed the first and best-known formal theory of personality. Many later personality theories arose either to elaborate upon or to oppose Freud's views. He stirred controversy with his proclamation (soon withdrawn) of cocaine as a wonder drug for treating mood disorders[1] and his *psychodynamic perspective,* which asserted that our own minds play tricks on us, that unconscious processes that elude awareness guide our conscious lives, and that the human sex drive spurs personality development from infancy into adulthood.[2] A number of followers who initially intended only to expand upon his theory—like Carl Jung, Karen Horney, and Erik Erikson—each came to veer away as their ideas came to contradict his, often beginning with disagreements over sexuality's role.[3] Rather than minimize the importance of the unconscious mind like some neo-Freudians, Carl Jung emphasized it more heavily than Freud, adding a deeper dimension popular in the study of heroes: the collective unconscious shared throughout our species.[4] Despite controversies, both Freud and Jung remain influential to this day and provide frameworks for analyzing fictional characters and their stories.

Most psychologists are *not* Freudians. Freud's ideas frequently lacked *falsifiability*—disprovability, meaning that no conceivable empirical outcome could have contradicted him. He said stairways in dreams represent sexual intercourse.[5] You can't prove that wrong any more than you can prove that no organ grinder ever played cribbage in any of your ancestors' kitchens. Einstein asserted that faster-than-light travel is impossible. Because a single supraluminal jaunt would refute his assertion, the idea itself—whether right or wrong—was scientific. One important reason why Carl Jung broke away from Freud was that Jung, although a religious man, felt that dogma in any form—in Freud's case, his insistence that sexual foundations underlay all psychological development—had no place in an empirical discipline.

Nevertheless, we can easily speculate on what Freud might have said about Batman. He said a great deal about how traumatic experiences will affect boys at around the age Bruce was when his parents died.

Freud's Psychodynamic Foundations

The cornerstone of Freud's *psychoanalysis* was his view that the *unconscious* mind continually influences us in ways the *conscious* mind does not realize. In his view, early experiences shape personality and create inner conflicts we wrestle with throughout our lives. This unconscious turmoil stirs up difficulties in conscious life.

He felt that we have two main instincts driving our behavior: a *life instinct* that he called *Eros* for the Greek god of erotic love and a *death instinct* he called *Thanatos* for the Greek god of death. He had much more to say about the life instinct. We spend all our time being alive and only a certain portion of it focusing on death and destruction. The life instinct or *libido* (all mental energy) would drive sex, activity, construction, creativity, hunger, and all the activities involved in keeping us and our species going—the kind of things for which playboy Bruce Wayne pretends to live. So Batman's ongoing effort to save lives, as a life-oriented activity, would be his form of sexual expression on Planet Freud. Seeing this as one wide-ranging instinct, Freud considered it all sexual in nature. The death instinct, on the other hand, would prompt aggression, destruction, and preoccupation with morbid topics. Dwelling on this could create antisocial or suicidal inclinations. The death instinct can serve life. Sometimes you need to fight off the wolves. Sometimes you must demolish one thing in order to build another. Batman's aggression and his terrifying image help him shield others from fates like his family's.

A Freudian might take the view that the three-part Batman character (Bruce façade, Batman as superhuman symbol, and the real man behind both) represents the three major structures of personality—not that they directly are the three structures, simply that they could symbolize them. At the beginning of life, personality consists of nothing but *id*, the innate animal self driven by those inborn instincts.* It operates on the *pleasure principle*, seeking immediate gratification, immediate fulfillment of needs and desires. Playboy Bruce would embody the id. Around age three, we develop the *ego*, the executive structure that includes the conscious mind and learns to operate on the *reality principle*. Whereas an infant has no concept of patience, no initial tolerance for waiting, children will learn that we can often achieve greater satisfaction by waiting. Because Batman is the main self, the identity that all Bruce's other efforts support, he might represent the ego. When his surrogate mother, Dr. Leslie Thompkins, gestures to the bat insignia on his chest and says, "This isn't the real you, Bruce," he tells her, "It's the only me

---

*Keep in mind that these are Freudians' concepts, not universally recognized throughout psychology even though I can't reasonably insert "according to Freud" into every sentence.

there is, Leslie."[6] Batcave Bruce, the hero unmasked and partially costumed down in the Batcave, the one place he might speak freely or reveal his injuries, sits at his giant computer using analysis and rational thought to achieve things his fists cannot—guided by the basic morality exemplified by surrogate father Alfred, who represents his conscience. This part of the superhero could represent that conscience, his *superego*. Both id and superego influence the ego, which must balance their respective wants to forge its own path, something strong-willed Batman with his great strength of ego should handle well.

Why is Batman so strong-willed? Where did he get such discipline and self-control? Freud would credit Bruce's toilet training. Freud believed we experience a series of *psychosexual stages of development* that sculpt our psyches and have lasting impact throughout our lives, each stage focusing on a different *erogenous zone* (sexually excitable area) with a distinct manner by which we go about satisfying those life-and-death instincts. In any stage, a person might develop a *fixation*, failing to outgrow that stage emotionally whether because of trauma, underindulgence (which creates a lingering ache to satisfy unfulfilled needs), or overindulgence (which makes the child too comfortable to want to mature).

Age	Stage	Developmental Tasks According to Freud
0–18 months	Oral	*Id*, the inborn, instinctive part of personality, dominates and operates on the *pleasure principle*, seeking immediate fulfillment of needs and desires. Oral activities (sucking, eating, crying, biting) satisfy life and death instincts. Fixation results in *oral-passive* (e.g., smoking, overeating) or *oral-aggressive* (biting, criticizing) habits.
18 months–3 years	Anal	Toilet training teaches self-control, promoting development of the *ego*. Fixation produces *anal-retentive* (clenched, uptight, overcontrolled, excessively neat) or *anal-expulsive* (impulsive, impatient, undercontrolled, slovenly) personality.
3 to 5 or 6	Phallic	The child resolves sexual and aggressive feelings toward parents by becoming more like the same-gender parent, incorporating morals and values to develop the *superego*.
5 or 6 to puberty	Latency	Sex drive is latent, not manifest, thus freeing the psyche to learn social and academic skills.
Puberty until ???	Genital	The sex drive returns.

Whether Bruce's parents died when he was 6 as Frank Miller writes[7] or 8 according to Dennis O'Neil[8] and others, the boy would have recently passed through the phallic stage's most intense conflict, which Freud considered early life's most important issue. He believed phallic stage fixation could produce *narcissism* (obsessive self-love), *flamboyance* (running around wearing a cape surely qualifies), or *homosexuality* (despite a lack of subsequent evidence to show that he was right about that). While he might have concurred with psychiatrist Fredric Wertham's contention that Bruce Wayne and Dick Grayson were living a homosexual "wish dream,"[9] Freud did not view homosexuality as deviant.

Freud's key ideas about the phallic stage originated in his treatment of a boy he called Little Hans in his writings.[10] Hans suffered such severe *equinophobia*, fear of horses, that he would barely go outside, horses being as common circa 1900 as cars are today. Freud concluded that the reason Hans was so afraid of being bitten by a horse was that he was in love with his mother and afraid his father was going to castrate him. Freud considered him a little Oedipus, after the figure from Greek tragedy who kills his own father and marries his mother*—hence, the *Oedipus complex*. Regardless of whether Freud was right about Hans's fear of a horse biting him symbolizing the deeper fear that his father might castrate him, Hans did have fantasies about marrying Mommy, animosity toward his father, and preoccupation with the fear that they might cut off part of his anatomy—although in his case, he had reason for the castration anxiety. He had been told that if he did not stop fidgeting with his "widdler," it would get cut off—and his little sister didn't have one. They'd done it before! Many sources erroneously credit Freud for proposing an equivalent *Electra complex*† for girls when, in fact, Freud refuted *Carl Jung's* Electra proposal.[11] Freud generalized Hans's phallic preoccupation to all children, positing that castration

---

*In *Oedipus Rex*, the character did not yet know they were his parents, but in Greek tragedy, the intent behind your sins does not matter. The gods will get you for them anyway.

†Jung spelled it *Electra* instead of the more traditional *Elektra*.

anxiety worried every little boy and *penis envy* irked every little girl. Hans eventually began acting more like his father, incorporating the man's manner and moral values, which Freud interpreted as an act of *identification*, becoming more like the father in order to get along with him. Each little boy supposedly develops his superego, the conscience, so Dad won't threaten his penis and each little girl develops hers so she can psychologically grow one.

In Freud's view, therefore, Bruce has undergone that entire conflict—including a wish to have his father out of the way and occasional resentment toward his mother for being with his father— but could have recently resolved this by identifying with his father and crystallizing his superego, his moral core. Now entering latency, that period of time when Freud of all people did not see much of anything sexual going on, the boy would no longer be the sex fiend he was back at age five. (Remember, we're still exploring Planet Freud for the moment—most of us do *not* consider preschoolers' underlying motivation primarily sexual in nature.) Instead, his mind is opening itself up to picking up new skills and learning about the great big world, right when a mugger's bullets shatters that world.

Batman vs. Hamlet, Act I: Murder Most Foul

"Dead! They're d-dead."
—Bruce Wayne, *Detective Comics* #33 (November 1939)

"Murder most foul, as in the best it is; but this most foul, strange, and unnatural."
—Ghost, *Hamlet*, Act I, Scene V

To help us speculate on what Freud might have said about Batman, we can glean clues by looking at what he had to say about another fictional character whose parents get murdered, a young man with different Oedipal issues, William Shakespeare's Prince Hamlet. Differences between Batman and Hamlet still prove useful in this task. In both stories, the hero's father gets murdered first—Bruce's father, Dr. Thomas Wayne, by a mugger who wants to steal the mother's pearls; Hamlet's father, King Hamlet, by the uncle who wants to steal the mother and the crown. Bruce witnesses the murder; Hamlet later learns his father's death had been a murder. Martha Wayne gets robbed and murdered; Hamlet's mother, Gertrude, marries her husband's murderer and later gets inadvertently murdered by him as well. Bruce has few doubts; Hamlet has them aplenty. Bruce knows that murder has occurred but not the killer's identity; Hamlet knows the killer's identity but needs to confirm that it was murder. Bruce Wayne is an active, decisive individual who knows what he wants, forms a plan, and pursues it; Hamlet is passive and uncertain, although to some extent he has good reason to proceed with caution. In case the spirit that visited Hamlet was not actually his father's ghost but was instead some demon trying to trick him into murdering a man, he first wants to prove murder happened at all. He and Bruce both want to be better than the killers they pursue. They both resist killing.

For centuries, scholars have contemplated why Hamlet goes through the elaborate ruse of acting insane while hesitating to kill his uncle even after establishing the man's guilt. Freud said Hamlet perceives his murderous uncle as "the man who shows him the repressed wishes of his own childhood realized."[12] The killer reminds the son, at least unconsciously, of the part of himself that wanted to eliminate his father and have his mother to himself. Freud would likely have considered it significant that Bruce Wayne's father dies first. By taking the mother's necklace—established by later stories to have been a gift from Thomas, a symbol of their affection—and shooting her too, the mugger would remind Bruce of any occasional resentment he'd felt toward her for choosing father over son.

Both newly fatherless sons take oaths. Whereas Bruce actively chooses to avenge his parents, Hamlet receives a spectral mandate to avenge. Note that in their respective oaths, neither son vows to slay his father's slayer, and neither promises to punish the man who has given his own Oedipal fantasy its reality. Bruce swears to take action, "to avenge their deaths by spending the rest of my life warring on all criminals," not to devote himself to hunting down the man who killed them. Hamlet vows inaction, in that he gets his friends to join him in swearing only that they won't tell anybody they saw a ghost.

Batman vs. Hamlet, Act II: The Defense Mechanisms

"Years ago, I created a mighty lie: an almost demonic creature
of violence and vengeance. . . .
But the lie was born to serve the greater good."
—Batman, *Batman: Absolution* (2003)

"Though this be madness, yet there's method in it."
—Polonius, *Hamlet*, Act II, Scene II

One area where many psychologists view Freud favorably is his proposal that we use a variety of automatic tactics to protect ourselves from anxiety, especially against threats to self-image, often without realizing we're using these *defense mechanisms* (or *ego defense mechanisms*). We all lie to ourselves sometimes. We avoid topics that unnerve us, devalue things we can't have ("sour grapes"), and shield ourselves from stress in many other ways. Sigmund's daughter Anna Freud deserves credit for giving names to numerous processes that her father had described without labeling and for identifying additional defense mechanisms he never addressed.[13]

Freud saw *Hamlet, Prince of Denmark* as a story of *repression*, whereby the unconscious mind hides disturbing wishes, thoughts, and experiences from conscious awareness. Unlike Oedipus, who kills his own father and marries his mother, Hamlet sees a man other than himself live out his childhood Oedipal fantasy, a fantasy Freud said Hamlet has repressed. "Thus the loathing which should drive him on to revenge is replaced in him by self-reproaches, by scruples no better than the sinner whom he is to punish."[14] Batman's story, on the other hand, is one of *displacement*, acting on one's feelings but focusing them on a different target because the original target is inappropriate or unavailable—for example, rather than pursue your roommate's boyfriend whom you find desirable, you convince yourself you're having those feelings about his buddy. Because Batman never brings his parents' killer to justice,* every hoodlum he hits serves as a substitute for the man who slayed them.

---

*Even the inconsistent accounts that depict Joe Chill's death show him slain by other criminals: *Batman* #47 (1948), *Batman: Year Two* (1987), *Batman Begins* (2008 motion picture).

Using defense mechanisms can be healthy, even necessary, to keep harsh reality from overwhelming us. The American Psychiatric Association's *Diagnostic and Statistical Manual of Mental Disorders* *(DSM)*[15] distinguishes the defenses that help us best cope with reality. These "mature" defenses, as Vaillant called them,[16] maximize our ability to feel good about life while staying aware of memories, feelings, and thoughts. Hamlet still has his wit, his sense of *humor*, with a particular fondness for wordplay, but for the most part he utilizes fewer of these healthier defenses than Batman does. Bruce Wayne lives a life of *altruism, self-assertion*, and, even as distant as Batman might seem, greater *affiliation* with his sidekicks, superhero teams, and the rest of Gotham's Bat-Family (Batgirl, Oracle, etc.) than anything Hamlet shows. Although each has a confidant (Alfred for Batman, Horatio for Hamlet), Hamlet more consistently than Batman cuts himself off from all others. *Thought suppression* helps Batman keep distractions from weakening his focus, but suppressed thoughts remain easily accessible to the conscious mind, unlike all the things Hamlet keeps repressed. Batman exemplifies one definition of the defense *introjection* in that he identifies so strongly with a particular image or symbol that he has incorporated it into his identity. Spending at least 15 years training himself in *anticipation* of his crime-fighting mission differs markedly from Hamlet's often aimless hesitation. During that anticipatory period, Bruce Wayne passes up opportunities to develop friends and girlfriends, discarding college acquaintances even though he wants them, "and the ache he felt seemed to fill his entire being. He learned to ignore the ache, and the pain of loss and isolation. These were the conditions of his life, and he accepted them."[17] Social and sexual drives get rerouted into training for his mission—this is an example of *sublimation*, feeling one need or impulse but channeling that energy into some other activity.

Both Bruce and Hamlet use *mental inhibitions*, the mildly neurotic defense mechanisms that compromise information, keeping fears and other potential threats hidden from our awareness. Like a police detective who must separate whatever feelings he has about a case from the thoughts and actions needed to do his job, Batman has feelings but must *isolate* those affective reactions from the brutal reality he faces. He tries not to let shock slow him down or anger blind his perception. He and Hamlet both channel emotional energy into analysis, but Hamlet overanalyzes to the point of *intellectualization*, using reason to avoid confrontation with an unconscious conflict. Both use *reaction formation*, a type of sublimation in which the person has one impulse but does the opposite instead, as when they each drive away women they find appealing—in Hamlet's case, cruelly so.

Hamlet uses more dysfunctional defenses than Batman— *apathetic withdrawal* after his father dies, *idealization* of that father, *devaluation* of the mother, *rationalization* (making excuses) for his hesitation to avenge his father even after satisfying himself that his uncle committed murder, and *passive aggression* throughout. Hamlet is suicidal. Batman is not. He survived that night in the alley and remains a survivor night after night.

Batman vs. Hamlet, Act III: Theatricality and Deception

"Theatricality and deception are powerful agents. You must become more than just a man in the mind of your opponent."
—Ducard (Liam Neeson), *Batman Begins*

"We are all errant knaves; believe none of us."
—Hamlet, *Hamlet,* Act III, Scene I

Both put on performances, one to expose a villain and the other to scare all villains. Hamlet plays the mad prince; Wayne plays both the bored play-boy and the dark symbol that must become "more than a man." Decep-tion permeates their relationships, especially those that should be most intimate (with notable exceptions being their respective confidants), and yet they both enlist help in their deceptive practices. Playing "mad" helps Hamlet hide his suspicions toward his uncle but does nothing to help him expose or destroy the man. When a troupe of traveling actors happens to come along, Hamlet requests that they perform a specific play so that he might gauge his uncle's reaction when they depict a murder similar to his father's. Even those whom Batman deceives as Bruce Wayne, including Commissioner Gordon, help him with performances of his own.

When Hamlet finally uses violence, striking an eavesdropper behind an arras while hoping it's the uncle he still cannot bring himself to confront face to face, he begins to illustrate the advantages of Batman's healthier, more consistently active coping strategies. Hamlet kills the wrong person. Soon he shows signs of *psychosis* (mental illness or at least a temporary state in which the person is grossly out of touch with reality) when his father's ghost reappears, but, unlike the Act I appearance when three others saw the ghost with him, his mother sees no ghost. Either she, having betrayed her late husband by remarrying so soon, is not permitted to see the ghost or Hamlet is having a *hallucination*, a psychotic symptom involving a false perception disconnected from real-world stimuli. Batman does not have *delusions*, beliefs grossly out of touch with reality, nor does he hallucinate—not unless exposed to some supervillain's hallucinogenic toxin, spell, or telepathic whammy—but those are career hazards every superhero faces from time to time.

Batman vs. Hamlet: Curtains

"My thoughts be bloody, or be nothing else!"
—Hamlet, *Hamlet,* Act IV, Scene IV

"Chill, I want to tell you a story without an ending. Maybe you can supply it."
—Batman to his parents' killer, *Batman* #47 (1948)

Bruce Wayne carries out a long-term plan that includes avoidance of killing; what little plan Hamlet forms falls apart after he finally, blindly kills. Hamlet's fate demonstrates why Batman draws the line he will not cross: Once the killing starts, the wrong people can suffer—a mistake no one can undo. Of the seven characters killed in *Hamlet*'s latter half, five are not the originally intended or hoped-for targets. Only at the play's end, when Hamlet stabs his uncle and then succumbs to his own envenomed wound, do the intended victims die.

Batman gets no Act V. His story in the comic books does not close. Numerous comics have presented variations of the character's possible future but never his canonical end. In fact, even those unofficial future tales tend not to end with his death.[18] Parallel universe stories that do depict deaths of other worlds' Batmen often confirm that DC's main Batman has followed the wiser path.[19]

"The rest is silence."

—Hamlet, *Hamlet,* Act V, final scene

". . . here, in the endless cave, far past the burnt remains of a crimefighter whose time has passed. . . . It begins here—"
—Batman's narrative, *The Dark Knight Returns,* final page

The Inner Child: Robin

"He was about the same age I was when my parents died. His parents—circus acrobats—had been murdered. And I wanted to make a difference in his life. The way, if my parents had lived, they would have made a difference in mine."
—Batman, *Batman* #618 (2003)

Whereas Sigmund Freud emphasized the importance of life's earliest years and would have dwelled on the Waynes' deaths, Carl Jung[20] considered *individuation* (individual personality growth, integrating diverse aspects of oneself to form a whole and healthy identity) a lifelong process and would have cast his gaze wider across the entire course of Bruce Wayne's life. Despite acknowledging that early experience influences us, Jung felt that psychological disturbances are more rooted in the present than in the past and that therapists should spend more time helping clients with the direction they're taking into the future.[21]

Both would have said that Robin the Boy Wonder reminds Batman of himself and the reason for his mission. Robin is a living *symbol* of the boy Bruce had been when he lost his parents and the boy he might have become under other circumstances. After all, Dick Grayson looks like young Bruce, his parents resemble Bruce's, and both are about the same age when they witness their respective parents' murders. Subsequent Boys Wonder Jason, Tim, and Damian all look like young Bruce, and Batman swiftly fires the only official Girl Wonder, blond Stephanie Brown.[22] Through Robin, Batman receives vicarious *wish fulfillment* as he helps the boy get what young

Bruce did not: guidance, crime-fighting as a father-and-son activity, justice, and thus closure. In their first case together, Batman and Robin send the Graysons' killer to jail.

Freud and Jung would have disagreed a bit on why Batman welcomes that symbol of his own childhood. Looking at how past crisis lingers with us via processes like fixation and repression, Freud might say that little boy Bruce, having never outgrown that night, always remains an important part of Batman's fixated psyche. Jung, on the other hand, felt that past conflicts tend to influence us most when *present* difficulties bring them up again. *Regression*, another defense mechanism, involves seeking comfort by reverting to behavior from an earlier point in life, like the toilet-trained child who resumes bedwetting during her parents' divorce or the ex-smoker who lights up while going bankrupt. Jung agreed that boys experience the Oedipus conflict, but he felt that it was unlikely to play an important role later unless the man reacted to current parental issues (e.g., Hamlet's ire toward his mother for remarrying so soon) by regressing or emotionally returning to a conflict long since left behind.

For Batman, Robin is not an unconscious symbol but rather a conscious reminder. In Robin's debut,[23] the narrative tells us, "The Batman thinks back to the time when his parents, too, were innocent victims of a criminal," and he tells Dick, "My parents too were killed by a criminal. That's why I've devoted my life to exterminate them." By helping the boy get justice, Batman returns to his parents' murder and gets to experience what a better post-murder outcome could have felt like.

Jung would also examine Robin's role as a symbol of the Child archetype and that child's place in the hero's journey.

Jung's Archetypes: Shadow of the Bat

"Patients suffering delusional episodes often focus their paranoia on an external tormentor, usually one conforming to Jungian archetypes."
—Dr. Jonathan Crane, a.k.a. the Scarecrow (Cillian Murphy),
Batman Begins (2008 motion picture)

Carl Jung (1875–1961) mentioned Superman in his work, seeing Superman as the main personality and Clark Kent as Superman's Shadow,[24] but we can only speculate on how he'd have assessed Batman. Of particular importance is Jung's theory that the *collective unconscious*, an inborn stratum of the psyche inherited by all human-kind, prepares us to perceive and create themes that fit abstract, instinctive patterns called *archetypes* that organize the things we see and do.[25] Certain themes and character types emerge in the legends and myths of every culture in the history of the world. Jung said the archetypal pattern is not "a question of inherited ideas, but of inherited possibilities of ideas."[26] The Joker is no more an inherent feature of every human psyche than is the mischievous Norse god Loki, but each has qualities common to rascally characters that stir trouble, challenge heroes, and push mortals on to greater heights in tales told throughout time. They are symbols of the *Trickster* archetype. Each fits within its mold, imperfectly sculpted with touches added and bits trimmed away by myriad storytellers over the course of many years.

Jungian therapy involved helping the client both face reality and delve into the unconscious. In early treatment, the client encounters the principal features of the *personal unconscious* (the part of the unconscious gathered over a lifetime, not inherited): the Shadow and the Persona. The *Shadow* represents your dark side, not necessarily your evil side but the part of you that is hidden, out of the light, the sum of those characteristics you wish to conceal from both the world and yourself. We fear it. In *Dr. Jekyll and Mr. Hyde*, a potion that Henry Jekyll hopes might eliminate evil releases a person's darkest inclinations instead and lets his Shadow take control. Appropriately enough, given that Walter Gibson's *The Shadow* helped inspire the Dark Knight's creation,[27] Batman is a Shadow character. Bruce Wayne confronts his own darkest nature early in life, chooses to work with it, and uses it to instill fear in others. His bright and dark sides work together to fight evil.

Superheroes commonly have Shadow foes, enemies that are twisted counterparts to themselves: Flash, Reverse-Flash; Green Lantern, Sinestro the Yellow Lantern; brutal gamma-mutated Hulk, supersmart gamma-mutated Leader. These twists take many forms.

Superman has both Bizarro, a dim-witted superstrong freak who does harm through his ignorance, and Lex Luthor, a non-superpowered scientist who does intentional evil for self-serving purposes—each a funhouse distortion from a different angle. Because Batman is himself a Shadow character, his Shadow foes become more freakish, more complicated than strong/dumb/amoral or mortal/smart/immoral. Inspired by a movie poster featuring Spencer Tracy's Jekyll on half his face and his version of Hyde down the other, Two-Face mirrors the entire character, both Batman and Bruce Wayne at the same time but with both his sides furthering evil. By letting a coin toss absolve him of guilt and responsibility for his bad side's actions, the villain's unscarred "good" Harvey Dent side also serves wrongdoing.

The Joker—laughing, murderous, psychopathic, brightly colored Clown Prince of Crime—shadows only Batman, not the whole character. The Joker has no alter ego. Despite some depictions, most notably when mobster Jack Napier becomes the Joker in Tim Burton's *Batman*, the comic book Joker has no secret identity, no confirmable past prior to the incident that turned him green-haired and chalk-white, and, for his first decade of publication, no origin at all.* "Sometimes I remember it one way, sometimes another," he tells Batman in Alan Moore's graphic novel *The Killing Joke*. "If I'm going to have a past, I prefer it to be multiple choice!" Because the Joker does not want Batman to have an alter ego, he threatens the lives of those who might expose the hero's unmasked identity. He does not want to see Batman by daylight. He refuses to recognize any brighter facets of Batman's Persona.

The *Persona* is the mask, essentially a collection of masks that the ego wears when interacting with the outer world. You wear many masks. You bring different set of qualities to different situations, and they all might be equally genuine. The face you wear

---

*Artist Jerry Robinson during our 2009 San Diego Comic-Con panel ("Is the Joker a Psychopath? You Decide!"): "Bill and Bob and myself, we . . . decided deliberately not to explain it, not to write an origin. We thought that would detract from the whole aura, the mystery of the Joker—where did he come from, how did he get that way? No, we did not explain that, quite deliberately. The origin story was written by a subsequent writer many years later."

on Saturday night may not be the face you wear on Sunday morning. The Persona helps keep the Shadow hidden. If balance between the two breaks down, a Persona-dominated person will worry too much what people think or a Shadow-dominated person might recognize no law beyond his own instant gratification.[28] The Joker hates the nice, bright masks people wear. He strives to smash masks, trying to unleash people's Shadow selves on the assumption that they're all monstrous at heart.

After the client faces those features of the personal unconscious, a Jungian therapist helps the person look at deeper aspects of the collective unconscious, beginning with the contrasexual archetypes, each gender's innate sense of the opposite sex. Jung said every man carries an archetypal representation of woman, his *Anima*, and each woman carries one of man, her *Animus*. He said each gender has a sense of what it would mean for the two to join as soul mates, a divine couple in a relationship called the *Syzygy*, named for alignment of the planets. Batman's attraction to Catwoman, established when he lets her escape in her first appearance even though he has "nice girl" Julie Madison in his life at the time, hints at his Anima's nature. Because he thinks of Batman as his true self, he desires a woman more like his Shadow than his Persona, but because he is more than merely Shadow, he can never fully trust her or keep any woman continuously in his personal life. The Golden Age Batman and Catwoman had to retire from crime-fighting and crime respectively before they could balance their complex nature and spend most of their remaining years as a happy couple.[29]

The maturing individual encounters representations of all the archetypes while progressing toward wholeness of being. The *Self* is the archetype of the individual's greatest potential, where all aspects come together as one. The *Hero* story archetype reflects the individuating person making that trek from balancing Shadow and Persona to become, eventually, possibly, the Self.

The Hero's Journey

Elaborating upon Jung's writings on heroes, Joseph Campbell (1904–1987) referred to the *Monomyth*, the *Hero's Journey*, as the archetypal myth at the foundation of every heroic tale.[30] In *The Hero with a Thousand Faces* (1949),[31] he described the steps heroes tend to take:

- *departure*, meaning the separation from their early lives (the Waynes get murdered, Bruce leaves Gotham);
- *initiation*, a series of trials that lead to achievement of the ultimate boon, the goal of that hero's quest (Bruce trains under many teachers until ready to don cape and cowl);
- *return*, coming back to bestow his boon upon others (Batman comes to Gotham).

Having gained wisdom, skills, and any other divine gifts, the hero returns to become a master of two worlds. Comics scholar Peter Coogan has observed that the entire journey takes place within the hero's origin story: "The classical monomyth, identified by Joseph Campbell, clearly serves as a model for the origin stories of superheroes."[32]

Batman: Year One and *Batman Begins* offer glimpses into that journey, if only its first and final parts. Aside from their brief origin stories, the most prominent superheroes' adventures rarely explore many steps within the monomythic arc—the television program *Smallville* a notable exception in its portrayal of young Clark Kent growing into his Superman role. Batman is a hero complete. As if to satisfy the inherent craving for tales of becoming heroes, the creators added a hero *in*complete, a student for Batman to mentor, a Boy Wonder who will grow up.

CASE FILE 9–1 Two-Face

Real name: Harvey Dent

First appearance: *Detective Comics* #66 (August 1942)

Origin: Handsome District Attorney Harvey "Apollo" Dent fights to clean up corruption as "the Face" of honor and justice in Gotham City. Not above bending rules to advance that goal and frustrated by mobsters who bribe authorities so they can operate above the law, he becomes an early ally helping the bat-masked vigilante[1] who "crosses a line we can't."[2] After a crime boss scars the attorney's face with acid, leaving his "face divided into beauty and ugliness,"[3] Dent wants to hurt others. Relinquishing responsibility for his own actions, he begins making decisions based on the toss of a two-headed coin: clean side up, do good; scarred side up, do wrong.

> *"The only morality in a cruel world is chance. Unbiased. Unprejudiced. Fair."*
>
> —Harvey Dent/Two-Face (Aaron Eckhart), *The Dark Knight*
> (2008 motion picture)

❖   ❖   ❖

If Dent now believes random chance controls people's actions and fates, then he believes in external causality. Your *locus of control* is your generalized expectancy or set of beliefs regarding your ability to influence events.[4] With *internal* locus, you tend to think your own skills and efforts determine the quality of your health, achievements, social interactions, and other life circumstances. With *external* locus, you attribute causality to things beyond your control, like weather, other people, predestination, or "blind, stupid, simple, doo-dah, clueless luck!"[5] Successful people tend to make internal attributions, taking personal responsibility for completing tasks and reaching goals. Few people are 100% internal or 100% external. We often mix and match however makes us feel best. For example, regardless of our general tendencies, we nevertheless tend to make internal attributions about favorable outcomes ("I made an A") and external attributions about unfavorable ones ("the professor gave me an F"). Harvey Dent, having climbed the career ladder to become district attorney and ambitiously determined to challenge all its corruption, appears to have had an internal locus before tragedy taught him that life is random and he should trust only fate.

Maybe that experience changed his basic beliefs. On the other hand, he may be using that "lesson" as an excuse to lash out at the world. Now that he has begun to steal and kill, to exercise power over life and death, he might still believe in Harvey Dent even though he'd rather not. Because holding himself accountable for his transgressions disturbs Dent, Freud might say that the character asserts the reverse of his core belief as a defense mechanism. *Reaction formation*, outwardly transforming a belief or inclination into its opposite, helps him avoid judging himself by his own standards. In other words, Dent at heart still believes himself responsible for his actions, accountability he prefers not to think about, so he lets a coin toss excuse his actions. He generally does not care which evil things he does as long as he gets to do some. When he tries to force others to see the randomness of life, he is trying to convince himself.

Although writers sometimes refer to Two-Face as having "multiple personalities,"[6] depictions of him rarely meet any diagnostic criteria for what is now called dissociative identity disorder (DID; see Case Study 2–1: King Tut). With DID, good Harvey would take control for periods of time, and his bad side would take its turn, with at least one identity unable to recall things that happened when the other took over, but no, both sides consistently stay with him. Exceptions in the literature do appear. More than a year after plastic surgery repairs his face, a year when he fights crime rather than committing it, an overstressed Dent hears his dark side telling him to let it out to play until he scars himself deliberately to become Two-Face once more.[7] While some DID patients report hearing their *alter* personalities, their other selves, that is not an essential feature for a DID diagnosis. The first story to present Harvey Dent and Two-Face as separate entities taking distinct turns controlling one body was "The Great Leap," in which Harvey Dent asks Nightwing to protect a woman from a mob killer who later turns out to be Two-Face.[8]

Could Two-Face's dual nature have evolved into DID over time? That's hard to say. After all these years, we barely understand multiple personality. Dissociative experience is so subjective that professionals cannot even agree on whether it exists. As mentioned when we looked at the Persona archetype, we all have variable personality states. If your Sunday morning self suppresses thoughts about your Saturday night self's actions, there's nothing to stop you from slapping a name on your Saturday side. I sometimes demonstrate this by asking a student volunteer questions in front of a class. When I ask to speak to that student's angry self, the person frowns, neck stiffens, and tone toughens up. When I request the student's five-year-old self, the eyebrows lift, head bobs, and tone becomes childlike. Everyone does that—under no hypnosis and with no preparation. When I ask for the angry or child self's real name, half the volunteers will offer a new name. Now imagine doing this in a therapeutic situation, especially while hypnotized. If Dent deals with Arkham Asylum therapists who believe he has DID, their therapeutic techniques may train him to emphasize division between his halves. When therapy causes or exacerbates mental illness, we refer to that process as *iatrogenesis.*[9]

Harvey Dent seeks excuses. Attributing his misdoings to another self could absolve good Harvey even further than leaving decisions to his deliberate coin toss. After all these years, Harvey may be trying to convince himself he has multiple personality.

10

The Kids

Why Robin?

"Young men with a mind for revenge don't need encouragement. They need guidance."

—Alfred (Michael Gough), *Batman Forever*
(1995)

 **W**hy does Batman work with a partner—and why is his crime-fighting partner a kid? Batman never sets out to recruit any partner. The partners each want to work with him. Each has been a youngster who already possesses the skills to combat or commit crimes, along with a personal grievance against evildoers. Each Robin picks Batman, not the other way around, with one notable exception that Batman would come to consider his greatest failure.

Robin Begins

"I had always thought Robin was a real pain-in-the-ass, but I now realize what a brilliant creation it was, because it really does give a human context to Batman's character."
—Frank Miller on including a Robin in the apocryphal
The Dark Knight Returns (*Comics Interview*, 1986)

The question of "Why Robin?" is at least as important outside the fiction as within it. Why did the grown men writing those early comic books add a child to the stories and why did readers accept the addition? A character's *narrative function*, its storytelling purpose, *is* a psychological function. Not only does the act of telling stories have both therapeutic[1] and harmful[2] potential for both storyteller and audience depending on the circumstances and nature of the story told, but the storyteller crafts the stories and characters to suit the audience's psychological processes, including motivations, emotions, and cognitive abilities.[3] Narrative intent and success depend on the storyteller's *theory of mind*, his or her personal theory regarding other people's mental activity. Your personal theory of mind involves attributing mental states, including thoughts, feelings, motives, knowledge, and perception, to oneself, others, and even fictional characters.[4] Creating a fictional character (therefore constructing an imaginary psyche) and crafting a story to evoke specific reactions from living, nonfictional readers will depend— whether intuitively or intentionally—on your *metacognition*, what you know and think about how cognitive processes like knowing and thinking work.[5]

The original answer to "Why Robin?" is that Bill Finger quickly tired of writing Batman's thought balloons. He wanted Batman to talk. Whenever he works alone, Batman is silent and more violent. Short on candid interactions with others, he can seem as distant to readers as he does to the criminals he intimidates. The alternative, revealing all his thoughts and feelings through thought balloons, can expose the mystery man too much. A partner provides the balance to reveal his nature as needed while still maintaining his mystique. Finger recounted, "Robin was an outgrowth of a conversation I had with Bob. As I said, Batman was a combination of Fairbanks and Sherlock Holmes. Holmes had his Watson. The thing that bothered me was that Batman didn't have anyone to talk to, and it got a little tiresome always having him thinking. I found as I went along, Batman needed a Watson to talk to."[6]

Bob Kane thought the partner should be a boy to whom their readers could relate. Finger agreed. *Identification*, connecting one's own identity to someone else's by perceiving shared characteristics, makes us feel bonded to others—even those we don't personally know, including celebrities and fictional characters.[7] With that goal in mind, artist Jerry Robinson (who helped Kane design the partner's costume) suggested they name the boy after Robin Hood so that readers would associate this new character with both a popular hero and real boys.[8] "Robin was more human," Robinson recalled, "a real boy's name, rather than one that implied some powers."[9] So in April 1940, Batman's twelfth month of publication, he became a surrogate papa.

Dick Grayson

In *Detective Comics* #38, to intimidate a circus owner into paying protection money, gangsters tamper with trapeze ropes so they'll break during acrobats John and Mary Grayson's "death-defying" triple spin. The Flying Graysons plunge to their deaths before the collective eyes of their son, Dick, and that night's entire audience, which happens to include Bruce Wayne. When Dick wants to go to the police with what he knows about the gangsters, Batman warns him that a mobster called Boss Zucco runs the town. "If you told what you knew, you'd be dead in an hour." Batman plans to hide the boy, but then he thinks back to his own origin.

> Batman: My parents too were killed by a criminal. That's why I've devoted my life to exterminate them.
> Dick: Then I want to also! Take me with you—please!
> Narrative: The Batman is reluctant but the troubled face of the boy moves him deeply.
> Batman: Well, I guess you and I were both victims of a similar trouble. All right. I'll make you my aid [*sic*]. But I warn you, I lead a perilous life!
> Dick: I'm not afraid.[10]

In an image reminiscent of one readers saw when they learned Batman's origin just five months earlier, the new boy swears an oath to "fight against crime and corruption and never to swerve from the path of righteousness!" Training progresses quickly for the boy, who has been doing acrobatics since he was four years old, with Bruce acknowledging that Dick "could probably teach me a thing or two," and soon they take Boss Zucco to jail. The Graysons swiftly receive the justice that the Waynes never got. Their son will not grow up forever aching to avenge them. In fact, he cheerfully ends his first adventure by declaring, "I can hardly wait till we go on our next case. I bet it'll be a corker!"

Where the pulps that originally shaped Batman's stories had been "grim, lacking in humor," Finger noted that Robin, with his ebullient smile and bright red, yellow, and green costume, altered the comic's look and mood. "The dialogue was easy, fluid, and flowing. It brightened up the strip and added characterization to the main figure of Batman."[11] Kane had not intended to change the tone of the book, nor had they introduced Robin in order to humanize Batman. Rather, these consequences evolved naturally.

Sales double, Batman starts smiling, and oh, the sidekicks! Apprentice crime-fighters pop up all over the place. Captain America gets Bucky fighting Nazis by his side; the Human Torch finds Toro; Sandman, Sandy; Green Arrow, Speedy; Mr. Scarlet, Pinky; Aquaman, Aqualad; and so on. Superheroes get busy endangering children left and right. The most successful of these spunky orphan characters have adventures apart from their mentors. Robin enjoys many solo adventures[12] and the competition's Bucky and Toro lead the Young Allies.[13] Whether in *The Adventures of Tom Sawyer*, *The Goonies*, *Spy Kids*, *Our Gang* shorts, or a whole host of modern YA fiction, we more readily suspend disbelief and accept fictional youngsters having adventures when the kids venture off on their own. Adults get in the way, for both readers and young protagonists. This would become increasingly important over the upcoming decades as comic book readership grew older.

Through the 1950s, the sidekicks appear less frequently, whether because superhero comics in general had lost some of their popularity or because psychiatrist Fredric Wertham's 1954 book *Seduction of the Innocent* with its insinuations about Batman and Robin's lifestyle raised questions of pedophilia in readers' minds regarding all these superheroes and their young wards (see Case File 10–2: Dr. Fredric

Wertham). The major comic book companies start separating the sidekicks from their mentors. In the 1960s, Marvel Comics kills off Bucky[14] and Toro[15] while DC emancipates its minors and makes them start growing up. Robin the Boy Wonder becomes the Teen Wonder, leading the Teen Titans as a whole team of sidekicks operating independently of their mentors.[16] These kids age. The Titans "seemed to be about thirteen years old when they formed their superteam in 1965, and by 1970 they seem to be about eighteen—they interacted with college kids as equals—a match of narrative and chronological time."[17] Through the 1960s, in an era of disillusionment, time progresses for characters at both DC and Marvel. In a climate of American assassinations and conflict in Vietnam, the superchildren grow up with the audience.

The readership's average age kept going up and comics matured with them. The "rather illogical tradition of adult superheroes taking on teenage sidekicks, often with no powers, in the dangerous fight against the very powerful forces of evil"[18] grew harder to accept. Illogical circumstances unquestioned by preschool children in the *preoperational stage* of cognitive development, those too young to consider others' viewpoints and perform more logical mental operations, wouldn't cut it, and even the simple logic and deduction accepted by elementary school–age children in the *concrete operational stage* grew shaky. An aging audience meant that in addition to wanting more mature subject matter and more sophisticated storytelling, adolescent and older readers utilizing the systematic reasoning of the *formal operational stage*[19] might reevaluate previously accepted story elements and decide, "That's just stupid." With the newness of formal operations upon them and without the perspective of more years, adolescents can have difficulty looking past a "stupid" obstacle.

In 1969, with the campy *Batman* TV series now canceled, writer Dennis O'Neil and artist Neal Adams brought the comic book Batman back to his darker roots. DC ships Dick Grayson off to college.[20] Robin continues to fight crime but on his own, with Batgirl, or as the Teen Titans' leader into the 1980s until the young man walks away from his Robin identity,[21] taking on a new masked persona to operate under the name Nightwing.[22] During those Teen Wonder years, while Batman often operates on his own in the pages of *Batman* and *Detective Comics*, Alfred grows in importance and evolves, in the Batcave and at Bruce's home, into Batman's Watson even though he doesn't go out prowling the night by Batman's side and trade quips in combat. Denny and other writers had to write a lot of thought bubbles. Readers got to enjoy more interactive dialogue over in Batman's team-up series *The Brave and the Bold* until it ended in 1983, the year for big changes in the Bat-titles.

As Nightwing, Dick Grayson is a strong and popular character, fighting crime without the burden of Batman's darkness—in many ways, Bruce Wayne's hopes fulfilled.

Jason Todd #1

With *The Brave and the Bold* team-ups having ended and Dick Grayson having outgrown his sidekick role, the narrative needs that had inspired Robin's original creation resurfaced and "the disadvantages of having Batman operate without a sidekick to talk to became apparent again."[23] Enter Jason Todd.[24] Mandated by DC executives to make the new kid "a carbon copy of Dick Grayson,"[25] writer Gerry Conway and artist Don Newton introduced Jason as yet another boy whose acrobat parents get killed by criminals. Through his circus connections, Dick—not Bruce—first meets Jason and his parents before the deaths. The first Batman ever sees of this new kid is when a grieving Jason in Robin-like costume jumps out to attack his parents' killer. Batman "experiences a surge of déjà vu: The caped figure crashing into the unconscious Killer Croc could be another boy, from long ago—"[26] Where Dick reminded Batman of young Bruce Wayne, Jason reminds Batman of young Dick Grayson.

That was Jason version #1, commonly known as "pre-Crisis Jason Todd." Associating this character so strongly with Dick Grayson for the readers by making Jason identify with Dick within the fiction allowed for a relatively smooth transition from the first Robin to the second—too smooth for dramatic purposes, some of the storytellers came to decide.

Seeing the second Robin for the first time strikes Batman at his core. © DC Comics.

Replacement Robin Rebooted: Jason Todd #2

1986 changed DC superheroes. *Crisis on Infinite Earths* collapsed DC's rich Multiverse, all of its parallel universes and alternate futures, into a single universe, one merged timeline with new character histories. Outside that new universe's official canon, DC published arguably the most influential deconstructions of superheroes with *Watchmen*, which explored how brutal and unpleasant superheroes' lives would be in general, and *The Dark Knight Returns*, a "possible future" tale that changed how readers looked at Batman in particular. These gritty alternate reality tales' respective authors, Alan Moore and Frank Miller, each decried one repercussion of their own work: Darkness spread through superhero comics.[27] Satire shaped the source.

It was in this climate that *The Road to Perdition* author Max Allan Collins wrote Jason Todd's post-Crisis origin.[28] Out went the happy-go-lucky circus kid. In his place, this new history delivers a cigarette-smoking street urchin in the process of boosting the Batmobile's tires the first time Batman meets him.

Readers disliked this new Jason Todd. Dick Grayson pre-Crisis chooses his own time to give up the mantle of Robin and take on a more mature role. He passes the Robin torch to his successor by introducing Jason #1 into Batman's life and, when the time comes for Jason to take over as Batman's official partner, gives Jason a Robin costume and encourages him to assume the name.[29] Post-Crisis, Batman unceremoniously fires an injured Dick Grayson and forbids him from using the Robin name. Readers considered this new version of the story and Jason Todd's nature to be an insult to Dick Grayson in every way. No longer identified with the first Robin as his anointed successor, this second Robin instead becomes his usurper. Discovering the readers' dislike of new Jason, the writers played to it, making Jason progressively brattier over the next year.

Readers voted to kill Jason Todd.[30] Although a slight majority of individual respondents apparently voted to spare this Boy Wonder, it seems that some enthusiastic voters—whether driven by sheer hatred of the character or by the feeling of power over determining the outcome—repeatedly voted, "Off with his head."[31] Maintaining someone else's status quo might not foster a feeling of power the way forcing a change can.[32] People like to see that they matter, that they exert real influence on the world outside themselves—those high in need for power (NPow) especially so[33] (see Case File 6–1: Bane). The second issue in DC Comics' *Batman* story "A Death in the Family" ended with Jason possibly dying in an explosion. A vote via 900 numbers determined the outcome, and two weeks later, the world learned Robin was dead. Much of the public, generally unaware that the comics had a new Robin, thought the original had died. Numerous news reports and even the documentary *Batmania: From Comics to Screen* erroneously reported Dick Grayson dead. Bob Kane hated the stunt. *The Dark Knight Returns* author Frank Miller expressed utter disgust: "An actual toll-free number where fans can call in to put the axe to a little boy's head. . . . To me, the whole killing of Robin thing was probably the ugliest thing I've seen in comics, and the most cynical."[34]

More than 16 years after Jason's published death, he would return from the dead as an antihero and enemy (see Case File 10–1: Red Hood).

Tim Drake

In light of Jason Todd's reader-dictated demise, writer Marv Wolfman returned to elements that had worked when Gerry Conway introduced the original Jason: He went to the circus. Preschooler Tim Drake witnesses the Flying Graysons' deaths, an event that gives him nightmares for years. Upon later realizing that Dick Grayson has become Robin, Tim deduces Batman's identity and extrapolates from there. Years pass. Jason Todd dies. Batman fights on without Robin but is now harder, more violent, wearier, and less careful, injuring himself more frequently than before. Thirteen-year-old Tim tries to convince Dick Grayson that Batman needs Grayson to become Robin again, but instead himself becomes the third Robin. The first time Bruce meets Tim, as had also been the case with Jason #1, Tim's in a Robin costume.[35]

Like Barbara Gordon, the original Batgirl, Tim initially dons cape and mask not because of any personal tragedy, not out of any need for vengeance, but because he has skills and putting them to use helping others seems like the right thing to do. Tim wants to become the world's greatest detective. For Tim and Barbara, crime-fighting starts out as a form of *altruism*, unselfishly helping others despite risk and cost to oneself. Tim is smart and friendly, a good partner who takes orders well, a strong leader for the new class of Teen Titans, and in the real world a popular character. "Dick Grayson was always so perfect in every way," said comic book writer Chuck Dixon, "and of course Jason Todd was too imperfect. Tim Drake is sort of in the middle. I feel like he's a real teenager."[36]

Figures in Tim's life keep dying[37] because that's how superhero comic books work (with some coming back from the dead because that's also how comic books work).[38] Instead of playing Robin at Dick Grayson's side while others believe Bruce is dead, Tim takes the name Red Robin and quests for proof that Bruce lives,[39] and then continues under the new name following his adoptive father's return. After Tim, there would be no more trips to the circus to shop for new sidekicks. Future Robins would, like Jason #2, come from the children of criminals.

Stephanie Brown

The daughter of a lesser known Bat-foe called the Cluemaster, high-schooler Stephanie Brown dons a purple costume as the Spoiler to "spoil" her father's crimes.[40] With some training from Batman, she continues fighting evil. Tim Drake becomes her sometimes-boyfriend before she finds herself pregnant from a prior relationship.[41] The ex-boyfriend having left Gotham after a cataclysmic earthquake wrecked the city, Stephanie goes ahead with the pregnancy without him. Tim helps, providing support and coaching her in Lamaze classes. In the end, she gives the child up for adoption.[42] Through Stephanie, the *Robin* series addressed teenage pregnancy and adoption sensitively and somewhat realistically while also stirring controversy for covering them at all. That controversy, however, paled in comparison to the maelstrom over Stephanie's death.

When Tim Drake's father orders him to quit being Robin, Stephanie insists on taking up the Robin mantle. Though wary, having previously deemed her too reckless and unskilled to fight crime, Batman briefly makes her his first Girl Wonder, only to fire her for disobeying him in two missions.[43] Unlike the Boys Wonder, all created to suit that narrative need for Batman to have a partner he can talk to, Stephanie became Robin to serve a different storytelling function: to give her upcoming death more impact. Having already decided to kill her off soon, the creative team first made her a Robin for three issues.[44] In the chaos of a citywide gang war, the Black Mask tortures Stephanie, trying to extract information about Batman, but she escapes. Before succumbing to those injuries, Stephanie in her hospital bed asks Bruce, "Was I ever really Robin?" Despite having evaded Alfred's accusation that he'd let her play Robin only as a ruse to manipulate Tim Drake, Batman assures her, "Of course you were," and soon she dies.[45]

Ah, but Stephanie's wounds had not been severe enough to kill her, after all! When Batman tries to determine why Stephanie died, Bruce Wayne's maternal figure Dr. Leslie Thompkins claims to have killed the girl by purposely withholding medical treatment that would have kept her alive, sacrificing Stephanie's life supposedly to teach Batman to stop involving children in his war on crime.[46] Fans howled because murder was wholly out of character for benevolent-as-Mother-Teresa, loving humanitarian Leslie Thompkins. By establishing that Stephanie should have survived, though, that story inadvertently set things up for her return under another writer. Chuck Dixon brought Stephanie back by staying true to the characters' personalities: As it turns out, Leslie has actually made a supreme act of altruism by giving up her medical practice, her reputation, her worldly possessions, and the life she had in Gotham in order to fake Stephanie's death and help the girl escape the chaos. Leslie heads to Africa, where she and Stephanie help the needy.[47] Only after Stephanie returns to fight Gotham's crime again does Leslie come home.

Why would a criminal's child become a crime-fighter in the first place?

At its most basic, Stephanie does so as her own *teenage rebellion*: She fights crime to fight her father. Teens rebel for many reasons, not the least of which is to say, "I'm not you." *Individuality* consists of two dimensions: *self-assertion*, the ability to have and express a point of view; and *separateness*, perception and expression of how that person is different from others.[48] Even as the maturing adolescent needs individuality, he or she still needs to feel connected to others. By assuming her Spoiler identity, Stephanie names herself for her efforts to spoil the Cluemaster's crimes, conveying both distinctiveness from and yet connectedness to her criminal father. She becomes Spoiler out of anger. Between his long incarcerations and time spent planning and committing robberies, his Cluemaster activities have directly kept him from being there for her as a father. Where other youths might commit crimes as their way of *acting out*, Stephanie acts out by stopping them. Along the way, though, she discovers that she enjoys being a hero, and heroism becomes part of her blooming personality. Of course, she's also defying her other parent by running off on these adventures without her mother's knowledge, much less her permission.* Some might consider Stephanie's early sexual activity and resultant pregnancy[49] to be a form of acting out too. Teens whose fathers have been absent exhibit higher pregnancy rates.[50] Even though Stephanie becomes Batgirl instead of Spoiler for a while, her final act as Batgirl before Barbara Gordon

---

*"Really, whose mother would allow her child to be Batman or Robin, anyway?"— Danny Fingeroth, *Superman on the Couch* (2004), 67.

resumes the role[51] is to spoil her father's criminal activity one more time.[52]

Damian Wayne

Ra's al Ghul marries the Caped Crusader to al Ghul's daughter Talia al Ghul—without our hero's consent but within the law of that unnamed land.[53] The graphic novel *Son of the Demon* left readers fascinated by the possibility that somewhere out in the world, Bruce might have a son from that marriage. In that story, his pregnant bride Talia grows to fear that Batman's overprotective manner makes him vulnerable and will surely get him killed, so she tells him she has miscarried, they agree to end the marriage, and he goes home. Later, however, she gives birth to their son, whom she gives up for adoption.

In 2006, author Grant Morrison reintroduced the child as an eight-year-old boy, Damian. Talia presents Damian to Bruce to distract Batman from interfering with a kidnapping plot she has in the works.[54] Damian has spent his short life alternately spoiled like a young prince and rigidly disciplined by assassins training him. Whether Bruce really is the father and, for that matter, whether Talia really is the mother goes unconfirmed. For all we readers know, Damian is really her nephew or little brother. Her own father Ra's might not know the truth. Bruce tells Tim he knows Damian's parentage and yet does not tell Tim what that means. "Tim, I know the kid's very tough to be around," Bruce explains. "He was raised by international terrorists in his grandfather's League of Assassins. Brutalized, indoctrinated, then used as a weapon in his mother's insane war on me. If he is my son—even if he is not—he deserves some love and respect."[55]

Damian is a deadly little boy. He kills—in fact, beheads—a criminal called the Spook and nearly kills Tim because that's how they did things in the League of Assassins. Damian tells Tim that "we showed our enemies no mercy. Now that I'm here, he doesn't need a surrogate. We killed anyone who got in our way." More than any other Robin, Damian is too dangerous to leave unguided. During a period when people think Bruce is dead, Dick becomes Batman, 10-year-old

Damian becomes Robin, and roles get reversed, with a more upbeat Batman leading a dark little Robin. Loath as Damian is to admit any weakness, he pines for his father's attention. When Bruce at last returns to Gotham, the time comes for Batman and son to fight crime together, with Batman in the position of needing to temper both himself and this newest Robin.[56]

Crime-Fighting Value

A superhero could use a partner for the same reasons a police officer does. The partner has your back. Working with a partner, you can watch multiple exits, improve the odds against multiple foes or out-number a criminal who works alone, and be in more than one location at the same time. One can aid the other as a lookout or scout. The senior partner learns by teaching, reinforcing his own strengths and maybe coming to understand his abilities better through the process of articulating them to someone else. The junior partner provides different knowledge, additional skills, an alternate point of view, a sounding board to help the senior think, and someone to complete the job's more menial duties. Having an apprentice benefits the mas-ter, as it has throughout the ages. The child sidekick could fit through smaller spaces, infiltrate groups a grown man could not, and play roles like the newsboy hawking papers right under hoodlums' noses. With a child, the duo's division of authority and responsibilities is clear.

The young partner offers the promise that the hero might create a long-term crime-fighting legacy. The master initiates the apprentice into the trade. Cusp-of-adolescence initiation rites promote *identity foreclosure*, forming a lifetime commitment before one is old enough to analyze the choice. The apprentice will carry on the work with the expectation that one day the apprentice will succeed the master.

Personal Value

Working with others can make Batman more cautious, more conscious of the big picture and what's going on outside his personal space. It keeps him sharp because he has someone else to watch out for and to fit into that big picture. Batman gets injured less often when he has a Robin. For a hero who expects never to settle down and raise a family, taking on a sidekick helps fulfill any paternal needs he might nevertheless feel.

Pederasty?

Despite Fredric Wertham's serious assertion that Batman and Robin's lifestyle is a homosexual fantasy and popular (usually not serious) speculations about homosexual or pedophilic subtext, the creators intended nothing of the sort. Kane considered Wertham perverted for even thinking such a thing (see Case File 10–2: Dr. Fredric Wertham).

Wish Fulfillment

Vicariously Batman can experience wish fulfillment by letting the boy experience things Bruce had only wished for, starting with closure. He helps the boy get the justice young Bruce didn't. In their first adventure, the original Dynamic Duo take down the gangster who had Dick's parents killed. Beyond that, Batman gives each Robin the mentor he himself didn't have and a father figure who's not on the payroll. With them all, he endeavors to provide mentorship of a kind Alfred couldn't give and let them enjoy their youth more than he ever did.

Identification

Robins look like Bruce. Specifically, they look like young, newly orphaned Bruce Wayne.*

Identification reminds Bruce why he does this: to keep others from suffering what he once suffered. He goes out to serve the kid he once was. Identification provides a connection to his inner

---

*The obvious exception, Stephanie, is Robin only briefly before Batman fires her. She didn't fit.

child—before his parents died, when they died, and afterward. When Tim Drake first shows up at Wayne Manor, trying to convince Dick to become Robin again, Tim says, "Dick, don't you see—he needs Robin. He needs him to remember what he used to be. Before his parents died."

The first time Batman meets Richard Grayson and the boy wants to join him in fighting crime, Batman "thinks back to the time when his parents, too, were innocent victims of a criminal." His identification with this boy gives him a connection to the murders themselves. He relies on reminders like that. Dick reminds Bruce of his own eight-year-old self, whereas the other Robins often remind Bruce of Dick Grayson. Dick, as the oldest son, doesn't have to live up to anyone else's example. The younger brothers all feel like they're expected to live up to his.

Growing Up Robin

Birth Order

One of psychotherapist Alfred Adler's enduring contributions to psychology is the notion that order of birth exerts powerful influence over social and personality development. Although empirical research varies in the degree to which it supports Adler's specific details, he nevertheless understood birth order enough that he could regularly amaze party guests by guessing their birth order based on their behavior. Birth order, while not mandating one's entire identity, exerts some influence.[57] To what degree it shapes personality, psychologists endlessly debate.[58]

Every Robin lives his or her earliest years, like Bruce himself, as an only child with no siblings. An *only child*, spending more time in the company of adults than would a kid with siblings, often matures earlier and manifests more adult attitudes and actions, except that the only child doesn't learn as well to share or compete. Accustomed to being the center of parental attention, depending on the quality and quantity of that attention, only children may find themselves disappointed in areas of life outside the home unless their skills happen to be particularly outstanding.

A *first-born child* faces *dethronement*, the loss of that special position from having been the only child. Parental attention and affection now get divided. Age diminishes this effect. The older the first-born is when the second comes along, the less he or she feels dethroned. A wide gap in age lets the first-born retain the sense of being the number-one child. Dick Grayson is grown before any other Robins come along. In fact, it is he who originally introduces both Jason Todd (pre-Crisis) and Tim Drake as his successors. Every Robin experiences dethronement by merit of having been the birth family's only child who becomes instead part of the Bat-Family, in which only Dick gets to be the first-born.

The *second-born child* whose arrival caused such upheaval for the first-born always has that first-born as an example to follow or fight. Seeing the older sibling as a role model, as competition, or even as a threat tends to make the second-born the most competitive child in the family, trying to avoid feeling eclipsed by the elder. This need to compete can be crushed, however, by an older sibling who excels even compared to peers. Jason Todd, the second-born Robin, feels daunted by Dick Grayson's stellar example. When Jason's murder goes unavenged, he has to wonder (after his resurrection, of course) if Bruce would have avenged Dick. Jason doesn't give Tim Drake much thought. He gives Dick plenty.

Even researchers who consider birth order important recognize that birth order effects become harder to predict as the family continues to grow. Dynamics within the family become more and more complicated. When Jason returns to Gotham, he discovers he has been replaced by Tim, effectively making Jason the middle son. The *middle-born* child who lacks "special" status as either the eldest or the youngest can feel like "the neglected birth order."[59] While Jason carves out his new niche as the black sheep of the family, he nevertheless shows characteristics some researchers have observed among the middle-born: more jealousy, less healthy self-esteem, less inclination to help family, and less affiliation with family in general.[60] With violent antihero Jason estranged from Batman, Tim becomes the middle son (among those still welcome in the Batcave) once Damian enters the picture, and as soon as Dick and Damian start spending time together, Tim becomes Red Robin and strikes off on his own.

The youngest or *last-born child* may be more mature than peers because of time spent with older siblings and their friends or less mature if babied by the family. No one gets pampered in the Bat-Family. Tim Drake briefly loses his position as the youngest child during Stephanie Brown's short stint as Robin and permanently when Damian arrives, compounding the difficulties an adoptive child faces when a child who is blood kin comes along. Even before Damian becomes a Robin, his apparent status as Bruce's biological son changes Tim's status. Damian, who wants to be seen as the only child, feels insecure about that, resents the others, and doesn't want to share with them. Tim, as the non-biological son, may feel usurped by this newcomer. When an older child is adoptive, the younger one often feels he or she should be seen as the most worthy, even teasing the elder with "I'm their real child, not you" to compensate for feelings that the adoptive child has been chosen, directly selected based on his or her own circumstances and qualities to become that parent's child, whereas the biological child has not. When Tim asks why Damian acts like "such a jerk," the boy tells him, "Because you don't deserve any of this. You're adopted! But when you're gone, I'll take my rightful place at my father's side—as Batman's son! I'll inherit everything." Throughout history, many later-born princes have seen older brothers as obstacles to the throne.

Dick, in accepting Jason and then Tim, shows little sign of feeling dethroned. He has already relinquished the Robin role and moved into his adult life before the little brothers start showing up. When he, Bruce's first adoptive son, becomes Batman in Bruce's absence, though, he shows some signs of dethronement around Damian, allegedly Bruce's first biological heir. Repeatedly calling the boy a "brat" to his face, Dick regresses a bit, acting less like a mature father figure and more like a teenage son who resents having to babysit a little stepbrother.

Psychosocial Stages

Batman as we know him skips the steps of growing up. He's a child whose parents die and then he's a crime-fighting hero, with scant attention to the years in between. While this suits Sigmund Freud's view that personality takes shape early in childhood, psychodynamic contemplation of the lives of Batman's sidekicks could benefit from Erik Erikson's more elaborate stage theory. Freud said little about adolescence. Mentored by Sigmund's daughter Anna Freud, who pioneered *adolescent psychology* as a distinct area of study, Erikson continued to call himself a loyal Freudian[61] even as his ideas departed substantially from Freud's psychoanalytic foundations. Sigmund Freud and Bruce Wayne, like other mentors and father figures throughout the ages, each watch their students take the lessons they've learned and build them into something new.

Instead of seeing sex drive as the impetus behind personality development, Erikson felt that interactions with our fellow human beings shape us more than anything else—hence his theory of *psychosocial stages of development* as opposed to Freud's psychosexual stages. He also didn't believe personality is mostly fixed by age six. The middle childhood and adolescent stages showed more active personality development than Freud had observed, and Erikson added adult stages as well. More optimistic than Freud, Erikson believed our personalities grow and change throughout our whole lives (see tables 10.1, 10.2, and 12.1).

Before Bruce loses his parents and before any of the Robins meet him, they've each completed the earliest psychosocial stages and have developed important aspects of their respective personalities. Early in life, Bruce and Tim learn to trust their parents. Dick, who spends

TABLE 10.1. ERIKSON'S STAGES OF PSYCHOSOCIAL DEVELOPMENT PART 1: EARLY CHILDHOOD—BEFORE THE BAT-FAMILY MISSION

Ages	Stage	Basic Strengths	Maldevelopments
0–18 months	Trust vs. Mistrust	Hope	Withdrawal
18 months to 3 years	Autonomy vs. Shame and Doubt	Will	Compulsion Shameless willfulness
3–6 years	Initiative vs. Guilt	Purpose	Ruthlessness, Inhibition
(continued in table 10.2)			

even more time with his parents, is more optimistic, hopeful, and trusting. Whereas newly orphaned Bruce is wary of adults who take an interest in him and his inheritance, Dick is immediately ready to trust police and a masked stranger who dresses like Dracula. Even though Stephanie and Jason have learned that people like their loving* but criminal fathers will let them down, the mothers who've raised them demonstrated that reliable people do exist and people can make themselves overcome their own failings (as when Stephanie's mother overcomes drug addiction), and so they both have hope, even if Jason's takes a dangerous turn. Least trusting of them all is Damian, the one raised by servants and assassins, and yet even that cynical child still hopes others will prove themselves worthy. According to Erikson, they would have all developed these various and sometimes conflicting tendencies during the first year and a half of life, in the *Trust vs. Mistrust* stage, depending on how consistently their primary caregivers met the infants' physical, emotional, and social needs.

A favorable outcome in one stage gives the individual abilities and characteristics that raise the odds of achieving favorable outcomes in subsequent stages as well. Toddlerhood carries the individual through the *Autonomy vs. Shame and Doubt* stage, when the child learns to feel good and secure about doing things on his or her own (autonomously) or learns to feel unsure about acting independently, whether feeling shame (self-conscious about doing something bad) or doubt (uncertainty about one's own ability to function independently). The struggle to develop autonomy can result in a weak will overburdened by shame, a strong but healthy will, or shameless willfulness as the insecure person tries too hard to assert independence. The extreme defiance individuals can show during adolescence grows from roots planted back during the "terrible twos." The Batcave reeks of strong wills. Every Robin defies Batman at times, but usually within the range of healthy self-assertion because sometimes their grim mentor needs people to

---

*The Cluemaster, for example, returns to Gotham City meaning to avenge his daughter's supposed death and later covers his prison cell's wall with photos of her in action as Batgirl (*Batgirl* #24, 2011).

stand up to him. Insecure Jason's unresolved grief over his parents leads him to become progressively defiant and distant, mistaking distance for autonomy, whereas a secure person can feel independent without cutting others off. Damian is willful all along, and yet bows in shame when Bruce chastises him, "You dishonor your sensei with your loss of composure!"[62] Stephanie, despite carrying some self-doubt and constructing her original Spoiler identity to radiate her separateness from her father instead of ignoring him, possesses enough healthy autonomous qualities to help her mature into a young woman capable of operating independently and working with others, even Damian.[63]

In the *Initiative vs. Guilt* stage of the later preschool years, roughly ages three to six, the child develops a greater sense of purpose, learning to think ahead and undertake new tasks even if the child's approach is not yet logical. Guilt, a new emotion, creeps in as the child becomes increasingly conscious of moral concerns. Bruce's decision to become Batman shows great initiative, as does Stephanie's to become Spoiler. Not satisfied with reading about Batman on the news after Jason dies, Tim Drake takes it upon himself to head for Wayne Manor and try to re-create a Dynamic Duo. Batman and all Robins show great initiative in taking on challenges, forming plans, and developing strategies. They all show hero initiative. While they also show varying capacities for guilt, they'll let it inspire them instead of holding them back.

TABLE 10.2. ERIKSON'S STAGES OF PSYCHOSOCIAL DEVELOPMENT PART 2: LATER CHILDHOOD AND ADOLESCENCE—THE BOY/GIRL/ TEEN WONDER YEARS

Ages	Stage	Basic Strengths	Maldevelopments
about 6 to puberty	Industry (Industriousness) vs. Inferiority	Competence	Inertia
puberty to 18ish	Identity Achievement vs. Role Confusion	Fidelity Devotion to friends or causes	Fanaticism Repudiation by indifference, defiance

For adult stages, see table 12.1 in chapter 12.

Dick and Damian first meet Batman when each boy is about the same age Bruce was when he lost his parents. Dick trains for months and Damian has two years of additional experiences before becoming Robin, but each is well within the *Industry vs. Inferiority* stage when he officially becomes Batman's sidekick. During this time, interpersonal awareness, deductive reasoning, and ability to play by rules can flourish. Parents, instructors, and in this case mentors determine how well the children perceive their own growth. When Dick's training begins, Bruce praises the boy's acrobat skill, telling Dick, "You could probably teach me a thing or two!"[64] The first time Bruce sees Damian perform as Robin, he assures this boy who so clearly aches for parental attention and approval, "You made the right choices. I'm proud of you."[65] Even Dick, however much Damian's arrogance might annoy him, doles out positive reinforcement for his sidekick's more astute deductions and better decisions.

Entering the caped crusade at such a young age, each has constructed his own sense of competence around his related interests, talents, and skills. Although he could later redefine himself during the identity crisis of adolescence, for him to do so entirely would mean abandoning the foundation for his personal sense of self-efficacy. A young Tiger Woods could have decided, "I'm going to give up this golf game I'm so good at," but not easily.

Of the various Robins, fear of feeling inferior may exert its greatest influence on Damian, however superficially ironic that may seem. In Dick's case, he'd had no previous Robin to whom he could compare himself. Damian is the first since Dick to become Robin this early in life. Damian's often arrogant manner suggests that he has been taught that he's supposed to feel superior without receiving guidance regarding the healthier aspects of self-esteem.

Jason, Tim, and Stephanie are all adolescents early in Erikson's *Identity Achievement vs. Role Confusion* stage when they start fighting crime. Having already developed their overall sense of competence and industry, they are now trying to figure out who they are as individual human beings. During this time, the youth forms his or her self-image, integrating ideas about self and what others think of them, with expanding awareness of his or her place in the world. Shaping identity is difficult, complicated, and sometimes stressful beyond explanation. Those who emerge from this stage form a strong sense of identity, though continuing to grow and add to that identity, and are better equipped to face adulthood with confidence and security. Dick and Tim, having enjoyed the most support and healthiest development all along the way, are the Robins who can most easily become stable adults. Peers play a critical role in shaping personality and helping adolescents define themselves. Aside from whatever high school experiences they live through in their civilian identities, Dick and Tim each enjoy the support of crime-fighting peers, the Teen Titans.

> Dick (to Batman): Unlike the JLA, the Titans aren't just about a promise to the world—it's also about a promise to each other—to ourselves. We swore on our childhood nightmares that we'd be there for one another. If I don't honor that, I don't honor who I am.[66]

Individuals failing to achieve cohesive sense of self, those who continue to struggle with Erikson's *identity crisis** or who have given up on figuring themselves out, show great confusion over their roles in life. That would be Jason Todd. Dying keeps him from growing up. Time in a grave, in a coma, and then brain-damaged before the Lazarus Pit heals him mean he has missed out on his high school years. Physically he may be grown but emotionally he's barely any older than he was when the Joker first killed him.

What Lies Ahead for the Robins?

Growing into two capable youths, each with a strong sense of self, Stephanie and Tim should have many of the qualities that would help them fare well if they ever get to enter the next psychosocial stage, *Intimacy vs. Isolation*, when those in their twenties and thirties either become increasingly capable of experiencing interpersonal intimacy with others or become psychologically isolated, cut off emotionally, and unable to open up. Aside from the sheer difficulty any superhero

---

*Best-selling author Brad Meltzer's limited series *Identity Crisis* happens to be the story that kills Jack Drake and orphans Tim.

faces in achieving a balance between masked and civilian lives, the greatest impediment for Stephanie's future intimacy may lie not in any problem with herself but in finding a compatible partner who can appreciate a strong and strong-willed woman. Many can. Plenty cannot. The major obstacle for Tim should be his own guilt and fear that his lifestyle might bring harm to his loved ones—again. Playing superhero already brought his father's killer to the door.[67] Jason Todd, who missed out on much of his own adolescence during his death, coma, and brain-damaged period, is far behind his peers in terms of personal growth. He has enjoyed the fewest opportunities to develop everyday social skills and seems unlikely to have any semblance of a "normal" relationship. Finding someone with the kind of patience he needs will not be easy. Most likely, he will enter into relationships with women as volatile as himself, and their relationships will seem as explosive as gasoline mating with fire.

Dick Grayson, the eldest Robin, has shown himself capable of long-term romantic relationships. Unfortunately for him, his lifestyle (plus the writers' need to keep the stories lively) keeps getting in the way. As he's about to marry longtime girlfriend Starfire, their minister gets murdered.[68] Later he becomes engaged to Barbara Gordon but, again, superheroics interfere. Nevertheless, he remains more likely than Bruce to enter successful intimate relationships. Bruce's personality is the first thing that interferes with his relationships. At least Dick Grayson goes for the "good girls."

> Dick: "Hold it. I've got one more thing to say. You and Alfred gave me a home and you gave me what we don't mention. The L word. You were the best family I could have had. Thanks."[69]

CASE FILE 10–1 Red Hood

Real name: Jason Peter Todd

First appearance: as Jason, *Batman* #357 (March, 1983); as Robin, *Batman* #368 (February,1984); as corpse, *Batman* #428

(Holiday, 1988); as Red Hood, *Batman* #635 (December, 2004); as Nightwing, *Nightwing* #118 (May, 2006); as Red Robin, *Countdown to Final Crisis* #17 (January, 2008).

Origin: This version of Jason Todd, the son of a loving mother who dies of poor health and a small-time hoodlum whom Two-Face has murdered, is a street orphan stealing the Batmobile's tires when the Dark Knight first meets him. Lonely after Dick Grayson outgrows the Robin role and becomes Nightwing, Batman decides that Jason stands his best chance in life if Bruce Wayne adopts the boy. After Jason persists in trying to work on Batman's cases, Bruce teaches him to redirect his criminal skills into crime-fighting. Though initially spunky, optimistic, and as gung-ho as Dick Grayson ever was, Jason turns increasingly distant, disrespectful, and disobedient. In one of his final appearances as Robin, he may have tossed a drug dealer to his death* after the man, protected by diplomatic immunity, sadistically drives his abused girlfriend to suicide. "He slipped," Jason claims.[1] When Jason soon discovers that the late Catherine Todd wasn't his biological mother, he sets off on a trek across the globe in search of his birth mom. He repeatedly crosses paths with the Joker, in a series of coincidences that strain credulity far beyond the suspension of disbelief comics already require, until the clown beats the boy nearly to death with a crowbar and then finishes the job with a bomb. Batman arrives too late. Jason is dead.

✿   ✿   ✿

Jason gets better.

Reality-wrenching events of the series *Infinite Crisis*[2] resurrect Jason inside his coffin. He claws his way out and up through the earth only to emerge from his grave brain-damaged. His mind and personality do not fully return until Talia al Ghul immerses him in

---

*"It was left vague as to whether or not Jason pushed someone off a balcony. The writer, Jim Starlin, thought he did—I thought he didn't."—Dennis O'Neil, interviewed by Pearson & Urrichio (1991).

her father's Lazarus Pit.° Finally, fully restored, Jason is stunned to learn that the Joker still lives. That hurts. The question that sears at Jason is not how he came back from the dead, but why he has gone unavenged. Confused, disappointed, and angry at Batman, the young man adopts a new identity as the Red Hood, taking a name the Joker once used, and returns to Gotham as a brutally violent vigilante who also shakes down the mob. When Batman assumes Jason is angry that he failed to prevent this ex-Robin's death, Jason tells him, "Bruce, I forgive you for not saving me. But why . . . why on God's Earth is he still alive!!??"

> Jason: Ignoring what he's done in the past. *Blindly*, stupidly, disregarding the entire graveyards he's filled, the thousands who have suffered, the friends he's crippled, I thought . . . I thought killing *me*—that I'd be the last person you'd ever let him hurt. If it had been you that he beat to a bloody mass, if it had been you that he left in agony, if he had taken *you* from this world, I would have done nothing but search the planet for this pathetic pile of evil, death-worshipping garbage and sent him off to hell.[3]

Diagnoses

When Batman first meets the boy, Jason shows behaviors associated with *conduct disorder*, a repetitive, persistent pattern of violating societal norms and the rights of others, but of no more than moderate severity. On the one hand, Jason chooses his lifestyle of fending for himself rather than becoming a ward of the state, while on the other hand, he is not out to hurt anyone. Severe conduct disorder would involve acts of cruelty or inflicting considerable harm—behavior more heinous than truancy, running away, or stealing to get by.

At first, Jason readily adapts to his new role as Batman's partner and Bruce Wayne's son and no longer shows any disruptive behavior

---

°The 2010 animated film *Under the Red Hood*, which follows the comic book story arc closely in dialogue and plot, presents the Lazarus Pit as the source of the resurrection itself.

disorder, but over the course of the next year he becomes "very moody, resentful, reckless," with "a dangerously high level of aggressive energy to work off," and Batman worries that Jason's attitude "is about to get him killed."[4] Batman tells Alfred he "may have started Jason as Robin before he had a chance to come to grips with his parents' deaths." Bouts of crying over his parents' photo yet refusing to talk about it, together with his moodiness, may indicate that Jason has developed *posttraumatic stress disorder.* Anger and aggression may be the tools he's using to repel depression or feelings of guilt over having replaced his parents with his adoptive dad. The overall pattern of negativistic, hostile, and defiant behavior fits *oppositional defiant disorder*—like conduct disorder, one of the disruptive behavior disorders—and this stubborn, disobedient pattern gets him killed.

Technically, the grown Jason fits the criteria for *antisocial personality disorder* through his aggressiveness, deceitfulness, repeated unlawful behavior, and lack of remorse, although we have to evaluate these in the context of the world in which he lives. Superheroes, like spies and undercover police, use aggression and deceit as tricks of the trade. He is a man on a mission. Like Marvel Comics' Punisher or Batman's inspiration, the Shadow, he slays evildoers. "I've killed. Not murdered," he originally insists, although he also threatens that "death may come to those who stand in my way of doing what's right."[5] Judging him by the standards of normal society, even comparing him to superheroes, he still seems fairly antisocial.

When authorities lock him in Arkham Asylum on the grounds that he will be safer there than in a prison's general population, he successfully petitions the court for transfer to Gotham City Corrections on the grounds that he is legally sane.

> Jason (to Batman): I murdered criminals. Granted, I got dressed up in a goofy outfit to do it, but look in a mirror, *Nosferatu*—that doesn't get me in the rubber room. I have passed all of my psych exams—multiple times. I am simply homicidal. Will I kill again? Sure. Am I a bad person? Oh, yeah. So keep me locked up. Just not here. I will not be housed in your kennel for freaks.[6]

In adopting his killer's old Red Hood *nom de plume*, antihero Jason has taken from the life of the villain who took his life. He takes more from the Joker than that. Beyond his own mounting body count and aside from giving the Joker some payback at the end of another crowbar, Jason is trying to teach people, especially Batman, some lessons. The Joker and Jason want Batman to break his rules. Both want substantiation for their respective opinions that rules and order do not work, although neither would keep seeking such support if fully secure in his beliefs. They're trying to tear down not Batman himself, but rather his restraint. They want to see his darkness unleashed. He is the standard by which they judge themselves. Unable to make sense of the world in which he lives and unable to see the world as Batman does, Jason is trying to get Batman to see that Gotham is ugly and that its most dangerous criminals need to die. Like the Joker, he tries to prove that people are uglier inside than Batman wants to believe. Were Batman to kill the Joker, he'd prove both the Joker and Jason right.

Supposedly to teach Bruce the price of enlisting others' help in the conflict between Batman and the Red Hood, Jason abducts Green Arrow's sidekick. The former second Robin tells Mia Dearden, the second Speedy, "Tonight you're going to get some learning." He tries to get Mia to see how much she has in common with him so she might be better prepared to kill enemies when necessary to keep herself alive. Jason's lessons tend to be about the need to kill.

> Jason (to Mia): My surrogate dad comes from the same damned upbringing as your self-righteous mentor. I'm like you. I was born out on the streets, too. . . . I know that sometimes we have to do the bad things just to get by. And I know that sometimes very bad things have to be done to do a great right. I don't think either of our "fathers" will ever understand that. But you do.[7]

Whereas the Joker tries to reshape the world in his own image by imposing his visage upon his victims, equipment, and fish, Jason redefines himself to be like others: At different points in his life, he replaces Dick Grayson as Robin, assumes the Joker's old Red Hood identity, dons the Nightwing costume and name while Dick Grayson is on sabbatical with Bruce and Tim, traipses the Multiverse in the costume of Earth-51 Batman's late partner Red Robin, and tries to win the right to wear his Batman's cowl when people think Bruce dead. After Dick wins that cowl and becomes Batman with Bruce's son Damian as his Robin, Jason transforms his Red Hood outfit into a more traditional superhero costume and gets his own sidekick, a girl called Scarlet. Later, as Bruce resumes his place as Gotham's one and only Batman, Jason follows and distorts another chapter from Bruce's life when he leads the Outlaws, the antihero equivalent of the Outsiders superteam Batman sometimes leads.[8] The Outlaws include former Teen Titans, notably Green Arrow's first sidekick and Dick Grayson's former girlfriend. Jason's repeated efforts to recast himself to fit other people's molds show some similarities to *borderline personality disorder* (previously discussed in connection with *Batman Forever*'s Riddler), a condition involving a vague, poorly formed identity. While Jason may be too consistent in his actions, manner, and moods to fit that particular disorder well, spending much of his youth brain-damaged and comatose has made him miss out on a critical period in personality development.

The greatest superhero backstories each include a defining moment. A rocket blasts off from a dying planet, a boy kneels crying over his slain parents, another boy's parents fall when trapeze ropes break, a clown shoots and cripples the police commissioner's daughter, a teenager stares in shock at the face of the burglar who killed his Uncle Ben. Jason's defining moments, the events we always think of in connection with him, are of a boy stealing tires from the Batmobile and a clown, the same clown who shot the commissioner's daughter, later beating the boy to death with a crowbar.° Just as readers cannot leave these moments behind, Jason, with no powerful redefining moment, also surely never will.

°An explosion moments later is what kills Jason, but the preceding beating by crowbar is the defining image.

CASE FILE 10-2 Dr. Fredric Wertham

Real name: Fredric Wertham (originally Wertheimer), M.D.

First appearance: Munich, Germany (March 20, 1895)

Origin: This psychiatrist's 1954 book, *Seduction of the Innocent*, a condemnation of comic books as the root of much juvenile delinquency in America, rocked the comics industry and instigated many changes. Among other things, Wertham contended that Batman and Robin live out a homosexual fantasy, and people have kept talking about that ever since.

Is Batman Gay?

No.

Is Robin Gay?

No.

But what about . . . ?

✿   ✿   ✿

No. To those who read the stories as written, these questions can seem stupid—in which case the greater question might be why people keep asking. That greater question could ignite considerable and fascinating debate while remaining objectively unanswerable. Comic book writer Alan Grant, one of numerous interviewees* Silver Bullet Comics once surveyed regarding Batman's sexuality, said, "In my 40 years as a Batman reader, that question never occurred to me. Then, during my time as writer on the Batman titles, I was interviewed for an American college rag. The first question was 'Is Batman gay?' Well, the Batman I wrote for 13 years isn't gay. Denny O'Neil's Batman, Marv Wolfman's Batman, everybody's Batman all the way back to Bob Kane—none of them wrote him as a gay character."[1] *The Dark Knight Returns* author Frank Miller has said, "Batman isn't gay. His sexual urges are so drastically

---

*None of whom seriously said yes, Batman's gay.

sublimated into crime-fighting that there's no *room* for any other emotional activity. Notice how insipid are the stories where Batman has a girlfriend or some sort of romance. It's not because he's gay, but because he's borderline pathological, he's obsessive. He'd be *much* healthier if he were gay."[2] DC Comics stories consistently present the Batman-Robin relationship as that of father and son, master and apprentice, mentor and mentee. Readers over the years have had fun pulling examples out of context, like a panel in which twin beds look like the same bed shared by both characters,[3] but consider this: If we could generate over a hundred thousand panel images from your life, assorted snapshots displayed out of context, aren't there more than a few we could misinterpret in wildly creative ways?

Popular discussion of the Caped Crusader's sexual orientation started with psychiatrist Dr. Fredric Wertham, who authored studies on homicide, helped pioneer courtrooms' use of expert witnesses in forensic psychiatry, provided information that helped the Supreme Court end school desegregation,[4] judged comic books to be the root of mid-20th-century juvenile delinquency, and shook the comic magazine industry to its foundation. Wertham studied under eminent psychiatrist Emil Kraepelin, worked with Adolf Meyer, and met with Sigmund Freud, all of whom exerted powerful influence over him—even though he ignored Freud's personal recommendation to keep psychiatry out of the popular press.[5] A social reformer who fought for civil rights, Wertham immigrated to the United States after World War I and made his name as a consulting psychiatrist for the New York court system. His psychiatric clinic was among the first to provide psychiatric examinations for all convicted felons, and his recommendations helped lead to the modernization of many facilities and their methods. A charitable mental health clinic Wertham established in Harlem became "the most successful in the nation to provide psychotherapy for the underprivileged . . . the only center in the city where both Negroes and whites may receive extended psychiatric care."[6] Known in Harlem as "Doctor Quarter" for the nominal fee he charged to encourage responsibility rather than administer service completely for free, Wertham kept this clinic open for about a decade, during which time he studied how segregation affected children and developed his ideas on how comic books, especially horror comics, cultivated juvenile delinquency.

In the course of his work with juvenile offenders, Wertham noted how avidly delinquents read comic books and how excitedly they described the sometimes gory content (often in response to Wertham's leading questions). Because the delinquents had all read comic books, Wertham concluded that the comics exerted unhealthy influence. One of the many flaws in this reasoning is that Wertham did not measure them against a *control group* (comparison group) of non-delinquents, the greater flaw being that he did not systematically collect enough quantitative measurements. In the 1940s and early 1950s when he made these observations, every delinquent child would also have seen baseball games (as would the non-delinquents), so why not blame baseball? After a child broke into a meat market so his companions would reward him with comic books and candy, why did Wertham blame the comic books instead of that wicked candy?[7] Hardly the first to criticize comic books but surely the most influential, Wertham started shaking things up with a 1948 *Saturday Review of Literature* article and grew increasingly more vocal, giving lectures and writing more articles over the next seven years, culminating with his famous book *Seduction of the Innocent* in 1954. During hearings before the Subcommittee to Investigate Juvenile Delinquency of the Committee on the Judiciary, Wertham testified, "I think Hitler was a beginner compared to the comic book industry."[8]

Seduction of the Innocent focused on horror and crime comics, devoting only a small portion of the book to superheroes, but in that small portion lies some of the book's most famous content. Wertham called Superman a fascist, scoffed at letting children read stories that "teach them the Green Lantern will help" save them,[9] said Batman and Robin lived a homosexual fantasy lifestyle, and called Wonder Woman the "Lesbian counterpart of Batman."[10] He never called Batman and Robin gay. He said their lifestyle was *like* "a wish dream of two homosexuals living together."[11] Wertham inferred a homoerotic subtext that the characters' creators never intended, a charge as easily leveled against other popular stories about men sharing adventures with their fellow men (e.g., war movies, cowboy movies, the Three Musketeers, the Three Stooges). "Only someone ignorant of the fundamentals of psychiatry and the psychopathology of sex can fail to realize a subtle atmosphere of homoeroticism which pervades the adventures of the mature 'Batman' and his young friend 'Robin.'" These Freudian fundamentals to which he refers, *especially* early psychoanalytic views on the psychopathology of sex, remain controversial among a majority of psychological professionals and inadequately supported by empirical study.[12] "At home they lead an idyllic life," Wertham said of the lifestyle Bruce Wayne and Dick Grayson enjoy, "in sumptuous quarters, with beautiful flowers in large vases, and have a butler, Alfred." "To avoid being thought queer by Wertham," Andy Medhurst, like others, suggests that Bruce and Dick needed to "never show concern if the other is hurt, live in a shack, only have ugly flowers in small vases, call the butler 'Chip' or 'Joe' if you have to have one at all, never share a couch, keep your collar buttoned up, keep your jacket on, and never, ever wear a dressing gown."[13]

Wertham complained about villains taking Robin hostage, not because that depicted child endangerment (which would have been a valid concern about Batman's relationship with Robin), but instead because he found something inherently sexual in the act of rescuing one's friends—a staple in adventure stories through any medium. Just as he says, "They constantly rescue each other from violent attacks by an unending number of enemies. The feeling is conveyed that we men must stick together because there are so many villainous creatures who have to be exterminated," when describing how "the Batman type of story helps to fixate homoerotic tendencies," he complains that "Where Batman is anti-feminine, the attractive Wonder Woman and her friends are definitely anti-masculine. Wonder Woman has her own female following. They are all continuously threatened, captured, almost put to death. There is a great deal of mutual rescuing, the same type of rescue fantasies as in Batman."[14],°

Dismissing strong good girl characters like intrepid reporter Vicki Vale, Wertham carped, "In these stories there are practically no decent, attractive, successful women. A typical female character is the Catwoman, who is vicious and uses a whip. The atmosphere is homosexual and anti-feminine. If the girl is good-looking she is undoubtedly the villainess."[15] Some truth may hover in there, for reasons other than Wertham's perceived homosexual subtext. Bob Kane distrusted women. Batman's creator, who enjoyed dating women like Marilyn Monroe, didn't know how to befriend them. "You always need to keep a woman at arm's length. We don't want anyone to take over our souls, and women have a habit of doing that," Kane said in his autobiography. "With women, when the romance is over, somehow they never remain my friends."[16]

By paving the way for the creation of the Comics Code Authority as a tool for the comic book industry to regulate its own content, a code Wertham himself neither supported nor endorsed, as he objected to censorship and felt pessimistic about the comic book companies' ability to regulate themselves, Wertham's campaign for parents to take responsibility and supervise their children's reading got Catwoman evicted from the comics for more than a decade. Never mind the whip—that, she could have gone without. The code, by forbidding suggestive postures, demanding realistic drawings of women with no exaggeration of any physical qualities, banning glamorous or sympathetic criminals, and requiring punishment for all crime every time, left little room for the sexy thief who steals Batman's heart.

°I can't flatly refute everything Wertham insinuated about Wonder Woman. Psychologist William Moulton Marston, who created her under his pseudonym Charles Moulton, was all in favor of lesbians and bondage.

11

The Women
Why the Cat?

Why does Batman go for "bad girls"? Why does anyone? They're trouble. Maybe he likes dangerous women because *he* is dangerous. A better question might be why anyone would go for him. Aside from his intelligence, good looks, strong voice, interesting friends, generous nature, big house, sprawling estate, cool car ("It's the car, right? Chicks love the car."),[1] massive fortune, aptitude for everything. . . . Okay, there are reasons to date the guy[2] but don't expect that relationship to last. And buy extra insurance: life, health, dental, auto, fire, theft, dismemberment, abduction, the works.

Sexy Devils

Empirical research reveals more about bad boys' appeal than equivalent bad girls'. Those who study "bad boys" in this context mean rebels, males whose temper and antisocial actions make trouble and who don't treat women with the kindness, sensitivity, or reverence "nice guys" will show. While bad boys usually have more sexual experience than nice guys, sexual activity isn't the foremost defining criterion for being considered a bad boy, whereas researchers who write about "bad girls" distinguish them from "nice girls" in terms of sexual expressiveness and promiscuity. The women most important to Batman, though sexually active, are not wantonly promiscuous. They have standards. No, they're bad girls in much the same way Batman's a bad boy, and therein lies the mutual attraction. "You are part of the night, just like me. We're not afraid of the dark—we come alive in it," Catwoman tells him, "we're thrilled by it."[3]

Confidence is attractive, as is a dominant, take-charge manner.[4] The man exhibiting dominant behavior (not to be confused with domineering) comes across as poised, strong, masculine, and capable of facing challenges, fulfilling his role as provider and defender, and fighting off the wolves. If a problem calls for heroics, the good man who seems timid, unassertive, and full of self-doubt, like Superman's alter ego Clark Kent, might appear less capable of successfully rising to the occasion than the bad one who's bold, aggressive, and free from doubt. Right or wrong, a brute may seem more capable of performing a gentle act than the gentleman seems able to succeed at a brutal one. Mild-mannered Clark Kent spends years adoring Lois Lane while she ignores him. No woman ignores Bruce Wayne. Superman is a good boy who honors his birth parents and embodies his adoptive parents' values. Batman is a bad boy with a good cause: avenging his parents whether they'd approve or not.

Gender roles (originally called *sex roles* but that sounded sexual, which confused people) are behavioral expectations for males and females, varying across cultures and over time, with some biology-dependent consistency.[5] They're not exactly *stereotypes* (beliefs as to what the members of specific groups are like), but rather expectations for how members of each gender are *supposed* to act. *Gender role masculinity* consists of the behavioral traits considered favorable for men; *gender role femininity*, those considered favorable for women. People expect men to be forceful, assertive, aggressive, dominant, independent, willing to take risks, and ready to defend their beliefs (a set of characteristics Bruce Wayne fulfills in every way where Clark Kent often does not), and women to be understanding, sympathetic, sensitive, compassionate, warm, tender, eager to soothe hurt feelings, and loving toward children.[6] A psychologically *androgynous* person has many characteristics from both sets, which can be attractive as well—probably among the many reasons Batman finds Catwoman so appealing. Clark's love interest, Lois, raised to best the boys like the son her father General Lane never had, shows even more traditionally masculine traits while remaining all woman.[7]

People tend to become more androgynous with age—many men warming up over time, many women growing assertive and independent—and this gives hopes to many a woman who starts off with a bad boy and dreams he'll become a better man later on. Part of the bad boy's appeal can be that the woman hopes to save him, as if helping him fulfill his potential would make her feel more accomplished as a woman and net her the ideal man. Hoping the hypermasculine man picks up some of her feminine strengths may seem more achievable and more fun for her than trying to "be the man" in the relationship while prodding a softer guy to take on that role. Neither Talia nor Selina wants a kinder, gentler Batman. It's he who talks about reforming them.

Nice guys have fewer sexual partners. Part of being nice is the fact that they'll place manners, respect, conversation, and concern ahead of passion. More willing to wait until long after the first date to seek intercourse, they therefore have sex less often because of times when there is no second date. By waiting for the perfect time to talk to a woman, to ask her out, to kiss her, and more, they miss opportunities—not that they all mind waiting, but expecting perfection in any human interaction guarantees failure and disappointment. Rebels take the lead. They're confident, bold, and indifferent. They'll test limits and push boundaries in all areas of their lives. If a woman spurns them, so what? Instead of moping and pining for one person, they'll go on to the next one. Numerous women prefer bad boys for immediate sexual gratification and nice guys for serious, committed relationships.[8] Niceness or agreeableness affects relationship success in several ways: Those interested in long-term relationships tend to seek nicer partners, plus the less agreeable individuals are more interested in casual sexual relationships with less commitment anyway.[9]

The bad boy poses a challenge. Superman makes people feel safe, but safe doesn't feel like a challenge. Security isn't mysterious. "It's wanting something you can't really have," actress Lee Meriwether (Catwoman in *Batman: The Movie*) commented when discussing why a woman would want a long-term relationship with Batman or any other bad boy.[10] We value the things we work harder to get. Procuring a collector's item after months of meticulous searching makes it a greater prize than if you'd ordered it online within three minutes of first Googling. Things that come easily to us, we undervalue. The more we suffer for something without sufficient external justification, the more we increase its perceived value so we don't feel like idiots for putting up with it. Members of groups who undergo harsher initiation rituals express greater loyalty afterward as a way of rationalizing their experiences; abandoning the group you suffered to join can make you feel foolish for having gone through that suffering in the first place.[11,*] When Clark Kent runs off to turn into Superman, his unreliability and perceived cowardice make him unappealing, and yet when Bruce Wayne lets people down, he comes across as indifferent or aloof, which might enhance his attractiveness to those who need to believe they're not hanging around for his money.

Leon Festinger's *cognitive dissonance theory* says feelings of tension (*dissonance*, the opposite of consonance or harmony) arise when you're conscious of two inconsistent ideas—like "I love him" and "he's so rude to me." We could downplay one idea ("ah, that wasn't really rude") or upgrade the other idea to justify tolerating the situation ("I love him so much, he's worth it"), each of which means altering an attitude so our actions make sense.[12] Where some theories might predict that we wouldn't like anything we associate with reprimands, cognitive dissonance theory predicts some circumstances in which we'll value those things, like when children

---

*Please note that this is not an argument in favor of hazing. Appropriate, nicer team-building activities can promote team cohesion (Van Raalte, Cornelius, Linder, & Brewer, 2007).

who receive strong admonishment to leave a toy alone want the toy more than if admonishment is mild.[13] The boy or girl your parents warn against becomes sexier. Forbidden fruit becomes more appealing.

Danger is sexy. "Batman feels most intensely alive when he's in danger and he's in danger when he's with bad girls. They help him feel alive," says psychologist Robin Rosenberg.[14] Arousal from one source fires up our feelings about other things, a process of *excitation transfer* (mentioned in chapter 5), which may account for the popularity of makeup sex or having sex while still angry. Danger makes people sexier. The excitement of riding a roller coaster with someone who's not your romantic partner can make that person more desirable.[15] Any male movie lead who encounters a femme fatale can count himself lucky if he's still breathing and not behind bars at the story's end. The thrill of danger makes her more exciting along the way, then cognitive dissonance makes some of those saps decide, "She was worth it."

Blinded by Beauty

What's more attractive, physical appearance or personality traits? Appearance is visible first. Discovering the personality takes time. Physical appearance is therefore the number-one determinant of *initial* attraction to someone else. People tend to choose romantic partners who are a "good match" for themselves in attractiveness and other traits, *the matching phenomenon.*[16] In happy couples who are not equally attractive, the less attractive partner usually has compensating qualities or assets.[17] Attractiveness exerts greater influence on those who seek short-term, less committed relationships.[18] Standards of attractiveness, varying somewhat between cultures, show some universal standards in that signs of health and fertility are attractive, especially *symmetry*: When one side of the face neatly mirrors the other side (e.g., eyes line up, ears match, one side of the skull isn't bulbous relative to the other) or likewise with the rest of the body (e.g., shoulders the same height and width), people not only find this physical balance pleasing[19] but also tend to expect people who have these even features to be more sociable, intelligent, lively, confident, and mentally balanced.[20]

Physical attractiveness carries benefits beyond the obvious mating advantages.[21] Attractive people and tall people fill more prestigious occupations and earn higher incomes.[22] Better-looking individuals on average develop better social skills, enjoy more success, and suffer less mental illness, perhaps because people treat and judge attractive children and adults more favorably.[23] When dealing with attractive children, adults use greater tact, show them more warmth, and consider their transgressions less naughty even when both attractive and homelier children have committed identical antisocial acts,[24] and their teachers presume the attractive ones to be smarter and more successful academically.[25] Pretty people get away with more. Researchers have found that jurors and mock jurors will consider good-looking defendants less dangerous,[26] believe attractive plaintiffs more sincere,[27] and recommend that they receive lesser sentences.[28] Juries punish more severely those offenders who hurt beauties, awarding larger damages to attractive negligence victims[29] and assigning lengthier sentences to sexual assaulters who have attacked better-looking victims.[30] The strength of these physical attractiveness effects on juries depends on the nature of the crime. Deliberating over burglary, an offense where attractiveness would not directly help or hurt a perpetrator commit the crime, subjects assign more lenient sentences than with a crime like swindling, in which attractiveness would logically help the con artist succeed.[31]

Beauty distracts Batman. The first time he meets Catwoman, he lets her get away while he muses over her lovely eyes.[32] In modern continuity, Selina Kyle has never gotten arrested, nor has her identity as Catwoman ever been publicly exposed, none of which would be possible if Batman set his mind on locking her up. Likewise, the first time he defeats criminal mastermind Ra's al Ghul and prepares to take Ra's to the authorities, al Ghul's beautiful daughter and accomplice Talia asks, "And I? Am I also to be imprisoned?" Batman replies by pulling Talia close for a big kiss before he carries an unconscious Ra's off without her.[33]

With his favorite women, Batman
finds alternatives to incarceration.[34]
Neal Adams & Dick Giordano art ©
DC Comics.

The Bat's Black Book: Women Who Love Batman

Bruce Wayne's fiancée during Batman's first year in *Detective Comics*, Julie Madison, breaks off the engagement in frustration over the seemingly carefree playboy's failure to do anything more worthwhile with his life. She leaves to become an actress, taking the name Portia Storme (supposedly after a character in Shakespeare's *The Merchant of Venice*, but really because Portia was the name of writer Bill Finger's girlfriend/ future ex-wife). Bruce never shares the secret of his dual identity with his fiancée, Julie. Was he saving that for the wedding night?

While still involved with Julie, Batman becomes smitten with the Cat, a jewel thief who crosses his path during an ocean cruise, from the first moment he sees her.* After letting the Cat escape, he ends

---

*After he removes her old lady disguise, that is, while telling her, "Quiet or papa spank!"

the story musing over her: "Lovely girl! What eyes! Say, mustn't forget I've got a girl named Julie! Oh, well. She still had lovely eyes! Maybe I'll bump into her again sometime."[35] Soon she returns as the cat burglar called Catwoman. Linda Page, Bruce's next girlfriend after Julie, breaks up with him because of Catwoman after seeing him woo "Elva Barr," a disguised Selina, during one of his many attempts to reform her.[36] The character kept changing. Unlike adversaries such as the Penguin, who arrived fully formed, top hat, monocle, umbrellas, and all, Catwoman/Selina Kyle evolved over the course of several years while artists kept redesigning her and writers figured her out.

> *"We knew we needed a female nemesis to give the strip sex appeal. So Bill and I decided to create a somewhat friendly foe who committed crimes but was also a romantic interest in Batman's rather sterile life. She was a kind of female Batman, except that she was a villainess and Batman was a hero. We figured that there would be this cat and mouse, cat and bat byplay between them—he would try to reform her and bring her over to the side of law and order. . . . We felt that she would appeal to the female readers and that they would relate to her as much as to Batman. We also thought that male readers would appreciate a sensual woman to look at. So, she was put into the strip for both the boys and girls, as a female counterpart to Batman."*
>
> —Bob Kane[37]

By the time they finally fleshed the character out, they had to let her go. 1954's new Comics Code Authority left no room for sexy, likable crooks. "With paranoia building, DC Comics decided it would be prudent to 'retire' a sexy and evil female character like Catwoman until such time, if any, that sanity returned to society and its standards."[38]

Once the Code drove Catwoman out of the comics for some years to come, Bob Kane and his creative team introduced a more respectable and less lust-inspiring heroine to fill the "kind of female Batman" role: the first Batwoman, Kathy Kane, a former circus acrobat with an inheritance and a dream of imitating Batman.[39] Bruce's dates with Kathy (who doesn't know he's Batman) and

Batman's interactions with Batwoman, introduced by a creative team eager to reassure readers of Batman's heterosexuality,[40] failed to satisfy readers. Back when the previous woman who'd interested him most had been a thief on the opposite side of the law, their romantic tension had spiced up the conflict as that line of law kept them apart. With a fellow crime-fighter, though, the flirtations seemed trite. Having no hero-versus-villainess complication in their way, why wouldn't they pursue their passion, tear off those masks when alone, and become a real couple? "Readers looking for mystery and adventure were beginning to wonder why they should put up with such soap opera, and why Batman wasn't out at night wrestling with Catwoman instead."[41] Claiming that Batman had renounced romance while fighting crime[42] didn't cut it.

A smiling Batman Family portrait in a 1961 *Batman Annual* demonstrated how far the Dark Knight had strayed from his dark roots. With Batman and Batwoman beaming like dad and mom with Robin and Kathy's niece Bat-Girl seated between them, Alfred and Commissioner Gordon on hand like elderly uncles, and family pet Ace the Bat-Hound at the kids' feet (plus Bat-Mite floating in the air like a helium balloon from the family's trip to the fair, not that most families have their own magical imp), a reader "capable of taking this seriously might have concluded the vengeful Batman of yore had at last been healed and made whole, but the less fanciful fact was that the series had somehow taken a wrong turn, switching from super heroes to situational comedy."[43] A few writers dabbled in plunking a Betty/Veronica element into the comics by pitting reporter Vicki Vale against Batwoman, both vying for Batman's attention while Robin predicted "a big Batwoman-Vicki Vale feud in the days ahead."[44] Decreased circulation saved the day. Prompted by flagging sales, editor Julius Schwartz engineered a rescue attempt that did away with the series' cartoony look, terminated the fantastic tales that pitted Batman against space aliens and mutated him into everything from a baby to a colossus to some kind of zebra man,[45] and unceremoniously fired supporting characters associated with that period. Among them, Batwoman vanishes without mention. Fifteen years later, she returns briefly, only to get stabbed to death.[46]

Commissioner Gordon's daughter Barbara takes over as Gotham's strong, independent heroine, but with "absolutely no romantic interest in Batman," as she tells Catwoman after Selina attacks her on the incorrect assumption that Batgirl wants the Caped Crusader for herself.[47] (Romantic possibilities with Batman pose even less of an issue for a much later Bat-heroine, a new Batwoman who turns out to be another Kane woman, lesbian Kate Kane.)[48] As far as Barbara's concerned, Batman is a colleague of her dad's, not boyfriend material. At that time, while Julie Newmar's Catwoman toys with Adam West's Batman, making him hot under the cowl on TV, Batman in the comics seems untempted by the feline felon. Batman's love life hits rock bottom and stays in its worst slump ever until after yet another revitalization and darkening of Batman's printed adventures.

Along comes Talia al Ghul. As opposed to Batwoman, who lives among Gotham's upper class and goes out to fight hoodlums, or Catwoman, who steals from the upper class and looks out for the downtrodden in Gotham's East End, exotic Talia takes Batman out into the world. Before meeting Talia and then her father, Ra's al Ghul, a villain fit for James Bond, Batman would more likely have visited another planet than any foreign land. Through them, he goes international. Talia falls in love with Batman. Ra's takes an interest in Batman, uncovers his Bruce Wayne identity, and approves of Batman not only as a potential son-in-law but as his own heir.[49] Ra's repeatedly lures Batman into adventures that test his worth to al Ghul or pit him against al Ghul's own rivals. One of his schemes gets Batwoman Kathy Kane killed, eliminating a possible competitor for Batman's heart, perhaps unintentionally, right before Ra's pronounces Bruce and Talia Batman and wife.[50] Though the marriage dissolves, Talia years later presents Bruce with a boy, Damian, who she says is their son.

Perhaps the most famous of Bruce Wayne's uncostumed, non-criminal girlfriends is intrepid *Gotham Gazette* reporter Vicki Vale. An actress Bob Kane dated, called Norma Jean when he first met her and later famous by the name Marilyn Monroe, inspired him to add a beautiful woman to the comic book's cast. Naming her Vicki Vale and making her a photojournalist after a character from the *Batman and Robin* serial, while forgetting to tell the colorist that Bob wanted a blonde,[51] they introduced the redhead reporter in *Batman* #49. Vicki sometimes dates Bruce, always finds Batman captivating, and repeatedly suspects they're one and the same. Since the early 1960s, she appears occasionally in the comics but rarely sticks around. In the 1989 motion picture *Batman*, though not obvious to all viewers, Vicki deduces Batman's identity. Another reporter, Alexander Knox, tells her Bruce saw his parents murdered. While they study an old newspaper photo of that boy Bruce, his eyes haunted by what he witnessed, Knox wonders what that kind of thing does to a kid, and the answer hits Vicki. "She makes a connection" and "knows now but hides it," the script confirms.[52] She heads straight to Wayne Manor, where Alfred escorts her down into the cave. More than sixty years pass in our time between the comic book Vicki Vale's first appearance and when she finally proves Batman is Bruce.[53] Hurt that he never confided in her on his own, she nearly publishes an exposé until she decides Batman's mission is more important than any Pulitzer she might win.[54]

While discussing whether Selina or Talia is Batman's true love during a Comic-Con panel,[55] *The Dark Knight Rises* executive producer Michael Uslan offered a third choice: Silver St. Cloud, a platinum-blond event planner Bruce meets on a yacht,[56] a beautiful, empowered woman sharp enough to notice details other people miss. When Silver finally gets a good look at Batman, she spots something

Batman enters Silver St. Cloud's room like Dracula appearing onstage.[57] Steve Englehart script, Marshall Rogers & Terry Austin art © DC Comics.

Vicki Vale also noticed when she first hit the scene: Batman has her boyfriend Bruce's jaw. Like Dracula watching his prey for a moment before asking permission to enter, Batman steps through a window into her room—a highly stylized, darkly romantic scene, Batman in full costume daunted by Silver in her towel. She knows he's Batman and he knows she knows, but neither will say so.[58] She trusts that this living legend must have good reasons if he chooses not to tell her. As with Vicki, he won't admit to anything if he can avoid doing so. He does not share secrets with either of them until it's far too late. Silver St. Cloud and Vicki Vale are too healthy to share Bruce's life.

Other women pass through. Bruce's relationships with women like Julie Madison and Linda Page, who dated Bruce briefly after Julie left, are empty of the passion Batman shows Selina Kyle and Talia al Ghul. His heart isn't in his carefree Bruce Wayne façade. Never mind all the arm candy, the models and many others he shows off at restaurants and parties, only to have him yawn and ditch them once they're away from cameras and prying eyes. He cancels dates and runs out on the women he genuinely likes as well. Between the many women he abandons early in the evenings and the series of boys he adopts, Bruce Wayne in his world would *definitely* face rumors akin to the gay fantasy speculations Dr. Wertham stirred up.

No, his heart is in his real work, Batman's mission, and he can only give his heart to women who dwell in that world. So why doesn't he love the heroines? During one of Catwoman's 1970s appearances, Batman stops to "wonder for a few panels about the two women in his life, Catwoman and Talia, daughter of Ra's al Ghul. Both were on the 'wrong' side of the law and he couldn't fathom his attraction to them— or what to do about it."[59]

Birds of a Feather, Bats of a Leather

Comics scholar Peter Coogan contends that the women Batman loves, like the enemies he hates, remind him of himself: "The women he dates are versions of Bruce Wayne, they're society women, or versions of Batman like Catwoman, like Batwoman, and so just as he's drawn to his life as Batman and pushed away from his life as Bruce

Wayne, the women he's really attracted to are versions of Batman. So it's really in some ways a relationship with himself."[60]

Is Batman attracted to these women for their similarities to himself or for their differences? One saying holds that birds of a feather flock together even though another says opposites attract. Which is more powerful when it comes to making a relationship work—*complementarity*, the supposed tendency for people with great differences to complete what is missing in each other,[61] or *similarity*? Despite the popularity of the "opposites attract" notion and whatever anecdotal contradictions spring into your mind, researchers have been broadly unable to support the notion. Strong inclinations for opposites to marry, mate, or even befriend one another have never been reliably demonstrated, with the exception of heterosexual pairing (i.e., the majority of people mate with the opposite sex).[62] We prefer others as a function of how similar they are to ourselves. "Smart birds flock together. So do rich birds, Protestant birds, tall birds, pretty birds."[63] Differences within couples can grab our attention, creating the impression that "they're as different as night and day," as when liberal pundit James Carville married conservative political consultant Mary Matalin. Clearly the two had their differences, but keep in mind that, among many other similarities they share, both had been advisors to U.S. presidents and were therefore members of a tiny club sharing similar abilities, interests, activities, events, and social exchanges. Few people on earth had more life experience in common with either of them.

Doesn't Batman have more in common with heroines than with criminals? Well, it's not like he goes for every voluptuous villainess he meets. Talia has noble intentions of saving the world from its people, even if that means using her father's eco-terrorist organization to advance her goals. Natalia Knight, a.k.a. Nocturna, a thief who shares Batman's last kiss before *Crisis on Infinite Earths* resets history, takes a maternal interest in his adopted son Jason, and her efforts to protect the boy apparently get her killed.[64] When a love interest turns out to be truly evil, like husband-murdering con artist Jillian Maxwell, his affection flips into anger.[65] Bad girls attract his interest, but evil girls incur his wrath. He might let Talia, Nocturna, and Selina get away, but not the true psychopaths. Catwoman's depiction over the decades has been inconsistent. Writers have waved her back and forth between degrees of good and bad similarly to how they've kept fluctuating the size of Batman's supporting cast. He's a loner, he has Robin, he has a whole Bat-Family, he's a loner. She's a crook, she's a heroine, she's an antiheroine, she's a crook. Since the 1990s, writers have settled on antiheroine, making her position within Gotham's underworld as precarious as Batman's with the authorities, while still varying how much that antiheroine steals and from whom.

In terms of similarity, the simplest reason Batman goes for lawbreaking ladies like Selina and Talia instead of crime-fighting comrades like Batgirl or Wonder Woman is that superheroines are good people, "and deep down, I'm not."[66]

Intimacy Issues

Secrets keep ruining his relationships, usually his secrets.

Intimacy—opening up to reveal personal information, share feelings and private thoughts, and let someone else inside—is no easy feat for him. As both Batman and Bruce, he stays guarded. In Erikson's *Intimacy vs. Isolation* stage, young adults seek companionship and love or let fears of rejection and disappointment isolate them from others. Sometimes an individual fails to mature beyond a specific stage, so its crisis and all the associated struggles carry on. Despite Erikson focusing on two extreme resolutions to each crisis, he recognized a wide range of outcomes and felt that most people settle somewhere in between. As Batman moves from young adulthood toward middle age, he keeps oscillating on how much companionship he wants in his tiny inner circle.

As a relationship grows, self-disclosing partners reveal more and more, deepening the relationship. Communication is key. One of the most reliable findings in intimacy research is that disclosure begets disclosure—the *disclosure reciprocity* effect. We reveal more to those who have revealed to us.[67] Revealing too much information or intensely personal details too soon comes across as indiscreet, unstable, and nothing special, *informationally promiscuous.*

"Appropriate intimacy progresses like a dance: I reveal a little, you reveal a little—but not too much. You then reveal more, and I reciprocate."[68] When the other person has a monumental secret that will alter your understanding of that individual as a person but you have no such secret to share in return, you two cannot dance to the same rhythm. Learning that secret becomes a relationship milestone, dividing the relationship pre-discovery from the relationship post. Will you feel privileged to find out or hurt that the other didn't tell you sooner? Depending on the nature of the secret and the personalities involved, for a normally reserved person to tell us that something about us made them feel like opening up and sharing personal confidences makes us feel good.[69] Before the revelation, disclosure was a bit one-sided because nothing the other person revealed then compares to the big reveal, as if a big lie of omission had hung through every past conversation. Upon the big reveal, the table turns and disclosure is now one-sided from the other person because you have nothing to give in return. "I'm Batman." "I have bunions."

Making the revelation can feel liberating and open the floodgate to everything else that person has withheld. Humanistic psychologist Sidney Jourard wrote that dropping our masks, letting someone else know us as we really are, nurtures love.[70] For others, though, the habit of keeping secrets runs so deep that the person remains distant. Sasha Bordeaux, a bodyguard Lucius Fox hires to protect Bruce Wayne,[71] learns Bruce's secret, becomes his lover, and starts fighting crime by his side,* none of which helps her feel close to him when he's most intent on his work. They don't discuss the toll his campaign against crime takes on himself and others. "He never talks about that, about what he's sacrificed, about what he's denied himself, about the friends he's driven away, or the isolation he feels," Sasha muses. "He doesn't talk about much, anyway."[72] Couples who reveal the most to each other tend to express greater relationship satisfaction and experience more enduring relationships.[73] Batman does not cultivate intimacy, nor do his romantic relationships endure.

---

*And later becomes a cyborg secret agent, but that's a different story.

Does Batman feel closer to Selina or Talia? Consider the history of what he shares with them and when. He unmasks himself for Selina through one version of their history after another;[74] Talia whips off his mask while he lies unconscious the first time they meet. He tells Selina his secret identity;* Talia's father discovers it and tells her himself.[75] The Golden Age Batman chooses to marry Catwoman, and together they raise a daughter.[76] For the modern Batman, even marrying Talia happens minus his consent. She and the League of Assassins raise Bruce's son for eight years before she reveals the boy's existence. Batman deliberately reveals his face, his name, his headquarters to Selina Kyle, Catwoman, not Talia al Ghul.

Even with Selina, he keeps letting opportunities to bond slip by. Best-selling novelist Brad Meltzer's game-changing limited series *Identity Crisis* revealed that several Justice League members, by means of the magician Zatanna's enchantments, have been altering supervillains' memories and personalities to make them less dangerous,[77] along with erasing Batman's memory of having discovered their unethical transgressions.[78] After the Secret Society of Super Villains retaliates against the League for violating their minds,[79] a remorseful Zatanna visits Catwoman and confesses to having altered her personality as well, turning her from villain into hero.[80] After throwing Zatanna out, Selina tries to figure out who she really is. All the good she has done in the East End, all the people she has helped—who really did those things? "They were inside me, Bruce. Inside my mind," she says after breaking into Wayne Manor to ask him, as the person who knows her best, who she really is. "My God, Bruce, can you imagine such a thing?" A moment passes before he says only, "You'd be surprised," without telling her they've done it to him too. Despite his reassurances that she's the same woman she has always been, in control of her own mind and life, she leaves frustrated, thinking, "Bruce. He tried, but I don't think he could really connect with my problem. Who's going to mess with his mind?"[81]

---

*More than once through multiple incarnations, although as of 2011's *Catwoman* #1, Selina once again doesn't know. So she'll get to find out all over again sometime.

The Love Triangle

Commitment, passion, and intimacy, three distinct components to love, in different degrees combine into seven different kinds of love in Robert Sternberg's triangular theory of love, primary colors mixing to make a love spectrum. *Passion*, an intense physical, mental, and emotional rush characterized by excitement and euphoria, generally is greatest early in a couple's relationship, sometimes bittersweet thanks to uncertainties about commitment and intimacy, frustrating if it's one-sided. Passionate feelings promote physical intimacy. For the relationship to grow, cognitive and emotional intimacy should flourish as well. *Interpersonal commitment*, feeling bonded or emotionally dedicated to someone else, develops more gradually—not to be confused with forms of *constraint commitment*: social pressure to stay together, material obligations like signing a lease, or feeling trapped.[82] Passion shares strong emotion, intimacy shares secrets, and interpersonal commitment shares life time via extraordinary life milestones,

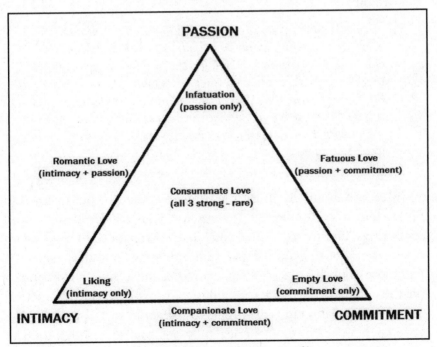

Sternberg's Triangular Theory of Love.[84]

shared responsibilities, and ordinary, everyday events: wedding, child-bearing, errands, housework, evening meals, watching TV, hanging out. Lasting relationships likely see passion fade, intimacy stabilize, and commitment build, with the focus of satisfaction shifting over time from early ardor into enduring companionship based on shared experiences and values.[83] In the long run, across both individualistic and collectivistic cultures, companionate love predicts greater life satisfaction than passion alone.[85]

Batman's romances, including his relationships with Selina and Talia, have shortcomings in all three components. He holds back in every area. His vigor and drive, which can channel into hot passion, seldom do. He has fallen for women often enough to prove he needs passion, try as he might to sublimate that desire. When Bruce, under a touch of Poison Ivy's pheromonal manipulation, calls her beautiful and sexy, Alfred remarks, "I thought you'd left all that behind, sir. Your energy being required elsewhere, so to speak," to which Bruce responds, "Even a Batman can dream!"

> *"Bruce Wayne's very capable of falling in love. You might even say that's his Achilles' heel, almost his Kryptonite. He can have the greatest technology, the greatest weapons in the world, but his heart has no shield. His heart can be broken. So if you're Bruce Wayne, falling in love is a very dangerous thing because it's possible that the person that you fall in love with will get hurt—as a direct function of that person's affiliation with you."*
>
> —Benjamin R. Karney, social psychologist[86]

Men are generally more ready than women to fall in love, to believe love conquers all, to regard love as miraculous and mysterious, and to say "I love you" first.[87] Women tend to be more pragmatic about relationships, contemplating long-term security, and more doubtful that love can overcome any obstacle.[88] Focusing on the passion, on the joy of falling in love instead of practical aspects of attachment, can predispose people to fall out of love, leaving them disillusioned once they get past the exhilaration of newness,[89] so men on average are both first to want exclusive commitment and first to engage in infidelity.[90] Women want more out of love, more details, more thought, more communication, and more intricate nuances between them. They want better-scripted love stories in both real life and fiction.[91] Romantic novels and movies may appeal more to women because men, readier to interpret passion as romance and readier to hear "Hello" as "Let's have sex,"[92] have less left to yearn for. Men tend to want *side-by-side relationships*

While Selina recovers from heart surgery, Bruce confirms her place in his heart.[95] From *Detective Comics* #850. Paul Dini script, Dustin Nguyen & Derek Fridolfs art © DC Comics.

based on activities performed together, whereas more women desire *face-to-face relationships* with deeper communication—"Let's go do something" versus "Let's talk."

To which woman is Bruce most committed?

Having a son with Talia would create a connection that never goes away, but not one that unites them as a family, much as Damian wishes it could. Talia puts Batman in the same position her father always has: Join the family to run their organization, fighting crime and contamination by taking charge of the world, or go to war against one another. Talia's relationship with Batman always gets wrapped up in both their relationships with her criminal mastermind father. Talia can have a falling-out with Ra's and Ra's can take time off from life itself. Alive or dead, though, with them he's always there. Why do the al Ghuls persist in pushing Batman to assume control of the father's deadly cartel? They're confident they understand Batman. He keeps proving them wrong, but people believe what they want and dislike reassessing their beliefs despite evidence to the contrary (*belief perseverance* again). That's why he can still surprise them. Selina understands him on more levels. Talia asks him why facing psychopathic supervillains is so much easier than facing his own emotions, but Selina can empathize with him there. She's on her guard too, another child of Gotham who loses her parents and builds herself into something new.

Bruce often dates Selina. They go out and do things together. Talia does not accompany him to concerts or dinner parties. She doesn't snuggle up to him for a chat in front of a fireplace in Wayne Manor like Selina[93] or have rooftop sex like Catwoman.[94] Selina and Bruce, Catwoman and Batman, both in their masks and out—across one universe, timeline, and retcon after another, from comic books to cartoons to three different movies, they fall for each other time and time again. As story continuity keeps rebooting so Gotham doesn't have a 90-year-old vigilante capering around town, they get to keep falling in love. Writers craft new accounts of how these two come together because the cat-and-bat courtship is a fun fiction to create. Selina Kyle is Batman's love story. Finger and Kane knew what they were doing.

When Bat met Cat. From *Batman* #1 (1940). © DC Comics.

CASE FILE 11–1 **Catwoman**

Real name: Selina Kyle

First appearance: *Batman* #1 (Spring, 1940)

Origin: While Bruce Wayne is born to wealth and loses his
parents through a criminal's brutal act, Selina Kyle comes from
Gotham's poorest slum in the city's East End where she loses her
parents one at a time, each through their own separate actions.
Abused mother Maria Kyle commits suicide, abusive father Brian
Kyle later drinks himself to death, and Selina's the person who
discovers each corpse. (The horror of finding Maria drenched in
her own blood and the revulsion at discovering dead, filthy Brian
stinking of alcohol may be why Selina one day quips, "Live fast.
Die young. Leave a good-smelling corpse.")[1] Despite resentful
Brian's view of his wife as aloof, interested only in "her crazy
dreams of wealth and luxury—and her cats," the few depictions
of Maria present a mother appropriately interested in her
daughter's well-being, a woman who encourages Selina's
excellence in gymnastics and who tries to shield her daughters
from Brian's abuse. Newly orphaned, independent Selina tries
fending for herself on the streets of Gotham, only to get caught
stealing food and sent to a facility for runaways and other

underage offenders. Running afoul of an embezzling administrator, Selina strikes out on her own once again, taking residence in a condemned property at age 13. From its roof, "the million lights of Gotham beckoned like fallen stars, or the shimmer gems of her dreams, cast upon the black velvet of dangerous byways. Someday, she vowed, she would rake them all right into her cold heart."[2] She advances from brash, dangerous thefts in broad daylight to artful, clever burglaries by night.

✿   ✿   ✿

That's one version of her origin, recent and more enduring than others. Previous variations include other men who harm her as well, from Earth-2 Selina's abusive first husband to *Batman Returns* Selina's boss who tries to murder her when she uncovers his crimes, violence that drives her to stand up for herself, mistreatment that justifies her lifestyle and keeps her character sympathetic. She has never been a fiend out to hurt anyone who couldn't afford it, nor some bored socialite who turns to crime to get a few sociopathic kicks.

Batman: Year One presents her as a dominatrix who turns to burglary wearing a cat costume after witnessing Batman in action gets her to thinking. In each canon, Batman inspires her to create the costume. If he could be a bat, why couldn't she be a cat? Whether she was ever a prostitute is a subject of heated debate. After publishing only a few stories presenting her as a prostitute, DC took the position that Catwoman was never a prostitute, that she hung out among prostitutes while hiding from authorities and sometimes posed as one to rob would-be customers. Moreover, a *dominatrix* or *pro-domme*—a woman paid to perform the dominant role in *BDSM* (derived from overlapping terms *bondage/discipline*, *dominance/submission, sadism/masochism*) with a submissive—is not usually a prostitute. Plenty of dominatrices have *no* sexual intercourse with their clients,[3,4] their work involving less erogenous contact than a lap dance. Many people pay to get back rubs; others pay to get whipped and spanked. Psychiatrically, *sexual sadism* (the need to inflict pain upon others in order to achieve sexual gratification) and *sexual masochism* (the need to receive pain to reach sexual gratification) are only clinically pathological when they're so invasive that the person is unable to experience or enjoy relations without these behaviors.[5] The majority of people who engage in consensual, non-coercive BDSM activities do not suffer these deep-seated sexual disorders.[6] Occasionally shouting "Spank me!" falls within the range of variety in bedroom behavior not known to increase anxiety, depression, lifestyle difficulties, or any other pathological issue for most people.

As a thief, does Catwoman qualify for a mental illness? Despite her saying, "Yeah, well, I'm a regular kleptomaniac,"[7] no, she's not. Kleptomaniacs don't steal for instrumental purposes. Selina does. *Kleptomania* (*compulsively* stealing items not needed for personal use, monetary value, anger, or revenge) is a type of *impulse-control disorder*. As with many addictive behaviors, the kleptomaniac feels rising tension beforehand, then pleasure, gratification, or relief upon committing the deed.[8] It's an adrenaline rush without practical function. Kleptomaniacs don't fence stolen goods. Frequently they give away or discard the items, in some cases pointlessly hoarding (e.g., a drawer full of unused combs) or surreptitiously returning their loot. They often have additional (*comorbid*) problems in areas of impulse control, substance use, anxiety, and mood disorders.[9] Kleptomania as a diagnosis for *nonsensical shoplifting* is controversial. One argument for considering it a mental illness is the fact that medications that treat obsessive-compulsive disorder seem to reduce some kleptomaniacs' urges to steal,[10] so perhaps professionals should view it as a variant of OCD.[11] On the other hand, the *recidivism* rate (committing more offenses after getting punished for a crime) among impulsive shoplifters is low, which deals a strong blow to the notion that it's an *irresistible* impulse.[12] Once arrested, most quit. Do most alcoholics give up drinking after their first drunk driving or public intoxication arrest? No. If kleptomania exists, it's rare. Most shoplifters interviewed freshly after apprehension do not meet its clinical criteria.[13] As a professional thief who knows what she's doing, Selina now engages in *adult antisocial behavior*, illegal activity that is *not* due to antisocial personality disorder, an impulse-control disorder, or any other mental illness.

Investigators generally understand *burglary*, "the unlawful entry of a structure to commit a felony or theft,"[14] as a sane act, a crime committed for material gain.[15] Most commonly it's an instrumental act, one performed in order to achieve some other purpose, driven by *extrinsic* (external, ulterior) motivation. The majority of burglars are not stealing items that hold *intrinsic* value (interest in the item itself) for the thieves. Most take money or things they can sell in order to meet other intrinsic needs or desires, whether they use the money to pay rent, buy drugs, or party hard. Intrinsic motives exist but are secondary in importance for the majority of burglars. Thrill, excitement, curiosity, peer approval, revenge, power, or control[16] will drive those who commit the crime primarily as an *expressive* (emotional) act. Expressive thieves are less likely to sell their stolen goods, in some cases discarding or vandalizing the items and in other cases keeping trophies. Expressive burglars fall into three main types: The *feral threat* destroys and defiles items throughout the residence; *riddlesmiths* show off their technical skill to the victims and investigators by setting up puzzles, mysteries, and booby traps, inventive in the way they leave enigmatic messages (in other words, if the Riddler stuck to burglary); and *dominators* violate the sanctity of homes because they find it empowering to threaten their victims, to leave them feeling terrified and unsafe.[17]

Selina's motivation, though usually practical, is not purely instrumental. Stealing serves emotional needs for her as well. "Mother, father, child, and cat-goddess guardian—everything I never had," she says, "and now it's mine. A home of stolen happiness."[18] Rich boy Bruce Wayne, free from worry over the most basic needs toward the bottom of Maslow's hierarchy of needs (see chapter 6), can afford to let his mission fill the void created by his parents' deaths. While he's hiring specialists to train him, young Selina's focusing on her survival—procuring food, clothing, shelter. For the sake of her own self-esteem, she owns her thievery emotionally instead of letting it own her. Cat-burglary becomes such a part of her that even when she has gone years without needing to steal to survive, even when she wants to stay on the right side of the law, she keeps becoming Catwoman so she can feel like herself. "I'm a thief—and stealing is what I do. Not so much for the prize or the possessions or even the profit, but for the art of doing it. Because I can. And because I'm good."[19] She tries running a business, she tries running for mayor, she tries dabbling in other legal and mask-free enterprises, but she keeps going back to running around as Catwoman. After one of her numerous faked deaths, six months out of costume makes her restless. Discussing Selina's sleeplessness, Dr. Leslie Thompkins suggests, "Your subconscious is probably trying to sort out who you are without that mask. It doesn't take Freud or Jung to figure that out." Thompkins, never one to endorse the mask-and-cape way of life, wouldn't take pride in knowing her advice for Selina to contemplate who she is without the mask instead inspires her to wear one again. Prowling rooftops by night, Selina weighs this decision while watching Batman fight the Riddler in the street below:

> Without him, I wouldn't have become who I am. And I owe him so much. But we've been at odds from the start . . . because my world is all just shades of grey, Batman. That's why you'll never really understand me. It's about good people being forced into bad situations. That's my territory—in between right and wrong. Which is a place you can never go. And we both know it. Just like I know I'll finally sleep tonight.[20]

Selina is fiercely independent. Before her bad experiences with an orphanage and juvenile detention, self-reliant Selina chooses to try making it on her own instead of seeking help from the state after losing her father. She may actually leave home or run away from previous foster care sometime earlier, after her mother dies but before she goes home to find her father dead. Her younger sister, Maggie, enters an orphanage without Selina, who says she "can't feed us both."[21] Stories about mentors who teach Selina fighting and thieving skills come and go, moving in and out of official canonicity as the stories change, because those teachers don't define her. Selina Kyle and Bruce Wayne each raise themselves on their own terms. She doesn't want the state running her life any more than he wants to surrender himself to the custody of people who seem more interested in the orphan boy's inherited fortune or any well-meaning adults who might get in the way of his life's mission.

Her independence distinguishes her from most female burglars. Older males operate alone more often than females and younger burglars do.[22] Most female burglars fall into two groups: *accomplices* (those committing the crimes out of subservience to others, usually males) and *partners* (equal participants in planning and committing the crime, co-offending but not taking orders). Otherwise, the offending patterns of female burglars resemble those of males.[23] More women get arrested for burglary than other serious felonies.[24] Gender discrepancies marginalize women's access to and participation in patriarchal criminal networks.[25] Aside from pragmatic reasons for stealing from criminals (like the fact that they won't report her to the police) or moral reasons (hurting only those who deserve it), one reason Selina likes to rob them may arise from resentment toward any boys club that won't let the girls play the same games—similarly to how the homeless little girl grows up to infiltrate and rob high society. Sometimes even she wonders why she has bothered to climb the Gotham social ladder when most of her real friends are on the East End.[26]

Selina Kyle is a strong human being. The cat identity becomes a symbol of her strength, so as Catwoman she becomes her own totem animal. Batman crosses the cat's path at a time when she needs a focal point to help her fill herself with the strength she already has inside. The sight of Batman fighting in the street is to Selina what a bat flitting into Wayne Manor once was to Bruce. Seeing a man fight dressed as his own totem, in a costume that lets him wear his strength on the outside, she knows she could, too. "A long time ago, before I put on this mask, I was afraid of everything."[27] The cat is her inner strength made visible. Like her, no matter what he might try to believe, Bruce Wayne doesn't don a costume only for its effect on others. Selina and Bruce wear costumes because of how those animal skins affect themselves.

12

The Fathers
Why Do We Fall?

"For an orphan, this guy has a lot of father figures."[1]
—comic book writer Len Wein, creator of
Lucius Fox[2]

 Growing up without his parents, Bruce doesn't get to learn from their example of how couples interact, work together, and resolve conflicts. A child with a single parent can learn from how that parent manages relationships. Bruce has no live example, good or bad, only early memories. A younger child doesn't give a lot of thought to how other people interact and relate to one another, and even the best parents may conceal many things from younger children, from friction when it arises between them to their more affectionate moments as well. As Bruce grows, his understanding of his parents does not progress naturally by observing, appraising, and reassessing them with a maturing point of view. If Alfred dates anyone while Bruce is growing up, he probably shields Bruce from seeing any signs of it, like those single parents who prefer not to introduce their dates to the kids.

They get him started, though. He trusts them, they encourage him to be autonomous instead of doubting himself, and he develops great initiative (the earliest psychosocial stages in Erikson's theory: *Trust vs.*

237

Mistrust, Autonomy vs. Shame and Doubt, Initiative vs. Guilt—see chapter 10); not perfectly in all areas, though, or he'd be less ready to distrust all adults interested in taking him in.[3] In debates over whether Bruce Wayne's parents were raising him Catholic or Episcopalian, those who focus on his great guilt as their proof that he must be Catholic, aside from stereotyping, are underestimating many people's capacity for guilt.[4] Anger motivates him more than guilt, and more than anger, the need to look out for others because there was no one to look out for the family Wayne takes priority. "My anger outweighs my guilt," he tells Henri Ducard in *Batman Begins*. Would-be father figure Ducard, out to replace the Waynes' ideals with his own while overestimating how much he and Bruce have in common, tries to manipulate the type of guilt he assumes Bruce has buried beneath his rage in order to turn the young man against his birth father. "Your parents' death was not your fault. It was your father's! Anger does not change the fact that your father failed to act." This "truth" Ducard wants him to confront doesn't convince Bruce Wayne. He stays loyal to his parents' memory, even if he has yet to reconcile his need for violence with the values they promoted. He quests not for their ghosts' approval—so he thinks.

Attachment

What happens when catastrophic circumstances cut children off from their parents? *Attachment theory*, an important idea in developmental psychology regarding the dynamics of long-term relationships, arose in answer to such a question. During the Blitz of World War II, when Nazi Germany spent months repeatedly bombing London plus other British military and industrial centers, trying to damage the British war economy and demoralize the British into surrendering, the air raids' ongoing threat kept citizens afraid for their lives and terrified for the safety of those who meant most to them: their children. Over a quarter of London's population evacuated to the countryside. Not all displaced families had anywhere to go, but some citizens who lived in those more remote areas volunteered to take in war orphans and to house other people's children. Later, families reunited. Physically, the children had come out fine. Psychologically, they had not. Separated from their parents at a crucial developmental period, they grew into adolescents and young adults displaying an alarming variety of psychological disorders and relationship difficulties.[5] Familial disruption during the formative years had thrown them off track.

Trying to make sense of the mass child evacuation's long-term consequences, psychologist John Bowlby launched a long line of studies on parent-child bonds. Mary Ainsworth, building on his work, concluded that people have different *attachment styles*, patterns in how people bond and seek closeness from others.[6] Infants attach to adults who meet their needs with consistent, sensitive care. The strength of infants' attachment to familiar people, particularly their primary caregivers, predicts their tendencies to connect to others throughout their lives. Consistent with Erik Erikson's idea that infants develop lifelong readiness to trust or mistrust depending on how dependably parents provide for them, parental responses sculpt their children's attachment styles which, in turn, shape the growing individuals' feelings, thoughts, and expectations in later relationships.[7] Ainsworth originally identified three main patterns: one secure and two insecure styles.[8] The *securely attached* child, feeling safe and supported, will freely explore the environment and engage with strangers when the primary caregiver is present. Visibly distressed if the parent leaves the child in a strange situation, this child will be happy upon the parent's return. The *anxious-ambivalent* child has mixed feelings, having received enough attention and interaction to want the parent but too inconsistently to trust. Afraid to explore, wary of strangers, and distressed if the parent departs, this child keeps close and yet, after the parent returns from briefly stepping outside, shows the parent resentment and resists when the parent initiates interaction. The *anxious-avoidant* child has been neglected. The child avoids or ignores caregivers and other adults, doesn't explore much, shows little emotion when parents depart or return, and in fact shows limited emotional range regardless of the situation. Because expressions of feelings and needs have gone too often unrewarded, the child expects communication to have little effect. In adulthood, people can avoid intimacy for different reasons: The avoidant adult who wants connections to others but is too scared to interact is *fearful-avoidant* while the one who really doesn't care is *dismissing-avoidant*.[9] Mary Main later added a fourth childhood style, *disorganized*, for children who lack any coherent pattern of coping with others. The ambivalent and avoidant styles, while less effective than the secure, are nevertheless strategies for human interactions. Disorganized children mostly know fear. Their caregivers come across to them as either frightened or, like Scarecrow Jonathan Crane's grandmother, frightening. Interactions are so erratic that the child develops no interpersonal perspective, no general expectations about human behavior, no coherent sense of self.[10]

The securely attached person shows grief following serious losses, feels less anger toward whomever they lost, and suffers less depression than the insecure types.[11] Bereavement leads to greater personal growth among the securely attached, although throughout all the styles, violent death yields more complicated grief responses than nonviolent.[12] As noted with the consequences of the London Blitz evacuations, disruptions to family life in violent times can reroute attachment styles and muddle or ruin interpersonal expectations. Some people adapt to loss and interruptions by withdrawing from others, attempting to use avoidance to reduce the pain and fear of further loss—it helps some, it hinders others.[13] Trauma, unresolved mourning, and other disruptions increase disorganization.[14] When previous expectations no longer fit new circumstances, the child's very personality may go into turmoil.

Bruce Wayne shows characteristics of both secure and dismissing-avoidant attachment. For someone who so values his independence and self-sufficiency, he has spent a lot of time learning from mentors, teaming up with other crime-fighters, training apprentices, and relying on the assistance and cooperation of a police commissioner and family butler. He cycles between dealing only with those last two and working with a sprawling, extended Bat-Family. If he completed the *Experiences in Close Relationships Scale*[15] (one test that measures attachment styles in adults) with complete honesty, he'd peg every avoidance item on the list as a good fit for himself. Consider these sample avoidance statements:

- I prefer not to show a partner how I feel deep down.
- Just when my partner starts to get close to me, I find myself pulling away.
- I don't feel comfortable opening up to romantic partners.
- I don't mind asking romantic partners for comfort, advice, or help. (*reversed*)
- I tell my partner just about everything. (*reversed*)
- I find it relatively easy to get close to my partner. (*reversed*)

Terrible things exist in this world. He knows that well. Crime, despair, and decadence abound. As if all the gangsters and drug lords and killers of the kind who took his parents weren't enough, sadists and serial monsters motivated by delights darker than economic need and greed are out there to destroy lives for their own amusement or to satisfy other cravings. Despite all that, Batman is, in his own way, oddly optimistic. He believes in love. He believes in warm, trusting families who deserve better than to suffer at the whims of the dangerous minority. He believes in rehabilitation, even offering it to the Joker right after the clown has shot and paralyzed Barbara Gordon. "We could work together. I could rehabilitate you. You needn't be out there on the edge any more. You needn't be alone. We don't have to kill each other."[16] It's a qualified belief, though, as he can be skeptical—and rightly so—when criminals like the Riddler and Penguin profess to turn a new leaf and go straight. He keeps an eye on them while hoping it works out for the better. The mugger who taught him bloodshed adds to Bruce's education about life without erasing the lessons his optimistic parents already imparted. As Bruce tells his would-be father figure during *Batman Begins*, his enemy who, in the name of justice, wants to destroy the city his parents believed in, "Gotham isn't beyond saving. Give me more time. There are good people here."

Antisocial personality disorder appears more commonly among dismissing-avoidant adults, but Batman's better-known nemeses act like ambivalent children, both resenting him and aching for his attention. The comic book incarnation of Henri Ducard (an unethical mentor who taught Bruce detective skills, *not* secretly Ra's al Ghul) observes that Batman functions as a lightning rod for grandiose criminals ostensibly motivated by greed, revenge, or power when "their true agenda is always the same: to cast Batman in the role of nemesis. Hence the puns, the riddles, the flagrant clues in their collective wake—daring their foe to penetrate the obvious. He always triumphs. If he failed, they'd be bereft. The *pas de deux* would have no point. Like naughty children, who tempt the wrath of a stern, demanding father. They seek only to shock him by the enormity of their transgressions. It's the moment of acknowledgement they crave."[17]

The Bad Fathers

Ducard is one example of a failed father figure. Training Bruce as a manhunter, detective Henri Ducard shows him the uses of viciousness, cunning, and deception. Amoral, ruthless Ducard works for criminals as often as he does the law. Outraged when Ducard's effort to track a fugitive leads unnecessarily to the man's death, Bruce shouts, "You become as bad as anyone you hunt!" The smug mentor tells him no, "I have not become—I always was. I am. As are you." Both eventually regret having parted on such terms.[18] Years later, Ducard deduces Batman's identity but keeps it to himself.

By investigating purchases of supplies and equipment Batman needs, Ra's al Ghul has already figured his identity out before they first meet. A voice in the Batcave greets him, "Welcome home, Bruce Wayne—or shall I address you as the Batman?" A mission to find who has abducted al Ghul's daughter Talia and Batman's ward Dick Grayson turns out to have been staged by Ra's to test Batman's potential as a worthy son-in-law and successor to run al Ghul's vast organization.[19] His subsequent appearances reveal both the depths of his organization's criminal nature and the heights of Ra's al Ghul's drive to save the world from its people. Time and again, Batman rejects him. Time and again, al Ghul insinuates himself into Batman's life in ways unlike any other foe. When al Ghul plots to kill billions of those darn people who crowd the planet, he digs into the Waynes' graves and steals their bodies to throw Batman off his game, and when he needs the Justice League out of the way in that same story arc, he steals Batman's own files on how to neutralize them one by one, thereby alienating Batman from that surrogate family of heroes for some time to come.[20] Their relationship grows progressively antagonistic, and yet after al Ghul's death* Batman performs what would ordinarily be a filial duty: cremating Ra's's remains. A letter scheduled to reach Batman in the event of al Ghul's death helps Batman fix a dangerous ecological shift. "Batman was the only person he could entrust with this task, which was the legacy to bestow upon his surrogate son."[21]

Merging Henri Ducard and Ra's al Ghul into a single character in the motion picture *Batman Begins*, instead of being two unrelated characters as they are in the comic books, gave Bruce an amalgamate bad father figure who would teach him skills but dares to challenge Bruce's loyalty to his birth father. This chapter keeps coming back to *Batman Begins*, the story that best demonstrates the ongoing father-son issues underlying our hero's campaign. Hunting for the knowledge and skills that will let him face and use fear, Bruce is also searching for a father's guidance. Warm Thomas Wayne versus cold Henri Ducard, a.k.a. Ra's al Ghul, clash across time to teach him different lessons. Ducard's violent methods, disdain for compassion, and grand plan to hurt the Waynes' city all drive Bruce back to the values from his true upbringing.

> Ducard/al Ghul (Liam Neeson): When I found you in that jail, you were lost, but I believed in you. I took away your fear and I showed you a path. You were my greatest student. It should be you standing by my side saving the world.
> Bruce (Christian Bale): I'll be standing where I belong, between you and the people of Gotham.

Ducard's League of Shadows has created the conditions that drove Joe Chill to commit robbery and murder. "Create enough hunger and

---

*It's a comic book. Death is more like a vacation until Ra's returns later—which he does.

everyone becomes a criminal." Topping off this revelation that his manipulations indirectly killed Bruce's parents, Ducard sets Wayne Manor ablaze and heads out to destroy their city. He leaves Bruce to die, having given up on him.

The Good Fathers

Bruce in *Batman Begins* must rely on all his good fathers at the film's climax.

After failed father figure Ducard/al Ghul leaves Bruce to burn to death, Alfred Pennyworth—the man who has helped Bruce raise himself as best he can—rushes into the burning building to save him. Bruce despairs that he has failed to protect "everything my family, my father built," so Alfred reminds him, "The Wayne legacy is more than bricks and mortar, sir," then channels wisdom from Thomas Wayne to convince him.

> Alfred: Why do we fall, sir? So that we can learn to pick our-
> selves up.
> Bruce: You still haven't given up on me.
> Alfred: Never.

Alfred Pennyworth saves Bruce Wayne; then Lucius Fox and James Gordon each help Batman save Gotham's people. These three occupy different places in Bruce's life, filling distinct roles as they father his different personas. The film's three-scene epilogue gives each good father his own denouement and ends with him preparing for the future. Lucius Fox takes his place as Wayne Enterprises' CEO, securing the future of the family business. Alfred helps Bruce sift through Wayne Manor's smoldering remains, where Bruce finds Thomas Wayne's old stethoscope, and Alfred suggests that as long as they're rebuilding the manor, they should take this opportunity to improve the Batcave. Gordon shines the Bat-Signal, right where he'll start and end the next film, as he frets about escalation and reveals the Joker's calling card. In each of Nolan's movies, this Jim Gordon sets up the sequel.

1939 comic book readers first met Bruce Wayne through Commissioner Gordon. Bruce appears to be nothing but Gordon's rich friend, a literary foil, a sounding board for Gordon's exposition about that mystery man in the bat costume. The final panel, after Gordon's last exit, reveals Bruce in the vigilante's costume. In the comics, Gordon works with Batman, Alfred helps out in the Batcave and maintains the Wayne Manor household, and Fox ties Bruce to his parents' charities and business. Lucius Fox's role as gadget guru, the *Batman Begins* version of James Bond's Q, suited the film's story and made so much sense that comic book Batman seems incomplete without a Q of his own, although that's not Fox's role in the comics. He runs the Wayne family business. In his bow tie leading a Wayne Enterprises business meeting at the end of *Batman Begins*, that's the comic book Lucius Fox. Trusting him lets Bruce focus on his real work just like his father, wealthy beyond belief, finds greater meaning in his own life by working as a physician.

> Bruce: Is that where you work?
> Thomas: No, I work at the hospital. I leave the running of our
>   company to much better men.
> Bruce: Better?
> Thomas: Well, more interested men.

When cool, imperturbable Lucius Fox enters the comics to save Wayne Enterprises from financial ruin, consequence of Bruce's neglect, he adds a new dimension to Bruce Wayne's world and character.[22] By making Bruce conscious of their business and the business world despite the Wayne heir's efforts to ignore the whole shebang, Fox forces Bruce as Bruce Wayne to become a bit more of a real human being within their fictional universe. Fox guards the Waynes' finances, not Batman's secrets. In most accounts, he's not privy to Bruce's dual identity. Visiting the offices of the *Daily Planet* in Metropolis one time, Bruce watches Perry White. Seeing that smart, no-nonsense man who supervises Clark Kent's reporting, a man surely smart enough to realize Superman is Kent and trustworthy enough to keep it to himself, leads Bruce to think similarly about Fox. Bruce wonders if he and Clark might enjoy fuller lives if they were to confide in these great men. It's a tough call. Yes, Bruce might become a better-rounded human being if he could be more open with someone else who knows him first as Bruce instead of Batman. On the other hand, though, he could start feeling more like he's really Batman around Fox, in which case there'd be even less Bruce than before. To some degree, this happens in the film *The Dark Knight*. By not admitting the secret, comic book Bruce has to listen to Fox's business concerns instead of saying, "I don't care, I'm Batman. Pretend I'm still here and cover for me." Distractedly hearing Fox while waiting for the sun to set so Batman can come to life, Bruce will accidentally learn some things, much like Alfred hopes that if Bruce pretends to have fun long enough, he might wind up having some. Compliance breeds acceptance; role-playing recasts reality—another by-product of *cognitive dissonance*.[23]

> Alfred: When you told me your grand plan for saving Gotham, the only thing that stopped me from calling the men in white coats is when you said that it wasn't about thrill-seeking.[24]

When and how does Bruce tell Alfred, "I want to sneak around in a mask—lend me a hand?" There's no definitive account of this because it probably happens by degrees. A mourning boy says he wants to go into law enforcement. Nobody's going to put down that dream. By most accounts, Bruce is college age before he concludes that dispensing justice in Gotham's corrupt climate means he must operate outside the law. His interactions with Alfred show mutual support. Alfred freely chastises him and gives unsolicited advice few servants would dare utter, expressing disagreement and worry through gentle rebukes and soft sarcasm, and Bruce doesn't view him as the hired help. Bruce sees himself as the man in charge, but he's like that with everybody.

Alfred's *parenting style* (his general approach to child rearing) is mostly *authoritative* (*not* authoritarian), encouraging his surrogate son's independence with warmth, nurturance, and verbal give-and-take, while also exerting authority, enforcing rules, and making *maturity demands* (expectations for age-appropriate conduct). Difficult as it may be to imagine Alfred telling Bruce at 10 or 11, "No, you may not," Bruce's social competence and self-control suggest that Alfred found ways to place limits and exert discipline, nothing corporal to be sure. The authoritative parent communicates well, listens receptively to the child's questions and requests, and teaches through explanation. The authoritative parent teaches the child more than what to do or not do; this parent teaches the child to think about *why*. The fact that Bruce is so accustomed to getting his own way might suggest that Alfred and Bruce's birth parents before him preferred to risk erring a little on the side of permissiveness. A *permissive* parent sets no limits, fails to guide and discipline, and rarely controls, restricts, or punishes the child. Some permissive parents are warm and responsive, available to help the child without seeing themselves as responsible for shaping who that child will become (*democratic-indulgent* permissiveness), while others are distant, uninvolved, even ignorant about what the child does (*rejecting-neglecting* permissiveness).[25] Bruce's responsive, supportive father and more nurturing mother set limits, maybe not enough. Sam Hamm (screenwriter for *Batman* and *Batman Returns*) concluded that "Bruce had become Batman as a result of being spoiled. He had grown up with sufficient money and leisure to luxuriate in his own tragedy, to wallow in the false sense that it made him somehow unique. In other words, Bruce had never learned to cut his losses."[26] Bruce shows too much self-discipline to have been completely spoiled. Alfred likely applied authoritative guidance based on logic, ethics, and Bruce's inherent guilt.

> *"And then, when they were under the ground, he became my guardian and friend, nagging constantly and sometimes caustically, never letting me neglect my schoolwork, always keeping my obsession in check. . . . With him, I remained driven but disciplined, anchored to vital reality through his sternness and arch humor, my soul tempered by his firm kindness and steadfast humanity."*
> —Bruce Wayne in *The Forensic Files of Batman*[27]

Except for communicating and explaining lessons to Bruce, Ducard in *Batman Begins* otherwise shows an unforgiving, *authoritarian* style: His word is law and his demands are high. Authoritarian parents are aloof, not affectionate or nurturing. Ducard scorns compassion. Authoritarians punish misconduct sternly, perhaps abusively, without adequately discussing logical and moral reasoning for right and wrong behavior much better than "because I said so" and without adequately rewarding approved conduct. The child has insufficient reason to internalize authoritarian lessons and may be ready to rebel. Domineering fathers tend to produce sons who passively acquiesce to the fathers and later may acquiesce to others, mimic the domineering styles, or overcome that domination, either by removing those fathers from their lives or by successfully standing up to them so they can redefine the relationship and move forward. Beneath Ducard's communicative veneer, he's still authoritarian. Beneath Bruce's receptiveness to instruction, he's ready to rebel for a higher cause. As soon as Bruce rejects Ra's al Ghul's League of Shadows and leaves Ducard behind on the icy mountain, there's Alfred at the airstrip ready to take him home.

> *"He's the good father that Bruce comes to depend on. Bruce's real father died before they could establish an adult relationship, and Liam Neeson's Ducard is stern and demanding, didactic and challenging, but not a father figure with any sympathy. If Bruce Wayne is anyone's son, it is Alfred's."*[28]
> —Danny Fingeroth, author of *Superman on the Couch*

The Mothers

Martha Wayne gets short shrift in *Batman Begins*. In several scenes, Bruce and Dad do all the talking while she blinks and looks pretty. In that movie as in *Detective Comics* #33's origin story, Thomas gets shot for moving to shield her and she gets shot for screaming over his fate, two fearful reactions, different facets of the fight-or-flight response—those are their roles. They die for each other. *Batman Begins*, like *Star Wars* and so many other tales of young men becoming heroes, is a father-and-son story. *Reconciliation with the father* is integral to the classic monomyth, the Hero's Journey (chapter 9), as the hero loses his father and must move away from his father's teachings before reuniting with his father's spirit and, now with his own self-defined perspective, making peace. Heroes need mothers too! Harry Potter offers an outstanding example of the orphan hero who idealizes both of his lost parents and must come to understand they were human beings with human foibles before he can relate to their ghosts from a more mature point of view.[29] Only then can he appreciate the magnitude of what they did for him. If Harry Potter can do it, why can't Bruce Wayne? Because Harry doesn't snarl and bust teeth.

Dr. Leslie Thompkins, the first person to notice Bruce and first to comfort him at the crime scene where his parents just died, stays involved in his life as a maternal figure, helping Alfred oversee the boy's upbringing, but without living at Wayne Manor, she doesn't take on an adoptive or foster role. Bruce does not readily include her in his secrets, and when she finds out he's Batman, she disapproves. For wearing his costume into her home, she admonishes him, and yet he does it unapologetically.[30] Leslie provides medical and emotional aid to many of his costumed colleagues, in hopes that she might help them stay safe and on an even keel until one day when they might discard those bothersome costumes. A staunch pacifist, she's the mother who worries about the child's well-being so much that she gets in the way of his fun.

Stereotypically, the father occupies a place in the child's life as disciplinarian, playmate, and provider, a stereotype borne out by research. Grown sons want their fathers' acknowledgment and their mothers' nurturance. Even if some specific issue gives a son reason to reconcile with his mother, that reconciliation with her won't characterize him as a man, not unless he'd lived henpecked by an overbearing mother, but heroes are supposed to come from stronger stock. That's how people often see these situations, so these are the themes we find woven into the stories. Sons don't as universally need to stand up to their mothers to establish who they are and redefine their relationships. Sons' self-concepts have more to do with their dads, even absent dads, than with their moms.[31] The father, whether hero or villain himself, provides the hero with a reference for how to become a man, the mother does not, and Bruce Wayne is all man.

Batman and Sons: The Legacy

Bruce doesn't know what to do with grown sons. His parents' example teaches him how to deal with children. For many reasons, he learns less about parenting from Alfred than from Thomas and Martha:

- The Waynes' early lessons lay his basic psychosocial foundations.
- Bruce grows distant from others during the years after the murders, hence the more dismissing-avoidant of his traits.
- Driven by his parents' demise, Bruce fixates on them.
- Alfred, whose approach seems more permissive than the Waynes', goes along with Bruce's intentions of raising himself.
- With Martha and Thomas gone, Alfred in his domestic role becomes Bruce's mother figure as Bruce endeavors to father himself through his adolescence.
- The Waynes aren't around when he gets old enough for any adolescent rebellion to kick in.
- Bruce leaves home at 14, after only six years in Alfred's care.
- Why try to parent the Robins the same way Alfred parented him when Alfred's right there to do that himself?

Batman relates better to the Robins when they're children. Because he doesn't grow into relating to his mother and father as fellow adults, he doesn't know how to relate to his sons as adults either. Letting those relationships mature poses problems for him. When he thinks he needs to give them their own space and let them become their own men, they feel like he's rejecting them—"they" meaning Dick Grayson and Tim Drake. Jason Todd has just gotten his adolescent rebellion rolling strong when he gets himself killed. During Jason's time dead underground, comatose post-resurrection, and then in antihero training, he becomes a young man, so he and Bruce skip that process of relationship growth and Jason carries adolescent rebellion on into a whole other set of problems. Dick and Tim have trouble getting Bruce to see what's wrong. Reconciling with this father isn't easy for them because Batman's hardheaded, he doesn't get what he's doing wrong, and the standard need to say, "I'm my own man now, give me space," gets thwarted by the fact that how clumsily and bossily he gives them that space has created this friction.

Once Talia al Ghul introduces Batman to the son she says is theirs, things change.

Talia al Ghul and Catwoman Selina Kyle each become mothers. Bruce may have fathered either, both, or neither of these of their children. No internal monologue on the mothers' parts at the time confirms that either believes her own paternity claim, that Bruce fathered Talia's child or that he didn't sire Selina's, nor does DNA testing (not that such tests or DNA markers themselves can't be faked in the DC Universe). This might explain Bruce's strangely distant manner with Damian and how uninvolved he is for a long time, entrusting Damian to the care of Dick and Alfred. Dick becomes Batman for a time with Damian as his Robin. Bruce doesn't take a more active role in Damian's life until he resumes his place as Gotham City's Batman.[32] Nevertheless, he accepts Damian as a son and goes along with Selina's claim that someone else fathered her daughter Helena. After enemies' attacks repeatedly endanger her little girl, he helps Selina find adoptive parents to take in Helena, now toddling about and starting to talk.[33]

Batman starts acting middle-aged. After a period through which everyone but Tim initially thinks he's dead, he returns reinvigorated. He accepts his sons in the new roles they've assumed, and instead of getting in their way immediately, he decides to build something new: Batman, Inc., an international alliance of many Batmen. How well he manages that, given his spotty history of leading teams, is another issue.

> "It's because of the Batman that the city has the protectors it needs, I know, but I also realize that Dick, Tim and Barbara and all their friends have done more together to secure our home than I ever could have on my own. This became a journey of self-identity, secret or otherwise, and my time away has helped me see everything through new eyes. The web that binds crime and justice, truth and lies, fear and hope is too strong for one man to unravel its threads. Now, more than ever, I'm prepared to accept help in expanding and accomplishing my mission. Now, more than ever, I'm prepared to cast the Shadow of the Bat across the entire globe.
>
> —Batman's journal entry in epilogue, *Bruce Wayne: The Road Home: Ra's al Ghul* (2010)

The *midlife crisis*, some individuals' period of self-doubt, emotional turmoil, radical reexamination, and sudden transformation in their lives,[34] does *not* happen to most people, and differs from the psychosocial crisis of middle adulthood described by Erik Erikson: *Generativity vs. Stagnation.*[35] A midlife crisis drives the older Batman in Frank Miller's alternate future story, *The Dark Knight Returns*, back into his cape and cowl, but the Batman in mainstream canon starts showing generative concerns without first suffering any depressive episode. *Generativity* encompasses adults' desire to leave a lasting legacy of themselves. Beyond the ticking of the biological clock, the generative individual thinks broadly in terms of what he or she is contributing to the next generation, and commits to the continuation and improvement of the world that upcoming generation will inhabit.[36] Generative adults take an interest in guiding younger adults. By contrast, those in a state of psychological *stagnation* (a.k.a. *self-absorption*) dwell on their own self-interests, unconcerned about any lasting legacy for others in the future. Stagnation sets the stage for a classic midlife crisis. *The Dark Knight Returns*, despite its reputation as a cynical, nihilistic piece, actually presents an optimistic forecast, progressing Bruce Wayne from utter stagnation at the story's start to generativity both personal and global by the end. Faking death to leave his old life behind and stop inspiring old enemies (and old friends) to make new trouble, he leads new Robin Carrie Kelley, Green Arrow, and other followers into caverns where they will train, study, and build a do-gooder army he hopes might one day bring sense to a world plagued by "worse than thieves and murderers." He decides this will be a "good life—good enough."

> *"For me that was a hopeful ending. He's looking forward to his next adventures after realizing that the methods of the past are no longer appropriate. The book starts with Bruce Wayne contemplating suicide; at the end he's found a reason to live. He's adjusted to the times."*
> —Frank Miller, author of *The Dark Knight Returns*[37]

As table 12.1 shows, Erikson identified one final psychosocial stage for later adulthood, *Ego Integrity vs. Despair*, when people reflect on the lives they've lived and the time they have left, piecing

TABLE 12.1. ERIKSON'S STAGES OF PSYCHOSOCIAL DEVELOPMENT CONCLUDED: ADULTHOOD

Ages	Stage	Basic Strengths	Maldevelopments
Early Adulthood	Intimacy vs. Isolation	Love Affiliation	Exclusivity (social world shrinks), Promiscuity
Middle Adulthood	Generativity vs. Stagnation	Care Production	Rejectivity (rejecting specific groups)
Late Adulthood	Ego Integrity vs. Despair	Wisdom	Disdain

together a positive or negative review of themselves. They ask themselves, "Have I lived a full life?" Retrospective glances back at their lives that yield healthy (not narcissistic) self-appreciation, *ego integrity*, convey assurance of personal proclivity and value with an acceptance of life's mistakes as necessary steps along the way. Those who evaluate themselves harshly, seeing their lives as unproductive, berate themselves for failing to meet goals. In their *despair*, they become dissatisfied with life, often leading to depression and hopelessness.[38] Because readers want to read the adventures of a healthy, hale Batman, DC periodically shaves years off his age, so we'll never see the mainstream Batman officially enter this stage. Stories set in Batman's future present many different possibilities. The animated series *Batman Beyond* reveals a disgruntled Bruce Wayne. Finally retiring after a heart attack renders him unable to fight, this Bruce severs ties with the Justice League, forbids other Bat-heroes from assuming their costumed alter egos, and shutters the Batcave, vowing, "Never again." This Bruce Wayne, a recluse living in bitter isolation, stews in his despair. Most old-Batman tales, however, depict him still thinking about generative concerns. Having spent so many years braced for the possibility that his war on crime might get him killed,[39] he never prepares himself to start thinking like an old man. In *Kingdom Come*, he's the most prominent older hero, protecting Gotham with crime-fighting robots and moving about in a powerful exo-suit that helps him deny the limits of age. He criticizes Superman for clinging to outdated ideals instead of keeping up with the times, and ends that story warmheartedly teasing his ageless friends from Krypton and Paradise Island with his observation, before they can tell him themselves, that they're already working on the future generation by having a child on the way.

Some tales of possible futures depict former Robins, a Batsuit thief, and others succeeding Bruce in the cape and cowl, but in the present, no one can replace him for long. Batman keeps getting new sidekicks because each Robin grows up, each boy becomes a man. Each can leave the Robin identity behind as a hand-me-down for someone younger to wear because Robin is a kid. Batman is a man, and that man is Bruce Wayne.

CASE FILE 12–1 Ra's al Ghul

Real name: If he has a name earlier than Ra's al Ghul (translated in the comics as "The Demon's Head"), we don't know it for certain. Pronounced "razz" and "rahz" in *Batman Begins* and *The Dark Knight Rises*; "raysh" in *Batman: The Animated Series* and by creator Dennis O'Neil.

First appearance: *Batman* #232 (June, 1971)

Origin: Born in a tribe of Arabian desert nomads centuries before he first encounters Batman, scientist Ra's al Ghul discovers the Lazarus Pits with their ability to heal wounds and regenerate those at death's door.[1] He travels the world, fights wars, learns combat techniques, expands his scientific knowledge, and amasses vast wealth and power. The international criminal cartel he creates known as The Demon includes the mysterious League of Assassins[2] (*Batman Begins'* League of Shadows).

> "Everything I have done, I do for the greater good."
> —Ra's al Ghul in *Batman: Death and the Maidens* (2004)

✿   ✿   ✿

Whether he's 450 or 700[3] varies depending on who writes the story. Creator Denny O'Neil depicts him as 450–500,[4] with Ra's himself saying he's lived so long, he lost track during the Black Plague.

During his centuries, he sees generations of people come and go, civilizations rise and fall, while the planet spins on. Earth itself becomes his only lasting companion. He comes to see himself as a physician who must tend to his patient, the natural world, and a warrior who fights for its sake. The human race, he sees as a collective body with some parts better, more useful than others and many members as malignant cells that need to be cut out. Ra's sees Batman's refusal to kill and his efforts to save any life as shortsighted defense of the species' cancers. A ruthless environmentalist, Ra's al Ghul would eradicate billions to give the planet a good cleansing. "When a forest grows too wild, a purging fire is inevitable and natural."[5]

> "We know tricks—small cracks in science and nature through which we have learned to slip—that rejuvenate our bodies and minds. But no mortal can count himself worthy of infinite life without a greater goal sustaining his soul."
> —Ra's al Ghul in Year One: Batman/Ra's al Ghul (2006)

As science extends life span, improving both the quantity and quality of the years we might live, new patterns of later life emerge. Genetic engineering, biomedical rejuvenation, and nanotechnology could conceivably lengthen human life to the point that no current perspective on aging will apply.[6] In his own later years, psychologist Erik Erikson acknowledged that his eight-stage theory of psychosocial development could use the addition of a ninth for extreme old age, as the average life span had lengthened enough during his time to open up new avenues for investigation. His widow and regular collaborator, Joan Erikson, fleshed out his notes to speculate on this unnamed ninth stage in an expanded edition of his book The Life Cycle Completed.[7] In their eighties and nineties, elders commonly struggle with their losses of independence, abilities both physical and mental, and significant people from their lives. Even those in the best health know that death approaches. Individuals with great trust and hope see continued purpose to their lives and face this stage by seeking enlightenment. Despair figures prominently in the stage's unsuccessful path, a different kind of despair from that of the preceding Integrity vs. Despair crisis, one focused on losses and fear of death's finality. Some developmental psychologists have called this stage *Immortality vs. Extinction.*[8] Once past the average age of death, the eldest of the elders have outlived the majority of people they've ever known. Looking outside mortal life for meaning, those who achieve a sense of *immortality* enjoy the life they have and do not spend their days terrified about their upcoming demise because they see that they personally will continue to exist and matter beyond death. They expect continued existence by living on through their children, contributions they've made to their community, lessons they've taught other people, physical markers like a monument in a city park, the chain of nature (decomposing body joins the earth and nourishes new life), supernatural presence as a ghost or psychic residue, or unearthly afterlife. Those on the *extinction* side enjoy no such solace. They despair that they will simply cease to exist in every way, that they might as well never have lived.

Ra's ages and rejuvenates himself so many times. Where another person outliving eras might grow indifferent to anyone or anything outside himself, inoculated by the centuries to grief or any concern for all those mortals who blink by as scenery, Ra's al Ghul casts his gaze across the world and its history. He sees beauty. He's oddly hopeful that his efforts, pitiless as they may be toward individuals caught in his path, can ultimately secure the world's future, and from the first time Talia tells him about her bat-masked hero, Ra's has hope that this dark detective can help secure the legacy both by fathering al Ghul's grandchildren and by running al Ghul's organization to fulfill the old man's global dream.

> *"I have too few years left, daughter! I have gone to the Lazarus Pit often—too often! Soon it will no longer restore life to my body! I must begin putting into effect my plan— my plans to restore harmony to our sad planet! I have been called a criminal and genius—and I am neither! I am an artist! I have a vision—of an Earth as clean and pure as a snow-swept mountain or the desert outside!"*
>
> —Ra's al Ghul in *Batman* #244 (1972)

13

Why So Serious?

"Batman and Robin were part of the fun—they were the straight men, but we were the stars. No one ever hurt anybody. Not really. Nobody died. You look around—it's all different. It's all changed. The Joker's killing people, for God's sake! Did I miss something? Was I away when they changed the rules?"

—Riddler to news crew, *Secret Origins Special* #1 (1989)

I get two main reactions whenever people hear I've been writing a book on the psychology of Batman. Most think it's cool.* The exceptions roll their eyes or grunt, "Hunh," their way of saying, "How ridiculous" without uttering the words. Who wants to analyze a superhero? Why do we love this character, what does our interest in him say about ourselves, and what might writing a book analyzing a fictitious hero say about its author? Some would say we're taking this too seriously—"we" meaning me for writing this book and you for reading it. To those who'd belittle analysis of a comic book character by saying, "It ain't Shakespeare," we might point out that neither are a great many topics on which

---

* Because it is.

257

psychologists and other scholars have filled library aisles, topics that have not generated multibillion-dollar businesses, fueled heated debates, inspired children's dreams, and in one way or another entered the minds of at least half the people on this planet. The fact that cosplayers and kids at Halloween dress themselves as superheroes, along with those of us who'd pin a towel in place for a cape during our childhood playtime, should provide more reason to look at how this fiction impacts us, not less. Fiction with its big question of *"What if?"* is one of the most powerful forces in the world. Once upon a time, the ability to light a fire was fictitious.

Dark Knight, Bright Knight

There's also nothing wrong with sitting back and enjoying the work without picking it apart. Analysis can be the enemy of enjoyment. "I've never given any thought to the character's motivation," Burt Ward once told me regarding his playing Robin to Adam West's Batman. "I don't keep up with the comic books. I'm not a fan of the *character* character, if that makes sense. I'm an actor and I did a job. It's not for me to analyze the character. That's for the fans. That's for you."[1] Honestly, that approach suited the way their TV series depicted Robin. Its Boy Wonder's a present-oriented character focused on the task at hand, not driven by past trauma and not thinking ahead often enough. He lives in the now. In the comic books, young Richard Grayson quickly apprehends his parents' killer, copes with their deaths, and moves ahead with his life as a spunky little adventurer, rarely referring to that tragedy. The 1960s TV series mentions Batman's tragic past but never Robin's, and because its Robin doesn't always think ahead, Batman regularly chastises his shortsightedness, prompting many a "Gosh, yes" from the Boy Wonder.

Adam, on the other hand, developed an in-depth character analysis while preparing for his role. He consulted with Bob Kane and immersed himself in the comic books, old Batman movie serials, *The Shadow* pulp fiction, *The Adventures of Superman* pilot episode, and dual-identity novels like *The Scarlet Pimpernel.* Together with the idea of the costume as a liberating factor and cartoonist Jules Feiffer's observation that Batman's a bit full of himself,[2] Adam shaped his performance by identifying six recurring features (abbreviated and semi-paraphrased here):

1. Batman risks his life for the underdog freely and without hesitation.
2. His adventures, especially the early ones, are set in the urban jungle, often among the downtrodden, which gives many of the tales a Dickensian flavor.
3. Batman is as plausible as a superhero can be, and that carries responsibilities. Batman knows there are kids out there who think they can grow up to be like him, so he's always on his best behavior.
4. He's a creature of the night, at home in the shadows, a bit of the vampire in him. Batman believes he's frightening.
5. Like Sherlock Holmes, he's a detective. He's always thinking and analyzing, maybe at the expense of his good health.
6. Batman's blessed (or cursed) with the most memorable rogues gallery this side of Dick Tracy. There's always someone flamboyant for him to play off. As a result, he must stay low-key to achieve a balance.[3]

To this day, people debate the value of their 1966–1968 TV series' campy humor. The show has its fans, old and new, and it also has its detractors, old and new. Batman can be fun, but not everyone wants him to be funny. A future filmmaker, adolescent Michael Uslan bemoaning the ignominy one night in 1966 after seeing too many *whams* and *pows* flash across the screen, swore an oath that would define his life much like the one that drives Bruce Wayne:

> Someday, somehow, I would eliminate these three little words from the collective consciousness of the world culture: Pow! Zap! and Wham! I would restore Batman to his true and rightful identity as the Dark Knight . . . a creature of the night stalking criminals from the shadows as he was originally intended to be by his creators, Bob Kane and Bill Finger . . . and thanks to many people who believed in that cause, when

Batman and years later *Batman Begins* and *The Dark Knight* arrived in theaters, I believed I had done just that. 2012's *The Dark Knight Rises* would be the icing on the cake.[4]

Notice which movies he named there, the most serious Batman films—not that Uslan shuns fun with superheroes. "There's an important lesson to be learned from *The Dark Knight*. Unfortunately, not everyone in Hollywood gets it," he said with a sigh in his autobiography.[5] "The movie's stunning success does NOT mean that all comic book superhero films must be dark, gritty, and violent and set in contemporary times. But that's exactly what the industry people are claiming. If that's the case, duck and cover, because it may just spawn movies like 'Casper the Unfriendly Ghost!' But *Iron Man*, a huge success, which I saw three times in the first week, is just plain FUN! Aha! There's room for many tones in our superheroes." Again, there's that distinction of fun versus funny.

"Are we supposed to take this one seriously or not?" viewers ask of every comic book adaptation. *Batman Returns* and *Batman Forever* had a few inconsistencies when answering that question, and *Batman & Robin* failed because, unlike the 1960s TV series, which was strictly camp, or Nolan's movies, which strictly are not, those movies mixed camp into a film series that had not set out to be campy. The bat-symbol credit card Batman whips out to outbid Robin at a charity auction in Joel Schumacher's *Batman & Robin* spits on Uslan's adolescent vow. Self-conscious camp takes us outside the situation. "What got lost in *Batman & Robin* is the emotions aren't real," screenwriter Akiva Goldsman admitted. "The worst thing to do with a serious comic book is make it a cartoon."[6] Marvel Studios' Kevin Feige called it possibly the most important comic book movie ever made, "so bad that it demanded a new way of doing things. It created the opportunity to do *X-Men* and *Spider-Man*, adaptations that respected the source material and adaptations that were not campy." *Iron Man*, *X-Men*, and *Spider-Man* have their moments of humor within the context of specific situations, humor meant to play naturally off the characters' personalities or take jabs at some of the insanities of life, not by demeaning the characters and the importance of their lives. What humor we find in Nolan's

Batman movies grows organically out of the characterization, much of it humanizing Bruce's relationship with Alfred ("Accomplice? I'm gonna tell them the whole thing was your idea"), along with some morbid humor from villains (think Joker + pencil or Two-Face + seatbelt, "Your driver"). Too many dramatic stories' authors populate their worlds entirely with characters who have no sense of humor, but in real life, no matter what horrible thing happens, someone will need to cope through humor. Many a funeral is followed by graveside moments when mourners laugh through their tears while sharing moments from the lost loved one's life. Some humor celebrates life, some mocks it. Humor and drama can mix, depending on the nature of each.

"Now Mister Uslan has his Dark Knight. I, of course, am the Bright Knight," Adam West said, sitting beside Uslan before our packed Comic-Con audience the day they finally met in person. "We had a different take."* Even those who could enjoy both Uslan's Dark Knight and West's Bright Knight sometimes had problems with the odd humor that infected the Burton/Schumacher films, only a little bit in the first one, but then it kept spreading through them like a virus that eventually killed that four-movie series. Director Joel Schumacher, a man capable of making serious, intelligent films (*Flatliners*, *A Time to Kill*), gave the studio in *Batman Forever* and *Batman & Robin* the films he'd felt they wanted. Warner Bros. studio heads had desired something more upbeat than *Batman Returns.* Schumacher would have preferred to shoot *Batman: Year One*, but the studio had no reason to reboot a successful series after only the first two.† Eight years had to pass between 1997's *Batman & Robin* and 2005's *Batman Begins*, more than long enough to declare the Burton/Schumacher series legally dead the way Wayne Enterprises' CEO has Bruce Wayne declared dead in *Batman Begins*, Christopher Nolan's variation on *Batman: Year One*. Batman had to wander away, die, and come back reborn.

---

*For more on that historic meeting, see Uslan's autobiography, *The Boy Who Loved Batman*, chapter 6.
†"There was no desire to do [*Year One*] the first time around, and there was definitely no desire to do that the second time around."—Schumacher (2005).

Humor is a vital coping mechanism. It's subjective, quixotic, and tough to pin down. It can be dry or absurd, good-natured or mean. What's funny now won't be funny later. What's hilarious to you might bore me. If you map out comedic formulas, humorists overuse them and they grow less effective. Humor relies on many of the same elements of incongruity[7] and surprise that horror doles out. Humor can swing like a weapon, drawing deep,[8] and we may get defensive when it jabs at our heroes. An insult that belittles our heroes insults us for looking up to them. *Adaptive styles of humor* build people up, whether through *affiliative humor*, which enhances our perceptions of others, or *self-enhancing humor*, which promotes us. *Maladaptive styles of humor*, on the other hand, tear people down. That includes those weapons of attack (*aggressive humor*) meant to objectify, ridicule, or humiliate others and impediments to ourselves (*self-defeating humor*).[9] Because humor is an evaluative response appraising funny versus unfunny, emotionally we're ready to evaluate humor in other ways as well. Our basic adaptive inclinations have readied us to react to humor like we'd size up potential allies and enemies, which then primes individuals who have aggressive natures or poor self-esteem to see offense where none was intended, not that intent always matters. An office employee who cracks a sexually suggestive joke oblivious to how co-workers feel can nevertheless create a negative work environment,[10] just as those who make fun of our heroes, our costumes, our collections, our movies, our toys stab at us whether they know it or not. We can't assume they know it. Some people are just that dumb. Some people, however, know that others bond and strengthen one another through mutual kidding around.

People with *gelatophobia*, the overwhelming fear of getting laughed at, do not experience humor and laughter as shared enjoyment but rather as a threat. Gelatophobes are less cheerful and use more maladaptive than adaptive humor, not that they recognize humor as much of a coping mechanism in the first place.[11] Maybe those who tease you or mock your heroes are trying to attack. Then again, maybe they're trying to connect with you or to help build your defenses against humor others truly mean to be cruel. Sensitivity has its place, and so does insensitivity. We need some of both to get through this life. Cynical gallows humor, one of the most popular coping methods among emergency service professionals like firefighters, paramedics, and police, helps them vent feelings, elicit social support, and distance themselves from situations enough to ensure that they can act effectively.[12] That doesn't mean they never care.

Entertainment is emotional. Even the most cognitively oriented activity is entertainment to those who like it, maybe also to those who dislike the activity but enjoy griping about it. A complicated math problem entertains those who enjoy the challenge. Batman stories have entertained the world since 1939 and keep going strong. When DC Comics relaunched all their titles with new #1 issues in 2011, resetting character histories, erasing stories that didn't work, and cleaning up the burdensome continuity to blow a giant breath of fresh air through their whole comic book line, they decided that Batman's history needed the least tweaking and that they should stick with what was working, leave his titles largely unchanged.* The character's humanity, above all else, keeps us invested. The stories keep us thinking and keep evoking our emotions. Batman's still fun.

The success of Frank Miller's comic book series (or four-part graphic novel, whichever you prefer to call it), *The Dark Knight Returns*, revealed an audience ready for a darker take on Batman and helped pave the way for Tim's Burton film adaptation. While Frank was working on that, Alan Moore and Dave Gibbons created *Watchmen*—similar to *The Dark Knight Returns* in that it, too, deconstructed the superhero and neither story took place in mainstream superhero canon. Both Miller and Moore have bemoaned the fact that deconstruction should have preceded reconstruction, not imitators who just kept tearing up the fabric of their heroes in the mainstream canon.

---

*Debatable, I know. The New 52's Catwoman can learn Batman's identity all over again someday and the Riddler can grow his hair out (or send his question-mark Mohawk to the Eighties) more easily than the Joker's face can grow back, but Damian should thank his lucky stars, considering how many DC Universe kids found themselves erased from history, having never been born, Selina Kyle's daughter among them (*Catwoman* #5, 2012).

"The gritty, deconstructivist postmodern superhero comic, as exemplified by Watchmen, also became a genre. It was never meant to. It was meant to be one work on its own. . . . The apocalyptic bleakness of comics over the past 15 years sometimes seems odd to me, because it's like that was a bad mood that I was in 15 years ago."

—Alan Moore, interviewed by Robinson (2001)

"I've seen all these characters of my childhood fall into disarray. They've become neither fish nor fowl. Those of us who wanted to test the boundaries of what a superhero comic book could do unfortunately broke those boundaries and the results have not all been very good. We pushed against the old walls, and they fell—but nothing much has been built to replace them. And now the roof is leaking and the sewer's backing up."

—Frank Miller, interviewed by Brownstein (2000)

The year after Frank said that, the 9/11 attacks came along, and America needed heroes. Hollywood started filling the screens with superheroes. Comic book stories Miller considered the most cynical (Jason Todd's death by phone vote, Green Lantern Hal Jordan's transformation into a mass murderer)[13] got fixed. Jason and Hal both return from the dead, and it turns out retroactively that Hal was never really a mass murderer after all.[14] The need for hope and heroes didn't stop comic books from exploring new darkness and many shades of gray. Both *Identity Crisis* at DC Comics[15] and then *Civil War* at Marvel[16] put superheroes at odds with one another over issues of security: How far will you go to feel safe? What rules will you break or impose to protect the people who matter to you? Each in its own way explored a central theme from Miller's *The Dark Knight Returns* graphic novel and Nolan's *The Dark Knight* films, what psychologist Erich Fromm considered the basic human dilemma driving us throughout our lives, *freedom versus security.*[17] *Identity Crisis* and *Civil War* each damaged relationships between superheroes, as when Batman's fury toward other heroes for violating his and other people's rights boiled forth, but each story turned out to be a case of "darkest before the dawn." Each reinvigorated storylines throughout its respective company for a time and stories felt like they mattered, like they made real differences in characters' lives as they worked through the aftermath to find new ways of relating to one another over time so they could again unite for the common good. "We're sick to death of heroes who are not heroes, we're sick to death of darkness," comic book writer Mark Waid said when discussing the more heroic character depictions that would follow DC's *Identity Crisis* and *Infinite Crisis*. "Not that there's no room, not that Batman should act like Adam West, but that won't be the overall feeling. . . . No more 'we screwed each other over and now we must pay the consequences.' No, we're super-heroes and that's what we do."[18]

Admittedly, every dawn and every day come before more darkness, and then another dawn should follow. Unending publication demands it.

> *"The night is darkest just before the dawn. And I promise you, the dawn is coming."*
> —Harvey Dent (Aaron Eckhart), *The Dark Knight* (2008 motion picture)

14

The Assessment
Bats in His Belfry?

"People think it's an obsession. A compulsion. As if there were an irresistible impulse to act. It's never been like that. I chose this life. I know what I'm doing. And on any given day, I could stop doing it. Today, however, isn't that day. And tomorrow won't be either."

—Batman, *Identity Crisis* #4 (2004)

Time's up. Does Bruce Wayne have bats in his belfry?

Is he psychotic, homicidal, suicidal, or gravely disabled? No. Does he have posttraumatic stress disorder? Even though he shows some symptoms, no. Does he have multiple personality disorder? Even if that were the correct name for the disorder, no, that one's so far off target it's ridiculous. He's one man who plays several roles and brings different characteristics to different situations with full awareness and memory of what he's doing. How about some sort of obsessive condition? No, no more so than the most driven athletes, artists, or activists who make great sacrifices to fulfill their callings in life. If he were compulsive, he'd have too little control over his actions to function so effectively and for so long. People can have problems and personality shortcomings without fitting a psychiatric diagnosis. Admittedly, though, whether or not he qualifies as suffering any specific mental disorder by the *DSM* criteria the American Psychiatric Association sets forth kind of sterilizes the basic issue: Is Batman crazy?

> Adam West (actor who minored in psychology): I hate to use a common word like this, but Batman's as crazy as Joker. You guys know that. I mean, fighting crime 24/7 in a funny suit.
> Travis Langley: Says the man who wore the suit.
> Adam West: What was I thinking? (*laughs*)[1]

> Grant Morrison (comic book writer): By psychoanalyzing his enemies with his fists, Batman may have hoped to escape the probing gaze of the analyst himself, but it was not to be. There was, after all, something deeply mad about Batman.[2]

> Steven Englehart (comic book writer who majored in psychology): That has come up a lot over the years, whether Batman's insane, but in my opinion he is not. He stands right out as having pushed himself as far as he can go because that's how he becomes the hero that he is, and he knows that if he took one more step, he'd fall into the abyss. And so he stands at the edge of that abyss.[3]

> Norm Breyfogle (comic book artist): In the fictional world in which Batman lives, no, he's not crazy at all. If Batman were to exist in the real world, however, yes, he'd be crazy—and very soon he'd be either institutionalized or dead.[4]

> Dennis O'Neil (comic book writer): There is a big difference between obsession and psychosis. Batman knows who he is and knows what drives him and he chooses not to fight it. He permits his obsession to be the meaning of his life because he cannot think of anything better. He is also rife with natural gifts. He is possibly the only person in the world who could do what he is doing. But he is not for one

second ignorant of *why* he is doing it and even what is unhealthy about it, nor is he ever out of control.[5]

This book, which could have covered many more topics, must come to a close somewhere. Batman's allies could fill their own books. Much as I'd love to discuss those allies in greater depth, like Barbara Gordon with her new forensic psychology degree,[6] her *eidetic memory*[7] (so-called photographic memory), her decades as a paraplegic, and her value as a role model both in and away from her wheelchair, this book's about Batman. Despite her Bat-identity, that independent redhead hasn't been his sidekick, has no interest in dating him (a friend of her dad's—*ew*), and doesn't reflect pieces of his personality the way his enemies do, so she doesn't fit any chapter's topic. Good for her. Understanding Batman requires us to look hardest at him and his foes. The villains mirror and warp his darkness, his fears, his needs for puzzles to solve and criminals to hurt, and his hopes too. Having a dark side does not make him mentally ill as long as he manages it, as long as he walks that edge Englehart talked about without falling into the abyss. Where his enemies reflect Batman as he is, his sidekicks hearken back to young Bruce as he was and paths adult Bruce wishes that boy could have taken. Enemies fit his fears and nightmares; the sidekicks, his hopes and better dreams.

Why doesn't this book analyze Man-Bat? Where's Amygdala? Where's Ventriloquist Albert Wesker or that gal who took his place? Not only are they less famous than most of the Case Files' featured foes, they gave me nothing new I wanted to say that I hadn't covered elsewhere. The Scarecrow Case File explained the *amygdala*, the part of the brain that links our fears and other emotions to the stimuli that set them off—so cross off the villain called Amygdala. King Tut took care of *dissociative identity disorder*, multiple personality—a topic worth contemplating (despite its inaccuracy) for Man-Bat and Ventriloquist. The Mad Hatter, on the other hand, may be a mere D-list villain, but his history raises issues no other enemy's could. How about Talia? By featuring Catwoman in a Case File but not Talia, am I playing favorites with the women in Batman's life? Maybe. During one of our convention panels before a packed house, Dr. Robin Rosenberg asked the audience for a show of hands to pick which woman is Batman's true love.[8] Nearly every hand in the crowd went up for Selina. Talia got three. Talia's relationship with Batman stays so intertwined with his relations and interactions with other people—the League of Assassins, the Society, her father, their son—that readers have trouble getting inside her head, as does Bruce. Although, her creator Denny O'Neil envisioned that by age 43, Batman would either die in the line of duty or settle down with Talia and have three kids.[9]

The easy answer is to say he's crazy when the writers make him crazy and he's not when they make him not. True enough, but when we step back to gaze long upon the great Batman tapestry, when we look for the common thread woven through it by Kane, Finger, Fox, O'Neil, Englehart, and that endless line of creators, those who have come and gone as well as those who are still weaving, what do we see? We see a hero. We see someone we'd want on our side, a figure we'd love to call forth from our shadows and hurl at those who would do us wrong. We see that part of ourselves that wants to scare all of life's bullies away, and we like it.

He is driven—haunted—but we can no more label that drive a mental illness for him than we can for the revolutionaries who stand up to tyrants or the activists who fight against great odds to make this world a better place. Out of tragedy, great good can arise. Horrible events have spurred individuals like the founder of MADD on to great, albeit unusual, achievements. They discovered their lives' missions. A person can have an obsession without qualifying for a mental illness. Is that preoccupation productive? Without intrusive passions, where would we find the world's greatest art, music, and so many inventions? These obsessions each carry a price, a massive tradeoff somewhere in that person's life, a great deal of sacrifice, and sometimes, yes, mental illness. Taking 10,000 hours to master a skill[10] cuts out time for so many other things. Everyone has problems. Batman's differ from yours and some of them are huge—but in a crisis, who's going to fall apart first, him or you? Could anyone else face the horrors he encounters and manage the complexities of his life any better than he? No.

Aside from the fact that he lives in a reality periodically twisted by magic, psionics, temporal anomalies, and other Multiversal crises, where mad scientists, monsters, extraterrestrials, and immortals walk the earth, Batman at his most realistic deals with one complicated city. Widespread corruption does not exorcise easily. Where does one man who wants to make a difference start? Does he become a police officer with hands tied by superiors and a court system that won't convict the wicked, and why would corrupt officers all around him let

Having defeated the Joker yet again, the Batman departs with the vanishing night.[11] © DC Comics.

him shake things up when, with impunity, they can beat him to a pulp the way some attack Gordon in *Batman: Year One*? Does he follow a career in law and then spin his wheels while bogged down in paperwork and regulations, subject to judges the criminals have bought—like the one who releases Joe Chill in *Batman Begins*? Maybe he becomes an activist or a social crusader, but if the rest of the community is too afraid to back him up, he'll have trouble getting far. The community needs help overcoming their fears. They need to see the crooks cower. Bruce Wayne sees that the system itself must change. He has the resources to attack that system, to show the good citizens that the bad ones will run scared when push comes to shove. In the real world, many people die for trying to expose criminals in their neighborhoods or for voicing dissent against corrupt authorities. Entire families get wiped out over one person's objection. When people make waves in such a setting, they and their loved ones can wind up dead, maimed, or framed, so the situation calls for anonymity—and yet the people could use a face to inspire the masses. They need a sense of *somebody* specific who's out there rattling the cages, even somebody wearing a mask.

So when the actor who wore that mask during my childhood asked if I, as a professional in the field of psychology, would consider Batman crazy in terms of more formal psychological principles, what did I reply?

My answer then and now: "Not for the world in which he lives."

He lives in one deeply crazed world. We love what he does to the place.

Notes

Introduction
1. Fingeroth (2004), 22–23.
2. Smith, Pustz, Langley, Andrada, Catalfu, Combs, Geranios, Moran, & Stover (2007).
3. Duncan, Langley, Langley, Smith, Poole, Head, O'Nale, Ash, Sepe, Cash, Hill, Cate, Langley, & Fingeroth (2008); Langley, Duncan, Langley, Poole, Sepe, Head, Langley, Hill, Cate, Shurtleff, & O'Nale (2008); Langley (in press).
4. Langley, Rosenberg, Meriwether, Pantozzi, & Uslan (2011); Letamendi, Rosenberg, Langley, & Wein (2011); O'Neil, Uslan, Cash, Langley, Rosenberg, & Zehr (2010); O'Neil, Zehr, Langley, Letamendi, Rosenberg, & Bruen (2011).
5. Rosenberg, Langley, Robinson, Englehart, Uslan, & West (2009).
6. Bender, Kambam, & Pozios (2011).

1. Beneath the Cowl
1. O'Neil (2008), 1.
2. *Action Comics* #1 (1938).
3. Kane & Andrae (1989).

2. Which Batman?
1. *Batman* movie serial (June 16, 1943), Chapter 1, "The Electrical Brain."
2. Harry S. Truman Library (n.d.).
3. *Batman* movie serial (September 22, 1943), Chapter 15, "The Doom of the Rising Sun."
4. *Batman* movie serial (June 23, 1943), Chapter 2, "The Bat's Cave."
5. Harmon & Glut (1972).
6. Eisner (1986), 8.
7. Rosenberg et al. (2009).
8. *Batman* television series (September 28, 1967), episode 97, "The Wail of the Siren."
9. *Batman* television series (December 28, 1966), episode 67, "The Sandman Cometh."
10. *Batman* television series (February 15, 1967), episode 81, "The Joker's Last Laugh."
11. *Batman* television series (February 16, 1967), episode 82, "The Joker's Epitaph."
12. Langley & Rosenberg (2011).

13. Burton & Salisbury (2006), 76.
14. Di Novi (2005).
15. Boucher (2011).
16. For example, *All-Star Batman and Robin the Boy Wonder* #2, 8.
17. Burton & Salisbury (2006), p. 76.
18. Burton & Salisbury, 72–73.
19. Burton (2005).
20. Goldsman (2005).
21. Freud (1989/1965).
22. Rofé (2008).
23. McNally (2004).
24. Kreisman & Straus (1989), xv.
25. For example, Mendelson (2008).
26. Quoted by Dini & Kidd (1998), unnumbered page.
27. Matson, Rivet, & Fodstad (2010); Sachdev (2000).
28. Chavel (2008).
29. Boucher (2010).
30. *Showcase* #4 (1956).
31. *The Flash* #123 (1961).
32. *Justice League of America* #21 (1963).
33. *Adventure Comics* #462 (1979); *DC Super-Stars* #17 (1977); *Superman Family* #211 (1981).
34. *Batman* #217 (1969); *Green Lantern/Green Arrow* #85 (1971); *The Amazing Spider-Man* #97 (1971); *The Amazing Spider-Man* #121 (1973); *Batman* #251 (1973).
35. *Batman: Son of the Demon* (1987).
36. *Batman* #655–658 (2006).
37. *Batman and Robin* #1 (2009).
38. *Batman Incorporated* #1 (2011).
39. Nolen-Weathington (2008), 61.

Case File 2–1: King Tut

1. *Batman* television series (March 8, 1967), episode 87, "King Tut's Coup."
2. *Batman* television series (September 29, 1966), episode 42, "Tut's Case Is Shut."
3. *Batman* television series (March 7, 1968), episode 119, "The Entrancing Dr. Cassandra."

Case File 2–2: Mr. Freeze

1. *Batman* television series (February 2, 1966), episode 7, "Instant Freeze."
2. Beginning with *Detective Comics* #373 (1968).
3. *Batman: The Animated Series* (September 7, 1992), episode 14, "Heart of Ice."
4. Kübler-Ross (1969, 2005).
5. Loughnan, Haslam, Murnane, Vaes, Reynolds, & Suitner (2010).

3. The Trauma

1. Langley et al. (2011).
2. Kane & Andrae (1989), 104.
3. Daniels (1999), 31.
4. *Action Comics* #1 (1938); *Detective Comics* #33 (1939); *Amazing Fantasy* #15 (1962).

5. *Action Comics* #1 (1938); *Superman* #61 (1949); *The Man of Steel* (1986).
6. Porter (1981).
7. For example, Monaghan, Robinson, & Dodge (1979).
8. Holmes & Rahe (1967).
9. *Smallville*, episode 148, "Descent;" *Superman: Secret Origin* #2 (2009); *Batman* #619 (2003).
10. Clements & Burgess (2002); Eth & Pynoos (1994); Malquist (1986); Parson (1995).
11. Burman & Allen-Meares (1994).
12. Wolchik, Ma, Tein, Sandier, & Ayers (2008); Wolchik, Tein, Sandier, & Ayers (2006).
13. Thompson, Kaslow, Kingree, King, Bryant, & Re (1998).
14. Sandier (2001); Skinner & Wellborn (1994).
15. O'Toole & Cory (1998).
16. Corr, Nable, & Corr (1997); Goldman (1998).
17. Kübler-Ross (1969, 2005).
18. Bonanno (2001, 2007).
19. Lindstrøm (2002).
20. Johnson & Rosenblatt (1981).
21. Cengage (n.d.); Chan (2009); Superherologist (2011).
22. Allen (1999).
23. American Psychiatric Association (1994).
24. American Psychiatric Association (2000).
25. Rosenberg (2008b), 149.
26. *DSM-IV-TR*, 468.
27. Phillips (2008).
28. Bruce Wayne (Christian Bale) to Alfred (Michael Caine) in *Batman Begins* (2005 motion picture).
29. Lu, Wagner, Van Male, Whitehead, & Boehnlein (2009).
30. Harb, Cook, Gehrman, Gamble, & Ross (2009).
31. Shore, Orton, & Manson (2009).
32. Fingeroth (2008).
33. *Batman* #650 (2006).
34. Rosenberg (2008b), 151.
35. Kistler (2010).
36. Kramer (2005).
37. Bourne (1989) in *Batman* #440.
38. *Batman: Year Three* (1989).
39. Lipkus, Dalbert, & Siegler (1996).
40. Lerner (1980); Lerner & Miller (1978).
41. Burger (1981); Valor-Seguar, Exposito, & Moya (2011).
42. Lerner & Simmons (1966).
43. Lipkus (1991); Zuckerman & Gerbasi (1977).
44. Park (2010).
45. Ehlers, Mayou, & Bryant (1998); Griffin, Resick, & Mechanic (1997); Harvey, Bryant, & Dang (1998).
46. Dekel (2011); Helgeson, Reynolds, & Tomich (2006); Triplett, Tedeschi, Cann, Calhoun, & Reeve (2011).

47. Calhoun, Cann, & Tedeschi (2010).
48. Wortmann (2009); Oltmanns & Emery (2012), 172.
49. Experts contemplating Batman's religiosity and spiritual value include Asay (2012); Brewer (2004); Garrett (2008); Lewis & Kraemer (2010); Oropeza (2006); Saunders (2011).
50. Rosenberg in Langley et al. (2011).
51. Bayer, Klasen, & Adam (2007); Haen (2009); Horowitz (2007); Orth, Montada, & Maercker (2006).
52. McCullough (2008), 146.
53. Carruth & Valle (1986).
54. Walsh (2008).
55. Jones (2010).
56. Finkelstein (2000).
57. Walters (2010).
58. Quoted by Levitz (2008).
59. Roosevelt (February 14, 1884).
60. Roosevelt (February 17, 1884).
61. Library of Congress (n.d.)
62. Morris (2002, 2010); Riis (1901).
63. Letamendi et al. (2011).
64. Salkin (2006).
65. Bonanno et al. (2011).
66. Wingo, Fani, Bradley, & Ressler (2010).
67. Caltabiano & Caltabiano (2006); Nygren, Alex, Jonsen, Gustafson, Norberg, & Lundman (2005); Wagnild & Young (1993); Wagnild & Collins (2009).
68. Ong, Zautra, & Reid (2010); Zautra, Arewasikporn, & Davis (2010).
69. For example, *Batman: Year One* (1987); *Secret Origins* trade paperback (1989); *Batman: The Long Halloween* (1996–1997).
70. Adler (1924).

4. Why the Mask?

1. *Secret Origins* trade paperback (1989).
2. Quoted by Zehr (2008), p. xvi.
3. Zehr (2008), p. 261.
4. Cuddy-Casey & Orvaschel (1997); Nagy (1948).
5. Piaget (1952, 1954); Piaget & Inhelder (1969).
6. Kuhn (2000); Overton & Byrnes (1991).
7. Piaget (1932).
8. Haidt (2001).
9. *Secret Origins* trade paperback (1989).
10. Commons & Richards (2003); Kramer (1989).
11. *Secret Origins* trade paperback (1989).
12. McCulley (1919).
13. Starting with "The Living Shadow" by the prolific Walter B. Gibson under his pen name, Maxwell Grant (1933).
14. Mann (1981).
15. Zimbardo (1969).
16. Johnson & Downing (1979).

17. Postmes & Spears (1998).
18. Rosenberg (2009).
19. Langley et al. (2011).
20. Guerrero (2011).
21. DiDio, Levitz, and Friedman, each interviewed in the *Batman Unmasked* television special (2008).
22. Zimbardo (1971).
23. Zimbardo, Maslach, & Haney (1999), 18.
24. Zimbardo, personal communication (August 18, 1991).
25. *Batman* #600 (2002).
26. *Batman* #603 (2002).
27. *Batman* #605 (2002).

5. Why the Bat?

1. *Secret Origins* trade paperback (1989).
2. *Batman: Year One* (1987).
3. *Batman Begins* (2005 motion picture).
4. Choy, Fyer, & Lipsitz (2007).
5. Rosenberg (2008a).
6. For example, *Gotham Central* #1–2 (2003).
7. Menzies & Parker (2001); Stein & Matsunaga (2006).
8. *DSM-IV-TR*, 445.
9. Sternthal (1974).
10. Petty (1997).
11. Maddux & Rogers (1983); Rogers (1983).
12. Stukas, Snyder, & Clary (1999).
13. Baumrind, Larzelere, & Owens (2010).
14. Gershoff (2002); Marshall (2002).
15. Dillard & Anderson (2004).
16. Kassin (2008); Kassin, Meissner, & Norwick (2005).
17. Kassin, Appleby, & Perillo (2010); King & Snook (2009).
18. Inbau & Reid (1967); Inbau, Reid, Buckley, & Jayne (2001).
19. Beune, Giebels, & Taylor (2010); Bull & Milne (2004).
20. Kassin et al. (2010); Leo & Ofshe (1998).
21. Kassin et al. (2007).
22. Kassin et al. (2010).
23. U.S. National Academy of Sciences (2002); Weiner, Johnston, & Lewis (1995).
24. Vergano (2002).
25. Kleinmuntz & Szucko (1984).
26. National Research Council (2002); Saxe, Dougherty, & Cross (1985).
27. Ben-Shakhar (2008).
28. Maschke & Scalabrini (2005); *Penn & Teller: Bullshit!* television series (July 23, 2009), season 7, episode 5, "Lie Detectors."
29. Arrigo & Wagner (2007).
30. Janoff-Bulman (2007).
31. Ross (2005).
32. Janoff-Bulman (2007), 430.
33. Dratel (2006); Suskind (2006).

34. Bowden (2007); Cialdini (2001); McCauley (2007).
35. Hogan & Emler (1981).
36. Janoff-Bulman (2007).
37. *Batman* #633 (2004).
38. U.S. Department of Justice, Federal Bureau of Investigation (n.d.).
39. Sternberg (2003).
40. Hallett (2004).
41. Kaczynski (1995).
42. Dawes (1991).

Case File 5–1: Scarecrow
1. World's Finest Comics #3 (1941).
2. *Batman* #189 (1967).
3. *Batman: Gotham Knights* #23 (2002).
4. Detective Comics #571 (1987).
5. *Batman* #457 (1990).
6. World Health Organization (2004).
7. Romero & Butler (2007).
8. Bunting, Tolson, Kuhn, Suarez, & Williams (2000).
9. Stein, Seedat, & Gelernter (2006); Van Ameringen, Mancini, Oakman, & Farvolden (1999).
10. Monteleone, Santonastaso, Tortorella, Favaro, Farbrazzo, Castaldo, Caregaro, Fuschino, & Maj (2005).
11. Machado & Einsarson (2010).
12. Dell'Osso, Buoli, Baldwin, & Altamura (2010).
13. Lee & Keltner (2006).
14. Czerner (2002).
15. Siegal (2005); Siegel, Bhatt, Bhatt, & Zalcman (2007).
16. Davis & Whalen (2001); Myers (1964); Roberts & Nagel (1996).
17. Itoi & Sugimoto (2010).
18. Schachter & Singer (1962).
19. Bryant & Miron (2003).
20. Myers (2008).
21. *Batman* #262 (1975).
22. Feinstein et al. (2010).
23. *Blackest Night* #4 (2009).

Case File 5–2: Hugo Strange
1. *Detective Comics* #46 (1940).
2. *Detective Comics* #471 (1977).
3. *Detective Comics* #472 (1977); *Batman* #356 (1983).
4. *Batman: Legends of the Dark Knight* #11–15 (1990).
5. *Batman: Legends of the Dark Knight* #137–141 (2001).
6. *Batman: Gotham Knights* #8–11 (2000–2001)
7. Grey (1992). See also *Ed Wood*, 1994 motion picture directed by Tim Burton.
8. Smithkey (1998).
9. Helfgott (2008).
10. Keppel & Birnes (1997).

11. Douglas (2006); Keppel & Birnes (1997).
12. Holmes & Holmes (2002).
13. For example, see Donald Foster's (2000) evaluation of James Brussel's Mad Bomber profile.
14. Alison (2011).
15. Gladwell (2007); see also Turvey (2008).
16. Goodwill, Alison, & Beech (2009); Schlesinger (2009).
17. Torres, Boccaccini, & Miller (2006).
18. Gregory (2005).

6. The "Superstitious, Cowardly Lot"

1. Greening (1997).
2. Patterson, Kosson, & Newman (1987); Van Goozen, Fairchild, Snoek, & Harold (2007).
3. Bartol & Bartol (2010), 102.
4. Newman, Widom, & Nathan (1985).
5. Hughes & Johnson (1975).
6. Dollinger & LaMartina (1998); La Voie (1973).
7. For example, *Penguin: Pain and Prejudice* #1–2 (2011–2012).
8. Maslow (1954).
9. *Catwoman* #0 (1994).
10. *Shadow of the Bat Annual* #3 (1995).
11. *Penguin: Pain and* Prejudice #1–2 (2011–2012).
12. *Catwoman* #39 (1996).
13. Maslow (1966).
14. Cianci & Gambrel (2003).
15. *Secret Origins* trade paperback (1989).
16. May (1983).
17. *Batman Special* #1 (1984).
18. *New Year's Evil: Prometheus* #1 (1998).
19. *JLA: Earth* 2 (2000).
20. Watson (1913).
21. Bandura (1973).
22. Neisser (1967).
23. Marian Breland Bailey, B. F. Skinner's second graduate student, many personal communications (1994–2001).
24. Lewin (1951).
25. Gottesman (1991); Kendler (1983); Tienari, Wahlberg, & Wynne (2006).
26. Berkowitz (1962).
27. *DSM-IV-TR.*
28. Khan (n.d.)
29. Frick & Ellis (1999).
30. Harris (2006).
31. *DSM-IV-TR.*
32. McCabe, Hough, Wood, & Yeh (2001).
33. *Detective Comics* #875 & 879 (2011).
34. Hare (1991, 1996); Hare & Neumann (2006).
35. *Detective Comics* #875 (2011).

36. *DSM-IV-TR.*
37. Lahey, Moffitt, & Caspi (2003); Raine (2002); Van Goozen & Fairchild (2008).
38. *Detective Comics* #879 (2011).
39. Harris & Rice (2006).
40. *Detective Comics* #881 (2011).
41. Davis & Whalen (2001).
42. Messich, Tarter, & Carvlin (n.d.).
43. *Catwoman* #0 (1994).
44. *Batman: Cacophony* #1–3 (2008–2009).
45. *Batman: Cacophony* #1–3 (2008–2009).
46. *Batman and the Outsiders* #14 (1984).
47. *DSM-I*, 38.
48. Bartol & Bartol (2005), 119.
49. *Red Hood: The Lost Days* #1 (2008).
50. Hare (2003).
51. Skeem & Cooke (2010).
52. Cleckley (1941/1988).
53. Cleckley, 338–339.
54. Babiak & Hare (2006).
55. Felthous & Henning (2010).
56. Gacono et al. (2001).
57. Bartol & Bartol (2005), 122.
58. Rosenberg & Kosslyn (2011), 599.
59. Hare (1996); Hart (1998).
60. Fabiano, Robinson, & Porporino (1990); MacKenzie (2001).
61. Lipsey, Chapman, & Landenberger (2001); Spiropoulous, Spruance, Van Voorhis, & Schmitt (2005); Van Voorhis, Braswell, & Lester (2004).
62. Putkonen et al. (2010).
63. Harpur & Hare (1994).
64. *Batman: Year Two* (1987).
65. *Batman* #47 (1948); *Batman* #673 (2008).
66. *Batman: Year Two* (1987); *Batman: Full Circle* (1991).

Case File 6–1: Bane

1. *Batman: Gotham Knights* #48 (2004).
2. Murray (1938).
3. McClelland (1961); McClelland, Atkinson, Clark, & Lowell (1953).
4. *Secret Six* #36 (2011).

7. The Halloween Party

1. Debuted in *Batman* #59 (1950); turned assassin in *Detective Comics* #474 (1977).
2. *Batman: Shadow of the Bat* #1 (1992); *The Batman Chronicles* #3 (1996).
3. *The Brave and the Bold* #111 (1974).
4. For example, *Batman and Robin* #20 (2011).
5. *Batman: Poison Ivy* (1997).
6. *Detective Comics* #734–735 (1999); *Gotham City Sirens* #8 (2010).
7. Leary, Twenge, & Quinlivan (2006); Williams (2002).

8. *DSM-III* through *DSM-IV-TR.*
9. Blackburn & Coid (1997); Hare (1991).
10. Halgin & Whitbourne (2009), 322.
11. Millon (2004); Millon et al. (2000).
12. Market (2009).
13. Millon (1991).
14. *Detective Comics* #611 (1990).
15. *Robin* #130 (2004).
16. *Catwoman* #12–15 (2002–2003).
17. *DSM-III-R.*
18. Abrams & Bromberg (2007).
19. Segal, Coolidge, & Rosowsky (2000).
20. Zuckerman (1979), 27.
21. Daderman, Muerling, & Hallman (2001); Hobfoll, Rom, & Segal (1989).
22. Schultz & Schultz (2009); Zuckerman (1983).
23. Harpur, Hare, & Hakstian (1989).
24. *Detective Comics* #475 (1978).
25. *The Batman Adventures: Mad Love* (1994).
26. Zuckerman (2004).
27. *Detective Comics* #485 (1979).
28. *Secret Origins* #6 (1986).
29. *DSM-IV-TR*, 457.
30. *DSM-IV-TR*, 457.
31. Bonnie, Jeffries, & Low (2008); Clarke (1990).

Case File 7–1: The Riddler
1. *Batman: Riddler—The Riddle Factory* (1995).
2. *Countdown* #33 (2007).
3. Peterson, Kaasa, & Loftus (2009).
4. Geraerts, Raymaekers, & Merckelbach (2008); Laney & Loftus (2005).
5. Laney & Loftus (2008).
6. Takarangi, Polaschek, Garry, & Loftus (2008).
7. *Batman* television series (March 31, 1966), episode 24, "Give 'em the Axe."
8. *Batman* #619 (2003).
9. *Batman* #179 (1966).
10. *Batman: Gotham Adventures* #11 (1999).
11. Parikh (2008).
12. *DSM-IV-TR*, 462.
13. *Detective Comics Annual* #8 (1995).
14. *Detective Comics* #822 (2006).
15. For example, *Trinity* (2007–2008).
16. *Gotham City Sirens* #3 (2009).
17. Fromm (1964).
18. *Detective Comics Annual* #8 (1995).
19. *Joker's Asylum II: The Riddler* #1 (2010).
20. *Batman* #705 (2011).
21. *Batman* #452–452 (1990).

Case File 7–2: The Penguin
1. *Secret Origins Special* #1 (1989).
2. *Countdown* #29 (2007).
3. *Penguin: Pain and Prejudice* #1 (2011).
4. Just & Morris (2003).
5. Adler (1930, 1933/1939).
6. *Batman Annual* #11 (1987).
7. *Penguin: Pain and Prejudice* #5 (2012).

Case File 7–3: Poison Ivy
1. *Gotham City Sirens* #7 (2010).
2. *Batman* #608 (2002).
3. *Gotham City Sirens* #2 (2009).

8. The Madhouse
1. *Batman* #258 (1974).
2. Lovecraft (1937).
3. Lytle (2008).
4. *Arkham Asylum: Living Hell* #1 (2003).
5. Lytle (2008), 117.
6. Porter (2002).
7. Rush (1815).
8. Gamwell & Tomes (1995).
9. *Batman* #618 (2003).
10. Daily (2011).
11. *Batman: The Long Halloween* #3 (1998).
12. Bender, Kambam, & Pozios (2009); Daniels (2008); Davidson (2011); Lytle (2008).
13. Nichols (2006).
14. *Detective Comics* #1 (2011).
15. Daniels (2008), 205.
16. *Arkham Asylum: Living Hell* #4 (2003).
17. *Gotham City Sirens* #21 (2011).
18. Lazarus & Zur (2002).
19. *Arkham Asylum: A Serious House on Serious Earth*, 1989. Again.
20. *Detective Comics* #865 (2010).
21. *Detective Comics* #864 (2010).
22. *Detective Comics* #1–2 (2011).
23. Wang et al. (2005); Wilson, Dyszynski, & Mant (2003).
24. Harris et al. (2005); Marshall et al. (2005).
25. R. M. Langley, personal communication (June 24, 2011).
26. Green (2001).
27. Keefe et al. (2007); McEvoy et al. (2007).
28. Lehman (1998).
29. *Batman: Poison Ivy* (1997).
30. Meltzer (1982); Schmid & Wanderer (2007); Segredou, Livaditis, Liolios, & Skartsila (2008).
31. *Detective Comics* #824 (2006).

Case File 8–1: The Mad Hatter
1. *Secret Six* #6 (2007).
2. *Batman and Robin* #21 (2011).
3. *Gotham Central* #20 (2004).
4. *Secret Six* #4 (2006).
5. *DSM-IV-TR.*
6. *Secret Six* #3 (2006).
7. *Secret Six* #6 (2007).
8. *Arkham Asylum: A Serious House on Serious Earth* (1989); *Batman: Streets of Gotham* #4 (2009).
9. *Batman: Legends of the Dark Knight Halloween Special* #2 (1994).
10. Holmes & Holmes (2009); National Center for Missing and Exploited Children (1985).

Case File 8–2: Harley Quinn
1. *Gotham City Sirens* #7 (2010).
2. *The New Batman Adventures*, episode 21, "Mad Love" (January 16, 1999).
3. *Gotham City Sirens* #1 (2009).
4. *Batman: Harley Quinn* (1999).
5. *DSM-IV-TR*, 721–725.
6. *The Batman Adventures: Mad Love* (1994); *Suicide Squad* #6–7 (2012).
7. *The New Batman Adventures*, episode 21, "Mad Love" (January 16, 1999).
8. *Gotham City Sirens* #24 (2011).
9. *DSM-IV-TR*, 332–334.
10. *Suicide Squad* #1 (2011).
11. *Gotham City Sirens* #6 (2010).
12. Rosenberg, Langley, Robinson, Englehart, Ulsan, & West (2009).
13. *The Batman Adventures: Mad Love* (1994).

Case File 8–3: The Joker
1. *Detective Comics* #168 (1951).
2. *Batman: The Killing Joke* (1988).
3. *Batman and Robin* #13–14 (2010).
4. *Batman Black and White*, Volume 2 (2002).
5. *Batman* #649 (2006).
6. *Gotham City Sirens* #6 (2010).
7. *Detective Comics* #64 (1942).
8. Gold (1988), 9.
9. *Batman* #74 (1952–1953).
10. *Batman* #251 (1973).
11. *Batman: The Killing Joke* (1988).
12. *Batman* #427–428 (1988).
13. *Detective Comics* #741 (2000).
14. *The Brave and the Bold* #111 (1974).
15. *Batman: The Killing Joke* (1988).
16. Coogan (2006), 109.
17. *Detective Comics* #475 (1978).

18. For example, Ingersoll (2003).
19. Rosenberg et al. (2009).
20. Langley & Rosenberg (2011).

9. The Psychodynamic Duo
 1. Freud & Byck (1974); Thornton (1983).
 2. Freud (1940).
 3. Erikson (1959); Freud & Jung (1974); Horney (1939).
 4. Jung, Henderson, von Franz, Jaffé, & Jacobi (1964).
 5. Freud (1899/1965), 390.
 6. *Detective Comics* #574 (1987).
 7. *Batman: Year One* (1987).
 8. *Secret Origins* trade paperback (1989).
 9. Wertham (1954/2004), 190.
10. Freud (1909).
11. Jung (1913).
12. Freud (1899/1965), 299.
13. Freud (1936).
14. Freud (1899/1965), 299.
15. American Psychiatric Association (2000).
16. Vaillant (1977).
17. *Secret Origins* trade paperback (1989), 7.
18. For example, *Batman: The Dark Knight Returns* (1986), *Kingdom Come* (1996), *Batman* #300 (1978).
19. For example, the multiply-doomed Earth-51 in *Countdown to Final Crisis* #14 (2008).
20. Jung (1971).
21. Jung (1949/1961), 166, 178.
22. *Robin* #128 (2004).
23. *Detective Comics* #38 (1940).
24. Jung (1964).
25. Jung (1919).
26. Jung (1936).
27. Kane & Andrae (1989), 41.
28. Jung (1942/1968), 265.
29. *DC Super Stars* #17 (1977).
30. Campbell, Cousineau, & Brown (1990).
31. Campbell (1949).
32. Coogan (2006), 122.

Case File 9–1: Two-Face
 1. *Batman: Year One* (1987).
 2. *Batman: The Long Halloween* (1997).
 3. *Detective Comics* #66, 4.
 4. Rotter (1966).
 5. Two-Face (Tommy Lee Jones) in *Batman Forever* (1995 motion picture).
 6. *Batman Forever.*
 7. *Batman* #651–654 (2006).

8. *Nightwing* #147–150.
9. Mersky (1992).

10. The Kids: Why Robin?

1. Bergner (2007); Grassley & Nelms (2009); Parker & Wampler (2006).
2. Cole (2010); Stone (2011).
3. Bigger & Webb (2010); Djikic, Oatley, Zoeterman, & Peterson (2009); Isbell, Sobol, Lindauer, & Lowrance (2004); Oatley (2011).
4. Happé (1994); Premack & Woodruff (1978).
5. Flavell (1979); Pizzolato (2006); Woolley (1996).
6. Bill Finger, quoted by Kane & Andrae (1989), 46.
7. Krause (2010); Meissner (1970).
8. J. Robinson, personal communication (June 23, 2009).
9. Jerry Robinson, quoted by Couch (2010), 38.
10. *Detective Comics* #38 (1940).
11. Bill Finger, quoted by Daniels (1999), 38.
12. *Star Spangled Comics* #65–130 (1947–1952).
13. *Young Allies* #1 (1941).
14. *The Avengers* #4 (1964).
15. *Sub-Mariner* #14 (1969).
16. *The Brave and the Bold* #54 (1964).
17. Coogan (2006), 213.
18. Duncan & Smith (2010), 228.
19. Piaget (1930, 1952).
20. *Batman* #217 (1969).
21. *The New Teen Titans* #39 (1984).
22. *Tales of the Teen Titans* #44 (1984).
23. Daniels (1999), 147.
24. *Batman* #357 (1983).
25. D. O'Neil, personal communication (July 24, 2011).
26. *Detective Comics* #526 (1983).
27. Quoted, respectively, by Robinson (2001) and Brownstein (2000).
28. *Batman* #408 (1987).
29. *Batman* #368 (1984).
30. *Batman* #427–428 (1988).
31. Daniels (1999), 191.
32. O'Brien (2005).
33. Fodor & Farrow (1979); Stahl & Harrell (1982).
34. Sharrett (1991), 35, 40.
35. *Batman: Year Three* (1989).
36. Quoted in Daniels (1999), 170.
37. For example, his mother in *Detective Comics* #618–621 (1990) and his father in *Identity Crisis* #5 (2004).
38. For example, his ex-girlfriend Stephanie Brown in *Robin* #174 (2008). Tim's parents stay dead despite their brief stint as Black Lantern super-zombies (*Blackest Night: Batman* #1–3, 2009).
39. *Red Robin* #1 (2009).
40. *Detective Comics* #647–648 (1992).

41. *Robin* #58 (1998).
42. *Robin* #65 (1999).
43. *Robin* #126–128 (2004).
44. Johnston (2011).
45. *Batman* #633 (2004).
46. *Batman* #644 (2005).
47. *Robin* #174 (2008); *Robin/Spoiler Special* (2008).
48. Cooper & Grotevant (1989).
49. *Robin* #58 (1998).
50. Ellis et al. (2003).
51. *Batgirl* #1 (2011).
52. *Batgirl* #24 (2011).
53. *DC Special Series* #15—*Batman Spectacular* (1978); *Batman: Son of the Demon* (1987).
54. *Batman* #655–658 (2006).
55. *Batman* #657 (2006).
56. *Batman and Robin* #1 (2011).
57. Adler (1908).
58. Ernst & Angst (1982); Zajonc (2001).
59. Kidwell (1982).
60. Allred & Poduska (1988); McGuirk & Pettijohn (2008); Kennedy (1989); Kidwell (1982); Salmon (1998, 2003).
61. Anderson & Friedman (1997), 1063; Keniston (1983), 29.
62. *Batman* #657 (2006).
63. *Batgirl* #7 (2010); #17 (2011).
64. *Detective Comics* #38 (1940).
65. *Batman and Robin* #16 (2011).
66. *JLA/Titans* #2 (1998).
67. *Identity Crisis* #5 (2004).
68. *The New Titans* #100 (1993).
69. *Nightwing* #4 (1995).

Case File 10–1: Red Hood

1. *Batman* #424 (1988).
2. Explained in *Batman Annual* #25 (2006).
3. *Batman* #650 (2006).
4. *Batman* #426 (1988).
5. *Batman* #641 (2005).
6. *Batman and Robin* #23 (2011).
7. *Green Arrow* #71 (2007).
8. *Red Hood and the Outlaws* #1 (2011).

Case File 10–2: Dr. Fredric Wertham

1. Donald (n.d.).
2. Quoted by Sharrett (1991), 38.
3. *Batman* #84 (1954).
4. *Brown v. Board of Education*, 347 U.S. 483 (1954).
5. Wertham (unpublished manuscript).

6. Ellison (1953/1964).
7. Wertham (1954/2004).
8. Hajdu (2008).
9. Wertham (1954/2004), 237.
10. Wertham (1954/2004), 192.
11. Wertham (1954/2004), 189–190.
12. Fisher & Greenberg (1996); McCullough (2001); Mills (2005).
13. Medhurst (1991), 51.
14. Wertham (1954/2004), 193.
15. Wertham (1954/2004), 191.
16. Kane & Andrae (1989), 108.

11. The Women
1. Yes, I quoted the movie *Batman Forever.*
2. Pantozzi (2010).
3. *Catwoman* #40 (1996).
4. Norton & Pettegrew (1977); Sadalla, Kenrick, & Vershure (1987); Touhey (1974).
5. Bem (1974); Bem (1976).
6. Calvo-Salguero, García-Martínez, & Monteoliva (2008); Colley, Mulhern, Maltby, & Wood (2009).
7. *The Adventures of Superman* #424 (1987); *Smallville*, episode 68, "Gone" (September 29, 2004).
8. Herold (1999); Urbaniak & Kilmann (2003).
9. Urbaniak & Kilmann (2006).
10. Langley et al. (2011).
11. Aronson & Mills (1959).
12. Festinger (1957); Gerard & Mathewson (1966).
13. Aronson & Carlsmith (1963); Cooper (2010).
14. Langley et al. (2011).
15. Meston & Frohlich (2003).
16. Takeuchi (2006).
17. Murstein, Reif, & Syracuse-Siewert (2002).
18. Regan (1998).
19. Penton-Voak et al. (2001); Rhodes (2006).
20. Fink, Neave, Manning, & Grammer (2006).
21. Jokela (2009); Rhodes, Simmons, & Peters (2005).
22. Engemann & Owyang (2005); Persico, Postlewaite, & Silverman (2004).
23. Judge, Hurst, & Simon (2009); Langlois et al. (2000).
24. Dion (1972).
25. Clifford & Walster (1973); Rich (1975).
26. Sigall & Ostrove (1973).
27. Castellow, Wuensch, & Moore (1990).
28. Darby & Jeffers (1988); DeSantis & Kayson (1997); Erian et al. (1998).
29. Kulka & Kessler (1978).
30. Erian et al. (1998).
31. Sigall & Ostrove (1975).
32. *Batman* #1 (1940).
33. *Batman* #244 (1972).

NOTES TO PAGES 217–226

34. *Batman* #244 (1972).
35. *Batman* #1 (1940).
36. *Batman* #15 (1943).
37. Kane & Andrae (1989), 107.
38. Uslan (2004), 5.
39. *Detective Comics* #233 (1956).
40. Daniels (1999), 91; York (2000).
41. Daniels (1999), 92.
42. *Batman* #144 (1961).
43. Daniels (), 94.
44. *Batman* #119 (1958); *Detective Comics* #309 (1962).
45. *Batman* #128 (1959); *Batman* #147 (1962); *Detective Comics* #292 (1961); *Detective Comics* #275 (1960).
46. *Detective Comics* #485 (1979).
47. *Batman* #197 (1967).
48. 52 #11 (2006).
49. *Batman* #232 (1971).
50. *DC Special Series* #15 (1978).
51. Kane & Andrae (1989), 129–131.
52. Hamm & Skaaren (1988).
53. *Batman* #703 (2010).
54. *Bruce Wayne: The Road Home: Ra's al Ghul* (2010).
55. Langley et al. (2011).
56. *Detective Comics* #470 (1977).
57. *Detective Comics* #475 (1978).
58. *Detective Comics* #475 (1978).
59. Greenberger (1992).
60. Moderating Langley et al. (2011).
61. Winch (1958).
62. Buss (1985); Nangle et al. (2004).
63. Myers (2008), 401.
64. *Detective Comics* #556–557 (1985).
65. *Batman: Legends of the Dark Knight Halloween Special* #1 (1993).
66. *Batman* #612 (2003).
67. Audet & Everall (2010); Joinson (2001).
68. Myers (2008), 417.
69. Archer & Cook (1986).
70. Jourard (1964).
71. *Detective Comics* #751 (2000).
72. *Batman: The 10-Cent Adventure* #1 (2002).
73. Sprecher (2001); Sprecher & Hendrick (2004).
74. *Batman* #615 (2003); *Batman Returns* (1992 motion picture); *The Brave and the Bold* #197 (1983).
75. *Batman* #232 (1971).
76. *DC Super Stars* #17 (1977).
77. *Identity Crisis* #2 (2004).
78. *Identity Crisis* #6 (2005).

79. *JLA* #115–119 (2005).
80. *Catwoman* #50 (2006).
81. *Catwoman* #51 (2006).
82. Rhoades, Stanley, & Markman (2010).
83. Acevedo & Aron (2009); Coleman & Ganong (1990); Sternberg (1988).
84. Sternberg (1986); Sternberg (1997).
85. Kim & Hatfield (2004).
86. Karney (2008).
87. Ackerman, Griskevicius, & Li (2011); Brantley, Knox, & Zusman (2002).
88. Peplau & Gordon (1985).
89. Simpson, Campbell, & Berscheid (1986).
90. Emmers-Sommer, Warber, & Halford (2007).
91. Barbara (2008).
92. Abbey (1982).
93. For example, *Batman Returns* (1992 motion picture).
94. *Catwoman* #1 (2011).
95. *Detective Comics* #850 (2009).

Case File 11–1: Catwoman
1. *Catwoman* #18 (1995).
2. *Catwoman* #0 (1994).
3. Lindemann (2010).
4. *The World* (2010).
5. *DSM-IV-TR*.
6. Connolly (2006); Richters et al. (2008); Wright (2010).
7. *Catwoman* #46 (1997).
8. *DSM-IV-TR*, 667–669.
9. Dannon, Lowengrub, Lancu, & Kotler (2004); Grant & Odlaugh (2008); Yates (2000).
10. Grant (2006).
11. Dannon (2002); Durst et al. (2001).
12. Cameron (1964); Deng (1997); Russell (1973).
13. Sarasalo, Bergman, & Toth (1997).
14. U.S. Department of Justice, Federal Bureau of Investigation (2004).
15. Cromwell & Olson (2004); Merry & Harsent (2000).
16. Bernasco (2006); Miethe, McCorkle, & Listwan (2006).
17. Walsh (1980).
18. *Catwoman* #39 (1996).
19. *Catwoman* #38 (1996).
20. *Catwoman* #1 (2002).
21. *Gotham City Sirens* #22 (2011).
22. Alarid et al. (1996); Pope (1977).
23. Decker, Wright, Redfern, & Smith (1993).
24. Mullins & Wright (2003).
25. Laidler & Hunt (2001); Maher (1997); Miller (2001); Phoenix (2000).
26. *Catwoman* #1 (2002).
27. *Catwoman* #59 (1998).

12. The Fathers: Why Do We Fall?

1. Letamendi et al. (2011).
2. *Batman* #307 (1979).
3. *Secret Origins* trade paperback (1989).
4. Adherents (2005/2007); Waldman & Kress (2006).
5. Bretherton (1992); Calder (2003); Van Dijken (1998).
6. Ainsworth & Bowlby (1965).
7. Bretherton & Munholland (1999).
8. Ainsworth, Blehar, Waters, & Wall (1978).
9. Bartholomew & Horowitz (1991).
10. Main & Solomon (1986).
11. Wayment & Vierthaler (2002).
12. Field & Filanosky (2010).
13. Mancini, Robinaugh, Shear, & Bonanno (2009); Shear (2010).
14. Crawford & Benoit (2009); Madigan, Moran, & Pederson (2006).
15. Brennan, Clark, & Shaver (1998).
16. *Batman: The Killing Joke* (1988).
17. *Detective Comics* #600 (1989).
18. *Detective Comics* #599 (1989); *Secret Origins* trade paperback (1989).
19. *Batman* #232 (1971).
20. *JLA* #43–46 (2000).
21. Marano (2008).
22. *Batman* #307 (1979).
23. Aronson & Mills (1959); Gerard & Mathewson (1966); Zimbardo (2008).
24. Alfred (Michael Caine) in *Batman Begins* (2005 motion picture).
25. Baumrind (1991); Maccoby & Martin (1983).
26. *Batman: Blind Justice* (1992).
27. Moench (2004), 17.
28. Fingeroth (2005).
29. Markell & Markell (2008); Pahel (2006).
30. *Batman: Full Circle* (1991).
31. Newberger (2000).
32. *Batman and Robin* #1 (2011).
33. *Catwoman* #72 (2007).
34. Jaques (1965); Levinson (1986).
35. Erikson (1968).
36. Pratt, Danso, Arnold, Norris, & Filyer (2001).
37. Sharrett (1991).
38. Erikson (1950).
39. *Detective Comics* #574 (1987).

Case File 12–1: Ra's al Ghul

1. *Batman: Birth of the Demon* (1992).
2. First appearance: *Strange Adventures* #215 (1968).
3. *Batman Annual* #25 (2006).
4. *Azrael* #6, 1995; *Batman: Birth of the Demon* (1992).
5. *Batman Begins* (2005 motion picture).

6. De Grey (2007); Gaudin (2009).
7. Erikson & Erikson (1998).
8. Newman & Newman (1991).

13. Why So Serious?

1. Burt Ward, personal communication, after a darn nice introduction from Adam West (November 14, 2010).
2. Feiffer (1977).
3. West & Rovin (1994).
4. Uslan (2011), 62.
5. Uslan (2011), 231.
6. Boucher (2009).
7. Samson & Hempelmann (2011).
8. Weinstein, Hodgins, & Ostvik-White (2011).
9. Kuiper & Leite (2010).
10. Berdahl & Aquino (2009).
11. Ruch, Beermann, & Proyer (2009).
12. Rowe & Regehr (2010).
13. *Zero Hour* (1994).
14. *Green Lantern: Rebirth* #4 (2005).
15. *Identity Crisis* #1–7 (2004–2005).
16. *Civil War* #1–7 (2006–2007).
17. Fromm (1941); Langley (2010).
18. Kistler (2005).

14. The Assessment

1. Langley & Rosenberg (2011), 672–673.
2. Morrison (2011), 25.
3. Quoted in Langley & Rosenberg (2011), 669.
4. Breyfogle (2008).
5. Quoted by Pearson & Uricchio (1991), 19.
6. *Batgirl* #3 (2012).
7. *Batman* #197 (1967).
8. Langley et al. (2011).
9. O'Neil et al. (2011).
10. Ericsson, Krampe, & Tesch-Römer (1993).
11. *Detective Comics* #476 (1978).

References
Comic Books and Graphic Novels

Puzzled by the lack of volume numbers on these titles? DC doesn't number their series' volumes when they revive a canceled series or relaunch an existing title by starting over with a new #1 issue. Fans impose those volume numbers—sometimes that helps, but sometimes it only creates further confusion. Comics listed here appear in alphabetical order by title, but within in each title they're in chronological order arranged by cover dates instead of issue numbers because issue numbers create confusion. For example, all DC Universe titles started over at #1 in the fall of 2011, so *Detective Comics* #881 (the last issue of the original run that began with a pre-Batman *Detective Comics* #1 back in 1937) came out weeks before 2011's new *Detective Comics* #1. Issue numbers for a title like *Catwoman*, which has had at least four or five #1 issues (depending on whether you'd include a mini-series like *Catwoman: When in Rome* in the count) can prove particularly perplexing if you overlook the dates. Because of subtitles, title changes, numbering changes, resumption of old numbering, and other factors, only a comic book's cover date places it in historical context.

52 #11 (2006, July). "Batwoman Begins!" Script: Geoff Johns, Grant Morrison, Greg Rucka, & Mark Waid. Art: Keith Giffen, Joe Bennett, Todd Nauck, Marlo Alquiza, & Jack Jadson.

Action Comics #1 (1938, June). "Superman, Champion of the Oppressed." Script: Jerry Siegel. Art: Joe Shuster.

Adventure Comics #462 (1979, March). "Only Legends Live Forever!" Script: Paul Levitz. Art: Jim Aparo & Dick Giordano.

The Adventures of Superman #424 (1987, January). "Man O' War!" Script: Marv Wolfman. Art: Jerry Ordway & Mike Machlan.

All-Star Batman and Robin the Boy Wonder #2 (2005, October). "Episode Two." Script: Frank Miller. Art: Jim Lee & Scott Williams.

Amazing Fantasy #15 (1962, August). "Spider-Man!" Script: Stan Lee. Art: Steve Ditko.

The Amazing Spider-Man #97 (1971, June). "In the Grip of the Goblin!" Script: Stan Lee. Art: Gil Kane, Frank Giacoia, & John Romita.

The Amazing Spider-Man #121 (1973, June). "The Night Gwen Stacy Died." Script: Gerry Conway. Art: Gil Kane, John Romita, & Tony Mortellaro.

Arkham Asylum: A Serious House on Serious Earth (1989). Script: Grant Morrison. Art: Dave McKean.

Arkham Asylum: Living Hell #1 (2003, July). "Whole in the Head." Script: Dan Slott. Art: Ryan Sook.

Arkham Asylum: Living Hell #4 (2003, October). "Tic Toc." Script: Dan Slott. Art: Ryan Sook & Wade Von Grawbadger.

The Avengers #4 (1964, March). "Captain America Lives Again!" Script: Stan Lee. Art: Jack Kirby & George Roussos.

Azrael #6 (1995, July). "The Temptation." Script: Dennis O'Neil. Art: Barry Kitson & James Pascoe.

Batgirl #7 (2010, April). "Batgirl Rising: Core Requirements." Script: Bryan Q. Miller. Art: Lee Garbett & Trevor Scott.

Batgirl #17 (2011, March). "Batgirl: The Lesson—Frogs, Snails, & Puppy-Dog Tails . . ." Script: Bryan Q. Miller. Art: Pere Pérez.

Batgirl #24 (2011, October). "Unsinkable." Script: Bryan Q. Miller. Art: Pere Pérez.

Batgirl #1 (2011, November). "Shattered." Script: Gail Simone. Art: Ardian Syaf & Vicente Cifuentes.

Batgirl #3 (2012, January). "A Breath of Broken Glass." Script: Gail Simone. Art: Ardian Syaf & Vicente Cifuentes.

Batman #1 (1940, Spring). [The Joker and the Cat's untitled debut stories.] Scripts: Bill Finger. Art: Bob Kane & Jerry Robinson.

Batman #15 (1943, February–March). "Your Face Is Your Fortune." Script: Jack Schiff. Art: Bob Kane & Jerry Robinson.

Batman #47 (1948, June–July). "The Origin of Batman." Script: Bill Finger. Art: Bob Kane & Charles Paris.

Batman #49 (1948, October–November). "Fashions in Crime!" Script: Bill Finger. Art: Bob Kane & Charles Paris.

Batman #49 (1948, October–November). "The Scoop of the Century!" Script: Bill Finger. Art: Bob Kane & Charles Paris.

Batman #59 (1950, June–July). "The Man Who Replaced Batman!" Script: David Vern. Art: Bob Kane & Lew Schwartz.

Batman #74 (1952, December–1953, January). "The Crazy Crime Clown." Script: Alvin Schwartz. Art: Dick Sprang & Charles Paris.

Batman #84 (1954, June). "The Sleeping Beauties of Gotham City!" Script: David Vern. Art: Sheldon Moldoff & Stan Kaye.

Batman #119 (1958, October). "The Arch-Rivals of Gotham City." Script: unknown. Art: Sheldon Moldoff & Stan Kaye.

Batman #121 (1959, February). "The Ice Crimes of Mr. Zero." Script: Dave Wood. Art: Sheldon Moldoff & Charles Paris.

Batman #128 (1959, December). "The Interplanetary Batman." Script: Bill Finger. Art: Sheldon Moldoff & Charles Paris.

Batman #144 (1961, December). "Bat-Mite Meets Bat-Girl." Script: Bill Finger. Art: Sheldon Moldoff & Charles Paris.

Batman #147 (1962, May). "Batman Becomes Bat-Baby!" Script: Bill Finger. Art: Sheldon Moldoff & Charles Paris.

Batman #179 (1966, March). "The Riddle-less Robberies of the Riddler." Script: Gardner Fox. Art: Sheldon Moldoff.

Batman #181 (1966, June). "Beware of—Poison Ivy!" Script: Robert Kanigher. Art: Sheldon Moldoff & Joe Giella.

Batman #189 (1967, February). "Fright of the Scarecrow!" Story: Gardner Fox. Art: Sheldon Moldoff & Joe Giella.

Batman #197 (1967, December). "Catwoman Sets Her Claws for Batman." Script: Gardner Fox. Art: Frank Springer & Sid Greene.

Batman #217 (1969, December). "One Bullet Too Many!" Script: Frank Robbins. Art: Irv Novick & Dick Giordano.

Batman #232 (1971, June). "Daughter of the Demon!" Script: Dennis O'Neil. Art: Neal Adams & Dick Giordano.

Batman #244 (1972, September). "The Demon Lives Again!" Script: Dennis O'Neil. Art: Neal Adams & Dick Giordano.

Batman #251 (1973, September). "The Joker's Five-Way Revenge!" Script: Denny O'Neil. Art: Neal Adams.

Batman #258 (1974, October). "Threat of the Two-Headed Coin!" Script: Denny O'Neil. Art: Irv Novick & Dick Giordano.

Batman #262 (1975, April). "The Scarecrow's Trail of Fear!" Script: Denny O'Neil. Art: Ernie Chan & Dick Giordano.

Batman #300 (1978, June). "The Last Batman Story –?" Script: David V. Reed. Art: Walt Simonson & Dick Giordano.

Batman #307 (1979, January). "Dark Messenger of Mercy." Script: Len Wein. Art: John Calnan & Dick Giordano.

Batman #356 (1983, February). "The Double Life of Hugo Strange." Script: Gerry Conway. Art: Don Newton & Dick Giordano.

Batman #357 (1983, March). "Squid." Script: Gerry Conway. Art: Don Newton & Alfredo Alcala.

Batman #368 (1984, February). "A Revenge of Rainbows." Script: Doug Moench. Art: Don Newton & Alfredo Alcala.

Batman #404–407 (1987, February–May). "Batman: Year One." Script: Frank Miller. Art: Dave Mazzuchelli.

Batman #408 (1987, June). "Did Robin Die Tonight?" Script: Max Allan Collins. Art: Chris Warner & Mike DeCarlo.

Batman #424 (1988, October). "The Diplomat's Son." Script: Jim Starlin. Art: Doc Bright & Steve Mitchell.

Batman #426–429 (1988, December–January). "A Death in the Family." Script: Jim Starlin. Art: Jim Aparo & Mike DeCarlo.

Batman #436–439 (1989, August–September). "Batman: Year Three." Script: Marv Wolfman. Art: Pat Broderick & John Beatty.

Batman #440 (1989, October). Letter by Malcolm Bourne.

Batman #452–554 (1990, August–September). "Dark Knight, Dark City." Script: Peter Milligan. Art: Kieron Dwyer & Dennis Janke.

Batman #457 (1990, December). "Master of Fear." Story: Alan Grant. Art: Norm Breyfogle & Steve Mitchell.

Batman #496 (1993, late July). "Knightfall (Part IX)—Die Laughing." Script: Doug Moench. Art: Jim Aparo & Dick Giordano.

Batman #600 (2002, April). "Bruce Wayne: Fugitive—The Scene of the Crime." Script: Ed Brubaker. Art: Scott McDaniel & Andy Owens.

Batman #603 (2002, July). "Bruce Wayne: Fugitive—The Turning Point." Script: Ed Brubaker. Art: Sean Phillips.

Batman #605 (2002, September). "Bruce Wayne: Fugitive—Not Guilty!" Script: Ed Brubaker. Art: Scott McDaniel & Andy Owens.

Batman #608 (2002, December). "Hush (Part I): The Ransom." Script: Jeph Loeb. Art: Jim Lee & Scott Williams.

Batman #612 (2003, April). "Hush (Part V): The Battle." Script: Jeph Loeb. Art: Jim Lee & Scott Williams.

Batman #615 (2003, July). "Hush (Part VIII): The Dead." Script: Jeph Loeb. Art: Jim Lee & Scott Williams.

Batman #618 (2003, October). "Hush (Part XI): The Game." Script: Jeph Loeb. Art: Jim Lee & Scott Williams.

Batman #619 (2003, November). "Hush (Part XII): The End." Script: Jeph Loeb. Art: Jim Lee & Scott Williams.

Batman #624 (2004, April). "Broken City, Part Five." Script: Brian Azzarello. Art: Eduardo Risso.

Batman #633 (2004, December). "No Going Back." Script: Bill Willingham. Art: Kinsun Loh & Aaron Sowd.

Batman #635 (2005, February). "Under the Red Hood: Part 1—New Business." Script: Judd Winick: Art: Doug Mahnke & Tom Nguyen.

Batman #641 (2005, August). "Family Reunion, Conclusion: Face to Face." Script: Judd Winick. Art: Doug Mahnke & Tom Nguyen.

Batman #644 (2005, November). "War Crimes, Part 4: Judgment at Gotham." Script: Bill Willingham. Art: Giuseppe Camuncoli & Sandra Hope.

Batman #649 (2006, March). "All They Do Is Watch Us Kill, Part 2." Script: Judd Winick. Art: Doug Mahnke & Tom Nguyen.

Batman #650 (2006, April). "It Only Hurts When I Laugh." Script: Judd Winick. Art: Eric Battle & Rodney Ramos.

Batman #651–654 (2006, May–August). "Face the Face." Script: James Robinson. Art: Don Kramer, Keith Champagne, Michael Bair, & Wayne Faucher.

Batman #655–658 (2006, September–December). "Batman and Son." Script: Grant Morrison. Art: Andy Kubert & Jesse Delperdang.

Batman #673 (2008, March). "Joe Chill in Hell." Script: Grant Morrison. Art: Tony S. Daniel, Jonathan Glapion, & Sandu Florea.

Batman #703 (2010, November). "The Great Escape." Script: Fabian Nicieza. Art: Cliff Richards.

Batman #705 (2011, February). "Eye of the Beholder, Part Two: See No Evil." Script: Tony Daniel. Art: Tony Daniel & Sandu Florea.

The Batman Adventures: Mad Love (1994, February). Script: Paul Dini. Art: Bruce Timm & Glen Murakami.

Batman and Robin #1 (2009, August). "Batman: Reborn, Part One: The Domino Effect." Script: Grant Morrison. Art: Frank Quitely.

Batman and Robin #13–15 (2010, August–November). "Batman and Robin Must Die!" Script: Grant Morrison. Art: Frazer Irving.

Batman and Robin #16 (2011, January). "Black Mass." Script: Grant Morrison. Art: Cameron Stewart & Frazer Irving.

Batman and Robin #20–22 (2011, April–June). "Dark Knight vs. White Knight." Script: Peter J. Tomasi. Art: Patrick Gleason & Mick Gray.

Batman and Robin #23 (2011, July). "The Streets Run Red, Part 1: Ins and Outs." Script: Judd Winick. Art: Guillem March & Andrei Bresson.

Batman and Robin #1 (2011, October). "Born to Kill." Script: Peter J. Tomasi. Art: Patrick Gleason & Mick Gray.

Batman and the Outsiders #14 (1984, October). ". . . The Wrath of Zeus!" Script: Mike W. Barr. Art: Bill Willingham & Bill Anderson.

Batman Annual #2 (1961). "Greetings from the Batman Family." Art: Bob Kane (officially). [Even though Kane signed it, the image was probably drawn and inked by unidentified ghost artists.]

Batman Annual #11 (1987). "Love Bird." Script: Max Allan Collins. Art: Norm Breyfogle.

Batman Annual #25 (2006). "Daedalus and Icarus—The Return of Jason Todd." Script: Judd Winick. Art: Shane Davis & Mark Morales.

Batman Black and White Volume 2 (2002). "Case Study." Script: Paul Dini. Art: Alex Ross.

The Batman Chronicles #3 (1996, Winter). "The First Cut Is the Deepest: The Secret Origin of Mr. Zsasz." Script: Alan Grant. Art: Jennifer Graves & Wayne Faucher.

Batman Incorporated #1 (2011, January). "Mr. Unknown Is Dead." Script: Grant Morrison. Art: Yanick Paquette & Michel Lacombe.

Batman Special #1 (1984). ". . .The Player on the Other Side!" Script: Mike Barr. Art: Michael Golden & Mike DeCarlo.

Batman: Absolution (2003). Script: J. M. DeMatteis. Art: Brian Ashmore.

Batman: Birth of the Demon (1992, December). Script: Denny O'Neil. Art: Norm Breyfogle.

Batman: Blind Justice (1992). Script: Sam Hamm. Art: Denys Cowan & Dick Giordano. Quote from trade paperback introduction, pp. 2–3.

Batman: Cacophony #1–3 (2008, November–2009, January). Script: Kevin Smith. Art: Walt Flanagan & Sandra Hope.

Batman: Death and the Maidens #1–9 (2003, October–2004, August). Script: Greg Rucka. Art: Klaus Janson. *Batman: Full Circle* (1991). Script: Mike W. Barr. Art: Alan Davis & Mark Farmer.

Batman: Gotham Adventures #11 (1999, April). "The Oldest One in the Book." Script: Ty Templeton. Art: Rich Burchett & Terry Beatty.

Batman: Gotham Knights #8–11 (2000, October–2001, January). "Transference." Script: Devin Grayson. Art: Roger Robinson & John Floyd.

Batman: Gotham Knights #23 (2002, January). "Fear of Success." Script: Devin Grayson. Art: Roger Robinson & John Floyd.

Batman: Gotham Knights #48 (2004, February). "Family Reunion." Script: Scott Beatty. Art: Roger Robinson & John Floyd.

Batman: Legends of the Dark Knight #11–15 (1990, September–1991, February). "Prey." Script: Doug Moench. Art: Paul Gulacy & Terry Austin.

Batman: Legends of the Dark Knight #137–141 (2001, January–May). "Terror." Script: Doug Moench. Art: Paul Gulacy & Jimmy Palmiotti.

Batman: Legends of the Dark Knight Halloween Special #1 (1993). "Choices." Script: Jeph Loeb. Art: Tim Sale.

Batman: Legends of the Dark Knight Halloween Special #2 (1994). "Madness." Script: Jeph Loeb. Art: Tim Sale.

Batman: Poison Ivy (1997). Script: John Francis Moore. Art: Brian Apthorp & Stan Woch.

Batman: Riddler—The Riddle Factory (1995). Script: Matt Wagner. Art: Dave Taylor.

Batman: Shadow of the Bat #1 (1992, June). "The Last Arkham, Part One." Script: Alan Grant. Art: Norm Breyfogle.

Batman: Son of the Demon (1987). Script: Mike W. Barr. Art: Jerry Bingham.

Batman: Streets of Gotham #4 (2009, November). "Business." Script: Paul Dini. Art: Dustin Nguyen & Derek Fridolfs.

Batman: The 10-Cent Adventure #1 (2002, March). "Fool's Errand." Script: Greg Rucka. Art: Rich Burchett & Klaus Janson.

Batman: The Dark Knight #1–4 (1986, February–June). Script: Frank Miller. Art: Frank Miller & Klaus Janson.

Batman: The Killing Joke (1988). Script: Alan Moore. Art: Brian Bolland.

Batman: The Long Halloween #1–13 (1996, December–1997, December). Script: Jeph Loeb. Art: Tim Sale.

Batman: Vengeance of Bane #1 (1993, January). Script: Chuck Dixon. Art: Graham Nolan & Eduardo Barreto.

Batman: Year One—see *Batman* #404–407.

Batman: Year Two—see *Detective Comics* #575–578.

Batman: Year Three—see *Batman* #436–439.

Blackest Night #4 (2009, December). [Power Levels 100%]. Script: Geoff Johns. Art: Ivan Reis, Oclair Albert, & Joe Prado.

Blackest Night: Batman #1–3 (2009, October–December). "Who Burns Who." Script: Peter J. Tomasi. Art: Ardian Syaf, John Dell & Vicente Cifuentes.

The Brave and the Bold #54 (1964, July). "The Thousand-and-One Dooms of Mr. Twister." Script: Bob Haney. Art: Bruno Premiani.

The Brave and the Bold #111 (1974, February–March). "Death Has the Last Laugh." Script: Bob Haney. Art: Jim Aparo.

The Brave and the Bold #197 (1983, April). "Night of Passion . . . Night of Fear!" Script: Alan Brennert. Art: Joe Staton & George Freeman.

Bruce Wayne: The Road Home: Ra's al Ghul (2010, December). Script: Fabian Nicieza. Art: Scott McDaniel & Andy Owens.

Catwoman #0 (1994, October). "Cat Shadows." Script: Doug Moench. Art: Jim Balent & Bob Smith.

Catwoman #18 (1995, February). "Here Comes the Bride." Script: Chuck Dixon. Art: Jim Balent & Bob Smith.

Catwoman #38–40 (1996, October–December). "Catwoman: Year 2." Script: Chuck Dixon. Art: Jim Balent & Mark Pennington.

Catwoman #46 (1997, June). "Two Cats in One." Script: Doug Moench. Art: Jim Balent & Ray McCarthy.

Catwoman #59 (1998, July). "Only Happy When It Rains: Fight or Flight." Script: Devin Grayson. Art: Jim Balent & John Stanisci.

Catwoman #1 (2002, January). "Anodyne, Part 1." Script: Ed Brubaker. Art: Darwyn Cooke & Mike Allred.

Catwoman #12–16 (2002, December–2003, April). "Relentless." Script: Ed Brubaker. Art: Cameron Stewart.

Catwoman #50–51 (2006, February–March). "Backward Masking." Script: Will Pfeiffer. Art: Pete Woods.

Catwoman #72 (2007, December). "Crime Pays, Part One." Script: Will Pfeifer. Art: David Lopez & Alvaro Lopez.

Catwoman #1 (2011, November). ". . . and Most of the Costumes Stay on . . ." Script: Judd Winick. Art: Guillem March.

Catwoman #5 (2012, March). "This Has Got to Be Dirty." Script: Judd Winick. Art: Guillem March.

Civil War #1–7 (2006, July–2007, January). Script: Mark Millar. Art: Steve McNiven, Dexter Vines, John Dell, & Tim Townsend.

Countdown #33 (2007, November). "The Origin of the Riddler." Script: Scott Beatty. Art: Don Kramer. [The weekly series *Countdown*, which became *Countdown to Final Crisis*, numbered its issues in reverse, starting with #51 and ending with #1.]

Countdown #29 (2007, December). "The Origin of the Penguin." Script: Scott Beatty. Art: Scott McDaniel & Andy Owens.

Countdown to Final Crisis #17 (2008, January). "This Means War." Script: Paul Dini, Keith Giffen, Justin Gray, & Jimmy Palmiotti. Art: Rom Lim & Justin Palmiotti.

Countdown to Final Crisis #14 (2008, January). "Choke on It!" Script: Paul Dini, Tony Bedard, & Keith Giffen. Art: Pete Woods, Tom Derenick, & Wayne Faucher.

Crisis on Infinite Earths #1–12 (1985, April–1986, March). Script: Marv Wolfman. Art: George Pérez, Dick Giordano, & Jerry Ordway.

The Dark Knight Returns—see *Batman: The Dark Knight* #1–4.

DC Special Series #15—*Batman Spectacular* (1978, Summer). "I Now Pronounce You Batman and Wife!" Script: Dennis O'Neil. Art: Michael Golden & Dick Giordano.

DC Super Stars #17 (1977, December). "From Each Ending . . . a Beginning!" Script: Paul Levitz. Art: Joe Staton & Bob Layton.

Detective Comics #27 (1939, May). "The Case of the Chemical Syndicate." Script: Bill Finger. Art: Bob Kane.

Detective Comics #33 (1939, November). "The Legend of the Batman — Who He Is and How He Came to Be!" Script: Bill Finger. Art: Bob Kane.

Detective Comics #36 (1940, February). "Professor Hugo Strange." Script: Bill Finger. Art: Bob Kane, Sheldon Moldoff, Jerry Robinson, & Fred Guardineer.

Detective Comics #38 (1940, April). "Robin the Boy Wonder." Script: Bill Finger. Art: Bob Kane & Jerry Robinson.

Detective Comics #46 (1940, December). "Fear Dust." Script: Bill Finger. Art: Bob Kane, Jerry Robinson, & George Roussos.

Detective Comics #58 (1941, December). "One of the Most Perfect Frame-Ups." Script: Bill Finger. Art: Bob Kane, Jerry Robinson, & George Roussos.

Detective Comics #64 (1942, June). "The Joker Walks the Last Mile." Script: Bill Finger. Art: Bob Kane & George Roussos.

Detective Comics #66 (1942, August). "The Crimes of Two-Face!" Script: Bill Finger. Art: Bob Kane, Jerry Robinson, & George Roussos.

Detective Comics #168 (1951, February). "The Man Behind the Red Hood." Script: Bob Kane (officially). [Sources like comics.org credit Bill Finger, but Jerry Robinson (personal communication, June 23, 2009) told me Bill Finger did not write that story.] Art: Lew Sayre Schwartz & Win Mortimer. [Source of art credit: comics.org. *The Greatest Joker Stories Ever Told* (1988) credits Sheldon Moldoff & George Roussos, but Bob Kane did not hire Moldoff until 1953.]

Detective Comics #233 (1956, July). "The Batwoman." Script: Edmond Hamilton. Art: Sheldon Moldoff & Stan Kaye.

Detective Comics #275 (1960, January). "The Zebra Batman!" Script: Bill Finger. Art: Sheldon Moldoff & Charles Paris.

Detective Comics #292 (1961, June). "The Colossus of Gotham City!" Script: unknown. Art: Sheldon Moldoff & Charles Paris.

Detective Comics #309 (1962, November). "The Mystery of the Mardi Gras Murders." Art: Sheldon Moldoff & Charles Paris.

Detective Comics #373 (1968, March). "Mr. Freeze's Chilling Deathtrap!" Script: Gardner Fox. Art: Chic Stone & Sid Greene.

Detective Comics #457 (1976, March). "There Is No Hope In Crime Alley!" Script: Denny O'Neil. Art: Dick Giordano.

Detective Comics #470 (1977, June). "The Master Plan of Doctor Phosphorous!" Script: Steve Englehart. Art: Walt Simonson & Al Milgrom.

Detective Comics #471 (1977, July). "The Dead Yet Live!" Script: Steve Englehart. Art: Marshall Rogers & Terry Austin.

Detective Comics #472 (1977, September). "I Am the Batman!" Script: Steve Englehart. Art: Marshall Rogers & Terry Austin.

Detective Comics #474 (1977, December). "The Deadshot Ricochet." Script: Steve Englehart. Art: Marshall Rogers & Terry Austin.

Detective Comics #475 (1978, February). "The Laughing Fish." Script: Steve Englehart. Art: Marshall Rogers & Terry Austin.

Detective Comics #476 (1978, April). "The Sign of the Joker!" Script: Steve Englehart. Art: Marshall Rogers & Terry Austin.

Detective Comics #485 (1979, August–September). "The Vengeance Vow!" Script: Dennis O'Neil. Art: Don Newton & Dan Adkins.

Detective Comics #526 (1983, May). Script: Gerry Conway. Art: Don Newton & Alfredo Alcala.

Detective Comics #556–557 (1985, November–December). Script: Doug Moench. Art: Gene Colan & Bob Smith.

Detective Comics #571 (1987, February). "Fear for $ale." Script: Mike W. Barr. Art: Alan Davis & Paul Neary.

Detective Comics #574 (1987, May). Script: Mike W. Barr. Art: Alan Davis & Paul Neary.

Detective Comics #575–578 (1987, June–September). "Batman: Year Two." Script: Mike W. Barr. Art: Todd McFarlane & Alfredo Alcala.

Detective Comics #598–600 (1989, March–May). "Blind Justice." Script: Sam Hamm. Art: Denys Cowan & Dick Giordano.

Detective Comics #611 (1990, February). "Bird of Ill Omen." Script: Alan Grant. Art: Norm Breyfogle & Steve Mitchell.

Detective Comics #618–620 (1990, July–August). "Rite of Passage." Script: Alan Grant. Art: Norm Breyfogle, Dick Giordano, & Steve Mitchell.

Detective Comics #621 (1990, September). "Trial by Fire." Script: Alan Grant. Art: Norm Breyfogle & Steve Mitchell.

Detective Comics #647 (1992, Early August). "Inquiring Minds." Script: Chuck Dixon. Art: Tom Lyle & Scott Hanna.

Detective Comics #648 (1992, Late August). "Let the Punishment Fit the Crime." Script: Chuck Dixon. Art: Tom Lyle & Scott Hanna.

Detective Comics #734 (1999, July). "Mark of Cain." Script: Greg Rucka. Art: Dan Jurgens & Bill Sienkiewicz.

Detective Comics #735 (1999, August). "Fruit of the Earth." Script: Greg Rucka. Art: Dan Jurgens & Bill Sienkiewicz.

Detective Comics #741 (2000, February). "Endgame: 3—Sleep in Heavenly Peace." Script: Greg Rucka & Devin Grayson. Art: Damion Scott & Dale Eaglesham.

Detective Comics #751 (2000, December). Script: Greg Rucka. Art: Shawn Martinbrough & Steve Mitchell.

Detective Comics #817–820 (2006, May–August). "Face the Face." Script: James Robinson. Art: Leonard Kirk & Andy Clarke.

Detective Comics #822 (2006, October). "E. Nigma, Consulting Detective." Script: Paul Dini. Art: Don Kramer & Wayne Faucher.

Detective Comics #824 (2006, December). "Night of the Penguin." Script: Paul Dini. Art: Don Kramer & Wayne Faucher.

Detective Comics #831 (2007, June). "Kind of Like Family." Script: Paul Dini. Art: Don Kramer & Wayne Faucher.

Detective Comics #850 (2009, January). "Heart of Hush: The Demon in the Mirror." Script: Paul Dini. Art: Dustin Nguyen & Derek Fridolfs.

Detective Comics #864–865 (2010, June–July). "Beneath the Mask." Script: David Hine. Art: Jeremy Haun & John Lucas.

Detective Comics #875 (2011, May). "Lost Boys." Script: Scott Snyder. Art: Francesco Francavilla.

Detective Comics #879 (2011, Early September). "Skeleton Key." Script: Scott Snyder. Art: Francesco Francavilla.

Detective Comics #881 (2011, October). "The Face in the Glass." Script: Scott Snyder. Art: Jock & Francesco Francavilla.

Detective Comics #1 (2011, November). "Detective Comics." Script: Tony S. Daniel. Art: Tony S. Daniel & Ryan Winn.

Detective Comics #2 (2011, December). "Playtime's Over." Script: Tony S. Daniel. Art: Tony S. Daniel, Ryan Winn, & Sandu Florea.

Detective Comics Annual #8 (1995). "Questions Multiply the Mystery." Script: Chuck Dixon. Art: Kieron Dwyer.

Face the Face—see *Detective Comics* #817–820 and *Batman* #651–654.

The Flash #123 (1961, September). "Flash of Two Worlds!" Script: Gardner Fox. Art: Carmine Infantino & Joe Giella.

Flashpoint #5 (2011, October). Script: Geoff Johns. Art: Andy Kubert, Sandra Hope, & Jess Delperdang.

Gotham Central #1–2 (2003, Early–Late February). "In the Line of Duty." Script: Greg Rucka & Ed Brubaker. Art: Michael Lark.

Gotham Central #20 (2004, August). "Unresolved, Part Two." Script: Ed Brubaker. Art: Michael Lark & Stefano Gaudiano.

Gotham City Sirens #1 (2009, August). "Union." Script: Paul Dini. Art: Guillem March.

Gotham City Sirens #2 (2009, September). "Girls Talk." Script: Paul Dini. Art: Guillem March.

Gotham City Sirens #3 (2009, October). "Riddle Me This." Script: Paul Dini. Art: Guillem March.

Gotham City Sirens #6 (2010, January). "The Last Gag." Script: Paul Dini. Art: Guillem March.

Gotham City Sirens #7 (2010, February). "Holiday Story." Script: Paul Dini. Art: Guillem March.

Gotham City Sirens #8 (2010, March). Script: Guillem March & Marc Andreyko. Art: Guillem March.

Gotham City Sirens #21 (2011, May). "Hell Hath No Fury, Part Two." Script: Peter Calloway. Art: Andres Guinaldo & Lorenzo Ruggiero.

Gotham City Sirens #22 (2011, June). "Family Matters." Script: Peter Calloway. Art: Andres Guinaldo, Lorenzo Ruggiero, & Walden Wong.

Gotham City Sirens #24 (2011, August). "Friends, Part Two." Script: Peter Calloway. Art: Andres Guinaldo & Lorenzo Ruggiero.

Green Arrow #71 (2007, April). "Seeing Red, Part III—Change Partners." Script: Judd Winick. Art: Scott McDaniels & Andy Owens.

Green Lantern: Rebirth #4 (2005, March). "Force of Will." Script: Geoff Johns. Art: Ethan Van Sciver & Prentis Rollins.

Harley Quinn #6 (2001, May). "Who Wants to Rob a Millionaire?" Script: Karl Kesel. Art: Terry & Rachel Dodson.

Identity Crisis #1–7 (2004, August–2005, February). Script: Brad Meltzer. Art: Rags Morales & Michael Bair.

Infinite Crisis #1–7 (2005, December–2006, June). Script: Geoff Jones. Art: Phil Jiminez, George Pérez, Ivan Reis, & Jerry Ordway.

JLA #43–46 (2000, July–October). "Tower of Babel." Script: Mark Waid. Art: Howard Porter & Drew Geraci; Steve Scott & Mark Propst.

JLA #115–119 (2005, August–December). "Crisis of Conscience." Script: Geoff Johns & Allan Heinberg. Art: Chris Batista & Mark Farmer.

JLA: Earth 2 (2000, December). Script: Grant Morrison. Art: Frank Quitely.

JLA/Titans #2 (1999, January). Script: Devin Grayson & Phil Jiminez. Art: Phil Jiminez & Andy Lanning.

Joker's Asylum: Penguin #1 (2008, September). "He Who Laughs Last . . .!" Script: Jason Aaron. Art: Jason Pearson.

Joker's Asylum II: The Riddler #1 (2010, August). "The House the Cards Built." Script: Peter Calloway. Art: Andres Guinaldo & Raul Fernandez.

Justice League #1 (2011, October). "Justice League, Part One." Script: Geoff Johns. Art: Jim Lee & Scott Williams.

Justice League #5 (2012, March). "Justice League, Part Five." Script: Geoff Johns. Art: Jim Lee, Scott William, Sandra Hope, Mark Irwin, & Joe Weems.

Justice League of America #21 (1963, August). "Crisis on Earth-One!" Script: Gardner Fox. Art: Mike Sekowsky & Bernard Sachs.

The Killing Joke—see *Batman: The Killing Joke.*

Kingdom Come #1–4 (1996, May–August). Script: Mark Waid. Art: Alex Ross.

The Long Halloween—see *Batman: The Long Halloween.*

The Man of Steel #1 (1986, October). "Prologue: From Out the Green Dawn . . ." Script: John Byrne. Art: John Byrne & Dick Giordano.

The New Teen Titans #39 (1984, February). "Crossroads." Script: Marv Wolfman. Art: George Pérez & Romeo Tanghal.

The New Titans #100 (1993, August). "The Darkening, Part Four: Something Old, Something New, Something Borrowed, Something . . . Dead!" Script: Marv Wolfman. Art: Tom Grummett & Bill Jaaska.

New Year's Evil: Prometheus #1 (1998, February). Script: Grant Morrison. Art: Arnie Jorgenson.

Nightwing #4 (1995, December). "Dead Simple." Script: Dennis O'Neil. Art: Greg Land, Mike Seller, & Nick Napolitano.

Nightwing #118 (2006, May). "Gang's All Here." Script: Bruce Jones. Art: Joe Dodd & Bit.

Nightwing #147–150 (2008, October–2009, January). "The Great Leap." Script: Peter J. Tomasi. Art: Don Kramer, Jay Leisten, & Rodney Ramos.

Penguin: Pain and Prejudice #1 (2011, December). "Cold World." Script: Gregg Hurwitz. Art: Szymon Kudranski.

Penguin: Pain and Prejudice #2 (2012, January). "Beautiful Boy." Script: Gregg Hurwitz. Art: Szymon Kudranski.

Penguin: Pain and Prejudice #5 (2012, April). "Touch of Death." Script: Gregg Hurwitz. Art: Szymon Kudranski.

Red Hood and the Outlaws #1 (2011, November). "I Fought the Law and Kicked Its Butt!" Script: Scott Lobdell. Art: Kenneth Rocafort & Blond.

Red Hood: The Lost Days #1 (2010, August). "The First Step." Script: Judd Winick. Art: Pablo Raimondi.

Red Robin #1 (2009, August). "The Grail (Part I of IV)." Script: Christopher Yost. Art: Ramon Bachs.

Robin #58 (1998, October). "They Didn't Know It Was Him." Script: Chuck Dixon. Art: Staz Johnson & Stan Woch.

Robin #65 (1999, June). "A Blessed Event." Script: Chuck Dixon. Art: William Rosado & Stan Woch.

Robin #126–127 (2004, July–August). "The Girl Wonder!" Script: Bill Willingham. Art: Damion Scott.

Robin #128 (2004, September). "Night of the Scarab!" Script: Bill Willingham. Art: Damion Scott.

Robin #130 (2004, November). "The Only Light in Gotham." Script: Bill Willingham. Art: Jon Proctor, Robert Campanella, & Rodney Ramos.

Robin #174 (2008, July). "Who Is the Spoiler?" Script: Chuck Dixon. Art: Chris Batista & Cam Smith.

Robin/Spoiler Special (2008, August). Script: Chuck Dixon. Art: Rafael Albuquerque & Victor Ibanez.

Secret Origins #6 (1986, September). "Secret Origins Starring the Golden Age Batman." Script: Roy Thomas. Art: Marshall Rogers & Terry Austin.

Secret Origins Special #1 (1989). "When Is a Door?" Script: Neil Gaiman. Art: Mike Hoffman & Kevin Nowlan.

Secret Origins trade paperback (1989). "The Man Who Falls." Script: Dennis O'Neil. Art: Dick Giordano.

Secret Six #1–6 (2006, July–2007, January). "Six Degrees of Devastation." Script: Gail Simone. Art: Brad Walker & Jimmy Palmiotti.

Secret Six #36 (2011, October). "Caution to the Wind, Part Two: Blood Honor." Script: Gail Simone. Art: J. Calafiore.

Shadow of the Bat Annual #3 (1995). "Year One: Poison Ivy." Script: Alan Grant. Art: Brian Apthorp & Stan Woch.

Showcase #4 (1956, October). "Mystery of the Human Thunderbolt!" Script: Robert Kanigher. Art: Carmine Infantino & Joe Kubert.

Star Spangled Comics #65–130 (1947–1952). Scripts & Art: Various.

Strange Adventures #215 (1968, November–December). "A New Lease on Death." Script & Art: Neal Adams.

Sub-Mariner #14 (1969, June). "Namor vs. the Human Torch!" Script: Roy Thomas. Art: Marie Severin & Mike Esposito.

Suicide Squad #1 (2011, November). "Kicked in the Teeth." Script: Adam Glass. Art: Federico Dallocchio, Ransom Getty, & Scott Hanna.

Suicide Squad #6–7 (2012, April–May). "The Hunt for Harley Quinn." Script: Adam Glass. Art: Tom Raney.

Superman #61 (1949, November–December). "Superman Returns to Krypton!" Script: Bill Finger. Art: Al Plastino.

Superman Family #211 (1981, October). "The Kill Kent Contract!" Script: E. Nelson Bridwell. Art: Kurt Schaffenberger & Dan Adkins.

Superman: Secret Origin #2 (2009, December). "Superboy and the Legion of Super-Heroes." Script: Geoff Johns. Art: Gary Frank & John Sibal.

Tales of the Teen Titans #44 (1984, July). "The Judas Contract: There Shall Come a Titan." Script: Marv Wolfman. Art: George Pérez, Mike DeCarlo, & Dick Giordano.

Trinity #1–52 (2008, August–2009, July). Script: Kurt Busiek. Art: Mark Bagley & Art Thibert.

Watchmen #1–12 (1986, September–1987, October). Script: Alan Moore. Art: Dave Gibbons.

World's Finest Comics #3 (1941, Fall). "Riddle of the Human Scarecrow." Script: Bill Finger. Art: Bob Kane, Jerry Robinson, & George Roussos.

Year One: Batman Scarecrow #1 (2005, July). Script: Bruce Jones. Art: Sean Murphy.

Year One: Batman/Ra's al Ghul (2006). Script: Devin Grayson. Art: Paul Gulacy & Jimmy Palmiotti.

Young Allies #1 (1941, Summer). "The Coming of Agent Zero." Script: Otto Binder. Art: Jack Kirby (as Charles Nicholas).

Zero Hour #4–0 (1994, September–October). Script: Dan Jurgens. Art: Dan Jurgens & Jerry Ordway.

Determining who really wrote and drew all the older Batman stories is not always possible, as Will Brooker has noted at length in *Batman Unmasked: Analyzing a Cultural Icon* (2001), because the published works originally credited Bob Kane without identifying his ghost writers and artists until well into the 1960s. Tracking those names down is difficult, sometimes impossible. While wikis are tricky, they're still valuable sources for helping find back issues and a great starting point for discovering additional resources, so we must thank the many volunteers who, often anonymously, edit sites like the Grand Comics Database (comics.org), DC Comics Database (dc.wikia.com), and Batman Wiki (batman.wikia.com). Wikipedia's WikiProject Comics helped the hunt in ways they may never know. Comic Book Resources (comicbookresources.com), Comic Vine (comicvine.com), Mike's Amazing World of DC Comics (dcindexes.com), and many others aided in the quest to credit the correct creators.

References
Not Comic Books or Graphic Novels

Abbey, A. (1982). Sex differences in attributions for friendly behavior: Do males misperceive females' friendliness? *Journal of Personality and Social Psychology, 42*, 830–838.

Abrams, R. C., & Bromberg, C. E. (2007). Personality disorders in the elderly. *Psychiatric Annals, 37*, 123–127.

Acevedo, B. P., & Aron, A. (2009). Does a long-term relationship kill romantic love? *Review of General Psychology, 13*, 59–65.

Ackerman, J. M., Griskevicius, V., & Li, N. P. (2011). Let's get serious: Communicating commitment in romantic relationships. *Journal of Personality and Social Psychology, 100*, 1079–1094.

Adherents. (2005, November 30/2007, August 20). *The religious affiliation of comic book character Bruce Wayne: Batman.* Retrieved July 11, 2011, from Adherents: http://www.adherents.com/lit/comics/Batman.html.

Adler, A. (1908). *Understanding human nature.* New York: Fawcett, 1959.

Adler, A. (1924). *The practice and theory of individual psychology.* London: K. Paul, Trench, Trubner & Company.

Adler, A. (1930). Individual psychology. In C. Murchison (Ed.), *Psychologies of 1930* (pp. 395–405). Worcester, MA: Clark University Press.

Adler, A. (1933/1939). *Social interest: A challenge to mankind.* J. Linton & R. Vaughan (Trans.). Paterson, NJ: Littlefield, Adams.

Ainsworth, M., Blehar, M., Waters, E., & Wall, S. (1978). *Patterns of attachment.* Hillsdale, NJ: Erlbaum.

Ainsworth, M., & Bowlby, J. (1965). *Child care and the growth of love.* London: Penguin Books.

Alarid, L., Marquart, J., Burton Jr., V., Cullen, F., & Cuvelier, S. (1996). Women's roles in serious offenses: A study of adult felons. *Justice Quarterly, 13*, 431–454.

Alison, L. (2011). *The forensic psychologist's casebook: Psychological profiling and criminal investigation.* Devon, UK: Willan.

Allen, J. (1999). *Coping with trauma: A guide to self-understanding.* Washington, D.C.: American Psychiatric Association.

Allred, G. H., & Poduska, B. E. (1988). Birth order and happiness: A preliminary study. *Individual Psychology, 44,* 346–354.

American Psychiatric Association. (1952). *Diagnostic and statistical manual of mental disorders* (DSM-I). Washington, D.C.: American Psychiatric Association.

American Psychiatric Association. (1980). *Diagnostic and statistical manual of mental disorders* (DSM-III) (3rd ed.). Washington, D.C.: American Psychiatric Association.

American Psychiatric Association. (1987). *Diagnostic and statistical manual of mental disorders* (DSM-III-R) (3rd ed., revised). Washington, D.C.: American Psychiatric Association.

American Psychiatric Association. (1994). *Diagnostic and statistical manual of mental disorders* (DSM-IV) (4th ed.). Washington, D.C.: American Psychiatric Association.

American Psychiatric Association (2000). *Diagnostic and statistical manual of mental disorders* (DSM-IV-TR) (4th ed., text revision). Washington, D.C: American Psychiatric Association.

Andersen, D. C., & Friedman, L. J. (1997). Erik Erikson on revolutionary leadership [retrospective review of four books by Erikson]. *Contemporary Psychology, 42,* 1063–1067.

Archer, R. L., & Cook, C. E. (1986). Personalistic self-disclosure and attraction: Basis for relationship or scarce resource. *Social Psychology Quarterly, 49,* 268–272.

Aronson, E., & Carlsmith, J.M. (1963). Effect of the severity of threat on the devaluation of forbidden behavior. *Journal of Abnormal and Social Psychology, 66,* 584–588.

Aronson, E., & Mills, J. (1959). The effect of severity of initiation on liking for a group. *Journal of Abnormal and Social Psychology, 59,* 177–181.

Arrigo, J. M., & Wagner, R. V. (2007). Psychologists and military interrogators rethink the psychology of torture. *Peace and Conflict: Journal of Peace Psychology, 13,* 393–398.

Asay, P. (2012). *God on the street of Gotham: What the big screen Batman can teach us about God and ourselves.* Carol Stream, IL: Tyndale House.

Audet, C. T., & Everall, R. D. (2010). Therapist self-disclosure and the therapeutic relationship: A phenomenological study from the client perspective. *British Journal of Guidance & Counseling, 38,* 327–342.

Babiak, P., & Hare, R. D. (2006). *Snakes in suits: When psychopaths go to work.* New York: HarperCollins.

Barbara, G. (2008). Gender differences in the verbal expression of love schema. *Sex Roles, 58,* 814–821.

Bartholomew, K., & Horowitz, L. M. (1991). Attachment styles among young adults: A test of a four-category model. *Journal of Personality and Social Psychology, 61,* 226–244.

Bartol, C. R., & Bartol, A. M. (2005). *Criminal behavior* (7th ed.). Upper Saddle River, NJ: Pearson.

Baumrind, D. (1991). The influence of parenting style on adolescent competence and substance use. *Journal of Early Adolescence, 11,* 56–95.

Baumrind, D., Larzelere, R. E., & Owens, E. B. (2010). Effects of preschool parents' power assertive patterns on adolescent development. *Parenting: Science and Practice, 10,* 157–201.

Bayer, C. P., Klasen, F., & Adam, H. (2007). Association of trauma and PTSD symptoms with openness to reconciliation and feelings of revenge among former Ugandan and Congolese child soldiers. *JAMA: Journal of the American Medical Association, 298,* 555–559.

Bem, S. L. (1974). The measurement of psychological androgyny. *Journal of Consulting and Clinical Psychology, 42*, 155–162.

Bem, S. L. (1976). Sex typing and androgyny: Further explorations of the expressive domain. *Journal of Personality and Social Psychology, 34*, 1016.

Bender, H. E., Kambam, P, & Pozios, V. K. (2009, July). *Unlocking Arkham: Forensic psychiatry and Batman's rogues gallery*. Panel presented at San Diego Comic-Con International, San Diego, CA.

Bender, H. E., Kambam, P, & Pozios, V. K. (2011, September 20). *Putting the Caped Crusader on the couch*. Retrieved October 24, 2011, from the New York Times: http://www.nytimes.com/2011/09/21/opinion/putting-the-caped-crusader-on-the-couch.html.

Ben-Shakhar, G. (2008). The case against the use of polygraph examinations to monitor post-conviction sex offenders. *Legal and Criminological Psychology, 13*, 191–207.

Berdahl, J. L., & Aquino, K. (2009). Sexual behavior at work: Fun or folly? *Journal of Applied Psychology, 94*, 34–47.

Bergner, R. M. (2007). Therapeutic storytelling revisited. *American Journal of Psychotherapy, 61*, 149–162.

Berkowitz, L. (1962). *Aggression: A social-psychological analysis*. New York: McGraw-Hill.

Bernasco, W. (2006). Co-offending and the choice of targets in burglary. *Journal of Investigative Psychology and Offender Profiling, 3*, 139–155.

Beune, K., Giebels, E., & Taylor, P. J. (2010). Patterns of interaction in police interviews: The role of cultural dependency. *Criminal Justice and Behavior, 37*, 904–925.

Bigger, S., & Webb, J. (2010). Developing environmental agency and engagement through young people's fiction. *Environmental Education Research, 16*, 401–414.

Blackburn, R., & Coid, J. W. (1997). Psychopathy and the dimensions of personality disorder in violent offenders. *Personality and Individual Differences, 25*, 129–145.

Bonanno, G. A. (2001). The crucial importance of empirical evidence in the development of bereavement theory: Reply to Archer (2001). *Psychological Bulletin, 127*, 561–564.

Bonanno, G. A. (2007). "The stage theory of grief": Comment. *JAMA: Journal of the American Medical Association, 297*, 2293.

Bonanno, G., Westphal, M., & Mancini A. (2011). Resilience to loss and potential trauma. *Annual Review of Clinical Psychology, 7*, 511–535.

Bonnie, R. C., Jeffries Jr., R. C. & Low, P. W. (2008). *A study in the insanity defense: The trial of John W. Hinckley Jr.* New York: Foundation Press.

Boucher, G. (2009, October 18). *For Akiva Goldsman, a beautiful turnaround*. Retrieved September 11, 2011, from the *Los Angeles Times*: http://articles.latimes.com/2009/oct/18/entertainment/ca-akiva18.

Boucher, G. (2010, March 10). *Christopher Nolan takes flight with Superman: "We have a fantastic story."* Retrieved September 12, 2011, from the Los Angeles Times: http://herocomplex.latimes.com/2010/03/10/christopher-nolan-takes-flight-with-superman-we-have-a-fantastic-story-1/.

Boucher, G. (2011, May 16). *"Batman": Michael Keaton on "The Dark Knight"—and a lost scene from 1989 film*. Retrieved December 16, 2011, from the *Los Angeles Times*: http://herocomplex.latimes.com/2011/05/16/batman-michael-keaton-on-the-dark-knight-and-a-lost-scene-from-1989-film/

Bowden, M. (2007, May). The ploy. *The Atlantic*, 54–68.

Brantley, A., Knox, D., & Zusman, M. E. (2002). When and why gender differences in saying "I love you" among college students. *College Student Journal, 36*, 614–615.

Breland Bailey, M. (1994–2001). Many personal communications.

Brennan, K. A., Clark, C. L., & Shaver, P. R. (1998). Self-report measurement of adult attachment: An integrative review. In J. A. Simpson & W. S. Rholes (Eds.), *Attachment theory and close relationships* (pp. 46–76). New York: Guilford Press.

Bretherton, I. (1992). The origins of attachment theory: John Bowlby and Mary Ainsworth. *Developmental Psychology, 28*, 759–775.

Bretherton, I., & Munholland, K. A. (1999). Internal working models in attachment relationships: A construct revisited. In J. Cassidy & P. R. Shaver (Eds.), *Handbook of attachment: Theory, research and clinical applications* (pp. 89–114). New York: Guilford.

Brewer, H. M. (2004). *Who needs a superhero? Finding virtue, vice, and what's holy in the comics*. Grand Rapids, MI: Baker.

Breyfogle, N. (2008, August 10). [normbreyfogle.community forum comment] Retrieved September 12, 2011, from http://normforum.adelaidecomicsandbooks.com/viewtopic .php?p=9655&sid=259bd3520a11e743ad3665af10f3eee0.

Brooker, W. (2001). *Batman unmasked: Analyzing a cultural icon*. New York: Continuum.

Brown v. Board of Education, 347 U.S. 483 (1954).

Brownstein, C. (2000, April 21). *Returning to the Dark Knight: Frank Miller interview— part 1*. Retrieved June 6, 2011, from Comic Book Resources: http://www .comicbookresources.com/?page=article&id=192.

Bryant, J., & Miron, D. (2003). Excitation-transfer theory and three-factor theory of emotion. In J. Bryant, D. Roskos-Ewoldsen, & J. Cantor (Eds.), *Communication and emotion: Essays in honor of Dolf Zillmann* (pp. 31–59). Mahwah, NJ: Erlbaum.

Bull, R., & Milne, R. (2004). Attempts to improve the police interviewing of suspects. In D. Lassiter (Ed.), *Interrogations, confessions, and entrapment* (pp. 182–195). New York: Kluwer Academic.

Bunting, C. J., Tolson, H., Kuhn, C., Suarez, E., & Williams, R. B. (2000). Physiological stress response of the neuroendocrine system during outdoor tasks. *Journal of Leisure Research, 32*, 191–207.

Burger, J. M. (1981). Motivational biases in the attribution of responsibility for an accident: A meta-analysis of the defensive-attribution hypothesis. *Psychological Bulletin, 90*, 496–512.

Burman, S., & Allen-Meares, P. (1994). Neglected victims of murder: Children's witness to parental homicide. *Social Work, 39*, 28–34.

Burton, T., & Salisbury, M. (2006). *Burton on Burton* (2nd revised edition). London: Faber & Faber.

Burton, T. (2005). Interviewed in *Shadows of the Bat: The Cinematic Saga of the Dark Knight*, part 4, "The Dark Side of the Knight." *Batman Returns* DVD bonus feature.

Buss, D. M. (1985). Human mate selection. *American Scientist, 73*, 47–51.

Calder, A. (2003). *Myth of the Blitz*. London: Pimlico.

Calhoun, L. G., Cann, A., & Tedeschi, R. G. (2010). The posttraumatic growth model: Socio-cultural considerations. In T. Weiss & R. Berger (Eds.), *Handbook of posttraumatic growth: Research and practice* (pp. 1–23). Mahwah, NJ: Erlbaum.

Caltabiano, M., & Caltabiano, N. (2006). *Resilience and health outcomes in the elderly*. Paper presented at the 39th Annual Conference of the Australian Association of Gerontology, Sydney, New South Wales.

Calvo-Salguero, A., García-Martínez, A. M. Á., & Monteoliva, A. (2008). Differences between and within genders in gender role orientation according to age and level of education. *Sex Roles, 58,* 535–548.

Cameron, M. O. (1964). *The booster and the snitch.* New York: Free Press.

Campbell, J. (1949). *The hero with a thousand faces.* Princeton, NJ: Princeton University Press.

Campbell, J. Cousineau, P., & Brown, S. (1990), *The hero's journey: Joseph Campbell on his life and work.* New York: Harper & Row.

Carruth, B., & Valle, S. K. (1986). *Drunk driving in America: Strategies and approaches to treatment.* London: Routledge.

Castellow, W. A., Wuensch, K. L., & Moore, C. H. (1990). Effects of physical attractiveness and defendants in sexual harassment judgments. *Journal of Social Behavior and Personality, 5,* 547–562.

Cengage. (n.d.). *Case study 4: The fictional case of Batman/Bruce Wayne.* Retrieved December 16, 2011, from Cengage Academic Resources: http://academic.cengage .com/resource_uploads/downloads/0534644902_48578.pdf.

Chan, S. (2009, January 26). *The Dark Knight of Gotham: Batman, the ultimate superhero homebody.* Retrieved August 10, 2011, from Sequential Art: http://www.sequentialart .com/article.php?id=1225.

Chavel, S. (2008, July 18). *Interview: Chris Nolan on "The Dark Knight."* Retrieved September 12, 2011, from UGO: http://www.cinecon.com/news/1652/interview-chris-nolan-the-dark-knight/.

Choy, Y., Fyer, A. J., & Lipsitz, J. D. (2007). Treatment of specific phobia in adults. *Clinical Psychology Review, 27,* 266–86.

Cialdini, R. B. (2001). *Influence: Science and practice* (4th ed.). Boston: Allyn & Bacon.

Cianci, R., & Gambrel, P. A. (2003). Maslow's hierarchy of needs: Does it apply in a collectivist culture? *Journal of Applied Management and Entrepreneurship, 82,* 143–161.

Clarke, J. W. (1990). *On being mad or merely angry: John W. Hinckley, Jr., and other dangerous people.* Princeton, NJ: Princeton University Press.

Cleckley, H. (1941/1988). *The mask of sanity.* 5th ed. reproduced for nonprofit educational use, retrieved August 8, 2011, from the Cassiopaean Experiment: http://www .cassiopaea.org/cass/sanity_1.PdF

Clements, P. T., & Burgess, A. W. (2002). Children's responses to family member homicide. *Family & Community Health, 25,* 32–42.

Clifford, M. M., & Walster, E. H. (1973). The effect of physical attractiveness on teacher expectation. *Sociology of Education, 46,* 248–258.

Cole, C. E. (2010). Problematizing therapeutic assumptions about narratives: A case study of storytelling events in a post-conflict context. *Health Communication, 25,* 650–660.

Coleman, M., & Ganong, L. H. (1990). Remarriage and stepfamily research in the 1980s: Increased interest in an old family form. *Journal of Marriage and the Family, 52,* 925–940.

Colley, A., Mulhern, G., Maltby, J., & Wood, A. M. (2009). The short form BSRI: Instrumentality, expressiveness and gender associations among a United Kingdom sample. *Personality and Individual Differences, 46,* 384–387.

Comics Interview. (1986). Spotlight: Dark Knight. *Comics Interview, 31,* 32.

Commons, M. L., & Richards, F. A. (2003). Four postformal stages. In J. Demick & C. Andreoletti (Eds.), *Handbook of adult development* (pp. 199–219). New York: Kluwer Academic/Plenum.

Connolly, P. H. (2006). Psychological functioning of bondage/domination/sado-masochism (BDSM) practitioners. *Journal of Psychology & Human Sexuality, 18*, 79–120.

Coogan, P. (2006). *Superhero: The secret origin of a genre.* Austin, TX: MonkeyBrain.

Cooper, C. R., & Grotevant, H. D. (1989, April). *Individuality and connectedness in the family and adolescent's self and relational competence.* Paper presented at the meeting of the Society for Research in Child Development. Kansas City, MO.

Cooper, J. (2010). Riding the D train with Elliot: The Aronsonian legacy of cognitive dissonance. In M. H. Gonzales, C. Tavris, & J. Aronson (Eds.), *The scientist and the humanist: A festschrift in honor of Elliot Aronson* (pp. 159–174). New York: Psychology University Press.

Corr, C. A., Nable, C. M., & Corr, D. M. (1997). *Death and dying, life and living* (2nd ed.). Pacific Grove, CA: Brooks/Cole Publishing Company.

Couch, N. C. C. (2010). *Jerry Robinson: Ambassador of comics.* New York: Abrams ComicArts.

Crawford, A., & Benoit, D. (2009). Caregivers' disrupted representations of the unborn child predict later infant-caregiver disorganized and disrupted interactions. *Infant Mental Health Journal, 30*, 124–144.

Cromwell, P., & Olson, J. N. (2004). *Breaking and entering: Burglars and burglary.* Belmont, CA: Wadsworth.

Cuddy-Casey, M., & Orvaschel, H. (1997). Children's understanding of death in relation to child suicidality and homicidality. *Death Studies, 17*, 35–45.

Czerner, T. G. (2002). *What makes you tick: The brain in plain English.* New York: Wiley.

Daderman, A. M., Muerling, A. W., & Hallman, J. (2001). Different personality patterns in non-socialized (juvenile delinquents) and socialized (air force pilot recruits) sensation seekers. *European Journal of Personality, 15*, 239–252.

Daily, J. (2011, October 31). Law and the Multiverse holiday special—Halloween edition. Retrieved December 2, 2011, from Law and the Multiverse: http://lawandthemultiverse.com/2011/10/31/law-and-the-multiverse-holiday-special-halloween-edition/.

Daniels, B. J. (2008). Arkham Asylum: Forensic psychology and Gotham's (not so) "serious house." In R. Rosenberg (Ed.), *The psychology of superheroes* (pp. 201–211). Dallas, TX: BenBella.

Daniels, L. (1999). *Batman: The complete history.* New York: DC Comics.

Dannon, P. N. (2002). Kleptomania: An impulse control disorder? *International Journal of Psychiatry in Clinical Practice, 6*, 3–7.

Dannon, P. N., Lowengrub, K. M., Lancu, L., & Kotler, M. (2004). Kleptomania: Comorbid psychiatric diagnosis in patients and their families. *Psychopathology, 37*, 76–80.

Darby, B. W., & Jeffers, D. (1988). The effects of defendant and juror attractiveness on simulated courtroom trial decisions. *Social Behavior and Personality, 16*, 39–50.

Davidson, R. (2011, January 18). *Supervillains and the insanity defense.* Retrieved December 2, 2011, from Law and the Multiverse: http://lawandthemultiverse.com/2011/01/18/supervillains-and-the-insanity-defense/.

Davis, M., & Whalen, P. J. (2001). The amygdala: Vigilance and emotion. *Molecular Psychiatry, 6*, 13–34.

Dawes, R. M. (1991). Social dilemmas, economic self-interest, and evolutionary theory. In D. R. Brown & J. E. K. Smith (Eds.), *Frontiers of mathematical psychology: Essays in honor of Clyde Coombs* (pp. 53–79). New York: Springer-Verlag.

De Grey, A. (2007). *Ending aging: The rejuvenation breakthroughs that could reverse human aging in our lifetime.* New York: St. Martin's Press.

Decker, S., Wright, R., Redfern, A., & Smith, D. (1993). A woman's place is in the home: Females and residential burglary. *Justice Quarterly, 10*, 143–162.

Dekel, S. (2011, April 4). Posttraumatic growth and posttraumatic distress: A longitudinal study. *Psychological Trauma: Theory, Research, Practice, and Policy.* Advance online publication.

Dell'Osso, B., Buoli, M., Baldwin, D. S., & Altamura, A. C. (2010). Serotonin norepinephrine inhibitors (SNRIs) in anxiety disorders: A comprehensive review of their efficacy. *Human Psychopharmacology, 25*, 17–29.

Deng, X. (1997). The deterrent effects of initial sanction on first-time apprehended shoplifters. *International Journal of Offender Therapy and Comparative Criminology, 41*, 284–297.

DeSantis, A., & Kayson, W. A. (1997). Defendants' characteristics of attractiveness, race, and sex and sentencing decisions. *Psychological Reports, 81*, 679–683.

DiDio, D. (2008). Interviewed in *Batman Unmasked: The Psychology of the Dark Knight* television special.

Dillard, J. P., & Anderson, J. W. (2004). The role of fear in persuasion. *Psychology & Marketing, 21*, 909–926.

Dini, P., & Kidd, C. (1998). *Batman Animated.* New York: Harper.

Di Novi, D. (2005). Interviewed in *Shadows of the Bat: The Cinematic Saga of the Dark Knight,* part 4, "The Dark Side of the Knight." *Batman Returns* DVD bonus feature.

Dion, K. K. (1972). Physical attractiveness and evaluations of children's transgressions. *Journal of Personality and Social Psychology, 24*, 207–213.

Dollinger, S. J., & LaMartina, A. K. (1998). A note on moral reasoning and the five-factor model. *Journal of Social Behavior & Personality, 13*, 349–358.

Donald, A. (n.d.). *Is Batman gay?* Retrieved August 7, 2011, from Silver Bullet Comics: http://www.comicsbulletin.com/panel/106070953757230.htm.

Douglas, J. (2006). *Crime classification manual* (2nd ed.). New York: Wiley.

Djikic, M., Oatley, K., Zoeterman, S., & Peterson, J. B. (2009). On being moved by art: How reading fiction transforms the self. *Creativity Research Journal, 21*, 24–29.

Dratel, J. (2006). The curious debate. In K. J. Greenberg (Ed.), *The torture debate in America* (pp. 111–117). New York: Cambridge University Press.

DSM-I—see American Psychiatric Association (1952).

DSM-III—see American Psychiatric Association (1980).

DSM-III-R—see American Psychiatric Association (1987).

DSM-IV—see American Psychiatric Association (1994).

DSM-IV-TR—see American Psychiatric Association (2000).

Duncan, R., Langley, T., Langley, N., Smith, N, Poole, J., Head, M., O'Nale, R., Ash, E., Sepe, T., Cash, T., Hill, K., Cate, C. L., Langley, A., & Fingeroth, D. (2008, July). *Capes and tights, caps and gowns.* Panel presented at the Comics Arts Conference, San Diego Comic-Con International, San Diego, CA.

Duncan, R., & Smith, M. J. (2010). *The power of comics: History, form, and culture*. New York: Continuum.

Durst, R., Katz, G., Teitelbaum, A., Zislin, J., & Dannon, P. N. (2001). Kleptomania: Diagnosis and treatment options. *CNS Drugs, 15*, 185–195.

Ehlers, A., Mayou, R. A., & Bryant, B. (1998). Psychological predictors of chronic posttraumatic stress disorders after motor vehicle accidents. *Journal of Abnormal Psychology, 107*, 508–519.

Eisner, J. (1986). *The official Batman batbook*. Chicago: Contemporary Books.

Ellis, B. J., Bates, J. E., Dodge, K. A., Fergusson, D. M., John, H. L., Pettit, G. S., & Woodward, L. (2003). Does father absence place daughters at special risk for early sexual activity and teenage pregnancy? *Child Development, 74*, 801–821.

Ellison, R. (1953/1964). Harlem is nowhere. In *Shadow and act* (p. 302). New York: Signet, New American Library.

Emmers-Sommer, T. M., Warber, K., & Halford, J. (2007). Reasons for (non) engagement in infidelity. *Marriage & Family Review, 46*, 420–444.

Engemann, K. M., & Owyang, M. T. (2005, April). *So much for that merit raise: The link between wages and appearance*. Retrieved December 4, 2011, from The Regional Economist: http://www.stlouisfed.org/publications/re/articles/?id=362.

Erian, M., Lin, C., Patel, N., Neal, A., & Geiselman, R. E. (1998). Juror verdicts as a function of victim and defendant attractiveness in sexual assault cases. *American Journal of Forensic Psychiatry, 16*, 25–40.

Ericsson, K. A., Krampe, R. H., & Tesch-Römer, C. (1993). The role of deliberate practice in the acquisition of expert performance. *Performance, 100*, 363–406.

Erikson, E. (1950). *Childhood and society*. New York: Norton.

Erikson, E. (1959). Identity and the life cycle: Selected papers. *Psychological Issues, 1* (Monograph 1).

Erikson, E. (1968). *Identity: Youth and crisis*. New York: Norton.

Erikson, E. H., & Erikson, J. M. (1998). *The life cycle completed* (extended version). New York: Norton.

Ernst, C., & Angst, J. (1982). *Birth order: Its influence on personality*. New York: Springer.

Eth, S., & Pynoos, R. S. (1994). Children who witness the homicide of a parent. *Psychiatry: Interpersonal and Biological Processes, 57*, 287–306.

Fabiano, E., Robinson, D., & Porporino, F. (1990). *Preliminary assessment of the cognitive skills training program: A component of living skills programming*. Ottawa: Correctional Service of Canada.

Feiffer, J. (1977). *The great comic book heroes*. New York: Dial Press.

Feinstein, J. S., Adolphs, A., Damasio, A., & Tranel, D. (2010). The human amygdala and the induction and experience of fear. *Current Biology, 21*, 34–38.

Felthous, A. R., & Henning, S. (2010). Introduction to this issue: International perspectives on psychopathy: An update. *Behavioral Sciences and the Law, 28*, 121–128.

Festinger, L. (1957). *A theory of cognitive dissonance*. Stanford, CA: Stanford University Press.

Field, N. P., & Filanosky, C. (2010). Continuing bonds, risk factors for complicated grief, and adjustment to bereavement. *Death Studies, 34*, 1–29.

Fingeroth, D. (2004). *Superman on the couch: What superheroes really tell us about ourselves and our society*. New York: Continuum.

Fingeroth, D. (2005, June 15). *Batman Begins: Redefining the Dark Knight*. Retrieved September 5, 2011, from Animation World Network: http://www.awn.com/articles/reviews/ibatman-beginsi-redefining-dark-knight.

Fingeroth, D. (2008). Interviewed in *Batman Unmasked: The Psychology of the Dark Knight* television special.

Fink, B., Neave, N., Manning, J. T., & Grammer, K. (2006). Facial symmetry and judgement of attractiveness, health and personality. *Personality and Individual Differences, 41*, 491–499.

Finkelstein, N. (2000). *The Holocaust industry*. Beccles, Suffolk, Great Britain: Clowes.

Fisher, S. P., & Greenberg, R. P. (1996). *Freud scientifically reappraised: Testing the theories and therapy*. New York: Wiley.

Flavell, J. H. (1979). Metacognition and cognitive monitoring: A new area of cognitive-developmental inquiry. *American Psychologist, 34*, 906–911.

Fodor, E. M., & Farrow, D. L. (1979). The power motive as an influence on use of power. *Journal of Personality and Social Psychology, 37*, 2091–2097.

Foster, D. W. (2000). *Author unknown: On the trail of anonymous*. New York: Holt.

Freud, A. (1936). *The ego and the mechanisms of defense*. New York: International Universities Press.

Freud, S. (1899/1965). *The interpretation of dreams*. New York: Discus.

Freud, S. (1909). Analysis of a phobia in a five-year-old boy. In *Jahrbuch für psychoanalytische und psychopathologische Forschungen*, Bd. i. Reprinted in *The sexual enlightenment of children* (1963). New York: Collier.

Freud, S. (1940). An outline of psychoanalysis. In *Standard Edition of the Complete Psychological Works of Sigmund Freud* (vol. 23, 141–207). London: Hogarth Press.

Freud, S., & Byck, R. (1974). *Cocaine papers by Sigmund Freud*. New York: Stonehill.

Freud, S., & Jung, C. G. (1974). *The Freud/Jung letters*. W. McGuire (Ed.). Princeton, NJ: Princeton University Press.

Frick, P. J., & Ellis, M. (1999). Callous-unemotional traits and subtypes of conduct disorder. *Clinical Child and Family Psychological Review, 2*, 149–168.

Friedman, C. (2008). Interviewed in *Batman Unmasked: The Psychology of the Dark Knight* television special.

Friedman, C. A. (2006). *Wisdom from the Batcave: How to live a super, heroic life*. Linden, NJ: Compass Books.

Fromm, E. (1941). *Escape from freedom*. New York: Rinehart.

Fromm, E. (1964). *The heart of man*. New York: Harper & Row.

Gacono, C. B., Nieberding, R. J., Owen, A., Rubel, J., & Bodholdt, R. (2001). Treating conduct disorder, antisocial, and psychopathic personalities. In J. B. Ashford, B. D. Sales, & W. H. Reid (Eds.), *Treating adult and juvenile offenders with special needs* (pp. 99–129). Washington, D.C.: American Psychological Association.

Gamwell, L., & Tomes, N. (1995). *Madness in America: Cultural and medicinal perceptions of mental illness before 1914*. Ithaca, NY: Cornell University Press.

Garrett, G. (2008). *Holy superheroes! Revised and expanded edition: Exploring the sacred in comics, graphic novels, and film*. Louisville, KY: Westminster John Knox Press.

Gaudin, S. (2009, October 2). *Nanotech could make humans immortal by 2040, futurist says*. Retrieved September 7, 2011, from ABC News: http://abcnews.go.com/Technology/AheadoftheCurve/immortality-nanotech-make-futurist/story?id=8726328.

Geraerts, E., Raymaekers, L., & Merckelbach, H. (2008). Recovered memories of childhood sexual abuse: Current findings and their legal implications. *Legal and Criminological Psychology, 13*, 165–176.

Gerard, H. B., & Mathewson, G. C. (1966). The effects of severity of initiation on liking for a group: A replication. *Journal of Experimental Social Psychology, 2*, 278–287.

Gershoff, E. T. (2002). Parental corporal punishment and associated child behaviors and experience: A meta-analytic and theoretical review. *Psychology Bulletin, 128*, 539–579.

Gibson, W. B. (as M. Grant). (1933, April 1). The living Shadow. *The Shadow Magazine.*

Gladwell, M. (2007, November 12). *Dangerous minds: Criminal profiling made easy.* Retrieved September 8, 2011, from the New Yorker: http://www.newyorker.com/reporting/2007/11/12/071112fa_fact_gladwell?currentPage=5.

Gold, M. (1988). The Joker's dozen. In M. Gold (Ed.), *The greatest Joker stories ever told* (pp. 6–10). New York: DC Comics.

Goldman, A. (1998). ABC of palliative care. Special problems of children. *British Medical Journal, 316*, 49–52.

Goldsman, A. (2005). Interviewed in *Shadows of the Bat: The Cinematic Saga of the Dark Knight,* part 5, "Reinventing a Hero." *Batman Forever* DVD bonus feature.

Goodwill, A. M., Alison, L. J., & Beech, A. R. (2009). What works in offender profiling? A comparison of typological, thematic, and multivariate models. *Behavioral Sciences & the Law, 27*, 507–529.

Gottesman, I. I. (1991). *Schizophrenia genesis: The origins of madness.* New York: W. H. Freeman.

Grant, J. E. (2006). Understanding and treating kleptomania: New models and new treatments. *Israel Journal of Psychiatry and Related Science, 43*, 81–87.

Grant, J. E., & Odlaugh, B. L. (2008). Kleptomania: Clinical characteristics and treatment. *Revista Brasileira de Psiuiatria, 30*, S11–S15.

Grassley, J. S., & Nelms, T. P. (2009). Tales of resistance and other emancipator functions of storytelling. *Journal of Advanced Nursing, 11*, 2447–2453.

Green, M. F. (2001). *Schizophrenia revealed: From neurons to social interactions.* New York: Norton.

Greenberger, R. (1992). End notes. In P. Kupperberg, *The greatest Batman stories ever told,* vol. 2 (pp. 249–253). New York: DC Comics.

Greenberger, R. (2008). *The essential Batman encyclopedia.* New York: Del Rey.

Greening, L. (1997). Adolescent stealers' and nonstealers' social problem-solving skills. *Adolescence, 32*, 51–55.

Gregory, N. (2005). Offender profiling: A review of the literature. *The British Journal of Forensic Practice, 7*, 29–34.

Gresh, L. H., & Weinberg, R. (2002). *The science of superheroes.* New York: Wiley.

Grey, R. (1992). *Nightmare of ecstasy: The life and art of Edward D. Wood, Jr.* Port Townsend, WA: Feral House.

Guerrero, T. (2011, September 6). *Exclusive: Scott Snyder goes in-depth on his plans for Batman in DC's "New 52."* Retrieved December 16, 2011, from ComicVine: http://www.comicvine.com/news/exclusive-scott-snyder-goes-in-depth-on-his-plans-for-batman-in-dcs-new-52/143552/.

Griffin, M. G., Resick, P. A., & Mechanic, M. B. (1997). Objective assessment of peritraumatic dissociation: Psychophysiological indicators. *American Journal of Psychiatry, 154*, 1081–1088.

Haen, C. (2009). Beyond retribution: Working through revenge fantasies with traumatized young people. *The Arts in Psychotherapy, 36*, 84–93.

Haidt, J. (2001). The emotional dog and its rational tail: A social intuitionist approach to moral judgment. *Psychological Review, 108*, 814–834.

Hajdu, D. (2008). *The ten-cent plague: The great comic-book scare and how it changed America.* New York: Farrar, Straus and Giroux.

Halgin, R., & Whitbourne, S. (2009). *Abnormal psychology: Clinical perspectives on psychological disorders* (7th ed.). New York: McGraw-Hill.

Hallett, B. (2004). Dishonest crimes, dishonest language: An argument about terrorism. In F. M. Moghaddam & A. J. Marsella (Eds.), *Understanding terrorism: Psychosocial roots, consequences, and interventions.* (pp. 49–67). Washington, D.C.: American Psychological Association.

Hamm, S., & Skaaren, W. (1988, October 6). *Batman* [unpublished screenplay] (5th draft).

Happé, F. (1994). An advanced test of theory of mind: Understanding of story character thoughts and feelings by able autistic, mentally handicapped, and normal children and adults. *Journal of Autism and Developmental Disorders, 24*, 129–154.

Harb, G. C., Cook, J. M., Gehrman, P. R., Gamble, G. M., & Ross, R. J. (2009). Post-traumatic stress disorder nightmares and sleep disturbances in Iraq war veterans: A feasible and promising treatment combination. *Journal of Aggression, Maltreatment, & Trauma, 18*, 516–531.

Hare, R. D. (1991). *The Hare Psychopathy Checklist—Revised.* Toronto, Ontario, Canada: Multi-Health Systems.

Hare, R. D. (1996). Psychopathy: A clinical construct whose time has come. *Criminal Justice and Behavior, 23*, 25–54.

Hare, R. D. (2003). *Manual for the Hare Psychopathy Checklist* (2nd ed. rev.). Toronto, Ontario, Canada: Multi-Health Systems.

Hare, R. D., & Neumann, C. N. (2006). The PCL-R Assessment of psychopathy: Development, structural properties, and new directions. In C. Patrick (Ed.), *Handbook of psychopathy* (pp. 58–88). New York: Guilford.

Harmon, J., & Glut, D. F. (1972). *The great movie serials: Their sound and fury.* Garden City, NY: Doubleday.

Harpur, T. J., & Hare, R. D. (1994). Assessment of psychopathy as a function of age. *Journal of Abnormal Psychology, 103*, 604–609.

Harpur, T. J., Hare, R. D., & Hakstian, A. R. (1989). Two-factor conceptualization of psychopathy: Construct validity and assessment implications. *Psychological Assessment: A Journal of Consulting and Clinical Psychology, 1*, 6–17.

Harris, G., & Rice, M. (2006). Treatment of psychopathy: A review of empirical findings. In C. Patrick, *Handbook of Psychopathy* (pp. 555–572). New York: Guilford.

Harris, J. C. (2006). Disruptive behavior disorders. In J. A. McMillan, R. D. Feigin, C. D. DeAngelis, & M. D. Jones Jr. (Eds.), *Oski's pediatrics: Principles & practice* (pp. 629–634). Philadelphia, PA: Lippincott, Williams, & Wilkins.

Harris, M. G., Henry, L. P, Harrigan, S. M., Purcell, R., Schwartz, O. S., Farrelly, S. E., Prosser, A. L., Jackson, H. J., & McGorry, P. D. (2005). The relationship between duration of untreated psychosis and outcome: An eight-year prospective study. *Schizophrenia Research, 79*, 85–93.

Harry S. Truman Library & Museum. (n.d.). *The War Relocation Authority & the incarceration of Japanese-Americans during WWII: 1942 chronology.* Retrieved

November 6, 2011, from the Harry S. Truman Library & Museum: http://www.trumanlibrary.com/whistlestop/study_collections/japanese_internment/1942.htm.

Hart, S. (1998). The role of psychopathy in assessing risk for violence: Conceptual and methodological issues. *Legal and Criminological Psychology, 3*, 121–137.

Harvey, A. G., Bryant, R. A., & Dang, S. T. (1998). Autobiographical memory in acute stress disorder. *Journal of Consulting and Clinical Psychology, 66*, 500–506.

Helfgott, J. B. (2008). *Criminal behavior: Theories, typologies, and criminal justice.* Thousand Oaks, CA: Sage.

Helgeson, V. S., Reynolds, K. A., & Tomich, P. L. (2006). A meta-analytic review of benefit finding and growth. *Journal of Consulting and Clinical Psychology, 74*, 797–816.

Herold, E. S. (1999). Dating preferences of university women: An analysis of the nice guy stereotype. *Journal of Sex & Marital Therapy, 25*, 333–343.

Hobfoll, S. E., Rom, T., & Segal. B. (1989). Sensation seeking, anxiety, and risk tasking in the Israeli context. In S. Einstein (Ed.), *Drug and alcohol use: Issues and factors* (pp. 53–59). New York: Plenum Press.

Hogan, R., & Emler, N. P. (1981). Retributive justice. In M. J. Lerner & S. C. Lerner (Eds.), *The justice motive in social behavior* (pp. 125–143). New York: Academic.

Holmes, R. M., & Holmes, S. T. (2009). *Profiling violent crimes: An investigative tool* (4th ed). Thousand Oaks, CA: Sage.

Horney, K. (1939). *New ways in psychoanalysis.* New York: Norton.

Horowitz, M. J. (2007). Understanding and ameliorating revenge fantasies in psychotherapy. *American Journal of Psychiatry, 14*, 7–13.

Hughes, R. C., & Johnson, R. W. (1975). Introversion-extraversion and psychiatric diagnoses: A test of Eysenck's hypothesis. *Journal of Clinical Psychology, 31*, 426–427.

ICD-10—see World Health Organization (2004).

Inbau, F. E., & Reid, J. E. (1967). *Criminal interrogation and confessions* (2nd ed.). Baltimore, MD: Williams & Wilkins.

Inbau, F. E., Reid, J. E., Buckley, J. P., & Jayne, B. C. (2001). *Criminal interrogation and confessions* (4th ed.). Gaithersburg, MD: Aspen.

Ingersoll, B. (2003, April 1). *The law is an ass installment #190.* Retrieved December 4, 2011, from worldfamouscomics.com: http://www.worldfamouscomics.com/law/back20030401.shtml.

Isbell, R., Sobol, J., Lindauer, L., & Lowrance, A. (2004). The effects of storytelling and story reading on the oral language complexity and story comprehension of young children. *Early Childhood Education Journal, 32*, 157–163.

Itoi, K., & Sugimoto, N. (2010). The brainstem noradrenergic systems in stress, anxiety and depression. *Journal of Neuroendocrinology, 22*, 355–361.

Janoff-Bulman, R. (2007). Erroneous assumptions: Popular belief in the effectiveness of torture interrogation. *Peace and Conflict: Journal of Peace Psychology, 13*, 429–435.

Jaques, E. (1965). Death and the midlife crisis. *International Journal of Psychoanalysis, 46*, 507–514.

Johnson, P. A., & Rosenblatt, P. C. (1981). Grief following childhood loss of a parent. *American Journal of Psychotherapy, 35*, 419–425.

Johnson, R. D., & Downing, I. L. (1979). Deindividuation and valence: Effects of prosocial and antisocial behavior. *Journal of Personality and Social Psychology, 37*, 1532–1538.

Johnston, R. (2011, July 15). *"Spoiler was gonna die"—Inside the DC writer meeting that killed Stephanie Brown.* Retrieved July 2, 2011, from Bleeding Cool: http://www.bleedingcool.com/2011/07/15/%E2%80%9Csome-kind-of-gang-war-in-gotham%E2%80%9D-and-%E2%80%9Cspoiler-was-gonna-die%E2%80%9D/.

Joinson, A. N. (2001). Knowing me, knowing you: Reciprocal self-disclosure in Internet-based surveys. *CyberPsychology, 4,* 587–591.

Jokela, M. (2009). Physical attractiveness and reproductive success in humans: Evidence from the late 20th century United States. *Evolution and Human Behavior, 30,* 342–350.

Jones, R. (2010, October 19). *Can Chicagoan qualify for Texan of the Year?* Retrieved August 12, 2011, from *Dallas Morning News:* http://dallasmorningviewsblog.dallasnews.com/archives/2010/10/can-chicagoan-q.html.

Jourard, S. M. (1964). *The transparent self.* Princeton, NJ: Van Nostrand.

Judge, T. A., Hurst, C., & Simon, L. S. (2009). Does it pay to be smart, attractive, or confident (or all three)? Relationships among general mental ability, physical attractiveness, core self-evaluations, and income. *Journal of Applied Psychology, 94,* 742–755.

Jung, C. G. (1913). The theory of psychoanalysis. *Psychoanalytic Review, 1,* 1–40.

Jung, C. G. (1919). Instinct and the unconscious. Reprinted in *The Structure and Dynamics of the Psyche.* CW 8. Princeton, NJ: Princeton University Press.

Jung, C. G. (1936). "Concerning archetypes with special reference to the anima concept." In *Part I: The Archetypes and the Collective Unconscious.* CW9. Princeton, NJ: Princeton University Press.

Jung, C. G. (1942/1968). *Alchemical studies.* CW 13. Princeton, NJ: Princeton University Press.

Jung, C. G. (1949/1961). *Freud and psychoanalysis.* CW 4. Princeton, NJ: Princeton University Press.

Jung, C. G. (1964). *Man and his symbols.* New York: Doubleday.

Jung, C. G. (1971). *Psychological types.* CW 6. Princeton, NJ: Princeton University Press.

Jung, C. G., Henderson, J. L., von Franz, M.-L., Jaffé, A., & Jacobi, J. (1964). *Man and his symbols.* New York: Doubleday.

Just, W., & Morris, M. R. (2003). The Napoleon complex: Why smaller males pick fights. *Evolutionary Ecology, 17,* 509–522.

Kaczynski, T. (1995, September 22). *Industrial society and its future.* Retrieved August 19, 2011, from the *Washington Post*: http://www.washingtonpost.com/wp-srv/national/longterm/unabomber/manifesto.text.htm.

Kakalios, J. (2009). *The physics of superheroes: Spectacular second edition.* New York: Gotham.

Kane, B., & Andrae, T. (1989). *Batman and me.* Forestville, CA: Eclipse.

Karney, B. (2008). Interviewed in *Batman Unmasked: The Psychology of the Dark Knight* television special.

Kassin, S. M. (2008). The psychology of confessions. *Annual Review of Law and Social Science. 4,* 197–213.

Kassin, S. M., Appleby, S. C., & Perillo, J. T. (2010). Interviewing suspects: Practice, science, and future directions. *Legal and Criminological Psychology, 15,* 39–55.

Kassin, S. M., Leo, R. A., Meissner, C. A., Richman, K. D., Colwell, L. H., Leach, A.-M., & La Fon, D. (2007). Police interviewing and interrogation: A self-report survey of police practices and beliefs. *Law and Human Behavior, 31,* 381–400.

Kassin, S. M., Meissner, C. A., & Norwick, R. J. (2005). "I'd know a false confession if I saw one": A comparative study of college students and police investigators. *Law and Human Behavior, 29*, 211–227.

Keefe, R.S.E., Sweeney, J. A., Gu, H., Hamer, R. M., Perkins, D. O., McEvoy, J., & Lieberman, J. A. (2007). Effects of olanzapine, quetiapine, and risperidone on neurocognitive function in early psychosis: A randomized, double-blind 52-week comparison. *American Journal of Psychiatry, 164*, 1061–1071.

Kendler, K. S. (1983). Twin studies of schizophrenia: A current perspective. *American Journal of Psychiatry, 140*, 1413–1425.

Keniston, K. (1983). Remembering Erikson at Harvard. *Psychology Today, 29*.

Kennedy, G. E. (1989). Middleborns' perceptions of family relationships. *Psychological Reports, 64*, 755–760.

Keppel, R. D., & Birnes, W. (1997). *Signature killers*. New York: Pocket Books.

Khan, L. (n.d.). *Conduct disorder*. Retrieved August 22, 2011, from Fittest Mind: http://fittestmind.net/Articles/conduct_disorder.htm.

Kidwell, J. (1982). The neglected birth order: Middleborns. *Journal of Marriage & the Family, 44*, 225–235.

Kim, J., & Hatfield, E. (2004). Love types and subjective well-being: A cross-cultural study. *Social Behavior and Personality, 32*, 173–182.

King, L., & Snook, B. (2009). Peering inside the Canadian interrogation room: An examination of the Reid model of interrogation, influence tactics, and coercive strategies. *Criminal Justice and Behavior, 36*, 674–694.

Kistler, A. (2005, September 21). *Alan Kistler's interview with Mark Waid*. Retrieved December 16, 2011, from Monitor Duty: http://www.monitorduty.com/2005/09/alan-kistlers-interview-with-mark-waid/.

Kistler, A. (2010, September 24). *Crazy sexy geeks: Superhero psychology 1—BATMAN!* Retrieved September 12, 2011, from YouTube: http://www.youtube.com/watch?v=JUxAnM2hKrk.

Kleinmuntz, B., & Szucko, J. J. (1984). A field study of the fallibility of polygraph lie detection. *Nature, 308*, 449–450.

Kramer, D. A. (1989). Development of an awareness of condiction across the life span and the question of postformal operations. In M. L. Commons, J. D. Sinnott, F. A. Richards, & C. Armon (Eds.), *Adult development: Vol. 1: Comparisons and applications of developmental models*. New York: Praeger.

Kramer, J. W. (2005, March 6). *Is Batman nuts?* Retrieved December 16, 2011, from Suspension of Disbelief: http://comicfacts.blogspot.com/2005/03/is-batman-nuts.html.

Krause, R. (2010). An update on primary identification, introjection, and empathy. *International Forum on Psychoanalysis, 19*, 138–143.

Kreisman, J. D., & Straus, H. (1989). *I hate you—don't leave me: Understanding the borderline personality*. New York: Avon.

Kübler-Ross, E. (1969). *On death and dying*. London: Routledge.

Kübler-Ross, E. (2005). *On grief and grieving: Finding the meaning of grief through the five stages of loss*. New York: Simon & Schuster.

Kuhn, D. (2000). Adolescent thought processes. In A. Kazdin (Ed.), *Encyclopedia of psychology* (pp. 52–59). Washington, D.C., & New York: American Psychological Association and Oxford University Press.

Kuiper, N. A., & Leite, C. (2010). Personality impressions associated with four distinct humor styles. *Scandinavian Journal of Psychology, 51*, 115–122.

Kulka, R. A., & Kessler, J. B. (1978). Is justice really blind? The influence of litigant physical attractiveness on juridical judgment. *Journal of Applied Social Psychology, 4*, 366–381.

La Voie, J. C. (1973). Individual differences in resistance-to-temptation behavior in adolescents: An Eysenck analysis. *Journal of Clinical Psychology, 29*, 20–22.

Lahey, B. B., Moffitt, T. E., & Caspi, A. (Eds.). (2003). *Causes of conduct disorder and juvenile delinquency.* New York: Guilford Press.

Laidler, K. J., & Hunt, G. (2001). Accomplishing femininity among the girls in the gang. *British Journal of Criminology, 41*, 656–678.

Laney, C, & Loftus, E. F. (2005). Traumatic memories are not necessarily accurate memories. *Canadian Journal of Psychiatry, 50*, 823–828.

Laney, C., & Loftus, E. F. (2008). Emotional content of true and false memories. *Memory, 16*, 500–516.

Langley, R. M. (2011, June 24). Personal communication.

Langley, T. (2010). Freedom versus security: The basic human dilemma from 9/11 to Marvel's Civil War. *International Journal of Comic Art, 11*, 426–435.

Langley, T. (in press). Our superheroes, our supervillains: Are they all that different? In R. Rosenberg (Ed.), *Our superheroes, ourselves.* New York: Oxford University Press.

Langley, T., Duncan, R. Langley, N., Poole, J., Sepe, T., Head, M., Langley, A., Hill, K., Cate, C. L., Shurtleff, J., & O'Nale, R. (2008, February). *How heavy is that cape? Challenges in empirical assessment of comics' influence and fans' behavior.* Panel presented at the Comics Arts Conference, WonderCon, San Francisco, California.

Langley, T., & Rosenberg, R. (2011). Reflections on the psychopathy of the Joker: A Comic-Con panel report. *International Journal of Comic Art, 13*, 654–676.

Langley, T., Rosenberg, R., Meriwether, L., Pantozzi, J., & Uslan, M. (2011, July). *Psychology of the Dark Knight: How trauma formed the Batman and why he's got a thing for "bad girls."* Panel presented at the Comics Arts Conference, San Diego Comic-Con International, San Diego, CA.

Langlois, J. H., Kalakanis, L., Rubenstein, A. J., Larson, A., Hallam, M., & Smoot, M. (2000). Maxims or myths of beauty? A meta-analytic and theoretical review. *Psychological Bulletin, 126*, 390–423.

Lazarus, A. A., & Zur, O. (2002). *Dual relationships and psychotherapy.* New York: Springer.

Leary, M. R., Twenge, J. M., & Quinlivan, E. (2006). Interpersonal rejection as a determinant of anger and aggression. *Personality and Social Psychology Bulletin, 10*, 111–132.

Lee, S. I., & Keltner, N. L. (2006). Biological perspectives: Serotonin and norepinephrine reuptake inhibitors (SNRIs): Venlafaxine and duloxetine. *Perspectives in psychiatric care, 42*, 144–148.

Lehman, A. F. (1998). Patterns of unusual care for schizophrenia: Initial results from the schizophrenia Port Outcomes Research Team (PORT) client survey. *Schizophrenia Bulletin, 24*, 11–20.

Leo, R. A., & Ofshe, R. J. (1998). The consequences of false confessions: Deprivations of liberty and miscarriages of justice in the age of psychological interrogation. *Journal of Criminal Law and Criminology, 88*, 429–497.

Lerner, M. J. (1980). *The belief in a just world: A fundamental delusion.* New York: Plenum Press.

Lerner, M. J., & Miller, D. T. (1978). Just world research and the attribution process: Looking back and ahead. *Psychological Bulletin, 85,* 1030–1051.

Lerner, M. J., & Simmons, C. H. (1966). Observers' reaction to the "innocent victim": Compassion or rejection? *Journal of Personality and Social Psychology, 4,* 203–210.

Letamendi, A., Rosenberg, R., Langley, T., & Wein, L. (2011, July 24). *The superhero battlefield: Resiliency in the face of loss and destruction.* Panel presented at San Diego Comic-Con International, San Diego, CA.

Levinson, D. J. (1986). A conception of adult development. *American Psychologist, 41,* 3–13.

Levitz, P. (2008). Interviewed in *Batman Unmasked: The Psychology of the Dark Knight* television special.

Lewin, K. (1951). *Field theory and social science.* New York: Harper & Row.

Lewis, A. D., & Kraemer, C. H. (Eds.) (2010). *Graven images: Religion in comic books and graphic novels.* New York: Continuum.

Library of Congress. (n.d.). *Timeline of Theodore Roosevelt's life.* Retrieved September 11, 2011, from the Library of Congress: http://memory.loc.gov/ammem/collections/troosevelt_film/trftime1880.html.

Lindemann, D. (2010). Will the real dominatrix please stand up: Artistic purity and professionalism in the S&M dungeon. *Sociological Forum, 25,* 588–606.

Lindstrøm, T. C. (2002). "It ain't necessarily so . . ." Challenging mainstream thinking about bereavement. *Journal of Health Promotion & Maintenance, 25,* 11–21.

Lipkus, I. M. (1991). The construction and preliminary validation of a Global Belief in a Just World Scale and the exploratory analysis of the Multidimensional Belief in a Just World Scale. *Personality and Individual Differences, 12,* 1171–1178.

Lipkus, I. M., Dalbert, C., & Siegler, I. C. (1996). The importance of distinguishing the belief in a just world, willingness to accommodate, and marital well-being. *Personality and Social Psychology Bulletin, 22,* 1043–1056.

Lipsey, M. W., Chapman, G., & Landenberger, N. A. (2001). Cognitive-behavioral programs for offenders. *Annals of the American Academy of Political and Social Science, 578,* 144–157.

Loughnan, S. Haslam, N., Murnane, T., Vaes, J., Reynolds, C., & Suitner, C. (2010). Objectification leads to depersonalization: The denial of mind and moral concern to objected others. *European Journal of Social Psychology, 40,* 709–717.

Lovecraft, H. P. (1937, January). The thing on the doorstop. *Weird Tales, 29* (1), 52–70.

Lu, M., Wagner, A., Van Male, L., Whitehead, A., & Boehnlein, J. (2009). Imagery rehearsal therapy for posttraumatic nightmares in U.S. veterans. *Journal of Traumatic Stress, 22,* 236–239.

Lytle, P. (2008). The madness of Arkham Asylum. In D. O'Neil & L. Wilson (Eds.), *Batman unauthorized: Vigilantes, jokers, and heroes in Gotham City* (pp. 109–120). Dallas, TX: BenBella.

Maccoby, E. E., & Martin, J. A. (1983). Socialization in the context of the family: Parent–child interaction. In P. H. Mussen (Ed.) & E. M. Hetherington (Vol. Ed.), *Handbook of child psychology: Vol. 4. Socialization, personality, and social development* (4th ed., pp. 1–101). New York: Wiley.

Machado, M., & Einsarson, T. R. (2010). Comparison of SSRIs and SNRIs in major depressive disorder: A meta-analysis of head-to-head randomized clinical trials. *Journal of Clinical Pharmacy and Therapeutics, 35,* 177–118.

Mackenzie, D. L. (2001). Corrections and sentencing in the 21st century: Evidence-based corrections and sentencing. *The Prison Journal, 81,* 299–312.

Maddux, J. E., & Rogers, R. W. (1983). Protection motivation and self-efficacy: A revised theory of fear appeals and attitude change. *Journal of Experimental Social Psychology, 19,* 469–479.

Madigan, S., Moran, G., & Pederson, D. R. (2006). Unresolved states of mind, disorganized attachment relationships, and disrupted interactions of adolescent mothers and their infants. *Developmental Psychology, 42,* 293–304.

Maher, L. (1997). *Sexed work: Gender, race and resistance in the Brooklyn drug market.* Oxford, England: Oxford University Press.

Main, M., & Solomon, J. (1986). Discovery of an insecure disorganized/disoriented attachment pattern: Procedures, findings and implications for classification of behaviour. In M. W. Yogman & T. B. Brazelton (Eds.), *Affective development in infancy* (pp. 95–124). Madison, CT: International University Press.

Malquist, C. P. (1986). Children who witness parental murder: Posttraumatic aspects. *Journal of the American Academy of Child Psychiatry, 25,* 320–325.

Mancini, A. D., Robinaugh, D., Shear, K., & Bonanno, G. A. (2009). Does attachment avoidance help people cope with loss? The moderating effects of relationship quality. *Journal of Clinical Psychology, 65,* 1127–1136.

Mann, L. (1981). The baiting crowd in episodes of threatened suicide. *Journal of Personality and Social Psychology, 41,* 450–463.

Marano, M. (2008). Ra's al Ghul: Father figure as terrorist. In D. O'Neil & L. Wilson (Eds.), *Batman unauthorized: Vigilantes, jokers, and heroes in Gotham City* (pp. 69–84). Dallas, TX: BenBella.

Markell, K. A., & Markell, M. A. (2008). *The children who lived: Using Harry Potter and other fictional characters to help grieving children and adolescents.* New York: Routledge.

Market, M. T. (2009, February 27). *Batman and personality disorders.* Retrieved June 6, 2011, from The Critical Thinker(tm): http://thecriticalthinker.wordpress.com/2009/02/27/batman-personality-disorders/.

Marshall, M. J. (2002). *Why spanking doesn't work.* Springville, UT: Bonneville Books.

Marshall, M., Lewis, S., Lockwood, A., Drake, R., Jones, P., & Croudace, T. (2005). Association between duration of untreated psychosis and outcome in cohorts of first-episode patients. *Archives of General Psychiatry, 62,* 975–983.

Maschke, G. W., & Scalabrini, G. J. (2005). *The lie behind the lie detector* (4th digital ed.). Retrieved August 18, 2011, from AntiPolygraph.org: http://antipolygraph.org/lie-behind-the-lie-detector.pdf.

Maslow, A. (1954). *Motivation and personality.* New York: Harper.

Maslow, A. (1966). *The psychology of science: A reconnaissance.* New York: Harper & Row.

Matson, J. L., Rivet, T. T., & Fodstad, J. C. (2010). Atypical antipsychotic adjustments and side-effects over time in adults with intellectual disability, tardive dyskinesia, and akathisia. *Journal of Developmental and Physical Disabilities, 22,* 447–461.

May, R. (1983). *The discovery of meaning: Writings in existential psychology.* New York: Norton.

McCabe, K. M., Hough, R., Wood, P. A., & Yeh, M. (2001). Childhood and adolescent onset conduct disorder: A test of the developmental taxonomy. *Journal of Abnormal Child Psychology, 29*, 305–316.

McCauley, C. (2007). Toward a social psychology of professional military interrogation. *Peace and Conflict: Journal of Peace Psychology, 13*, 399–410.

McClelland, D. C. (1961). *The achieving society.* Princeton: Van Nostrand.

McClelland, D. C., Atkinson, J. W., Clark, R. A., & Lowell, E. L. (1953). *The achievement motive.* Princeton, NJ: Van Nostrand.

McCulley, J. (1919). The curse of Capistrano. *All-Story Weekly.*

McCullough, M. E. (2008). *Beyond revenge: The evolution of the forgiveness instinct.* San Francisco: Jossey-Bass.

McCullough, M. L. (2001). Freud's seduction theory and its rehabilitation: A saga of one mistake after another. *Review of General Psychology, 5*, 3–22.

McEvoy, J. P., Lieberman, J. A., Perkins, D. A., Hamer, R. M., Gu, H., Lazarus, A., Sweitzer, D., Olexy, C., Weiden, P., & Strakowski, S. D. (2007). Efficacy and tolerability of olanzapine, quetiapine, and risperidone in the treatment of early psychosis: A randomized, double-blind 52-week comparison. *American Journal of Psychiatry, 164*, 1050–1060.

McGuirk, E. M., & Pettijohn, T. F. (2008). Birth order and romantic relationship styles and attitudes in college students. *North American Journal of Psychology, 10*, 37–52.

McNally, R. J. (2004). The science and folklore of traumatic amnesia. *Clinical Psychology Science and Practice, 11*, 29–33.

Medhurst, A. (1991). Batman, deviance and camp. In R. E. Pearson & W. Uricchio (Eds.), *The many lives of the Batman: Critical approaches to a superhero and his media* (pp. 149–163). New York: Routledge.

Meissner, W. W. (1970). Notes on identification I. Origins in Freud. *Psychoanalytic Quarterly, 39*, 563–589.

Meltzer, S. W. (1982). Group analytic approaches to psychotic patients in an institutional setting. *American Journal of Psychoanalysis, 42*, 357–362.

Mendelson, S. (2008, November 10). *Batman: The Complete Animated Series (DVD).* Retrieved November 26, 2011, from Film Threat: http://www.filmthreat.com/reviews/11348/.

Menzies, R. G., & Parker, L. (2001). The origins of height fear: An evaluation of neoconditioning explanations. *Behaviour Research and Therapy, 39*, 185–199.

Merry, S., & Harsent, L. (2000). Intruders, pilferers, raiders and invaders: The interpersonal dimensions of house burglary. In L. Alison & D. Cander (Eds.), *Profiling property crimes. Offender profiling series* (vol. IV, pp. 31–56). Dartmouth, UK: Aldershot.

Mersky, H. (1992). The manufacture of personalities: The production of multiple personality disorder. *British Journal of Psychiatry, 160*, 327–340.

Messich, A. C., Tarter, R. E., & Carvlin, M. (n.d.). *Conduct disorder and drug use.* Retrieved August 22, 2011, from Encyclopedia of Drugs, Alcohol, and Addictive Behavior: http://www.enotes.com/drugs-alcohol-encyclopedia/conduct-disorder-drug-use.

Meston, C. M., & Frohlich, P. F. (2003). Love at first fright: Partner salience moderates roller-coaster-induced excitation transfer. *Archives of Sexual Behavior, 32*, 537–544.

Miethe, T. D., McCorkle, R. C., & Listwan, S. J. (2006). *Crime profiles: The anatomy of dangerous places, persons, and situations.* New York: Oxford University Press.

Miller, J. (2001). *One of the guys: Girls, gangs, and gender.* New York: Oxford University Press.

Millon, T. (1991). *Manual for the Millon clinical multiaxial inventory.* Minneapolis, MN: National Computer Systems.

Millon, T. (2004). *Personality disorders in modern life.* New York: Wiley.

Mills, J. (2005). *Relational and intersubjective perspectives in psychoanalysis: A critique.* Lanham, MD: Jason Aronson.

Moench, D. (2004). *The forensic files of Batman.* New York: DC Comics.

Monaghan, J. H., Robinson, J. O., & Dodge, J. A. (1979). The Children's Life Events Inventory. *Journal of Psychosomatic Research, 23,* 63–68.

Monteleone, P., Santonastaso, P., Tortorella, A., Favaro, A., Farbrazzo, M., Castaldo, E., Caregaro, L., Fuschino, A., & Maj, M. (2005). Serotonin transporter polymorphism and potential response to SSRIs in bulimia nervosa. *Molecular Psychiatry, 10,* 716–718.

Morris, E. (2002). *Theodore Rex.* New York: Random House.

Morris, E. (2010). *The rise of Theodore Roosevelt.* New York: Random House.

Morrison, G. (2011). *Supergods: What masked vigilantes, miraculous mutants, and a sun god from Smallville can teach us about being human.* New York: Spiegel & Grau.

Mullins, C. W., & Wright, R. (2003). Gender, social networks, and residential burglary. *Criminology, 41,* 813–840.

Murray, H. A. (1938). *Explorations in personality.* New York: Oxford University Press.

Murstein, B. I., Reif, J. A., & Syracuse-Siewert, G. (2002). Comparison of the function of exchange in couples of similar and differing physical attractiveness. *Psychological Reports, 91,* 299–314.

Myers, D. (2008). *Social psychology* (9th ed.). New York: McGraw-Hill.

Myers, R. D. (1964). Emotional and autonomic responses following hypothalamic chemical stimulation. *Canadian Journal of Experimental Psychology, 18,* 6–14.

Nagy, M. (1948). The child's theories concerning death. *Journal of Geriatric Psychology, 73,* 3–27.

Nangle, D. W., Erdley, C. A., Zeff, K. R., Stanchfield, L. L., & Gold, J. A. (2004). Opposites do not attract: Social status and behavioral-style concordances and discordances among children and the peers who like or dislike them. *Journal of Abnormal Child Development, 32,* 425–434.

National Center for Missing and Exploited Children. (1985). *Child molesters: A behavioral analysis.* Washington, D.C.: Author.

National Research Council, Committee to Review the Scientific Evidence on the Polygraph. (2002). *The polygraph and lie detection.* Washington, D.C.: National Academies Press.

Neisser, U. (1967). *Cognitive psychology.* New York: Meredith.

Newberger, E. (2000). *The men they will become: The nature and nurture of male character.* Cambridge, MA: Da Capo Press.

Newman, B. M., & Newman, P. R. (1991). *Development through life: A psychosocial approach* (5th ed.). Pacific Grove, CA: Brooks/Cole.

Newman, J. P., Widom, C. S., & Nathan, S. (1985). Passive avoidance in syndromes of disinhibition: Psychopathy and extraversion. *Journal of Personality and Social Psychology, 48,* 1316–1327.

Nichols, D. S. (2006). Tell me a story: MMPI responses and personal biography in the case of a serial killer. *Journal of Personality Assessment, 86,* 242–262.

Nolen-Weathington, E. (2008). *Modern masters volume three: Bruce Timm*. Raleigh, NC: TwoMorrows.

Norton, R. W., & Pettegrew, L. S. (1977). Communicator style as an effect determinant of attraction. *Communication Research, 4*, 257–282.

Nygren, B., Alex, L., Jonsen, E., Gustafson, Y., Norberg, A., & Lundman, B. (2005). Resilience, sense of coherence, purposes in life and self-transcendence in relation to perceived physical and mental health among the oldest old. *Aging & Mental Health, 9*, 354–362.

Oatley, K. (2011). *Such stuff as dreams: The psychology of fiction*. West Sussex, UK: Wiley-Blackwell.

O'Brien, L. T. (2005). Perceiving self-interest: Power, ideology, and maintenance of the status quo. *Social Justice Research, 18*, 1–24.

O'Neil, D. (2008). Introduction. In D. O'Neil & L. Wilson (Eds.), *Batman unauthorized: Vigilantes, jokers, and heroes in Gotham City* (pp. 1–6). Dallas, TX: BenBella.

O'Neil, D. (2011, July 24). Personal communication.

O'Neil, D., Uslan, M., Cash, T., Langley, T., Rosenberg, R., & Zehr, E. P. (2010, July 24). *Batman and the empty nest syndrome*. Panel presented at the Comics Arts Conference, San Diego Comic-Con International, San Diego, CA.

O'Neil, D., Zehr, E. P., Langley, T., Letamendi, A., Rosenberg, R., & Bruen, M. (2011, October 14). *Batman vs. Iron Man: Can a person truly become either?* Panel presented at the Comics Studies Conference, New York Comic Con, New York, NY.

Oltmanns, T. F., & Emery, R. E. (2012). *Abnormal psychology* (7th ed.). Upper Saddle River, NJ: Pearson.

Ong, A. D., Zautra, A. J., & Reid, M. C. (2010). Psychological resilience predicts decreases in pain catastrophizing through positive emotions. *Psychology and Aging, 25*, 516–523.

Orth, U., Montada, L., & Maercker, A. (2006). Feelings of revenge, retaliation motive, and posttraumatic stress reactions in crime victims. *Journal of Interpersonal Violence, 21*, 229–243.

Orzopeda, B. J. (2006). *The Gospel according to superheroes*. New York: Peter Lang.

O'Toole, D., & Cory, J. (1998). *Helping children grieve and grow: A guide for those who care*. Bumsville, NC: Compassion Books.

Overton, W. F., & Byrnes, J. P. (1991). Cognitive development. In R. M. Lerner, A. C. Petersen, & J. Brooks-Gunn (Eds.), *Encyclopedia of adolescence* (vol. 1, pp. 151–156). New York: Garland.

Pahel, L. J. (2006). Harry Potter and the magic of transformation. In N. Mulholland (Ed.), *The psychology of Harry Potter* (pp. 311–326). Dallas, TX: BenBella.

Pantozzi, J. (2010, December 2). *14 reasons why Batman's my dream man*. Retrieved July 31, 2011, from Topless Robot: http://www.toplessrobot.com/2010/12/14_reasons_why_batmans_my_dream_man.php.

Parikh, R. K. (2008, July 18). *The medical maladies of Batman and his enemies*. Retrieved June 6, 2011, from Salon: http://open.salon.com/blog/rahul_k_parikh/2008/07/18/the_medical_maladies_of_the_batman_and_his_enemies.

Park, C. L. (2010). Making sense of the meaning literature: An integrative review of meaning making and its effects on adjustment to stressful life events. *Psychological Bulletin, 136*, 257–301.

Parker, T. S., & Wampler, K. S. (2006). Changing emotion: The use of therapeutic storytelling. *Journal of Marital and Family Therapy, 32*, 155–166.

Parson, E. (1995). Post-traumatic stress and copying in an inner-city child: Traumatogenic witnessing of interparental violence and murder. *The Psychological Study of the Child, 50,* 272–307.

Patterson, C. M., Kosson, D. S., & Newman, J. P. (1987). Reaction to punishment, reflectivity, and passive avoidance learning in extraverts. *Journal of Personality and Social Psychology, 52,* 565–575.

Pearson, R. E., & Uricchio, W. (1991). Notes from the Batcave: An interview with Dennis O'Neil. In R. E. Pearson & W. Uricchio (Eds.), *The many lives of the Batman: Critical approaches to a superhero and his media* (pp. 18–32). New York: Routledge.

Penton-Voak, I. S., Jones, B. C., Little, A. C., Baker, S., Tiddeman, B., Burt, D. M., & Perrett, D. I. (2001). Symmetry, sexual dimorphism in facial proportions and male facial attractiveness. *Proceedings of the Royal Society of London, 268,* 1–7.

Peplau, L. A., & Gordon, S. L. (1985). Women and men in love: Sex differences in close heterosexual relationships. In V. E. O'Leary, R. K. Unger, & B. S. Wallston (Eds.), *Women, sex, and social psychology* (pp. 257–291). Hillsdale, NJ: Erlbaum.

Persico, N., Postlewaite, A., & Silverman, D. (2004). The effect of adolescent experience on labor market outcomes: The case of height. *Journal of Political Economy, 112,* 1019–1053.

Peterson, T., Kaasa, S. O., & Loftus, E. F. (2009). Me too! Social modeling influences on early autobiographical memories. *Applied Cognitive Psychology, 23,* 267–277.

Petty, R. E. (1997). Attitudes and attitude change. *Annual Review of Psychology, 48,* 609–647.

Phillips, R. T. M. (2008). Interviewed in television special *Batman Unmasked: The Psychology of the Dark Knight* (2008).

Phoenix, J. (2000). Prostitute identities. *British Journal of Criminology, 40,* 37–55.

Piaget, J. (1930). *The child's conception of physical causality.* New York: Routledge.

Piaget, J. (1932). *The moral judgment of the child.* New York: Harcourt Brace Jovanovich.

Piaget, J. (1952). *The origins of intelligence in children.* New York: Harcourt Brace Jovanovich.

Piaget, J. (1954). *The construction of reality in the child.* New York: Basic Books.

Piaget, J., & Inhelder, B. (1969). *The child's conception of space* (F. J. Langdon & J. L. Lunzer, Trans.). New York: W. W. Norton.

Pizzolato, J. E. (2006). Crafting stories, constructing selves: Supporting girls' development through structure story writing. *Identity: An International Journal of Theory and Research, 6,* 187–206.

Pope, C. E. (1977). *Crime Specific Analysis: The characteristics of burglary incidents.* Analytic Report SD-AR-10, U.S. Department of Justice, Law Enforcement Assistance Administration, National Criminal Justice Information and Statistics Service. Washington, D.C.: U.S. Department of Justice.

Porter, J. N. (1981). Is there a survivor's syndrome? Psychological and socio-political implications. *Journal of Psychology and Judaism, 6,* 33–52.

Porter, R. (2002). *Madness: A brief history.* New York: Oxford University Press.

Postmes, T., & Spears, R. (1998). Deindividuation and antinormative behavior: A meta-analysis. *Psychological Bulletin, 123,* 238–259.

Pratt, M. W., Danso, H. A., Arnold, M. L., Norris, J. E., & Filyer, R. (2001). Adult generativity and the socialization of adolescents. *Journal of Personality, 69,* 89–120.

Premack, D. G., & Woodruff, G. (1978). Does the chimpanzee have a theory of mind? *Behavioral and Brain Sciences, 1,* 515–526.

Putkonen, H., Weizmann-Henelius, G., Repo-Tiihonen, E., Lindberg, N., Saarela, U., Eronen, M., & Häkkänen-Nyholm, H. (2010). Homicide, psychopathy, and aging—a nationwide register-based case-comparison study of homicide offenders aged 60 years and older. *Journal of Forensic Science, 55*, 1552–1556.

Raine, A. (2002). Biosocial studies of antisocial and violent behavior in children and adults: A review. *Journal of Abnormal Child Psychology, 30*, 311–326.

Regan, P. (1998). Minimum mate selection standards as a function of perceived mate value, relationship context, and gender. *Journal of Psychology and Human Sexuality, 10*, 53–73.

Rhoades, G. K., Stanley, S. M., & Markman, H. J. (2010). Should I stay or should I go? Predicting dating relationship from four aspects of commitment. *Journal of Family Psychology, 24*, 543–550.

Rhodes, G. (2006). The evolutionary psychology of facial beauty. *Annual Review of Psychology, 57*, 199–226.

Rhodes, G., Simmons, L. W., & Peters, M. (2005). Attractiveness and sexual behavior: Does attractiveness enhance mating success? *Evolution and Human Behavior, 26*, 186–201.

Rich, J. (1975). Effects of children's physical attractiveness of teachers' evaluations. *Journal of Educational Psychology, 67*, 599–609.

Richters, J., de Visser, R. O., Rissel, C. E., Grulich, A. E., & Smith, A. M. A. (2008). Demographic and psychosocial features of participants in bondage and discipline, "sadomasochism" or dominance and submission (BDSM): Data from a national survey. *Journal of Sexual Medicine, 5*, 1660–1668.

Riis, J. A. (1901). *The making of an American.* Retrieved September 11, 2011, from Bartleby.com: http://www.bartleby.com/207/13.html#Z54.

Roberts, W. W., & Nagel, J. (1996). First-order projections activated by stimulation of hypothalamic sites eliciting attack and flight in rats. *Behavioral Neuroscience, 110*, 509–527.

Robinson, J. (2009, June 23). Personal communication.

Robinson, T. (2001, October 24). *Alan Moore.* Retrieved June 17, 2011, from the A. V. Club: http://www.avclub.com/articles/alan-moore,13740/.

Rofé, Y. (2008). Does repression exist? Memory, pathogenic, unconscious, and clinical evidence. *Review of General Psychology, 12*, 63–85.

Rogers, C. (1983). *Freedom to learn for the 80s.* Columbus, OH: Merrill.

Rohmer, S. (1913). *The mystery of Dr. Fu-Manchu.* London: Methuen.

Romero, L. M., & Butler, L. K. (2007). Endocrinology of stress. *International Journal of Comparative Psychology, 20*, 89–95.

Roosevelt, T. (1884, February 14). Diary photo retrieved September 11, 2011, from the Library of Congress: http://memory.loc.gov/ammem/collections/troosevelt_film/trfdiary3.html.

Roosevelt, T. (1884, February 17). Diary photo retrieved September 11, 2011, from the Library of Congress: http://memory.loc.gov/ammem/collections/troosevelt_film/trfdiary2.html.

Rosenberg, R. S. (2008a). Interviewed in the television special *Batman Unmasked.*

Rosenberg, R. S. (2008b). What's wrong with Bruce Wayne? In D. O'Neil & L. Wilson (Eds.), *Batman unauthorized: Vigilantes, jokers, and heroes in Gotham City* (pp. 145–156). Dallas, TX: BenBella.

Rosenberg, R. S. (2009, November 1). The Liberation of Anonymity. Retrieved June 14, 2011, from Psychablog: http://psychablog.blogspot.com/2009/10/liberation-of-anonymity-part-ii.html.

Rosenberg, R. S., & Kosslyn, S. M. (2011). *Abnormal psychology*. New York: Worth.

Rosenberg, R., Langley, T., Robinson, J., Englehart, S., Uslan, M., & West, A. (2009, July 25). *Is the Joker a psychopath? You decide!* Panel presented at the Comics Arts Conference, San Diego Comic-Con International, San Diego, CA.

Ross, J. (2005). A history of torture. In K. Roth & M. Worden (Eds.), *Torture* (pp. 3–17). New York: The New Press.

Rotter, J. B. (1945). *Social learning and clinical psychology*. New York: Prentice-Hall.

Rotter, J. B. (1966). Generalized expectancies for internal versus external locus of control of reinforcement. *Psychological Monographs, 80* (whole no. 609).

Rowe, A., & Regehr, C. (2010). Whatever gets you through the day: An examination of cynical humor among emergency service professionals. *Journal of Loss and Trauma, 15*, 448–464.

Ruch, W., Beermann, U., & Proyer, R. T. (2009). Investigating the humor of gelatophobes: Does feeling ridiculous equal being humorless? *Humor: International Journal of Humor Research, 22*, 111–143.

Rush, B. (1815). *Medical inquiries and observations*. Philadelphia, PA: Thomas Dobson.

Russell, D. (1973). Emotional aspects of shoplifting. *Psychiatric Annals, 3*, 77–86.

Sachdev, P. S. (2000). The current status of tardive dyskinesia. *Australian and New Zealand Journal of Psychiatry, 34*, 355–369.

Sadalla, E. K., Kenrick, D. T., & Vershure, B. (1987). Dominance and heterosexual attraction. *Journal of Personality and Social Psychology, 52*, 730–738.

Salkin, A. (2006, December 13). *Web site hunts predators, and TV goes along*. Retrieved August 12, 2011, from the *New York Times*: http://query.nytimes.com/gst/fullpage.html?res=9D07E2DB1531F930A25751C1A9609C8B63.

Salmon, C. (1998). The evocative nature of kin terminology in political rhetoric. *Politics and the Life Science, 17*, 51–57.

Salmon, C. (2003). Birth order and relationships: Family, friends, and sexual partners. *Human Nature, 14*, 73–88.

Samson, A. C., & Hempelmann, C. F. (2011). Humor with backgrounded incongruity: Does more required suspension of disbelief affect humor perception? *Humor: International Journal of Humor Research, 24*, 167–185.

Sandier, I. N. (2001). Quality and ecology of adversity as common mechanisms of risk and resilience. *American Journal of Community Psychology, 29*, 19–61.

Sarasalo, E., Bergman, B., & Toth, J. (1997). Theft behaviour and its consequences among kleptomaniacs and shoplifters: A comparative study. *Forensic Science International, 86*, 193–205.

Saunders, B. (2011). *Do the gods wear capes? Spirituality, fantasy, and superheroes*. New York: Continuum.

Saxe, L., Dougherty, D., & Cross, T. (1985). The validity of polygraph testing: Scientific analysis and public controversy. *American Psychologist, 40*, 355–366.

Schachter, S., & Singer, J. E. (1962). Cognitive, social and physiological determinants of emotional state. *Psychological Review, 69*, 379–399.

Schlesinger, L. B. (2009). Psychological profiling: Investigative implications from crime scene analysis. *Journal of Psychiatry & Law, 37*, 73–84.

Schmid, G. B., & Wanderer, S. (2007). Phantasy therapy: Statistical evaluation of a new approach to group psychotherapy for stationary and ambulatory psychotic patients. *Forschende Komplementärmedizin, 14*, 216–223.

Schultz, D. P., & Schultz, S. E. (2009). *Theories of personality* (9th ed.). Belmont, CA: Wadsworth.

Schumacher, J. (2005). Interviewed in *Shadows of the Bat Part 5: Reinventing a Hero. Batman Forever* Special Edition DVD bonus feature.

Segal, D. L., Coolidge, F. L., & Rosowsky, E. (2000). Personality. In S. K. Whitbourne (Ed.), *Psychopathology in later life*. New York: Wiley.

Segredou, E., Livaditis, M., Liolios, K., & Skartsila, G. (2008). Group programmes for recovery from psychosis: A systematic review. *Annals of General Psychiatry, 7*, 1.

Sharrett, C. (1991). Batman and the twilight of the idols. In R. E. Pearson & W. Uricchio (Eds.), *The many lives of the Batman: Critical approaches to a superhero and his media* (pp. 18–32). New York: Routledge.

Shear, M. K. (2010). Exploring the role of experiential avoidance from the perspective of attachment theory and the dual process model. *Omega: Journal of Death and Dying, 16*, 357–369.

Shore, J. H., Orton, H., & Manson, S. M. (2009). Trauma-related nightmares among American Indian veterans: Views from the dream catcher. *American Indian and Alaska Mental Health Research, 16*, 5–38.

Siegal, A. (2005). *The neurobiology of aggression and rage*. Boca Raton, FL: CRC Press.

Siegel, A., Bhatt, S., Bhatt, R., & Zalcman, S. S. (2007). The neurobiological bases for development of pharmacological treatments of aggressive disorders. *Current Neuropharmacology, 5*, 135–147.

Sigall, H., & Ostrove, N. (1973). Effects of the physical attractiveness of the defendant and nature of the crime on juridic judgment. *Proceedings of the Annual Convention of the American Psychological Association—1973*, 267–268.

Sigall, H., & Ostrove, N. (1975). Beautiful but dangerous: Effects of offender attractiveness and nature of the crime on juridic judgment. *Journal of Personality and Social Psychology, 31*, 410–414.

Simpson, J. A., Campbell, B., & Berscheid, E. (1986). The association between romantic love and marriage: Kephart (1967) twice revisited. *Personality and Social Psychology Bulletin, 12*, 363–372.

Skeem, J. L., & Cooke, D. J. (2010). Is criminal behavior a central component of psychopathy? Conceptual directions for resolving the debate. *Psychological Assessment, 22*, 433–445.

Skinner, E. A., & Wellborn, J. G. (1994). Coping during childhood and adolescence: A motivational perspective. In D. Featherman, R. Lerner, & M. Perlmutter (Eds.) *Life-span development and behavior* (vol. 12, pp. 91–133). Hillsdale, NJ: Erlbaum.

Smith, M. J., Pustz, M., Langley, N., Andrada, M., Catalfu, C., Combs, W. S., Geranios, P., Moran, J. K., & Stover, K. (2007, July). *The culture of popular things: Ethnographic examinations of Comic-Con 2007*. Panel presented at the Comics Arts Conference, Comic-Con International, San Diego, California.

Smithkey, J. III. (1998). *Jack the Ripper: The inquest of the final victim Mary Kelly*. North Canton, OH: Key.

Spiropoulous, G. V., Spruance, L., Van Voorhis, P., & Schmitt, M. M. (2005). Pathfinders and problem solving: Comparative effects at two cognitive-behavioral programs among men and women offenders in community and prison. *Journal of Offender Rehabilitation, 42,* 69–94.

Sprecher, S. (2001). Equity and social exchange in dating couples: Associations with satisfaction, commitment, and stability. *Journal of Marriage & the Family, 63,* 599–613.

Sprecher, S., & Hendrick, S. S. (2004). Self-disclosure in intimate relationships: Associations with individual and relationship characteristics over time. *Journal of Social and Clinical Psychology, 23,* 857–877.

Stahl, M. J., & Harrell, A. M. (1982). Evolution and validation of a behavioral decision theory measurement approach to achievement, power, and affiliation. *Journal of Applied Psychology, 67,* 744–751.

Stein, D. J., & Matsunaga, H. (2006). Specific phobia: A disorder of fear conditioning and extinction. *CSN Spectrums, 11,* 248–252.

Stein, M. B., Seedat, S., & Gelernter, J. (2006). Serotonin transporter gene promoter polymorphism predicts SSRI response in generalized social anxiety disorder. *Psychopharmacology, 187,* 68–72.

Sternberg, R. (1986). A triangular theory of love. *Psychological Review, 93,* 119–135.

Sternberg, R. (1997). Construct validation of a triangular love scale. *European Journal of Social Psychology, 27,* 313–335.

Sternberg, R. J. (1988). *The triangle of love: Intimacy, passion, commitment.* New York: Basic Books.

Sternberg, R. J. (2003). A duplex theory of hate: Development and application of terrorism, massacres, and genocide. *Review of General Psychology, 7,* 299–328.

Sternthal, B. (1974). Fear appeal: Revisited and revised. *Journal of Consumer Research, 1,* 22–34.

Stone, M. H. (2011). The meaning of life and Adler's use of fictions. *The Journal of Individual Psychology, 67,* 13–30.

Stukas, A. A., Snyder, M, & Clary, E. G. (1999). The effects of "mandatory volunteerism" on intentions to volunteer. *Psychological Science, 10,* 59–64.

Superherologist (Langley, T.). (2011, August 13). *Does Batman have PTSD?* Retrieved August 12, 2011, from Rocket Llama Headquarters: http://www.rocketllama.com/blog-it/2011/08/13/does-batman-have-ptsd.

Suskind, R. (2006, September 10). The unofficial story of the al-Qaeda 14. *Time, 168* (12), 34–35.

Takarangi, M. K. T., Polaschek, D. L. L., Garry, M., & Loftus, E. F. (2008). Psychological science, victim advocates, and the problem of recovered memories. *International Review of Victimology, 15,* 147–163.

Takeuchi, S. (2006). On the matching phenomenon in courtship: A probability matching theory of mate selection. *Marriage & Family Review, 40,* 25–51.

Thompson, M. P., Kaslow, N. J., Kingree, J. B., King, M., Bryant, L., & Rey, M. (1998). Psychological symptomatology following parent death in a predominantly minority sample of children and adolescents. *Journal of Clinical Child Psychology, 27,* 434–441.

Thornton, E. (1983). *Freud and cocaine: The Freudian fallacy.* London: Blond and Briggs.

Tienari, P., Wahlberg, K., & Wynne, L. (2006). Finnish adoption study of schizophrenia: Implications for family interventions. *Family, Systems, & Health, 24,* 442–451.

Torres, A. N., Boccaccini, M. T., & Miller, H. A. (2006). Perceptions of the validity and utility of criminal profiling among forensic psychologists and psychiatrists. *Professional Psychology: Research and Practice, 37,* 51–58.

Touhey, J. C. (1974). Effects of dominance and competence on heterosexual attraction. *British Journal of Clinical Psychology, 13*, 22–26.

Triplett, K. N., Tedeschi, R. G., Cann, A., Calhoun, L. G., & Reeve, C. L. (2011, July 4). Posttraumatic growth, meaning in life, and life satisfaction in response to trauma. *Psychological Trauma: Theory, Research, Practice, and Policy.* Advance online publication.

Turvey, B. E. (2008). *Criminal profiling: An introduction to behavioral evidence analysis* (3rd ed.). Burlington, MA: Academic Press.

Urbaniak, G. C., & Kilmann, P. R. (2003). Physical attractiveness and the nice guy paradox: Do nice guys really finish last? *Sex Roles, 49*, 413–426.

Urbaniak, G. C., & Kilmann, P. R. (2006). Niceness and dating success: A further test of the nice guy stereotype. *Sex Roles, 55*, 209–224.

U.S. Department of Justice, Federal Bureau of Investigation (2004). *Uniform crime reporting handbook.* Retrieved June 14, 2011, from the Federal Bureau of Investigation: http://www.fbi.gov/about-us/cjis/ucr/frequently-asked-questions/ucr_faqs_incspec#burglary.

U.S. Department of Justice, Federal Bureau of Investigation (n.d.). *Terrorism 2002–2005.* Retrieved August 19, 2011, from the Federal Bureau of Investigation: http://www.fbi.gov/stats-services/publications/terrorism-2002-2005.

U.S. National Academy of Sciences. (2002). *The polygraph and lie detection.* Washington, D.C.: National Academic Press.

Uslan, M. (2004). Introduction. In A. Kawasaki (Ed.), *Catwoman: Nine lives of a femme fatale.* New York: DC Comics.

Uslan, M. E. (2011). *The boy who loved Batman.* San Francisco, CA: Chronicle.

Vaillant, G. E. (1977). *Adaptation to life.* Boston, MA: Little, Brown.

Valor-Seguar, I., Exposito, F., & Moya, M. (2011). Victim blaming and exoneration of the perpetrator in domestic violence: The role of beliefs in just world and ambivalent system. *Spanish Journal of Psychology, 14*, 195–206.

Van Ameringen, M., Mancini, C., Oakman, J. M., & Farvolden, P. (1999). Selective serotonin reuptake inhibitors in the treatment of social phobia: The emerging gold standard. *CNS Drugs, 11*, 307–315.

Van Dijken, S. (1998). *John Bowlby: His early life: A biographical journey into the roots of attachment theory.* London: Free Association Books.

Van Goozen, S. H. M., & Fairchild, G. (2008). How can the study of biological processes help design new interventions for children with severe antisocial behavior? *Development and Psychopathology, 20*, 941–973.

Van Goozen, S. H. M., Fairchild, G., Snoek, H., & Harold, G. T. (2007). The evidence for a neurobiological model of childhood antisocial behavior. *Psychological Bulletin, 133*, 149–182.

Van Raalte, J. L., Cornelius, A. E., Linder, D. E., & Brewer, B. W. (2007). The relationship between hazing and team cohesion. *Journal of Sport Behavior, 30*, 491–507.

Van Voorhis, P., Braswell, M., & Lester, D. (2004). *Correctional counseling & rehabilitation* (5th ed.). Cincinnati, OH: Anderson Publishing.

Vergano, D. (2002, September 9). *Telling the truth about lie detectors.* Retrieved August 18, 2001, from *USA Today*: http://www.usatoday.com/news/nation/2002-09-09-lie_x.htm.

Wagnild, G. M., & Collins, J. A. (2009). Assessing resilience. *Journal of Psychosocial Nursing, 47*, 28–33.

Wagnild, G. M., & Young, H. M. (1993). Development and psychometric evaluation of the Resilience Scale. *Journal of Nursing Measurement, 1*, 165–178.

Waldman, S., & Kress, M. (2006, June 19). BeliefWatch: Good fight. *Newsweek*, 12.

Walsh, J. (1980). *Break-ins: Burglary from private houses.* London: Constable.

Walsh, J. (2008). *Tears of rage.* New York: Pocket.

Walters, G. (2010). *Hunting evil: The Nazi war criminals who escaped and the quest to bring them to justice.* New York: Broadway.

Wang, P. S., Lane, M., Olfson, M., Pincus, H. A., Wells, K. B., & Kessler, R. C. (2005). Twelve-month use of mental health services in the United States: Results from the National Comorbidity Survey Replication. *Archives of General Psychiatry, 62*, 629–640.

Ward, B. (2010, November 14). Personal communication.

Watson, J. B. (1913). Psychology as the behaviorist views it. *Psychological Review, 20*, 158–177.

Watson, J. B. (1930). *Behaviorism* (revised edition). Chicago: University of Chicago Press.

Wayment, H. A., & Vierthaler, J. (2002). Attachment style and bereavement reactions. *Journal of Loss and Trauma, 7*, 129–149.

Weiner, T., Johnston, D., & Lewis, N. A. (1995). *Betrayal: The story of Aldrich Ames, an American spy.* New York: Random House.

Weinstein, N., Hodgins, H. S., & Ostvik-White, E. (2011). Humor as aggression: Effects of motivation on hostility expressed in humor appreciation. *Journal of Personality and Social Psychology, 100*, 1043–1055.

Wertham, F. (1948, May 29). The comics—very funny! *Saturday Review of Literature*, p. 6.

Wertham, F. (1954/2004). *Seduction of the innocent.* New York: Rinehart.

Wertham, F. (n.d.). *Episodes: From the life of a psychiatrist* [unpublished manuscript].

West, A., & Rovin, J. (1994). *Back to the Batcave.* New York: Berkley.

Williams, K. D. (2002). *Ostracism: The power of silence.* New York: Guilford.

Wilson, L., Dyszynski, K., & Mant, A. (2003). A 5-year follow-up of general practice patients experiencing depression. *Family Practice, 20*, 685–689.

Winch, R. (1958). *Mate selection: A study of complementary needs.* New York: Harper & Row.

Wingo, A. P., Fani, N., Bradley, B., & Ressler, K. J. (2010). Psychological resilience and neurocognitive performance in a traumatized community sample. *Depression and Anxiety, 27*, 768–774.

Wolchik, S. A., Ma, Y, Tein, J.-Y, Sandler, I. N., & Ayers, T. S. (2008). Parentally bereaved children's grief: Self-system beliefs as mediators of the relations between grief and stressors and caregiver-child relationship quality. *Death Studies, 32*, 597–620.

Wolchik, S. A., Tein, J., Sandler, I. N., & Ayers, T. S. (2006). Stressors, quality of the child-caregiver relationship, and children's mental health problems after parental death: The mediating role of self-system beliefs. *Journal of Abnormal Child Psychology, 34*, 221–238.

Woolley, J. E. (1996). Young children's awareness of the origins of their mental representations. *Developmental Psychology, 32*, 335–346.

The World. (2010, September 29). *Canadian prostitution law.* Retrieved September 4, 2011, from PRI's The World: http://www.theworld.org/2010/09/canadian-prostitution-law/.

World Health Organization. (2004). *Neuroscience of psychoactive substances use and dependence.* Geneva: Author.

Wortmann, J. H. (2009). Religion/spirituality and change in meaning after bereavement: Qualitative evidence for meaning making model. *Journal of Loss and Trauma, 14,* 17–34.

Wright, S. (2010). Depathologizing consensual sexual sadism, sexual masochism, transvestic fetishism, and fetishism. *Archives of Sexual Behavior, 39,* 1229–1230.

Yates, E. (2000). The influence of psychosocial factors on nonsensical shoplifting. *International journal of Offender Therapy and Comparative Criminology, 30,* 203–211.

York, C. (2000). All in the family: Homophobia and Batman comics in the 1950s. *The International Journal of Comic Art, 2,* 100–110.

Zajonc, R. B. (2001). Birth order debate resolved? *American Psychologist, 56,* 522–523.

Zautra, A. J., Arewasikporn, A., & Davis, M. C. (2010). Resilience: Promoting well-being through recovery, sustainability, and growth. *Research in Human Development, 7,* 221–238.

Zehr, E. P. (2008). *Becoming Batman: The possibility of a superhero.* Baltimore, MD: Johns Hopkins.

Zimbardo, P. G. (1969). The human choice: Individuation, reason, and order versus deindividuation, impulse, and chaos. In W. J. Arnold & D. Levine (Eds.), *Nebraska Symposium on Motivation* (vol. 17). Lincoln, NE: University of Nebraska Press.

Zimbardo, P. G. (1971, October 25). *The psychological power and pathology of imprisonment.* A statement prepared for the U.S. House of Representatives Committee on the Judiciary, Subcommittee No. 3: Hearings on Prison Reform, San Francisco.

Zimbardo, P. G. (1991, August 18). Personal communication.

Zimbardo, P. G. (2008). *The Lucifer effect.* New York: Random House.

Zimbardo, P. G., Maslach, C., & Haney, C. (1999). Reflections on the Stanford Prison Experiment: Genesis, transformations, consequences. In T. Blass (Ed.), *Obedience to authority: Current perspectives on the Milgram paradigm* (pp. 193–237). Mahwah, NJ: Erlbaum. Retrieved December 17, 2011, from Stanford Prison Experiment: http://www.prisonexp.org/pdf/blass.pdf (quote p. 18).

Zuckerman, M. (1979). *Sensation seeking: Beyond the optimum level of arousal.* Hillsdale, NJ: Erlbaum.

Zuckerman, M. (1983). *Biological cases of sensation seeking, impulsivity, and anxiety.* Hillsdale, NJ: Erlbaum.

Zuckerman, M. (2004). The shaping of personality: Genes, environments, and chance encounters. *Journal of Personality Assessment, 82,* 11–22.

Zuckerman, M., & Gerbasi, K. C. (1977). Belief in a just world and trust. *Journal of Research in Personality, 11,* 306–317.

Index

Note: Page numbers in *italics* refer to photographs.

About the Author

Superherologist **Travis Langley** teaches on the psychology of crime, mental illness, social behavior, and media (including comic books), not to mention a course titled *Batman*, at Henderson State University. He received his bachelor's degree in psychology from Hendrix College and his psychology doctorate from Tulane University. An organizer of the Comics Arts Conference, he regularly speaks as a panelist discussing the psychology of superheroes at conventions such as San Diego Comic-Con International, WonderCon, and New York Comic Con. As part of their ongoing

Photo by Alex Langley.

ERIICA Project (Empirical Research on the Interpretation and Influence of the Comic Arts), Dr. Langley and his students investigate how fans see themselves and their heroes. Travis has also been a child abuse investigator, courtroom expert, and undefeated champion on the *Wheel of Fortune* game show even though none of the puzzles they gave him were about psychology or superheroes.

Follow him as @Superherologist on Twitter and keep up with his latest adventures through Superherologist.com.

"Like" this book and get updates at Facebook.com/BatmanBelfry.